The Dead and the Living in Paris and London, 1500–1670

book is an innovative exploration in social history, showing how
ractices surrounding death and burial can illuminate urban culture
xperience. Vanessa Harding focuses on the crowded and turbulent
ls of early modern London and Paris, and makes use of rich con-
orary documentation to compare and contrast their experience of
ng with the dead. The two cities shared many of the problems and
ires of urban life, including high mortality rates, and a tradition
ristian burial, and there are many similarities in their responses to
. The treatment of the dead reveals the communities' preoccupa-
with the use of space, control of the physical environment, and the
ing of society and social behaviour. But the impact of Reformation
into question many traditional attitudes, and although London
irly successful in establishing a new consensus, burial of the dead
ame a serious point of conflict in Paris.

Dead and the Living is as much about London and Paris as about
th rituals, and Vanessa Harding emphasises the importance of the
graphic, physical and social context within which burial and fury practices evolve. She looks at actual churchyards, cemeteries and
ches, and at the responses of specific communities to burial. Vividly
strated, this work is a major contribution to the history of the early
dern city, and to our understanding of social and cultural change in
ban environment.

SSA HARDING is Senior Lecturer in London History at Birkbeck,
rsity of London, and a Fellow of the Royal Historical Society.

The Dead and the Living in Paris and London, 1500–1670

Vanessa Harding

CAMBRIDGE UNIVERSITY PRESS

CAMBRIDGE UNIVERSITY PRESS
Cambridge, New York, Melbourne, Madrid, Cape Town, Singapore, São Paulo

Cambridge University Press
The Edinburgh Building, Cambridge CB2 2RU, UK

Published in the United States of America by Cambridge University Press, New York

www.cambridge.org
Information on this title: www.cambridge.org/9780521811262

First published 2002
This digitally printed first paperback version 2006

A catalogue record for this publication is available from the British Library

ISBN-13 978-0-521-81126-2 hardback
ISBN-10 0-521-81126-0 hardback

ISBN-13 978-0-521-00974-4 paperback
ISBN-10 0-521-00974-X paperback

In memory of
Jill Harding

Contents

Illustrations

Acknowledgements

This study had a very precise and identifiable starting-point, recounted in Chapter 1. After that, it ramified into a number of different enquiries, some of which I have written up elsewhere, before returning to the first questions. The book, therefore, has taken longer to make than the human body allegedly takes to unmake: 'Faith, if he be not rotten before he die ... he will last you some eight year, or nine year' (*Hamlet*, Act 5, Scene 1). Without taking an unsavoury metaphor too far, I can at least claim to have been involved in an equally lengthy process of transformation of material, and ultimately, I hope, the constitution of new meaning.

Over that period I have incurred many debts which I now have pleasure in acknowledging. The book could not have been written without the two periods of study leave granted by Birkbeck College, the first of which was spent in archives in London and Paris and the second, some years later, in writing up in New York. In between came a stint of administration, demanding but not thankless, which certainly delayed progress, but it is fair to add that the book would not have been written without the stimulus of working in such a lively and intellectually productive department, with colleagues and students whose enthusiasm for the study of history never flags. I thank Birkbeck also for the research grants that supported my periods of study leave, and for conference grants to give papers on death and burial to new audiences. I thank the Maison Suger, of the Maison des Sciences de l'Homme in Paris, for offering me accommodation and facilities during my first study leave, and the Center for Medieval Studies at Fordham University, New York, and especially its director, Maryanne Kowaleski, for giving me an Honorary Visiting Fellowship and much-valued privileges and facilities during the second. A grant from the British Council (Canada) enabled me to give papers in Toronto and Montreal in 1997, where Sandy Johnston and Bob and Anne Tittler were my kind hosts and sponsors.

I gratefully acknowledge the assistance and resources of the Manuscripts, Print Room, and Printed Books sections of the Guildhall

Library, the Corporation of London Records Office, the British Library, the Public Record Office, the Family Records Centre, and Lambeth Palace Library in London; Birkbeck College Library, the Warburg Institute Library, and the University of London Library; the Bodleian Library, Oxford; the Archives Nationales, the Bibliothèque Nationale, the Bibliothèque de l'Arsenal, and the Bibliothèque Historique de la Ville de Paris, in Paris; and the New York Public Library and Fordham University Libraries in New York. For me, as for many historians, the Institute of Historical Research in London has been an invaluable resource, bibliographically, intellectually, and socially. For assistance with the illustrations, I particularly wish to thank François-Joseph Ruggiu; John Fisher of the Guildhall Library Print Room; Bernard Nurse of the Society of Antiquaries of London; and Jon Wilson and Christina Panagi of Birkbeck's Photographic Unit, as well as the copyright holders of the images themselves.

Along the way to completion I have benefited greatly from opportunities to present my ideas to seminars and conferences in London, Birmingham, Bournemouth, Cambridge, Leicester, St Andrews, Sussex, Budapest, Strasbourg, and Tours, and at the universities of Brown, Columbia, Concordia (Montreal), Dartmouth, Eugene (Oregon), Fordham, McGill, Oxford (Mississippi), and Toronto. At all of these I received useful comments, criticisms, and encouragement.

Declaring that I was working on death was sometimes a conversation stopper, but more often it evoked an interested and thoughtful response. Many generous offers of information and insight contributed to my understanding and argument. I hope I have acknowledged specific references in the footnotes, but I also take this opportunity of thanking James Amelang, David Andrews, Caroline Barron, Judith Bennett, Clive Burgess, Martha Carlin, Margaret Cox, Peter Earle, Mary Erler, Loreen Giese, Matthew Groom, Charlotte Harding, John Henderson, Cynthia Herrup, Ralph Houlbrooke, Derek Keene, Jenny Kermode, Jim Masschaele, Julia Merritt, Adrian Miles, David Mitchell, Karen Newman, Scott Newstrom, Margaret Pelling, François-Joseph Ruggiu, Barney Sloane, Anne Sutton, Danae Tankard, Andrew Thrush, Bob Tittler, Joe Ward, Bill White, and Christopher Wilson. I would like to thank John Schofield who took me and my students to see the New Churchyard excavation where my interest in death began, and Ann Johnston for a memorable visit to Père Lachaise, where I realised that there is actually only one famous person buried in Paris. I am grateful to the anonymous readers for Cambridge University Press for their comments and constructive criticisms, and to Richard Fisher for his long patience and support in seeing this through. Above all, though, I wish to xii Acknowledgements

thank Paul Strohm, who read the whole text at a late stage and through his insightful and incisive remarks helped me to see what it was I was really trying to say, and to say it better; and Jen Guttenplan, who, as well as encouraging me over a long period, also offered assistance in the last painful stages of editing and proofing.

Family, friends, and colleagues have amiably, if sometimes with puzzlement, put up with my preoccupation with this book for several years. They must all have learned more than they ever wished to know about death and burial. Their continuing interest, and their good company, warm hospitality, intellectual generosity, willingness to listen, readiness to argue, and refusal to accept an inadequate answer have been an invaluable stimulus and reward to my endeavours, vividly illustrating what is important in life, as well as showing that there is a lot of life in death. So my warmest thanks to them all and especially to Caroline Barron, Judith Bennett, Barry Coward, Peter Earle, Sam Guttenplan, Jen Guttenplan, David Hebb, Cynthia Herrup, Ann Johnston, Maryanne Kowaleski, David Ormrod, Gigliola Pagano, Dorothy Porter, Steve Rappaport, Paul Strohm, Jane Waldfogel, and David Wallace. I dedicate the book, however, to the memory of my mother. She was a life-giver and life-enhancer and long after her death her warmth and generosity of spirit are remembered by those who loved her.

Note

Dates

New-style dates are used throughout. London and Paris were following the Gregorian and Julian calendars respectively for most of the period covered here, but this has no significant impact on the discussion.

Spelling

Although this book is written primarily with an English-speaking reader in mind, there is inevitably much quotation from French writings. On the whole these are straightforward and have not been translated, after the first appearance of common terms, except where problems in translation contribute to the discussion. In quotations from sixteenth- and seventeenth-century French sources I have followed the original spelling but added an accent to distinguish the tonic from the atonic 'e' at the end of a word.

Money

Both England and France used a similar currency structure, with the measure of value being the pound (£) or *livre*, made up of 20 shillings (s.) or *sous* (occasionally *sols*), each of which contained 12 pence (d.) or *deniers*. In France this is slightly complicated by the existence of two currencies, the *livre tournois* and *livre parisis*, the latter really a relic currency, exchanged against *tournois* at the rate of 16 *sous parisis* to the *livre tournois*. In the contemporary sources used for this book, the kind of money in which transactions were made is not always specified, but it may be assumed to be the *livre tournois* unless otherwise stated (see P. Spufford, *Handbook of medieval exchange* (London: Royal Historical Society, 1986), p. 167).

The pound and *livre* were moneys of account, and both countries used gold and silver coins with a range of face values. Their effective monetary value varied according to the bullion content and the currency practices of governments. The face value of the English gold noble was 6s. 8d., while the French *écu d'or* was approximately 2 *livres*. The English mark was a notional sum or money of account worth two-thirds of a pound or 13s. 4d.

It is difficult to find any reliable way of establishing equivalents between French and English money for this period. At the end of the fifteenth century, the pound sterling's exchange value was 8 *livres tournois* (based on Spufford, *Handbook of medieval exchange*, pp. 179, 201). For purposes of comparison, however, it is the purchasing value rather than the exchange rate between sterling and the *livre tournois* that matters. Given serious inflation during the period (see S. Rappaport, *Worlds within worlds: structures of life in sixteenth-century London* (Cambridge, 1989), esp. p. 155; J.-P. Babelon, *Nouvelle histoire de Paris. Paris au XVIe siècle* (Paris, 1986), pp. 295–314), this is particularly hard to assess. In 1572, a French royal edict set the daily wage of a master mason and carpenter at 12 *sols tournois*, and that of a labourer at 6 *sols*, but these rates were probably unrealistically lower than the wages really offered (Babelon, *Paris au XVIe siècle*, p. 299). The mayor and aldermen set London wages in 1586 at 13d. a day for a mason, tiler, or plaisterer, and 14d. for a joiner. 'Common labourers' were to have 9d. a day (R. H. Tawney and E. Power (eds.), *Tudor economic documents*, 3 vols. (London, 1924), vol. I: *Agriculture and industry*, pp. 369–70). These too may be unrealistically low: cf. J. Boulton, 'Wage labour in seventeenth-century London', *Economic History Review* 49 (1996), 268–90. If they do offer a valid base for comparison, the equivalence rate of the pound sterling and the *livre tournois* was between 1 : 8 and 1 : 11. An alternative source for comparison would be the annual cost of an obit or anniversary commemoration. This appears to have been 10s. in London in 1548 (C. Kitching (ed.), *The London and Middlesex chantry certificate of 1548* (London Record Society 16, 1980), passim). Several obits were founded in the church of Saint-Gervais in Paris in the midsixteenth century for 10 or 12 *livres* rent (AN, LL 752, ff. 24–34v). Taken together, these would suggest either that ecclesiastical services were relatively more expensive in Paris than in London – perhaps because more was offered – or that an appropriate rate to compare sums in pounds sterling with sums in *livres tournois* for the mid- to late sixteenth century would be well over 1 : 10 and perhaps close to 1 : 20.

Measurements

Both England and France measured length in feet (*pieds*) and inches (*pouces*), the French foot being slightly longer than the English. I have used those units when quoting directly or indirectly from contemporary sources, but have normally expressed my own calculations in metric measures. One acre = 4047 m^2 or 0.405 ha; 1 yard (English) = 0.912 m; 1 ft (English) = 0.3048 m; 1 *pied* (French) = 0.3086 m. The French *toise* of approximately 1 fathom or 6 ft (1.949 m: *OED*) was used as a measure of both area and volume. For the former, it must have been equivalent to about 3.8 m^2, and for the latter, to 7.4 m^3. However, it is clear that many measurements were roughly taken or given, and close accuracy should not be expected. See *OED*; Cassell's *French and English Dictionary* (London, 1881); H. Ballon, *The Paris of Henri IV. Architecture and urbanism* (New York and Cambridge, Mass., 1991), p. 258.

Abbreviations

AN	Archives Nationales, Paris
BL	British Library, London
BN	Bibliothèque Nationale, Paris
BR	burial registers
Bodl.	Bodleian Library, Oxford
CA	churchwardens' accounts
CLRO	Corporation of London Records Office, London
Consistory Court Wills	*London Consistory Court Wills, 1492–1547*, edn I. Darlington (London Record Society 3, 1967)
GL	Guildhall Library, London
Harl Soc.	Harleian Society
LPL	Lambeth Palace Library, London
Machyn, *Diary*	*The diary of Henry Machyn, citizen and merchant-taylor of London, from A.D. 1550 to A.D. 1563*, edited by J. G. Nichols (Camden Society 42, 1848)
MoLAS	Museum of London Archaeology Service
PRO	Public Record Office, London
RCHM *City of London*	Royal Commission on the Historical Monuments of England, *An Inventory of the historical monuments in London*, vol. IV: *The city* (London: HMSO, 1924)
RDBVP	*Registres des délibérations du Bureau de la Ville de Paris*, edited by F. Bonnardot, A. Tuetey, P. Guérin et al., 20 vols. (Paris: Histoire Général de Paris, Imprimerie Nationale, 1883–1990)
VCH London	*Victoria history of London: including London within the bars, Westminster and Southwark*, vol. I, ed. W. Page (London: Constable, 1911)
VM	Vestry minutes

1   Introduction

A wide plain, apparently of churned mud, stretched almost to the horizon, bounded by the tall buildings of the twentieth-century city. In the distance mechanical diggers and hard-hatted workmen circled purposefully. In the foreground, the top layers of earth had been stripped off, to expose a profusion of human remains, a seeming jumble of skulls, vertebrae, and limb-bones. Looking more carefully, one could see that this was not in fact a pit or mass grave, with bodies tossed in anyhow. The skeletons were mostly laid out and oriented east–west in single graves, but these overlay and intercut each other in a dense pattern of use and re-use of the space. The ground had been opened frequently and repeatedly to accommodate successive burials, and each new cut must have exposed at best quite significant skeletal remains and at worst decomposing bodies. The residue of earlier burials had been shovelled aside to make way for new ones, so that the bones of scores of individuals were contained in this small space. The possibility that a similar density of burial material stretched further in all directions daunted the imagination.

This was the scene at Broad Street in the city of London in early 1986, as archaeologists from the Department of Urban Archaeology made the most of their opportunity to investigate the site, between the demolition of the nineteenth-century Broad Street railway station and the erection of the late twentieth-century Broadgate development.[1] A visitor to the excavation, I was both shocked and fascinated. For the first time I was brought literally face to face with one of the material realities of life in early modern London, the shortage of space to bury the dead, and the way in which it was handled. Further investigation of the antecedents of

---

[1] MoLAS site reference LSS 85. For the early modern use of the New Churchyard, see below, chapter 3. The burial ground went out of use in the mid-eighteenth century, appears to have been divided up as gardens for the surrounding houses by 1793, and was wholly built over by Broad Street Station by 1865. See H. A. Harben, *A dictionary of London* (London, 1908), pp. 70, 107, 356; CLRO, Comptroller's City Lands Plans, 142, 270; CLRO, Plans, Railways: North London Railway, City Branch, 1860 (678F, plan 122).

this site, which proved to be the New Churchyard established in 1569, raised a range of questions: how far was the initiative to create this burial ground typical of civic attitudes to burial and the safe disposal of bodies in that time and place? What factors determined who was buried there? Who managed burial in early modern London?

These specific questions led me to the burgeoning literature on death, and to the now widely shared recognition that the study of death can offer insights into the much broader area of the structure and relations of historical societies. This has long been accepted as a valid approach to understanding prehistoric and ancient societies, in which death rituals and burial practices are seen as exemplifying and reinforcing social formations, and as an important mechanism for ensuring social continuity and recovery in the face of mortality. The growing body of writings on death, mortuary practices, and eschatology in more modern periods suggested that major insights could be gained in this area too. As a result, I began to consider what part the experience of mortality and the management of burial played in shaping urban community and culture, especially in the medieval and early modern periods. I was particularly interested in the large and complex metropolitan context, where individuals had multiple identities and foci of loyalty, and where the interests and wishes of the state impinged upon local or municipal governmental interests. An issue of particular significance appeared to be the location of burial, and the decisions made about where burial could take place in the crowded physical environment of the early modern city. The questions that principally presented themselves to me as a historian of London included asking: who, or what interests, determined where any individual was buried? What practices evolved to deal with the problem of thousands – in some years, tens of thousands – of bodies to be buried? What rituals were devised to temper this brutal reality, and how were they reshaped over time? How much did this all cost, and can the value or success of a particular repertory of responses be assessed? What do the ways in which these problems were addressed tell us about the society, its preoccupations, its capacity for responding to social issues and crises? And what other discourses – of identity, community, hierarchy, power, privacy, consumption – were involved in dealing with the irreducibly material fact of death?

This book arises from those questions, and attempts to address them by investigating the material reality of death in the early modern city. It is intended as an exploration in urban history: to show that study of the practices surrounding death and burial can make an important contribution to understanding urban culture and experience. It is not a discussion of death as an ontological phenomenon, of attitudes to dying, or the negotiations with the hereafter; it is more an investigation of what it meant, in practical terms, to deal with death on a scale wholly unfamiliar to modern western societies. Responses to death, in the form of burial practices and funeral rituals, are clearly bound up with issues of personal and family or community identity, geography and the use of space, control of the physical environment, and the ordering of society and social behaviour. All of these topics are of central importance for the urban historian; their significance can only have been magnified by the huge scale of mortality in the early modern city. Death rates were commonly three to four times those prevalent now, and for some categories such as children, and during epidemics, were many times higher. I would argue that death played a particularly significant role in early modern urban societies, which experienced more and more-frequent deaths; lost more of their social and cultural capital to death; and faced a greater problem in disposing of the dead, than many others have done.

The topic invites comparative study, since all pre-modern cities and metropolises must have experienced similar problems, but reacted to them in characteristically and perhaps significantly different ways. The most appropriate comparator for early modern London is not another British city, but Paris. Though some differences are immediately apparent, the two had many features in common. One of the most important similarities between them is their great size: both appear to have reached and passed 450,000 inhabitants by 1670, making them the two largest cities in northern Europe and among the largest in the world known to contemporary Europeans. As the capitals of centralising nation-states, both cities were the foci of power and its contestation at many levels; they were at the centre of systems that drew in and redistributed goods and profits produced nationally; they were places where different value systems met, clashed, and modified each other. By this period both had a history of centuries of development and redevelopment on the same spot, resulting in a congested urban plan that was invested with meanings derived from traditional uses and ownerships but modified by newer practices. Each of the two was often conceived and represented, visually or verbally, as a unity, but this unity was belied by jurisdictional incoherence and anomaly on the ground. The size and the varied origins of the metropolitan population created a complex and pluralistic society, in which individuals had multiple identities and loyalties, not all pulling in the same direction. London and Paris shared many of the pressures and problems of urban living with smaller centres, but it is this complexity and multi-focality that puts them in a special category.

In this book, therefore, I examine the history of death and burial in London and Paris in the sixteenth and seventeenth centuries, and ask what this can add to our understanding of the divergent histories of these two cities. London was the starting point of the enquiry, and remains the better-documented subject of research, but the information and insights gained from study of Paris have had a major impact on the overall shape and conclusions of the work. Recent historical writing has suggested that early modern London's relative social stability may be attributable to its dynamic and integrative socal structure, offering opportunities for participation and advancement, as well as to the suppression or containment of political conflict among the city's rulers.[2] An obvious question to ask is whether Paris's much more traumatic experience of religious and political strife was in part the result of weaker social bonds or structures. Paris saw more frequent and savage conflict on the streets and at times the city was completely out of control. Not all forms of authority were challenged, but those that might be characterised as in intention inclusive and conciliatory – that is, the royal and municipal – were. Clearly the contribution of political contest at the national level and the exploitation of factional interests cannot be ignored, but, given the active participation of the people of Paris in large political events and their outcomes, an examination of social structures must be important to this question.[3] One way of approaching this huge topic is suggested here: some of the different assumptions and priorities that informed social relations and interactions in London and Paris may be revealed through comparison of their responses to the problem of mortality. The two communities were confronted by the same challenge, of how to survive the practical and psychic impact of enormously high mortality. Both needed to dispose safely of thousands of bodies a year, and to find ways of preserving social bonds and social harmony when death was constantly undermining relations and continuities. Though there are variations in the quality and survival of the documentary sources between the two cities, the topic is at least adequately documented in both, in comparable categories of sources,[4] and despite the increasing divergence of their political and religious institutions there is still much evidence of the common inheritance

---

[2] F. F. Foster, *The politics of stability. A portrait of the rulers in Elizabethan London* (London, 1977); V. Pearl, 'Change and stability in seventeenth-century London', *London Journal* 5 (1979), 3–34; S. Rappaport, *Worlds within worlds: structures of life in sixteenth-century London* (Cambridge, 1989); I. W. Archer, *The pursuit of stability. Social relations in Elizabethan London* (Cambridge, 1991); J. P. Ward, *Metropolitan communities. Trade guilds, identity and change in early modern London* (Stanford, 1997).

[3] R. Mousnier, *Paris au XVIIe siècle* (Paris, 1961); R. Mousnier, 'Recherches sur les structures sociales parisiennes en 1634, 1635, 1636', *Revue Historique* 507 (1973), 35–58; B. Diefendorf, *Paris city councillors in the sixteenth century. The politics of patrimony* (Princeton, 1983); M. Holt, *The French Wars of Religion, 1562–1629* (Cambridge, 1995).

[4] See appendix 5, A note on sources.

of belief and practice. An important aim of this study, therefore, is to consider whether what we can learn of burial practices in London and Paris can illuminate the different social and political experiences of the two cities in the early modern period, especially as regards social stability versus disorder and fragmentation. This in turn may enable us to reflect on what was generally urban or metropolitan about such practices, and what was specifically local or national. But an equally important question must be whether death was indeed a destabilising factor in the early modern metropolis, as one might expect given its numerical scale, or whether responses to it succeeded in transforming it into a positive and unifying phenomenon, 'making the networks of order denser'.[5]

The cities indeed shared a long tradition of Christian faith and liturgical observance, but their early modern experiences differed quite dramatically, in that London experienced a relatively peaceful and thoroughgoing Protestant Reformation while Paris was torn by religious strife in the sixteenth century and retained its identity as the most Catholic city at a high cost of violence. Though comparison of the course and outcome of religious Reformation in the two cities is not a primary aim of this study, theological changes obviously affected burial practice. Some of the fundamental assumptions that justified many of the components of the burial ritual were challenged by reformed thought. Traditional rituals of funeral and commemoration took it for granted that specific actions and prayers could accumulate spiritual merit to the benefit of the individual's salvation, and also that merit was transferable: the living could obtain merit on behalf of the dead. Attention to the place of interment reflected the belief that holiness could be physically located and was accessible through spatial practices, while physical memorials and funeral performances evoked intercession and beneficial prayer. An examination of the extent to which burial practice did in fact change in reformed London, and whether this was really different from developments in Catholic Paris, is an important theme of the book. The impact of religious challenge on the social value of ritual also has significance for the question of stability identified above.

My book's title, *The dead and the living*, indicates its organising principle. In a real sense it is about the dead rather than death, and specifically the dead of London and Paris. It seeks to locate social responses to the material reality of death in a particular setting: that of the crowded and turbulent worlds of the two largest cities in northern Europe. The book's strong focus on the location of burial is founded on the belief that the

[5] M. de Certeau, *The practice of everyday life*, translated by S. Rendall (Berkeley, 1984), pp. 94–5.

spaces within which funeral rituals and burial took place had an important effect on their form and experienced meaning, and that, reciprocally, ritual uses produced or constituted urban spaces. Equally, it insists on the importance of the social setting, the hierarchical, competitive, dynamic society of the metropolis, struggling to maintain stability in the face of huge population growth, religious and political differences, and gross disparities of wealth and status.

In this context the dead and the living may be seen as separate but interacting categories, needing to occupy the same urban space and to resolve or at least accommodate their different sets of interests and priorities. The dead obviously continued to exist in a physical sense, presenting an immediate problem of hygiene and safety whose resolution could not be delayed. In the longer term, the colonisation of spaces by the dead could get in the way of the needs and priorities of the living community. In a more intangible way, the dead continued to shape the present through the ongoing effects of their testamentary dispositions: an individual's right to control property did not cease with life, and pious and charitable bequests and provision for posterity had an influence far into the future. The living had their current needs to consider, and they tended to put these first, but they necessarily looked towards a time when they themselves would be dead, and aimed to make arrangements accordingly. They also frequently acted as trustees or representatives of the interests of deceased individuals, defending the rights of certain dead over the generality of the living. In spiritual terms, medieval and early modern communities posited a reciprocal relationship between the living and the dead which gave the latter a continuing role in the thoughts and actions of the former.

In discussing 'the dead' we are often shifting between two different understandings of the term, the individual and the category, and even the latter is capable of varied readings. The notion of the dead as an 'age-group' in society[6] encourages us to view them as one end of a continuum of human existence, rather than as wholly separate from it, a state to which all look forward, both for themselves and for society more generally. The dead are therefore as socially differentiated as the living: they include male, female, rich, poor, powerful, dependent, old, young. Throughout this book I have tried always to acknowledge the dead both as a single human category and also as several contrasting social categories. For every autonomous, economically and socially empowered, articulate and

---

[6] Attributed by Peter Marshall and Bruce Gordon to Natalie Zemon Davis, 'borrowing and building on a suggestion of André Varagnac': 'Introduction', p. 6, to B. Gordon and P. Marshall (eds.), *The place of the dead. Death and remembrance in late medieval and early modern Europe* (Cambridge, 2000).

discriminating individual (usually the adult male householder) there were many not so privileged: women, children, servants, paupers, strangers, criminals, and excommunicates. None of these received identical treatment in their burial and funeral, in place, ceremony, or memorialisation. Drawing distinctions between the dead was a formative and revealing activity on the part of the urban community.[7]

This focus on the dead contrasts with, but I hope complements, the approaches of other historians of death. Many important works, including, most recently, Ralph Houlbrooke's major study of *Death, religion and the family in England*[8] and David Cressy's of *Birth, marriage and death*,[9] have enormously enriched our understanding of the way in which death was understood by individual human subjects in the past. With a wealth of research and detail, they have shown how complex, how simultaneously universal and particular, was the early modern experience of death. I have avoided the examination of eschatology and systems of belief, and have little to say on attitudes to death, or on the personal side of the experience, since these issues have already been opened up for discussion, and many questions have been answered. Houlbrooke's discussion of the human and personal aspect of early modern death allows me to take for granted an appreciation of these issues, and my main theme is social practice rather than interiorised experience. In some ways my approach is nearer to Cressy's, and it would have been difficult to assert the importance of local particularities of experience and behaviour, as I aim to do, without the richly detailed context he and others have established.[10]

Long ago, French historians began to investigate death, and their findings have been widely influential, especially Philippe Ariès' *The hour of our death*,[11] a long sweep through the history of death in western society. The existence of Pierre Chaunu's monumental study, *La mort à Paris: XVIe, XVIIe, XVIIIe siècles*,[12] based on a major programme of collaborative research centred on wills and testamentary discourse, was effectively a precondition for this more comparative and materially based

[7] See V. Harding, 'Whose body? A study of attitudes towards the dead body in early modern Paris', in Gordon and Marshall, *The place of the dead*, pp. 170–87.

[8] R. A. Houlbrooke, *Death, religion and the family in England, 1450–1750* (Oxford, 1998).

[9] D. Cressy, *Birth, marriage and death. Ritual, religion and the life-cycle in Tudor and Stuart England* (Oxford, 1997).

[10] See also C. Gittings, *Death, burial and the individual in early modern England* (London, 1984); D. Stannard, *The Puritan way of death. A study in religion, culture, and social change* (New York, 1977).

[11] P. Ariès, *The hour of our death*, translated by Helen Weaver (London, 1983); originally published in France as *L'homme devant la mort* (Paris, 1977); J. McManners, 'Death and the French historians', in J. Whaley (ed.), *Mirrors of mortality: studies in the social history of death* (London, 1981), pp. 107–30.

[12] P. Chaunu, *La mort à Paris: XVIe, XVIIe, XVIIIe siècles* (Paris, 1978).

enquiry. Chaunu's book focuses on changing attitudes to death, using both the contemporary literature of the Ars Moriendi tradition and the testamentary evidence of the Parisian notarial sources to chart the appearance of a 'new eschatology', a changed apprehension of death and judgement, and the increasing secularisation of death in the eighteenth century. It is not specifically a study of the impact of death on Parisian society. Some aspects of its approach, notably the quantitative analysis of testamentary discourse, are vulnerable to the criticism that they read too literally a source that is textually and generically formulaic; equally, some of the book's larger claims and speculations, about major changes over time, might also be queried.[13] The present work, using an investigation of the practices associated with death and burial as a way of commenting on the social history of Paris itself, owes a considerable debt to Chaunu's work, and necessarily draws on the *mémoires de maîtrise* of his students, who made numerous individual studies of samples of wills from the notarial archives, but it is designed to answer a different set of questions. It has more in common with the objectives of Jacqueline Thibaut-Payen's *Les morts, l'église et l'état… dans le ressort du Parlement de Paris aux XVIIe et XVIIIe siècles* (1977), which explores the politics of death by investigating the administrative and legal framework regulating the management of death and burial in this period and geographical area. Thibaut-Payen's account of the different treatment accorded to the bodies of 'les sauvés' and 'les reprouvés' parallels the major contention of this work that burial was an important occasion for signalling differentiation and relative privilege.[14]

The period covered in this study extends from the early sixteenth century to the 1670s. It starts before the Reformation, in order to compare the common religious culture of London and Paris before the onset of religious controversy and to be able to distinguish historical practice from later assertions of 'traditional' usages. The progress and reception of political and theological Reformation are not specifically charted, but nevertheless form an essential background to many of the developments examined here. An issue that recurs in many contexts is the extent to which Protestants accepted, rejected, or revised the practices and rituals of their Catholic past; equally important, though, is how Protestant and reformed-Catholic traditions evolved over time. In the English historical

[13] Cf. M. Zell, 'The use of religious preambles as a measure of religious belief in the sixteenth century', *Bulletin of the Institute of Historical Research* 50 (1977), 246–9; McManners, 'Death and the French historians', p. 126.

[14] J. Thibaut-Payen, *Les morts, l'église et l'état: recherches d'histoire administrative sur la sépulture et les cimetières dans le ressort du Parlement de Paris aux XVIIe et XVIIIe siècles* (Paris, 1977).

tradition, one general understanding of the 'early modern' period ends
with the Restoration or the Revolution, but there are specific reasons
for ending this study around 1670. The date marks the effective end of
the age of plague in northern Europe, an important milestone. In London, the destruction of most of the city churches in the Fire of 1666,
and the subsequent reconfiguring of the ecclesiastical parishes, revised
the topography of burial in the city.[15] The contemporary development of
non-parochial burial grounds associated with nonconformist communities changed the parameters of burial practice in the capital. In Paris, in
1669, the state stepped in to take a section of the city's most treasured
and iconic burial site, the cemetery of the Innocents, for road widening;
at about the same time, the hospital of the Hôtel-Dieu finally accepted
the need to find a new burial site outside the city to replace its intramural site at la Trinité, opening one at Clamart in the southern faubourg
Saint-Marcel in 1673.[16] By the 1670s, pressure on the Huguenot community was becoming increasingly severe, culminating in the revocation
of the Edict of Nantes in 1685, and the elimination of the most significant non-Catholic community. The year 1670 also marks the beginning
of the collection of demographic statistics in France, to which contemporary 'political arithmeticians' made a prompt response, drawing useful
comparisons between the two cities.[17] Though the discussion is broadly
framed by the period c. 1520 to c. 1670, however, it has sometimes been
necessary to stray beyond these dates, either to illustrate medieval or pre-
Reformation practice in London, or to fill a gap in the patchy Parisian
sources by reference to a later pronouncement or analysis. It would undoubtedly be rewarding to extend the full study beyond the 1670s, but to
do so would be to move into a new world. The granting of religious toleration in England and its abandonment in France in the 1680s embodied
a significant divergence of approach to dissent and to the notion of an
integrated metropolitan and national community. Especially important
in late seventeenth-century Paris was the institution of a powerful police
system, with jurisdiction affecting public spaces, environmental hygiene,
assemblies, order, and discipline, all of them important factors in burial
practice.

[15] Cynthia Wall, *The literary and cultural spaces of Restoration London* (Cambridge, 1998),
argues for a wholesale reconceptualisation of the city of London as inhabited space after
the Fire.
[16] See chapter 3, below.
[17] See especially W. Petty, 'Two essays in political arithmetick concerning the people, housing, hospitals, etc. of London and Paris' (1687), reprinted in C. H. Hull (ed.), *The economic writings of Sir William Petty, together with observations on the Bills of Mortality*, 2 vols.
(New York, 1963–4), vol. II, pp. 501–13.

The book is structured in two main sections, which deal thematically rather than chronologically with a number of issues. Change over time is obviously a crucial aspect of my endeavour to set the funeral and burial practices of the two societies in their historical context. Pre- and post-Reformation contrasts in London, and the evolution of Catholic practice in Paris, therefore help to shape individual sections within chapters. However, the thematic approach has also meant abandoning the short-term chronology of the human life and the sequence of deathbed, funeral, interment, and post-mortem commemoration which provides a natural structure for many studies of death.

Following this introduction and chapter 2, which concerns the scale of the burial problem and its geographical, social, and administrative setting in the two cities, chapters 3 to 6 begin to consider how that problem was tackled. This section aims to show that we can gain useful insights into a number of important issues by considering the space of the dead. A metaphorised notion of 'space' as a category of enquiry has proved a very productive one for a number of studies, but these in turn have enriched the ways in which we can understand and write about geographical space.[18] Cities are pre-eminently defined as bounded geographical entities, but they are also characterised by a complex internal division and allocation of space, and by sensitivity to access to and use of different spaces. Burial practices are literally grounded in the city and help to reveal graded understandings of spaces as sacred or secular, central or marginal, private or common. The four chapters in this section examine separately and contrast the characteristics of burial in four locations: in parish churchyards; in civic and non-parochial churchyards; in churches; and in private chapels, vaults, and tombs, usually within churches. Each of these spaces had a different burial population, and each exemplifies a different aspect of the relationship between the living and the dead.

Parish churchyards, where the great majority of the urban population were buried, were a location where the interests of the dead were important, but often subordinated to those of the living. As open spaces within crowded cities, they attracted much secular and indeed profane activity. Those who were buried there were from the middling to lower ranks of society, and those in charge of churchyard burial were more easily able to direct and control burial practices there. There was still, however, a sense of community, of the churchyard space as belonging to both living and dead of that parish. The civic and non-parochial churchyards also

---

[18] Most notably, H. Lefebvre, *The production of space*, translated by D. Nicholson-Smith (Oxford, 1991). For a particularly relevant example of the use of notions of 'space' to structure discussion, see H. Phillips, *Church and culture in seventeenth-century France* (Cambridge, 1997).

accommodated the poorer dead, weak individually though overwhelming in numbers, very much at the mercy of the more powerful interests who controlled the space. These dead were very liable to be treated impersonally, as a material or environmental problem rather than a human one, especially since these spaces were often used for plague burials. But the presence of the dead also contributed to the meaning of these churchyards, especially at the Innocents in Paris. The physical remains of generations of dead Parisians gave the site a cultural and spiritual importance which the religious conflicts of the sixteenth century enhanced. In addition to the poor, therefore, it attracted burials from the middling and upper classes, and helped to shape the imagined and acted topography of the city around itself.

Church burial was a privilege usually reserved for wealthier and higher-status citizens, initially desired for spiritual reasons, but easily read as a mark of social status. Though social structures and the mechanisms of mobility differed greatly in London and Paris, in both cities there was dynamism and certainly aspiration; church burial represented a realisable ambition for a widening group. The people who were buried in church were the élite of the local community, concerned while alive to ensure that their expected privileges after death were protected. Those in charge of church burial had to manage a scarce spatial resource without offending powerful interests (with which they might well sympathise), but also without sacrificing the interests of the community they represented. Burial in vaults and chapels represented a further step in the privatisation of space in the church, allowing individuals and families to secure for themselves a spiritual and social benefit, the value of which was created and endorsed by the communal worship that such privatisation, in part, excluded. Church burial was a way of placing oneself in the middle of the community of the living, and of securing their continued attention, through monuments, inscriptions, and the performance of rites and services over the grave or in the name of the deceased. Consideration of the space of the dead, in a physical sense, reveals a widely shared vision of society as ascertainably differentiated and hierarchical. The spatial order reflected the social, in a paradigm of centrality and marginality, inclusion and exclusion.

The second section, chapters 7 to 9, considers the urban funeral. The individual's transition from living to dead was marked by rituals involving multiple meanings and interests, often overlapping and complementary, sometimes conflicting. These three chapters analyse the funeral as a means of making a personal statement, of individuality, affiliation, confession; as a phenomenon subject to external control and commercial exploitation; and as a social ritual of participation, the demonstration of solidarity, respect, or affection. The urban setting was important for all of these. For the funeral as personal statement it offered a great variety of components and accompaniments, and at the same time stimulated awareness of the possibility of choice. Urban wealth and craftsmanship contributed to this, and a sense of competitive consumption is not hard to find. At the same time, funerals were the special business of professional purveyors of heraldry and funeral trappings; how meaning survived and changed under the pressure of increasing commercialisation is an important question. The community of the family, parish, guild, and city found expression in rituals and processions, and, in addition to these, the city and its inhabitants were called on to participate in the larger funeral ceremonies of government and political circles. Widely shared as the traditions and observances of the funeral were, there were also counter-currents, from the earnest Puritan rejection of ceremony to the cynical insights of urban commentators. These were complex and composite cultural performances, which could be received and interpreted in many different ways.[19]

The concluding chapter of the book returns to some of the concerns stated at the outset: the role played by death and burial in early modern urban culture, and the extent to which different local practices interacted with different historical experiences. Death threatens to undermine continuity and stability, and the earlier chapters showed local community leaders trying, with varying strategies and degrees of success, to meet this challenge. Order was reaffirmed by the establishment of traditions and the observance of ritual, but it was always difficult to balance respect for sensibilities with the urgent need to ensure physical safety and environmental amenity. Significantly, appropriate treatment of the dead was considered such a fundamental aspect of a properly functioning community that when community was riven by religious or political faction, the treatment of the dead could become the focus of serious disorder. Burial did become a significant element in the clash between Catholic and Protestant in sixteenth-century Paris, with access to churchyard burial a source of conflict. This chapter argues for the relationship of death and burial with the issue of order and disorder in the early modern city. Drawing on the evidence of different practices and emphases explored earlier, it suggests that although burial ritual remained a binding force in London society, it was less effective in Paris, and that this was both part cause and part effect of Paris's more stratified and factionalised society.

---

[19] 'The concept of "culture" must take into account the differences of opinion in society; the unequal, yet overlapping awareness of the spectrum of available ideas, and the conflicts and syntheses that constantly occur among these alternatives': C. Stewart, review in *The Times Literary Supplement*, 11 August 2000, p. 28.

Alongside the development of this argument, the book also aims to identify and illustrate, as an objective of value in itself, the customs and practices surrounding death and burial in early modern London and Paris. This story is of some importance, since such practices formed a significant element in the cultural repertoire of these societies, a repeated motif in the rich tapestry of urban life. Death was certainly ever present, at a number of levels of consciousness, in the early modern city. Dealing with it took up a good deal of the cities' spiritual and economic resources, and played a fundamental part in shaping their sense of themselves as a moral community. Death impinged on the everyday life of their inhabitants, visibly, audibly, in terms of the spaces they could use and how they could use them. Searchers of the dead, gravediggers, sextons, clerks, clergy and lawyers all derived much of their income from death and dying. With large sums being spent on funerals, death provided a reliable source of business for heralds, *jurés-crieurs de corps et de vin*, drapers, coffinmakers, and eventually undertakers. The poor of both cities were supported by funeral doles and post-mortem distributions, and by employment in funeral ceremonies, while funeral feasting contributed to the network of sociable and charitable occasions that helped to sustain social relations. The authorities in parish communities had to make numerous day-to-day decisions about graves, bells, monuments, and memorials, and deal with challenges to control their churchyards, as well as trying to think strategically about the future. For them and for the cities' governors, the massive death toll of plague and other epidemics generated an enormous problem with effects that continued for years afterwards. In addition, of course, in their internal spiritual lives the citizens of London and Paris were constantly being exhorted to remember death, to consider the afterlife, to affirm by their actions and aspirations their membership of an eternal Christian community. It is their response, to the constant fact of death and the presence of the dead, that this book seeks to explore.

2   London and Paris, the setting of life and death

By the opening of the period investigated in this book, both London and Paris had a history of Christian funeral rites and burial stretching back for about a thousand years. A sense of the antiquity of their funerary practices was clearly important to both the church and the laity, though it is likely that some aspects they took for granted as timeless were of comparatively recent development. Most parish and conventual churches had not been established before the eleventh or twelfth century; many places of burial were more recent than that. Similarly, the liturgy of burial had evolved over time, reflecting the increasing dominance of the doctrine of purgatory and the eschatological preoccupations of the later middle ages. Both burial places and liturgical practices were modified – in some respects, transformed – in the early modern period, though the strength of tradition constrained both possibilities and choices. The similarities and differences between the treatment of the dead in early modern London and Paris relate to the broader structures – spatial, social, governmental – that shaped urban life. The extent to which disposal of the dead is a problem, after all, owes much to the level of mortality, the physical and environmental constraints on solutions, and the powers and capacities of the agencies required to cope with it.

Population and mortality

In the early sixteenth century, London was very much smaller than Paris, though still by far the largest and most prosperous city in Britain. It had weathered the difficulties of the later middle ages better than most other English cities, and by the mid-sixteenth century had probably recovered to its pre-Black Death maximum population of 70–80,000.[1] The great majority of this population total lived in the walled city and its immediate

[1] B. M. S. Campbell, J. A. Galloway, D. Keene, and M. Murphy, *A medieval city and its grain supply: agrarian production and distribution in the London region c. 1300* (London, Historical Geography Research Paper Series 30, 1993), p. 11.

14

fringe, with significant nuclei in Westminster and Southwark. Following serious epidemic mortality in the 1550s and 1560s, growth seems to have been rapid in the 1580s and 1590s, and by 1600 the population total may have reached 200,000. By 1660 it seems likely to have been over 400,000, perhaps over 450,000.[2] A plausible range for the early 1670s, based on data from the London Bills of Mortality, is between 475,000 and 550,000.[3] Explanations for London's early modern growth are complex, resting primarily on its commercial vigour and its increasingly dominant position, even in changing circumstances, in the national economy, and on the growth of the state and London's role as capital. A strongly rising population trend in the country as a whole provided the migration flows that fuelled London's population growth, but London continued to increase even when national population growth slackened and indeed reversed in the later seventeenth century.

The evidence for Paris indicates a much larger medieval population, but a more complex pattern of growth and change in the early modern period. From a figure of around 200,000 in 1500, it is suggested that Paris's population rose quite sharply to 250–300,000 by the middle of the sixteenth century. If this is true, Paris was then about four times the size of London. The upward trend may have been set back by the opening of the religious wars and the plague of 1561, but population had recovered to 300,000 or more by 1588, at the start of the Ligue's rebellion against Henri III. The siege of Paris from 1589 caused the population to drop to *c.* 200,000 in the early 1590s, but it was able to recover quite rapidly to 300,000 by 1600. Thereafter population rose again, to 400–450,000 in the early years of Louis XIV (1643–1715).[4] The figure of

---

[2] This section is based on the argument and sources cited in V. Harding, 'The Population of London, 1550–1700: a review of the published evidence', *London Journal* 15 (1990), 111–28. The figures offered diverge from those given by R. Finlay and B. Shearer, 'Population growth and suburban expansion', in A. L. Beier and R. Finlay (ed.), *London 1500–1700, the making of the metropolis* (London, 1986), pp. 37–59, but we agree on the upward *trend* over the period 1500–1700.

[3] The London yearly Bills were collected and printed as *A collection of the yearly Bills of Mortality from 1657 to 1758 inclusive* (London, 1759). Figures from both the London and Paris series are printed in John Graunt, 'Natural and political observations upon the Bills of Mortality' (1676), in Hull, *The economic writings of Sir William Petty*, vol. II, pp. 314–435. The mortality rates applied here, 33–8 per thousand per annum, represent a plausible range for the later seventeenth century: Harding, 'The population of London, 1550–1700'. R. Finlay, *Population and metropolis, the demography of London 1580–1650* (Cambridge, 1981), calculates population levels assuming birth rates of 30 to 35 per thousand: pp. 155–7.

[4] This account is based on B. Diefendorf, *Beneath the cross. Catholics and Protestant in sixteenth-century Paris* (Oxford, 1991), p. 9, synthesising J.-P. Babelon, *Nouvelle histoire de Paris. Paris au XVIe siècle* (Paris, 1986), pp. 164–6, and J. Jacquart, 'Le poids démographique de Paris et de l'Ile de France au XVIe siècle', in *Annales de démographie historique, 1980* (Paris, 1980), pp. 87–96.

c. 400,000 for around 1640 seems generally thought to be plausible.[5] By the 1670s, Paris's population was probably somewhere between 495,000 and 570,000.[6] Like that of London, Paris's growth was fed by migration from the country as a whole; its speedy recovery following the cessation of hostilities in the mid-1590s must have been due to immigration on a large scale, owing much to the restoration of confidence and commerce as well as to Henri IV's conscious promotion of his capital. By the late seventeenth century, however, Paris was growing more slowly, if at all, and it is likely that it had been overtaken in size by London by around 1680.[7]

Population totals and trends are part of the picture, but mortality rates and actual mortality levels are of equal or greater importance to this study. The significant population growth over the period *c.* 1500–1670 entailed a continually increasing annual death total and hence a worsening problem of accommodation for the dead. Around 1580 the city parishes of London were burying around 3,000 a year in the healthiest, non-plague, years; by the late 1590s, it was closer to 4,000. In the first decade of the seventeenth century (from 1604), annual burials averaged 7–8,000, though the actual range was from 5,219 (a low in 1604, following the population losses of the plague of the previous year) to 11,785 in 1609 (including over 4,000 deaths from a localised and relatively mild plague). Apart from major plague years, London (in the narrower definition adopted by the contemporary statistician John Graunt, which excluded Stepney and Westminster) was burying over 7,500 a year in the 1610s and 1620s, and often over 9,000; between 8,500 and 10,500 in the 1630s; between 11,000 and 14,000 in the 1640s; and between 10,000 and 15,000 for most of the 1650s. In the early 1660s Graunt's London buried between 11,500 and 15,200 bodies per annum, rising to an exceptional peak of 76,500 in the plague year of 1665.[8] By the early 1670s, London (in the broadest definition, including Westminster and the outlying settlements) suffered an annual mortality of around 18,000.[9] Though the total number of deaths

[5] R. Pillorget, *Nouvelle histoire de Paris. Paris sous les premiers Bourbons, 1594–1661* (Paris, 1988) pp. 97, 103; G. Dethan, *Nouvelle histoire de Paris. Paris au temps de Louis XIV* (Paris, 1990), pp. 177–9.

[6] See Graunt's figures and calculations in his 'Natural and political observations'. Paris figures are also printed in J. Bertillon, *Des recensements de la population: de la nuptualité, de la natalité, et de la mortalité à Paris pendant le XIX siècle et les époques antérieures* (Paris, 1907), pp. 11–15.

[7] Petty, 'Two essays in political arithmetick', pp. 501–13.

[8] Figures for 1578–1600 (discontinuous) are printed in Finlay, *Population and metropolis*, appendix 1, p. 155. Graunt, 'Natural and political observations', pp. 407–10 prints tables giving totals for London from 1604 to 1664; for comments on his accuracy, see ibid., p. 407n.

[9] Graunt, 'Natural and political observations', pp. 422–3.

tended to be lower in the years immediately following a plague, the problem of burial accommodation would have remained acute in those years, since the recent plague mortality and the associated elevation in deaths from other causes would have filled all available burial spaces.

No such detail is available for Paris before the 1670s, when according to the newly established series of monthly statistics in the Etat des Baptêmes it experienced some 17–20,000 deaths per annum.[10] At the risk of circularity, however, it is possible to propose that a city with 200,000 inhabitants, the suggested size of Paris c. 1500, would probably have been burying 6,600 to 7,600 bodies in most years; a city of 300,000, between 9,900 and 11,400; a city of 400,000, from 13,200 to 15,200. And the pressure on burial resources was unremitting: even when Paris's live population seems to have fallen, in the 1570s and 1580s, this was at least partly due to increased deaths in the city, as well as to outward movement and the interruption to immigration. The cumulative total of dead in either city over the period 1520–1670 was well over one million. Despite London's relatively small size in 1500, its sixteenth-century death toll must have reached several hundred thousand, especially since there were at least three major epidemics. In the seventeenth century, between 1603 and 1665, the death total (including the distant parishes) came to over 880,000.[11] Paris's mortality total must have been higher than London's, given its much larger size at the start of the period, and may have neared two million in all.

The number of deaths and burials occuring weekly or monthly was of importance to the local community in determining what demands were made upon its burial resources. Urban mortality had a marked seasonality, with deaths distributed very unevenly across the year. Graunt noted for London that 'the unhealthful season is the autumn', and the late summer/early autumn high is confirmed by examination of both parish registers and weekly Bills.[12] The returns of the Etat des Baptêmes for Paris in the 1670s tell a story of unpredictable seasonal variation, with monthly death totals for the city ranging from just over 1,000 to over 2,000; no month was invariably the worst or the best, though the peaks were usually of shorter duration than the lows.[13] Seasonal disparities were greatly

---

[10] See appendix 2.

[11] 886,601: calculated by adding the yearly totals for 1604–64 given in Graunt, 'Natural and political observations', pp. 407–10 (752,001) to the totals for the years 1603 (37,294) and 1665 (97,306) from ibid., table f, p. 426. Individual figures may be slightly inaccurate but the magnitude is not in doubt.

[12] Graunt, 'Natural and political observations', p. 369; cf. J. Landers, *Death and the metropolis. Studies in the demographic history of London, 1670–1830* (Cambridge, 1993), pp. 203–41, for new seasonal mortality patterns after the disappearance of plague.

[13] Graunt, 'Natural and political observations', pp. 424–5; BN (Réserve), LK[7] 6745.

increased in plague years, as discussed below. The local incidence of particular diseases – not only plague, but also infections and water-borne diseases – must also have contributed to local and seasonal variations in death totals.

The characteristics of those who died were also significant. Age- and gender-related variations in mortality were very marked; particular diseases may have affected the individual's attitude to and preparation for death. Gender is the easiest global calculation, since the London Bills give total deaths for males and females. For the middle years of the seventeenth century (1629–64), the ratio was remarkably consistent at 52 per cent males, 48 per cent females (equivalent to 108:100), including the plague year of 1636.[14] There were local divergences from this, of course, according to the character of the local population.[15] The age profile of the dead population is harder to establish, outside some broad but important generalisations. The very high level of infant and child mortality in this period has long been appreciated. In some parts of early modern London, fewer than 60 per cent of children born there survived to the age of fifteen.[16] 'Infantile' causes accounted for some 33 per cent of deaths in mid-seventeenth-century London, and plausibly another one-sixth of deaths from a range of other causes also fell on infants and children.[17] Across the whole metropolis it seems likely that 40 to 50 per cent of all deaths in non-plague years were of juveniles. Evidence from the few parish registers that give ages at death over a period suggests that a significant number of deaths occurred in every decade of adult life, from the twenties to the sixties, with a small population living to their seventies, eighties or above.[18] Widows formed an important sector of the population of early modern London, though not necessarily one with a consistent relationship to age. They tended to cluster in some of the poorer areas of London, which will have affected the gender and also the age profile of those areas.[19]

[14] Calculated from Graunt, 'Natural and political observations', table p. 411.

[15] See e.g. M. F. Hollingsworth and T. H. Hollingsworth, 'Plague mortality rates by age and sex in the parish of St Botolph's without Bishopsgate, London, 1603', *Population Studies* 25 (1971), table 1, p. 134.

[16] Finlay, *Population and metropolis*, pp. 50, 101.

[17] Graunt, 'Natural and political observations', p. 349.

[18] T. R. Forbes, *Chronicle from Aldgate: life and death in Shakespeare's London* (New Haven, 1971), table 4, p. 74; Hollingsworth and Hollingsworth, 'Plague mortality rates by age and sex', p. 135.

[19] V. Brodsky, 'Widows in late Elizabethan London: remarriage, economic opportunity and family orientations', in L. Bonfield, R. Smith, and K. Wrightson (eds.), *The world we have gained: histories of population and social structure* (Oxford, 1986), pp. 122–54; B. Todd, 'The remarrying widow: a stereotype reconsidered', in M. Prior (ed.), *Women in English society, 1500–1800* (London, 1985), pp. 54–92; J. Boulton, 'London widowhood

Life expectancy was related to social category, as expressed in a range of measures such as location of residence (with poverty mapped by rent values, tax exemption, and other proxies) and company membership. Children born in the poorer London parishes had markedly worse chances of surviving to the age of fifteen, with a corresponding impact on the overall life expectancy in those parishes.[20] Men who entered the freedom in the mid-sixteenth century as members of the greater city companies lived longer on average than those who entered the lesser, artisan companies, suggesting 'a predictable correlation between wealth and longevity'.[21] Epidemic death (plague or other) and subsistence crisis hit the poorer parishes hardest, and had the greatest relative impact on people in their middle years; this too would affect the age profile of the dead differently according to locality.[22] Although comparable data do not exist for Paris, other French studies reveal a pattern of life expectancy 'nuanced' by social status.[23] Extrapolation from the varied experience of other areas in France led Chaunu to suggest that adult deaths in Paris could have been in the minority (as in London), and that at least 40 per cent of deaths were of children under the age of four.[24] It seems reasonable to conclude that in Paris too, outside major epidemics, dearth, and war, the 'burial population' was made up of a wide spectrum of ages, but that half or more of the dead were under the age of fifteen.

One major difference between London and Paris in the experience of death, with a material impact on the question of burial, was the huge importance of hospitals and hospitalisation in the Parisian life-cycle. It seems likely that the approach to death, for a significant number of Parisians, was by way of the hospital; they were places to go in anticipation of death, not necessarily to seek a cure. Medieval hospitals offered hospitality, asylum, and assistance at least as much as medical treatment, and care of the dying was an important element in notions of charity. The total dying in the

revisited: the decline of female remarriage in the 17th and early 18th centuries', *Continuity and Change* 5 (1990), 323–55; B. Todd, 'Demographic determinism and female agency: the remarrying widow reconsidered . . . again', *Continuity and Change* 9 (1994), 421–50. D. Keene, 'The poor and their neighbours in seventeenth-century London' (unpublished seminar paper, Centre for Metropolitan History, London, n.d.).

[20] Finlay, *Population and metropolis*, pp. 50, 101, 108.

[21] Rappaport, *Worlds within worlds*, p. 71.

[22] J. A. I. Champion, *London's dreaded visitation. The social geography of the great plague in 1665* (London, Historical Geography Research Paper Series 31, 1995), pp. 53–80, who notes, however, significant local variations in the profile of plague victims. Cf. P. Slack, *The impact of plague on Tudor and Stuart England* (London, 1985).

[23] L. Brockliss and C. Jones, *The medical world of early modern France* (Oxford, 1997), p. 62.

[24] Chaunu, *La mort à Paris*, pp. 167–93.

Hôtel-Dieu and the other sick hospitals of Paris in the early modern period was very large. At the beginning of the seventeenth century, in years not known to be serious epidemic ones, between 1,000 and 1,500 bodies were taken from the Hôtel-Dieu for burial at the cemetery of la Trinité; this represents 10 per cent or more of the probable total death toll for a city of *c.* 300,000, as Paris may then have been.[25] Some of the Hôtel-Dieu dead were reclaimed for private burial, and others buried at the Innocents, so the total dying in the hospital must have been still greater. By the later seventeenth century, more than a quarter of all Parisians appear to have died in a hospital. Of the 21,477 recorded deaths in Paris in 1670, 4,812 or 22 per cent died in the Hôtel-Dieu; another 1,105, or 5 per cent, died in the other hospitals. Most of these dead came from the hospitals for the sick, and only a small number from the houses of the Hôpital-Général founded to enclose the poor in 1656–7.[26]

Though the Parisian hospitals were where people went to die, it is not clear at what stage of sickness an individual was removed there, or for what specific reason. According to one historian of the Ancien-Régime hospital, if a poor patient did not respond to treatment at home within three weeks, he or she was taken to the Hôtel-Dieu.[27] Numbers seeking hospital aid could evidently be swelled by general distress in the city. In 1587, the numbers of the sick poor 'qui affluent audict Hotel-Dieu' were estimated at 14–15,000, but a few years later, in 1592, a doctor's claim for wages was rejected because there were not many sick in the hospital.[28] The records of the Hôtel-Dieu refer to the sick 'presenting themselves' at the hospital, some with plague; subsequently it appears that it also received the wounded from the armed clashes during the disturbances of the Fronde. October 1661 saw some kind of epidemic, though not of plague, which again brought numbers of the sick to the hospital.[29] Some of the deaths at the Hôtel-Dieu must have been of women in childbed: the hospital had a 'salle des accouchées' and recorded a number of baptisms each month, while the new hospital of the Enfants Rouges had been

[25] Annual totals from the accounts of the Hôtel-Dieu, summarised in L. Brièle, *Collection de documents pour servir à l'histoire des hôpitaux de Paris*, 4 vols. (Paris 1881–7), vol. IV, pp. 44–61; L. Brièle and M. A. Husson, *Inventaire-sommaire des archives hospitalières antérieures à 1790. Hôtel-Dieu*, 2 vols. (Paris, 1866, 1884), vol. II, pp. 215–23.

[26] Etat des Baptêmes: BN (Réserve), LK⁷ 6745. For a brief account of the Hôpital-Général, see L. Bernard, *The emerging city. Paris in the age of Louis XIV* (Durham N.C., 1970), pp. 145–55. See also Brockliss and Jones, *The medical world of early modern France*, pp. 678–88.

[27] Bernard, *The emerging city*, p. 145, citing L. Pasturier, *L'assistance à Paris sous l'Ancien Régime et pendant la Révolution* (Paris, 1897), p. 187.

[28] Brièle, *Inventaire-sommaire*, vol. II, pp. 207–8.

[29] Ibid., vol. II, pp. 108, 110, 118.

created in 1535–7 for the orphaned children born in the Hôtel-Dieu.[30] The hospital was certainly a place of bad reputation, on account of its high death rate and crowded conditions. In 1670, epidemics of smallpox and scurvy flourished at the Hôtel-Dieu, and 114 of 800 scorbutics received at the hospital of Saint-Louis died.[31] Sir William Petty noted the large numbers dying in the Hôtel-Dieu, compared with the numbers entering, but drew the probably mistaken conclusion that this was due to 'want of as good usage and accommodation', and 'the evil administration of the hospital', rather than a different culture of hospitalisation from the one he knew. He attributed the greater propensity to hospitalise the sick in Paris to the city's poverty.[32] The Hôtel-Dieu must therefore have loomed large in popular Parisian visions of death, and the scale of hospitalisation clearly had a major impact on burial in the parishes. It would certainly have affected the social profile of the burial population there, relieving them of responsibility for burying a significant number of their poorer fellows.

However high normal mortality was, the impact of crises and epidemics was even greater, both in multiplying the number of deaths and in concentrating mortality, and thus the problem of disposing of the dead, into a short period. Both subsistence crises and plague had an impact on the spatial and social distribution of death. Plague also undoubtedly affected contemporary views of death, because it seemed both random and very lethal, and because it so rapidly debilitated and killed most of its victims.

Though both cities were to some degree protected by their national governments from the worst impact of dearth, London still suffered to a limited extent from food shortage and a related elevation of mortality, while for Paris the breakdown of national order had a devastating impact on the food supply. Food prices in London certainly rose throughout the sixteenth century, though not steadily, with the sharpest rises concentrated in the 1540s–50s and the 1590s.[33] The dearth years of 1595–7 led to widespread starvation and death in rural areas, especially in the north of England. However, the efforts of national and local government to ensure food supplies and to hold down prices in the capital, though not wholly successful, were apparently adequate to keep starvation at bay

---

[30] Ibid., vol. II, pp. 116, 119, 120; Etat des Baptêmes: BN (Réserve), LK⁷ 6745; Babelon, *Paris au XVIe siècle*, pp. 187–8.

[31] Bernard, *The emerging city*, pp. 223–33; Brièle, *Inventaire-sommaire*, vol. II, p. 123. The year 1670 was when both smallpox and scurvy were noted as important causes of death in the Etat des Baptêmes, suggesting that the experience of the Hôtel-Dieu was a major source for those comments: BN (Réserve), LK⁷ 6745.

[32] Petty, 'Two essays in political arithmetick', pp. 508, 510–11.

[33] See Rappaport, *Worlds within worlds*, ch. 5, 'The standard of living', esp. fig. 5.4, p. 155.

in London at least until the third year of the crisis. Athough the overall death toll was insignificant compared with the plague years of 1593 and 1603, 1597 was a year of raised mortality, especially in the poorer outlying parishes of the metropolis.[34] It was obviously the poor who suffered most: 4,014 householders were said to be 'wanting relief' in late 1595, and in 1598 a contemporary remarked on 'the poor and miserable people within this city who for want of food and like do daily perish'.[35] In the seventeenth century, the cost of living in London rose more rapidly than wages, and though there was no actual subsistence crisis food prices rose sharply in the later 1640s, presumably because of difficulties associated with the civil war.[36] More generally, however, there appears to be no significant correlation between nutritional status (based on the price of food) and epidemic mortality in London, with the exception of typhus, an acknowledged concomitant of dearth.[37] There is no way of knowing to what extent long-term malnutrition may have undermined resistance to and survival of non-epidemic diseases, or poor-quality food have contributed to gastric and intestinal disorders.

Paris appears to have been in a much riskier position than London with regard to its food supply, partly because of its greater size for most of the period, but even more because of challenges to the central authority that helped to guarantee its supplies. In bad harvest years (at least one in most decades in the sixteenth century, though less frequent in the seventeenth) grain prices doubled. The threshold of significantly increased mortality was a trebling of prices, reached in the siege of 1589–90. Stories of gruesome expedients to avert starvation circulated, and one in three Parisians is said to have died. If true, this implies a death toll of 100,000 or more.[38] The records of the Hôtel-Dieu note 'l'extreme necessité de bled' at that time, and the difficulty of ensuring food for the sick poor in the hospital. The crisis may itself have brought more poor to the hospital, seeking relief. This may also have been the case in 1649, when the hospital complained simultaneously of 'peu de blé' and of 1,700 lying sick there.[39]

---

[34] Ibid. pp. 157–9; A. B. Appleby, *Famine in Tudor and Stuart England* (Liverpool, 1978), pp. 135–9; M. J. Power, 'London and the control of the "crisis" of the 1590s', *History* 70 (1985), 371–85; M. J. Power, 'A "crisis" reconsidered: social and economic dislocation in London in the 1590s', *London Journal* 12 (1986), 134–45.

[35] Archer, *The pursuit of stability*, pp. 151–4.

[36] J. Boulton, 'Food prices and the standard of living in London in the "century of revolution", 1580–1700', *Economic History Review* 53 (2000), 455–92.

[37] A. B. Appleby, 'Nutrition and disease, the case of London, 1550–1750', *Journal of Interdisciplinary History* 6 (1975), 1–22.

[38] Chaunu, *La mort à Paris*, pp. 185–6; N. L. Roelker (ed.), *The Paris of Henry of Navarre, as seen by Pierre de l'Estoile. Selections from his mémoires-journaux* (Cambridge, Mass., 1958), pp. 188, 192. See below, p. 112.

[39] Brièle, *Inventaire-sommaire*, vol. II, pp. 103, 110, 208, 209.

Grain prices rose by 250 per cent during the Fronde, enough to have some impact on mortality, especially when the grain scarcity was associated with larger-scale warfare and disease.[40] Though statistics from wills are subject to question because of the smallness of each sample, they do apparently confirm this picture of crisis mortality in Paris in siege and civil war, though normally one would not expect those with sufficient substance to make a will to be starving.[41] As with London, the greatest impact of dearth must have been on those close to the margin of subsistence.

Both London and Paris experienced a succession of epidemics in the early modern period.[42] London was hit by the sweating sickness of 1551: according to the contemporary Henry Machyn, 872 people died there between 8 and 19 July 1551.[43] Almost certainly the most serious single episode of the early modern period in England was the national epidemic of 1556–9, which was severe enough to affect the population trend. This may have been a 'mixed' epidemic, with typhus, following the failed harvests of 1555 and 1556, plus influenza, a 'new ague' or 'new disease'.[44] Surviving London registers at this date are few and patchy, possibly the result of the epidemic itself, but also of the fact that the order to copy and keep early data, to which we owe many of the surviving registers, specified the accession of Elizabeth as the start date. There is, however, a perceptible peak in deaths in 1559 in some London registers, and it is clear from other sources that the city suffered badly: eleven of the city's aldermen died between 1555 and the end of 1559.[45]

The most severe epidemic disease, in its recurrence and overall fatality, was the one defined by contemporaries as plague or pestilence, and currently accepted by most historians as some form of bubonic plague.[46]

[40] Chaunu, *La mort à Paris*, pp. 185–6.   [41] Ibid. pp. 188–90.

[42] E. A. Wrigley and R. Schofield, *The population history of England, 1541–1871, a reconstruction* (Cambridge, 1981), pp. 15–32.

[43] Machyn, *Diary*, p. 8; A. Dyer, 'The English sweating sickness of 1551. An epidemic anatomized', *Medical History* 41 (1997), 361–83.

[44] Wrigley and Schofield, *Population history*, p. 207; F. J. Fisher, 'Influenza and inflation in Tudor England', *Economic History Review* 18 (1965), 120–9; Slack, *Impact of plague*, pp. 70–1.

[45] Slack, *Impact of plague*, table p. 147; Machyn, *Diary*, pp. 99, 105–6, 111, 115, 116, 166, 170–1, 173, 217.

[46] C. F. Mullett, *The bubonic plague in England. An essay in the history of preventive medicine* (Lexington, 1956); J. F. D. Shrewsbury, *A history of bubonic plague in the British Isles* (Cambridge, 1971); Slack, *Impact of plague*; A. Appleby, 'The disappearance of plague – a continuing puzzle', *Economic History Review*, 33 (1980), 161–73; P. Slack, 'The disappearance of plague – an alternative view', *Economic History Review* 34 (1981), 469–76. Graham Twigg, whose 'biological reappraisal' of *The black death* (London, 1984) argued against its identification as modern bubonic plague, also queries the identification of the early modern disease; cf. G. Twigg, 'Plague in London: spatial and

Though surviving London parish registers for the 1540s and 1550s are too few, too geographically scattered, and individually concern numbers too small for statistical analysis, their evidence suggests raised mortality in 1543 and 1548. Thereafter, the five major epidemics (1563, 1593, 1603, 1625, 1665), and one lesser one (1636) are quite well documented, along with more localised outbreaks, or periods of raised mortality, especially in the 1580s and from c. 1604 to 1612.[47] While the epidemic of 1665 was the last, and therefore in popular memory *the* great plague, and certainly caused the largest number of deaths, it is probable that 1563 and possibly 1603 were more severe relative to the population at the time.[48] Although there were few years when plague was wholly absent from the capital, and it made some contribution to overall mortality levels in non-epidemic years, the impact of the epidemics on communities already perhaps struggling to cope with ordinary urban mortality was very marked. Even in the least severe of the city-wide epidemics, in 1636, 10,400 deaths were attributed to plague and the overall mortality figure for the year was 2.6 times normal.[49] In 1665, 68,596 deaths were attributed to plague, and the total mortality for the year, 97,306, was nearly six times the annual average for the preceding decade.[50] The total figure would have included deaths from plague not so reported, and probably many deaths, especially of infants, old people, and those already ailing, resulting from the breakdown of support during the epidemic. Predictably, mortality was worse in some areas of the metropolis, though the focus of epidemic death shifted over time, from the ancient crowded city centre to the newer, poorer suburbs.[51] While the overall elevation of the death rate was striking, the impact on the local community was increased by the concentration of deaths within a short period. Plague epidemics in

temporal aspects of mortality', in J. A. I. Champion (ed.), *Epidemic disease in London* (London, 1993), pp. 1–17. Champion, *London's dreaded visitation*, carefully and rightly avoids explanations or inferences based on the epidemiology of bubonic plague in his account of the epidemic of 1665. In this study I have used the word 'plague' for the disease or epidemic so called by contemporaries, but have tried to avoid making any assumptions about its epidemiology that are not based on observation of its behaviour and incidence at the time.

[47] Slack, *Impact of plague*, table p. 147.

[48] I. Sutherland, 'When was the great plague? Mortality in London, 1563–1665', in D. V. Glass and R. Revelle (eds.), *Population and social change* (London, 1972), p. 311, believes that 1563 may have seen the highest rise in mortality, but that 'the many uncertainties make it unwise to single out any one of these plagues [1563, 1603, 1625, 1665] as clearly greater than the others'. Slack, *Impact of plague*, pp. 150–1, also points to the severity of 1603.

[49] Annual average mortality 1626–35 and total and plague mortality for 1636 calculated from the figures in Graunt, 'Natural and political observations', p. 408.

[50] Champion, *London's dreaded visitation*, p. 27.

[51] Slack, *Impact of plague*, pp. 152–63.

early modern London typically began in early summer, really took hold in the late summer, were at their worst in early autumn, and only began to decline with the onset of colder weather.[52] Although there were local chronologies, starting and ending earlier or later as the disease moved across the metropolis, in most parishes the majority of deaths occurred within a period of eight weeks or so.

Both the gross and the local impact of epidemic death are effectively impossible to chart for Paris in the way they are for London, owing to the loss of parish registers and other material, though numerous epidemics can be identified.[53] According to Biraben, plague was present in Paris for almost one year in three in the sixteenth and seventeenth centuries to 1670. There were major epidemics in 1529–33, 1553–5, 1560–2, 1580, and 1595–7, 'les années terribles'; plague was also present in several other years. It is striking that plague episodes in Paris, unlike London, appear to have lasted two or three years, but the relative severity of each epidemic season cannot be calculated.[54] The epidemic of 1566 may have claimed 25,000 lives; that of 1580, 30,000, according to Pierre l'Estoile, though contemporary estimates are rarely reliable.[55] The records of the Hôtel-Dieu mention plague or plague victims in the hospital in 1533, 1561, 1584, 1596, and 1598.[56] Plague recurred in 1604, 1606–8, 1612, and 1618–19, and from 1622 to 1632.[57] After outbreaks in 1636 and 1638, Paris, like London, was largely free from major plague epidemics during the 1640s and 1650s, apart from one in 1652, attributed to the Fronde. The 'paroxysme' of 1668 was the last visitation in the capital, though not in France.[58] As elsewhere, it is likely that the disease hit the poor hard, both because of their living conditions and because of the reported propensity of the rich to flee the city in an epidemic; plague was certainly treated as a police matter, because of the possibility of disorder and crime. It was understandably a terrifying disease to the authorities as well as the individual, overwhelming the human body and the social

---

[52] Ibid., p. 65; Graunt, 'Natural and political observations', table f, p. 426. For the local experience, see Champion, *London's dreaded visitation*; V. Harding, 'Burial of the plague dead in early modern London', in Champion (ed.), *Epidemic disease in London*, pp. 53–64.

[53] J. N. Biraben, *Les hommes et la peste en France et dans les pays européens et méditerranéens*, 2 vols. (Paris, 1975–6), vol. II, p. 111. Cf. F. Hildesheimer, *La terreur et la pitié? l'Ancien Régime à l'épreuve de la peste* (Paris, 1990); M. Lucenet, *Les grandes pestes en France* (Paris, 1985).

[54] Biraben, *Les hommes et la peste*, vol. 2, annexe IV, pp. 377–88. See also M. Fosseyeux, 'Les épidémies de peste à Paris', *Bulletin de la Société Française d'Histoire de la Médicine*, 12.2 (1913), 115–41.

[55] Babelon, *Paris au XVIe siècle*, p. 176.

[56] Brièle, *Inventaire-sommaire*, vol. II, pp. 103, 104, 189, 196, 211; Brièle, *Collection de documents*, vol. II, p. 53.

[57] Brièle, *Inventaire-sommaire*, vol. II, pp. 221–3.

[58] Chaunu, *La mort à Paris*, pp. 176–85, citing Biraben, *Les hommes et la peste*.

body, generating rational and irrational responses ranging from obsessive precautions to despair.[59]

Mortality in the early modern metropolis was therefore numerically high at all times, but its impact was increased because it was so unevenly distributed. Infants and children suffered most, but still more in poorer areas. Epidemic death also concentrated in certain quarters of the city. Patterns of disease contributed to marked seasonal variation. The massive overall growth of population magnified the scale of the burial problem, while the uneven distribution of resources increased the difficulties of many local communities. The high mortality totals of the early modern period certainly posed a major problem for the cities' governors, whose authority and adequacy were already under strain because of the rate of population increase and the changing composition of the urban population.

Authorities, boundaries, divisions

Topographical change was an inevitable result of population growth in both cities, though responses to it differed. Over this period, London was transformed from a relatively compact, centred settlement, with a large proportion of its population contained within its ancient walls, into a much more extended, sprawling metropolis, that had spread over green fields and open spaces and linked several outlying nuclei into one whole.[60] However, physical and demographic growth was not matched by an appropriate revision of administrative divisions and jurisdictions. In 1500 the boundary of the city of London – the area ruled by the mayor and aldermen based at Guildhall – included most of the built-up area and a considerable amount of open space outside the walls. This boundary was marked on the approach roads to the city by bars or movable barriers, but there were no fortifications or even discernible embankments around most of the circuit. After the inclusion of Southwark in the city's jurisdiction in 1550, this boundary was never altered, even though a dense mass of buildings subsequently spread far beyond it. The projected incorporation of the suburbs into a new metropolitan authority in the early seventeenth century failed, for political reasons, and by the later seventeenth century

[59] Biraben, *Les hommes et la peste*, vol. II, pp. 31, 105, 117–18, 124–5, 139, 173; Brockliss and Jones, *The medical world of early modern France*, pp. 37–43.

[60] M. D. Lobel (ed.), *The British atlas of historic towns*, vol. III: *The city of London from prehistoric times to c. 1520* (London, 1990); F. Barker and P. Jackson, *London, 2000 years of a city and its people* (London, 1983); V. Harding, 'City, capital and metropolis: the changing shape of seventeenth-century London', in J. F. Merritt (ed.), *Imagining early modern London: perceptions and portrayals of the city from Stow to Strype, 1598–1720* (Cambridge, 2001), pp. 117–43.

probably three-quarters of the capital's population lived outside the city and the jurisdiction of mayor and aldermen. This had an important effect on both the history and the historiography of London, in that there was a marked disparity between the resources (and in consequence the records) of government and its activities in the city centre and in the new suburbs.[61]

There was a closer match between Paris's topographical and administrative identities. The city wall of Philippe-Auguste (1180–1220) survived on the left bank, and still enclosed most of the early modern settlement, but on the right bank the early medieval wall had been succeeded in the late fourteenth century by a much wider circuit. In the mid-sixteenth century there was still space within Paris's walls for further development, and the walls themselves were renovated and extended from 1553, so there was no need to question the identity of the city in terms of jurisdiction. There were suburban settlements, *bourgs* and *faubourgs* outside the ramparts, but these areas were regularly incorporated into the city, so that effectively 'Paris' as ruled either from the Hôtel de Ville or the Châtelet comprised the whole urbanised area.[62] At the lower level too, although tradition and vested interest made reform of the internal administrative boundaries of the city difficult, it was not impossible. The extent of growth and change was recognised by revising the boundaries of *quartiers*, the principal administrative subdivisions of the city, and by creating new *dizaines*, subdivisions of the *quartier*. There were still many inconsistencies and disparities, including areas of exempt jurisdiction, and there were marked social differences between parts of the metropolis, but it formed a relatively coherent geographical–juridical entity throughout the period.[63]

However, when the local government of the two cities is compared, London proves easier to describe than Paris. London had a well-defined and powerful municipality, commanding considerable resources and with wide competence, even if its jurisdiction did not extend to the whole of the metropolis. Royal government usually operated through the agency

[61] N. G. Brett-James, *The growth of Stuart London* (London, 1935), passim; V. Harding, 'From compact city to complex metropolis: records for the history of London, 1500–1720', in M. V. Roberts (ed.), *Archives and the metropolis* (London, 1998), pp. 83–92.

[62] Babelon, *Paris au XVIe siècle*, pp. 195–292; D. Thompson, *Renaissance Paris. Architecture and growth, 1475–1600* (Berkeley, 1984); H. Ballon, *The Paris of Henri IV. Architecture and urbanism* (New York and Cambridge, Mass., 1991).

[63] R. Pillorget and J. de Viguerie, 'Les quartiers de Paris aux XVIIe et XVIIIe siècles', *Revue d'Histoire Moderne et Contemporaine* 17 (1970), 253–77; R. Descimon and J. Nagle, 'Les quartiers de Paris du Moyen Age au XVIIIe siècle. Evolution d'un espace plurifonctionnel', *Annales ESC* 34 (1979), 956–83; R. Descimon, 'Paris on the eve of Saint Bartholomew: taxation, privilege and social geography', in P. Benedict (ed.), *Cities and social change in early modern France* (London, 1992), pp. 69–104.

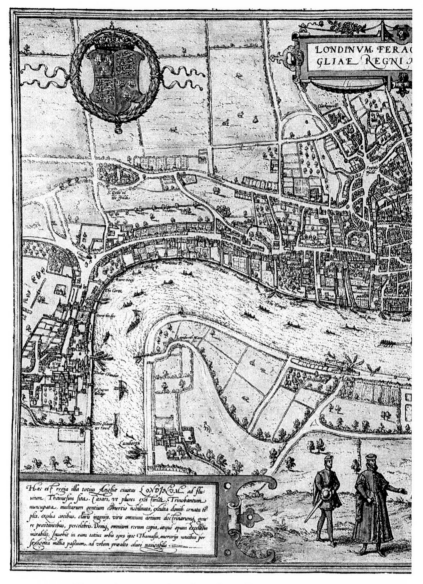

1   Sixteenth-century London, from Braun and Hogenberg, *Civitates orbis terrarum* (1572) (London, Guildhall Library). North is at the top.

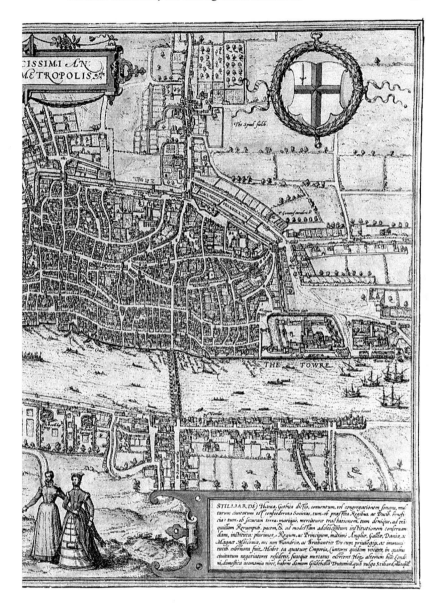

2   Sixteenth-century Paris, from Braun and Hogenberg, *Civitates orbis terrarum* (1572) (London, Guildhall Library). East is at the top.

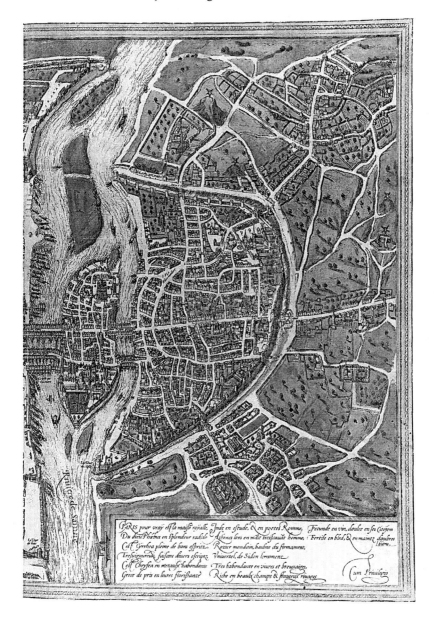

Paris pour vray est la maison royalle, Inde en estude, & en poetes Romme, Fecunde en vin, doulce en ses Croysen
Du dieu Phœbus en splendeur radiale Athenes lors en mœil trescauait homme, Fertile en bled, & en maintz dauieres
Cest Cyrrhea pleine de bons espritz, Rozier mondain, baulme du firmament, Leseru,
Tresuigneureux, faisant diuers escriptz Vnuersel, de Sidon lornement
Cest Chrysea en metaulx habondante Tres habondante en vuires et breuuaiges,
Grece de pris en liures florissante Riche en beaulx champs & fluuieux riuaiges, Cum Priuilesio

of the municipality, though it was inclined to intervene directly at times. Paris, on the other hand, had a relatively weak municipality, with much power assumed or exercised by the king's officers at the Châtelet, and also by the court of the Parlement of Paris, sitting in the heart of the city, or by the king himself.

The city of London[64] was ruled by a court or council of twenty-six aldermen, one of whom held the office of Lord Mayor for a year at a time and represented the city on all ceremonial occasions. New aldermen were recruited by the existing court rather than popularly elected, though there was a veneer of democratic consent. The position of alderman was normally held for life, unless business failure or other disaster forced a premature resignation, and once elected a man could expect to take his turn as Lord Mayor in some eight to twelve years from his election as alderman. Those aldermen who had already passed the mayoral chair formed an élite group, distinguished by their seniority and the knighthood which normally accompanied mayoral service. Below the Court of Aldermen came a much larger council, the Common Council, with over 200 members, an important forum in its own right, which gave consent to taxation and issues of major public import. An enlarged assembly known as Common Hall made or approved the appointment of sheriffs, mayors, civic bureaucrats, and parliamentary representatives. Common councilmen were elected at the annual meetings of the city's twenty-six wards, and held the position for several years, and sometimes for life, rather like the aldermen, though they were subject to re-election. For many of them, this was the highest office they held, but it was also a necessary step for those rising towards aldermanic rank. The activities of the municipality were supported by a bureaucracy, headed by the Chamberlain, the Common Clerk, and the Common Sergeant; the Recorder, usually a professional lawyer, was the chief legal officer of the city, and normally one of its four MPs.

The mayor and aldermen wielded real power within the city, as legislators and policy makers, as justices of the peace, as dispensers of patronage, as the court of appeal for lesser civic proceedings. The crown had a constant role, intervening with orders, requests, and suggestions, but the city normally acted independently though with due deference. The city's means of coercive enforcement were limited, and in a rapidly changing

[64] For this section see Rappaport, *Worlds within worlds* chs. 2, 6; Archer, *The pursuit of stability*, ch. 2; V. Pearl, *London and the outbreak of the Puritan revolution* (Oxford, 1961), ch. 2; Foster, *The politics of stability*, chs. 2, 3; J. Boulton, 'London', in P. Clark (ed.), *Cambridge urban history of Britain*, vol. II: *1540–1840* (Cambridge, 2000), pp. 315–46; I. Archer, 'The government of London, 1500–1650', and V. Harding, 'Controlling a complex metropolis, 1650–1750. Politics, parishes and powers', in *London Journal* 26 (2001), pp. 19–28, 29–37.

and expanding city there were many vexing and intractable problems, but there was a high degree of compliance. Outside the city, London was much less effectively governed.[65] Southwark on the south bank was partly incorporated into the city in 1550, as the twenty-sixth ward, but never had the infrastructures of administration and representation enjoyed by the other twenty-five. The vill or settlement of Westminster, formerly under the manorial adminstration of Westminster Abbey, was governed by the vestry of St Margaret Westminster, and by a Court of Burgesses from 1585. Though significant local powers were granted to this court, it never exercised as wide or effective a jurisdiction as the city itself. The remaining suburbs were administered by their parish vestries, especially after the institution of the Poor Laws in 1598/1601, and by justices of the peace, but their powers and effectiveness again fell far short of the city's. It has been argued that the city of London was almost over-governed by a multiplicity of officers in elective or salaried positions, but this level of provision was not matched in the new suburbs, whose local services were often much poorer.[66] Perhaps the most important effect, however, from the point of view of the study of death and burial, is that authority in moments of crisis, such as the plague epidemics, was divided and uncertain. While the Privy Council could order the municipality to act in respect of the area its jurisdiction covered, and rely on its being able, if not eager, to carry out its directions, for much of the metropolis there was no effective authority at that level to which such tasks could be delegated. The problem became even more acute as the suburbs spread and as the concentration of plague mortality shifted there.[67]

In early modern Paris,[68] power was exercised in separate spheres, not without contention, by the elected municipality or Bureau de Ville under the *prévôt des marchands* at the Hôtel de Ville, and the king's representative, the *prévôt de Paris* and his officers, at the Châtelet. The *prévôt des marchands* and the four *échevins* were elected for two-year terms by a limited electoral college, who also elected the twenty-four *conseillers de la ville*. The latter formed an advisory council rather than an executive or legislative one like the Court of Aldermen of London. The officers

[65] Brett-James, *The growth of Stuart London*, esp. pp. 127–50, 223–47.
[66] V. Pearl, 'Change and stability in seventeenth-century London', *London Journal* 5 (1979), 3–34.
[67] P. Slack, 'Metropolitan government in crisis: the response to plague', in Beier and Finlay, *London 1500–1700*, pp. 60–81; Slack, *Impact of plague*, pp. 154–7; Champion, *London's dreaded visitation*, pp. 42–52.
[68] This account is based on Babelon, *Paris au XVIe siècle*, pp. 263–92; Diefendorf, *Paris city councillors*, pp. 3–32, 42–59; Pillorget, *Paris sous les premiers Bourbons*, pp. 53–9; Bernard, *The emerging city*, pp. 29–55.

of the municipality included the *greffier* (secretary or clerk), the *receveur* (treasurer or chamberlain), and the *procureur du Roi et de la Ville* (representing the city to the agencies of national government). There were also local representatives of the *quartiers* and *dizaines* into which the city was topographically divided. The staff of the Châtelet included three *lieutenants*, *civil*, *criminel*, and *particulier*, and a corps of notaries. As this might suggest, the main police and legal activity of the metropolis was based there. The Bureau de Ville had responsibility for tax-raising, street-cleaning, and provisioning; it also had a corps of armed men, and used these and its other resources in the ceremonial programmes with which it was charged. Both areas of responsibility, however, were subject to appeal to or order from the Parlement of Paris, especially in disputes over rights that might lead to breaches of order. By the mid-seventeenth century the Parlement was exercising 'formidable administrative and police duties in the capital city', not merely acting as court of appeal: it had an interest in highways and public spaces, food supply, and public order, and indeed burial, usually working in a close relationship with the Châtelet.[69] In the last decade of the period covered by this study, Paris's government was subject to major reform, with the institution of a new *lieutenant général de police* at the Châtelet and the appointment of Nicolas de la Reynie to the post in 1667. Though this development did not in itself eliminate all the overlapping and disputed jurisdictions of the past, the powers exercised by the *lieutenant de police* marked the beginning of a new era in the government of the city, exemplified in *commissaire* Nicolas Delamare's four-volume *Traité de la police*.[70]

There was considerable overlap in the personnel of all these offices, undermining perhaps the autonomy of the municipality as such but also tending to consolidate authority in Paris in the hands of a group of notables. Members of the royal courts of Parlement, the Chambre des Comptes, and the Cour des Aides might seek election to a municipal office; over 60 per cent of sixteenth-century *conseillers de la ville* held office in one of the sovereign courts or the royal administration.[71] The elective nature of the municipal offices was threatened by royal intervention, and the increasing venality and heritability of office weakened the democratic or representative aspect of the city's government. Nevertheless, there were networks of kinship, patronage, and clientage that helped to sustain the

---

[69] A. N. Hamscher, *The Parlement of Paris after the Fronde, 1653–1673* (Pittsburgh, 1976), pp. 134–6. Cf. Thibaut-Payen, *Les morts, l'église et l'état*, passim.

[70] N. Delamare, *Traité de la police, où l'on trouvera l'histoire de son établissement, les fonctions et les prérogatives de ses magistrats, toutes les lois et les règlements qui la concernent* (BN, MS Fr 21609; 2nd printed edn, Paris, 1722–38). Cf. Bernard, *The emerging city*, pp. 29–55.

[71] Diefendorf, *Paris city councillors*, p. 44.

power of the governors of Paris. Though it appears that they were legally and administratively weaker than London's governors, they were not by any means powerless or lacking in independent perspective. The rulers of sixteenth-century Paris were certainly more prepared to resist royal authority, at least on confessional issues, than those of London.

Parishes and community

London and Paris shared the important characteristic of physical and social complexity arising from their size. With such great acreages and population numbers, each city was in fact a collection of smaller, overlapping, partly integrated communities, defined by geography or by some other identifying feature. There were considerable differences in the social and environmental character of localities across the face of the city, and this is of major importance for the study of a phenomenon as rooted in locality as burial practice. Individual parishes or streets had distinctive social compositions, whether the measure be wealth, occupation, house, or household size. The size and shape of the parish mattered, as did its social composition, since this was, for most people, the primary community of daily experience and the predominant context in which burial practices were negotiated.[72]

One of the effects of population growth was to change the nature of community at the local level. In part this was simply the overwhelming impact of numbers on the existing structures such as apprenticeship and service that facilitated naturalisation and assimilation. There was also an increase in immigrant groups that resisted assimilation. Significantly for the management of death, however, population growth altered the dynamic of the parish community. In medieval London, the common experience was to live in a parish of moderate size, with a population that could be known to each other, by category if not in individuality. There were just under one hundred parishes within the wall, and a further sixteen parishes or precincts outside the wall but partly or wholly within the city's jurisdiction. The parishes varied considerably in size, the smallest being only about 1 acre (0.4 ha) in extent, the largest, within the wall, not more than 12 acres (4.9 ha); the mean and median sizes were close at 3 to 4 acres (1.2–1.6 ha).[73] The mean size of parish populations within the wall in 1548 was around 300, within a range from 150 to 1,200. Outside the walls parishes were much larger, from 20 acres to over 100 (8–40 ha),

---

[72] See maps 1 and 2.
[73] See Lobel, *The British atlas of historic towns*. The parishes of the early modern city are listed (with acreages, taken from the 1881 Ordnance Survey) in Finlay, *Population and metropolis*, pp. 168–72.

but none of the extramural parishes within the city's jurisdiction was fully or very densely settled at the end of the middle ages. Parish populations there ranged from 1,200 to 4,500, but were concentrated along certain streets or clustered round the church, and there was much unbuilt land. Beyond the city lay another ring of extensive parishes, few of which were densely settled by the mid-sixteenth century; even St Dunstan Stepney, covering most of east London, probably had no more than 1,800–2,000 inhabitants, distributed between a number of scattered hamlets.[74] The concentration of settlement around the abbey and court at Westminster gave the parish of St Margaret a population of 3,300–3,500, though it is clear that even at this size the parish could function effectively as a community.[75] The Southwark parishes were also quite thickly settled; the most populous was St Olave Southwark, with an estimated 3,600–4,200 inhabitants.[76]

The city parishes had a coherent spatial identity, based on access and communication, as the physical framework for the lives and interactions of their inhabitants. In most cases formed before 1200, their topographical form and territorial integrity reflected their origin as geographical circumscriptions of communities of worshippers in a single church. Intramural parishes were compact in shape, and most churches were centrally placed, often at a crossroads or street junction. Parish boundaries ran behind houses rather than along streets. Even the larger suburban parishes focused on main roads and streets, with churches at key intersections.[77] Apart from the formation of a few new parishes from former religious precincts, the early modern growth of population and the spread of suburbs over green fields were not matched by an appropriate augmentation of the parish network. The population of inner-city parishes doubled or trebled; in the outer suburbs, it increased by a multiple of ten or more. Only in the later seventeenth century did some of the new suburban settlements obtain churches and parochial status, though conversely, following the Fire of 1666, a number of city-centre parishes were amalgamated for ecclesiastical purposes. In consequence, by 1670 most of London's population lived in parishes that were geographically extensive and extremely populous. The population of the inner-suburban parish of St Botolph

[74] C. J. Kitching (ed.), *London and Middlesex chantry certificate of 1548* (London, 1980), p. 169; cf. K. G. McDonnell, *Medieval London suburbs* (Chichester, 1978), pp. 119–21.

[75] G. Rosser, *Medieval Westminster, 1200–1540* (Oxford, 1989), esp. pp. 175, 248.

[76] M. Carlin, *Medieval Southwark* (London, 1996), pp. 143–4; J. Boulton, *Neighbourhood and society. A London suburb in the seventeenth century* (Cambridge, 1987), pp. 13–21. Boulton uses a larger multiplier to convert the 1548 communicant numbers into population figures than I have done.

[77] Cf. C. N. L. Brooke and G. Keir, *London 800–1215: the shaping of a city* (London, 1975), pp. 122–48; A. Prockter and R. Taylor, *The A to Z of Elizabethan London* (London, 1979); R. Hyde, J. Fisher, and R. Cline, *The A to Z of Restoration London* (London, 1992).

Aldgate could have been as high as 10,000 in the mid-seventeenth century, and some of the more distant parishes were very much larger. St Giles Cripplegate, St Martin in the Fields, and St Dunstan Stepney could each have had a population of 25–30,000.

Paris had fewer parishes than London at the start of the period, despite its much higher population, and there were even more marked disparities in acreage and the size of the congregation. Probably more than half the population of 250–300,000 lived on the right bank, also known as the Ville, where there were nineteen parishes. There were fourteen tiny parishes on the Ile de la Cité, and twelve within the wall on the left bank, plus the parish of Saint-Sulpice in the faubourg Saint-Germain. The evolution of parishes in Paris shows a much greater intervention of lordship and of the state. According to their historian, parish boundaries in Paris 'se confondaient presque toujours avec celles d'une domaine ecclesiastique', and included territorial outliers and irregularities as a result.[78] The parishes of the Ile de la Cité emerged in the twelfth century, under the shadow of Notre-Dame, formerly the parish church for the Cité; for that reason few of them had any burying space outside the church. The right bank parishes were partly based on lordship, partly on lay communities, and seem to have been formed through a process of rivalry and counter-assertion of rights and autonomy. The more ancient parishes had rights and powers that later ones did not. On the left bank, the parish church of Saint-Séverin became the seat of the 'archiprêtre méridional', and exercised authority over the neighbouring parishes, suppressing the territorial parochiality of Saint-Julien and Saint-Etienne-des-Grès by 1200. There was also more medieval reorganisation and re-formation of parish territories and boundaries than in London.[79]

These much earlier developments still had an impact on the parochial geography of the early modern period, in the disparate sizes and territorial irregularities of the parishes. The right-bank parish of Saint-Josse, representing a block of houses cut off from its parent parish of Saint-Laurent by the wall of Philippe-Auguste and made parochial in 1260, had only twenty-nine houses in the eighteenth century. Saint-Jean-en-Grève, originally a baptismal chapel of Saint-Gervais, was erected into a parish in 1213, but Saint-Gervais kept a block of territory within the daughter parish. Saint-Leu–Saint-Gilles on the right bank remained succursal to Saint-Barthélemy on the Ile de la Cité until 1617, even though it had long exceeded it in population.[80] The conception of the parish as representing domainal rights as well as a congregation was also significant. If parishes

---

[78] A. Friedmann, *Paris, ses rues et ses paroisses du Moyen Age à la Révolution. Origine et évolutions des circonscriptions paroissiales* (Paris, 1959), pp. xxviii, 41–3.
[79] Ibid., pp. 46–87, 233–8.   [80] Ibid., pp. 281–2, 285–93.

were staffed by regular clergy from the parent monastic house rather than by secular priests, which may have been more true in the middle ages than later, this must also have had an impact on the formation of community. Later parish formations were less topographically complex, and allowing for the overall much larger scale of parishes in Paris, outside the very centre, there was a reasonable response to growth. New urban parishes, or semi-autonomous succursals, were created as suburban hamlets were engulfed by the spread of the metropolis. Peripheral urban and suburban parishes in Paris were nevertheless very large, with populations in the thousands. Saint-Sulpice in the faubourg Saint-Germain could have had as many as 80,000 inhabitants by the late seventeenth century, and the parishes of Saint-Eustache and Saint-Paul with its annexe Sainte-Marguérite on the right bank not many fewer.[81]

Parishes remained one of the most important topographical and social units in the early modern city, in the world of the living but also for the larger society's response to the problem of the dead. Parishioners worshipped in their local church and took collective responsibility for its repair and beautification; in return for their attentions and offerings, they expected the rites of the church and the promise of burial. The small size of London's medieval parishes meant that the responsibility for burial was widely dispersed across the city, and that decisions about how it should be done were taken locally, with respect for sensibilities and an eye to the maintenance of social bonds. As population grew, however, especially in the suburbs, close relations between parishioners and the governors of the parish must have been hard to maintain. Many Parisian parishes, as noted above, were much larger and more populous even at the beginning of the period considered here, and the issue of burial rights, in England an intrinsic part of the understanding of *parochia*, was particularly difficult. Several had no burial space of their own, and were dependent on the cemetery of the Innocents, though parish clergy were active in defence of their rights to bury their parishioners, or to share in the profits if they chose burial elsewhere.[82]

The parishes had to shoulder the task of dealing with the dead, but very substantial disparities, in the scale of the burial problem and in the resources with which to meet it, opened up between parishes as time went on. In general the parishes with the greatest wealth were the

---

[81] Based on extrapolation from the annual burial totals in the Etat des Baptêmes for the 1670s (BN (Réserve), LK[7] 6745). For annual burial totals by parish for 1670, see appendix.

[82] See below, chapter 4; Thibaut-Payen, *Les morts, l'église et l'état*, pp. 26, 47–52, 65–72; R. M. Golden, *The godly rebellion. Parisian curés and the religious Fronde, 1652–1662* (Chapel Hill, 1981), pp. 97–122.

small, city-centre ones which had fewest burials to cope with.[83] Overall size of parish was certainly significant. In London between 1655 and 1664, thirty-four parishes dealt with on average fewer than 20 burials per annum, and the majority of those within the walls (eighty or more) with fewer than 50. Three large suburban parishes, however (St Dunstan Stepney, St Giles Cripplegate, and St Martin in the Fields), each buried an average of over 1,100 bodies per annum, and another eight parishes buried over 500 a year.[84] In Paris in 1670, with far fewer parishes, the disparity was even more marked. Twenty tiny parishes (almost all on the Ile de la Cité) each buried fewer than 50 bodies a year, while five large parishes (Saint-Sulpice, Saint-Eustache, Saint-Paul with Sainte-Marguérite, Saint-Nicolas-des-Champs, and Saint-Laurent en la Ville-neuve) each buried between 1,200 and 1,700 per annum. Another five parishes each buried between 500 and 1,000 bodies a year. The more populous parishes normally had a higher proportion of poor inhabitants, and fewer wealthy inhabitants to contribute to assessments or leave endowments, so they were struggling to cope with a much greater problem with more limited resources.[85]

Within the urban area itself, especially between the centre and the periphery, there were major variations in wealth, social character, and the physical environment. Tax and other assessments, compiled at different dates and for various purposes, can illuminate this, though no single-moment snapshot of the distribution of any social or economic value across the metropolis holds good for a long period. Indeed, mapping the changing distribution of severe plague mortality in the city of London, from the intramural centre in 1563 to the extramural parishes in the seventeenth century, has made a significant contribution to our understanding of the disease's social impact.[86] Nevertheless, these data offer a persuasive representation of the variation in local character within the urban area, and allow us to place specific parishes or areas on a scale of wealth and sufficiency, as well as giving a sense of the broader social topography of each city.[87]

---

[83] R. W. Herlan, 'Social articulation and the configuration of parochial poverty in London on the eve of the Restoration', *Guildhall Studies in London History* 2(2) (1976), 43–53; Slack, *Impact of plague*, pp. 154–64; Harding, 'Burial of the plague dead', pp. 53–64.

[84] Champion, *London's dreaded visitation*, pp. 104–7. See appendix 1.

[85] See appendix 2.

[86] Slack, *Impact of plague*, pp. 151–64; Champion, *London's dreaded visitation*, pp. 42–52.

[87] The parishes specially mentioned in the following discussion are for the most part those whose records, experience, or intrinsic interest mean they are frequently referred to in the discussion of burial and funerary practice below. A similar attempt at characterising the parishes of London, in the context of a discussion of parochial responses to the imposition of presbyterian organisation, is made by Tai Liu, *Puritan London. A study of religion and society in the city parishes* (London, 1986), pp. 23–50.

Neither London nor Paris conforms closely to the classic patterns of social topography in pre-industrial cities proposed by geographers such as Sjoberg and Vance.[88] Early modern London[89] was broadly concentric (Sjoberg's model), with a concentration of wealth in the city centre and wider areas of poverty on the outskirts, but the axis of prosperity was elongated westwards by the pull of Westminster and the court. The city's wealthy centre extended along the east–west line of Cheapside, running through the parishes of All Hallows Honey Lane, St Mary le Bow, St Pancras, St Mary Colechurch, and reaching east into the slightly less wealthy areas of St Michael Cornhill, St Andrew Undershaft and St Helen Bishopsgate. To the west of the city, Fleet Street (especially St Dunstan in the West), the Strand, and Westminster itself shared some of the city centre's characteristics of substantial households, property size, or rent value. Some of London's poorest parishes lay within the city wall, either up against it like All Hallows on the Wall, or on the river like St Peter Paul's Wharf, though overseas trade brought wealth to the eastern waterfront around St Mary at Hill. Outside the city wall to the north and east, the extensive parishes of St Botolph Bishopsgate and St Botolph Aldgate had large populations but low rent values and many poor households.

Early modern Paris[90] appears to have had a distinctive and not wholly concentric distribution of wealth and social class, though it was not very close to Vance's model of evenly distributed or mixed wealth and poverty either. The outermost streets were largely occupied by the poor, but the centre was unevenly mixed. This included some of the Ile de la Cité, and the area round the Hôtel de Ville on the right bank, especially the parishes of Saint-Gervais and Saint-Jean-en-Grève. The location of centres of power, especially royal or state power, was critical, giving rise to concentrations of nobles and professionals to the west and north-west of the centre, round the Louvre on the right bank and the Palais, seat of the Parlement of Paris, on the west end of the Ile de la Cité. Professionals

---

[88] G. Sjoberg, *The pre-industrial city. Past and present* (New York, 1960); J. E. Vance, 'Land assignment in the pre-capitalist, capitalist, and post-capitalist city', *Economic Geography* 47 (1971), 101–20. The applicability of these models to London is the starting-point for E. Jones, 'London in the early seventeenth century: an ecological approach', *London Journal* 6 (1980), 123–34.

[89] This characterisation is based on Jones, 'London in the early seventeenth century', 123–34; Finlay, *Population and metropolis*, pp. 70–82; M. J. Power, 'The social topography of Restoration London', in Beier and Finlay, *London 1500–1700*, pp. 199–223. Cf. Harding, 'City, capital and metropolis', pp. 117–43.

[90] See Descimon, 'Paris on the eve of Saint Bartholomew', pp. 69–104; J. de Viguerie and E. Saive-Lever, 'Essai pour une géographie socio-professionelle de Paris dans la première moitié du XVIIe siècle', *Revue d'Histoire Moderne et Contemporaine* 20 (1973), pp. 424–9. Their map is also reproduced and discussed in Pillorget, *Paris sous les premiers Bourbons*, pp. 114–19.

and *gens de qualité* also inhabited the inner streets of the south-west segment of Paris, an area including the university but also the residences
of lawyers and royal officers in the parishes of Saint-André-des-Arts and
Saint-Cosme. Further out to the south-west, though there were some people of quality, the high-class development of the faubourg Saint-Germain
had not really begun at this period. The north-west quarter of the city
was also mixed, with poorer households along the rue Saint-Denis and
around les Halles and the cemetery of the Innocents, but there were also
residents of wealth and status in the parishes of Saint-Eustache and Saint-
Germain-l'Auxerrois, towards the Louvre. Royal power and patronage,
expressed in the development of the Place Royale on the site of the former hôtel des Tournelles, and the planned Place de France, also made the
Marais and the north-eastern segment of Paris a wealthy area, attractive
to *gens de qualité*. The area south-east of the centre, including the Place
Maubert, was the least mixed, with low rent values and almost uniformly
occupied by working people.

But while overviews such as these confirm the existence of local variation, closer topographical and social analysis indicates that even within
the unit of parish or *quartier*, there were marked inequalities of wealth and
standing.[91] The classic, pre-industrial social pyramid of wealth, sharply
pointed with a very broad base, was reproduced locally across the city,
with each parish containing a spectrum of richer and poorer inhabitants.
London's smaller central parishes were less likely to include both the
very richest and the very poorest; the outer and suburban parishes, being much larger, could contain a wider spectrum but represented in very
different proportions. The west end of London exhibited strong contrasts of great wealth and severe poverty, while the eastern parishes were
increasingly, by the seventeenth century, expanses of uniform poverty,
though not necessarily destitution.[92] The mix of richer and poorer, or
gens de qualité and working people, varied across Paris, but since most
parishes were larger, and since, arguably, extremes of wealth and poverty
were greater than in London, their populations are likely to have been
more widely diverse. This again would seem to suggest that the emergence of community or commonality of interest within the parish was
more doubtful in Paris than in London, though obviously social homo-
geneity does not of itself guarantee consensus. Parish leadership and the
representation of a diverse congregation may, in Paris, have derived more
from confessional unity than from social solidarity.

[91] E.g. Boulton, *Neighbourhood and society*, pp. 99–119, 175–92; D. Keene and V. Harding, *Historical gazetteer of London before the Great Fire*, 1, *Cheapside* (Chadwyck-Healey
microfiche, 1987).

[92] Harding, 'City, capital and metropolis', pp. 117–43; C. Spence, *London in the 1690s.
A social atlas* (London, 2000), esp. pp. 63–114.

To some extent these local variations in social characteristics are consistent with a centripetal model of wealth and status at the centre and disenfranchised poverty on the periphery. Though the model is distorted by specific topographical and other features, especially in Paris, it is nevertheless true that most of the wealthy resided towards the city's centre, and that suburban areas tended to be more uniformly poor. The raggedly growing edges of the city were less socially integrated, less well policed, less subject to successful environmental control, than older parts of the metropolis. The equation of the spatial metaphor of centrality and marginality with the binary opposition of rich and poor, powerful and dispossessed, was something that strongly influenced the location of burial in the early modern city. Parish communities saw themselves as centred on the church, the most desirable place of burial, and on its immediate churchyard; there was resistance to pressure to transfer burials elsewhere. The most socially powerful were the best able to resist such pressures, while the least powerful were the most likely to be buried on the margin.

The parish was administered on behalf of the congregation at large by a group of elected representatives who in turn managed a staff of paid officers or servants. The longest-established of these posts was that of churchwarden or *marguillier* – two, three, or sometimes four laymen from the congregation who for a period of two or three years acted as financial and administrative managers of the resources of the parish community, with special responsibility for the church building. While the post of churchwarden in London was certainly one of local importance and immediate authority in the parish, it was not a very high rung on the civic *cursus honorum*. At the time of his holding office, a churchwarden was probably in the middle rank of householders; he would have been outranked in age and often status by his predecessors in office, and by others in the parish who had risen even higher.[93] In Paris the post of senior *marguillier* or *marguillier d'honneur* was held by local notables, while the day-to-day work was done by men of lesser status, known as *marguilliers comptable, de compte,* or *en charge*. In the parish of Saint-André-des-Arts, the senior *marguilliers* were usually *conseillers* or *avocats*, while some *marchands bourgeois* or *bourgeois de Paris* acted as working churchwardens.[94] In 1613 the *marguilliers* were named as M. de Montholon, *conseiller du roi*, and M. Haultemen (possibly Maître Pierre Hotman, also *conseiller du roi* at

[93] Foster, *Politics of stability*, pp. 31–2, 56. Assessments for the poor rate in St Mary Colechurch in 1653 ranged from 1s. 6d. to £1 9s. The serving churchwardens paid the median assessment of 5s. 10d. each: GL, MS 64, f. 52.

[94] AN, LL 692 (Obituary list, 1546), f. 1; AN, LL 687 (Délibérations, 1657–93), ff. 1–2. From 1613, notaries were not to be named *marguilliers* : AN, LL 686 (Délibérations, 1589–1627), f. 16. Cf. L. Brochard, *Saint-Gervais. Histoire de la paroisse, d'après de nombreux documents inédits* (Paris, 1950), p. 187.

the Châtelet), while the current *marguillier de compte* was a candlemaker. M. de Montholon contributed 400 *livres* to the rebuilding of the church; M. Haultemen gave 100 *livres*; the candlemaker gave 18 *sous*.[95]

While churchwardens had a good deal of authority, they derived this from the parish as a collectivity. But assemblies of householders could be unwieldy and disorderly, and increasingly, and perhaps sooner in Paris than in London, an intermediate group of householders formed a committee known as the vestry or *fabrique* in which policy was made. How representative this committee was varied from parish to parish in London; the growth of select vestries, which permanently excluded the majority of householders from membership and decision making, was a contentious issue, but 'all the heavily populated extramural parishes had select vestries by Elizabeth's reign'.[96] Parisian parishes certainly restricted access to meetings, either explicitly or by omission. Although seventy-one parishioners were present at a meeting at Saint-Gervais in 1500, to debate an offer to found a chapel in the church, meetings later in the century were much smaller, perhaps as a result of political and religious conflicts and the wish to eliminate opposition. In 1594 the *marguilliers* convened a meeting of 'plusieurs notables personnes paroissiens de ladite eglise et fabrique', which actually consised only of fourteen people, all but one of whom had already served as *marguillier*. In the early seventeenth century a similarly restricted group controlled the parish. In the parish of Saint-Etienne-du-Mont, a group of 'notables paroissiens' met monthly to discuss parish affairs.[97] In these circumstances, it was the élite members of the vestry or *fabrique* that made burial policy, for example by setting the charges for grave sites and other aspects of the funeral service, and the churchwardens or *marguilliers comptables* who implemented it. The latter kept the parish accounts and were responsible for the day-to-day running of the church and its activities, directing the work of clerks, sextons, and gravediggers. They also, in pre-Reformation London and in Paris, administered the pious endowments of the church, accepting responsibility for employing priests and ensuring that services were performed in accordance with the benefactor's instructions.[98]

The ornamentation and the quality of liturgical provision in any parish church, which contributed to its attractiveness as a centre of worship and commemoration, were a function of the wealth of its congregation, living and dead, and of their devotion, whether to reformed doctrine or traditional practices. Relations between the lay representatives of the

---

[95] AN, LL 686, ff. 14–16.   [96] Archer, *The pursuit of stability*, p. 69.
[97] Brochard, *Saint-Gervais. Histoire de la paroisse*, pp. 180–9. Cf. Diefendorf, *Beneath the cross*, pp. 35–6.
[98] See appendix 5.

parish and the clergy, especially the beneficed priest or *curé*, in whose appointment they usually had no say, could range from friendly co-operation to acrimony, especially as the range of confessional attachments widened.[99] As has been recognised elsewhere, the parish and its records constitute perhaps the most valuable resource for measuring the progress of Reformation in England, though exactly where the responsibility for collective compliance or resistance should be laid requires careful consideration.[100] Many London parish congregations in the later sixteenth and early seventeenth centuries had more advanced Protestant views than their rector or vicar. Some took the initiative in obtaining the kind of service they wanted, and relations between laity and clergy were radically reshaped during the English Revolution and the contest between Presbyterianism and Independency.[101] There was, perhaps, more overt controversy over how parishes should be run, and what character their worship and observance should take, in London, because these issues were up to a point open to negotiation. In Paris, where dissent was excommunicated rather than muffled, the religious enthusiasm of the majority was the strongest guarantor of the authority of the parish's leaders. The ability of an active *curé* to inspire devotion in his flock, and to encourage its expression in acts of piety or even of violence directed against heterodoxy, was a key factor in the conflicts of the sixteenth century.[102]

Early modern London and Paris shared many characteristics of urban identity and tradition deriving from their common membership of a pre-industrial, north-European, monarchical and Christian society. Such features as overall urban form, parochial structure, and the significant presence of the church were common to both, even if there were many important differences in the particulars. London had a tighter network of smaller parishes, Paris a greater number of private enclaves within the town; London had a more unitary structure of government within the city, Paris a more integrated idea of governance for the metropolis as a geographical whole. Each also had its own distinctive internal hierarchies, social, economic, or status-related, that reflected the nature of power in the state, and a unique distribution of wealth and authority. But they were recognisably part of the same world-system, part of the same

[99] Cf. e.g. Brochard, *Saint-Gervais. Histoire de la paroisse*, pp. 119–47; Golden, *The godly rebellion*, pp. 97–122.
[100] R. Hutton, 'The local impact of the Tudor Reformations', in C. Haigh (ed.), *The English Reformation revised* (Cambridge, 1987), pp. 114–38; E. Duffy, *The stripping of the altars: traditional religion in England, c. 1400–1580* (New Haven, 1992).
[101] *VCH London*, pp. 309–14 ; Tai Liu, *Puritan London*, esp. pp. 51–102, 103–25.
[102] Babelon, *Paris au XVIe siècle*, pp. 476–7; Roelker, *The Paris of Henry of Navarre*, pp. 185–260; Diefendorf, *Beneath the cross*, pp. 33, 36–8, 45, 147–58.

moral and economic culture, and subject to many similar tensions and pressures. Both cities experienced considerable population growth and in-migration, with a resulting challenge to the social networks and traditions that appeared to guarantee stability. The anxieties of government about the dangers posed by the unruly, unhealthy metropolis were often expressed in similar terms, even if specific solutions (building controls, Poor Law, plague orders, police measures) varied.

Nevertheless, even if neither London nor Paris was a fully integrated, uniform, and orderly social or physical entity, they were not completely incoherent, loose, and disconnected either. Authorities might have only limited jurisdictions, the sense of local community and variation might be strong, but there was a shared notion of a civic identity, created in part by geographical foci with a city-wide significance. These included food markets, the cathedral church (Notre-Dame was known as 'l'église de Paris', while St Paul's and its churchyard formed a major focus of civic assembly and religious publicity in London), the headquarters of the municipality, and in Paris the cemetery of the Innocents. Major thoroughfares crossed numerous invisible boundaries and traversed local topographies, linking disparate quarters into a knowable entity. These thoroughfares were often used as processional routes, for funerals as well as entries and inaugural parades, asserting the existence and importance of a larger civic as well as a local community. Parisians were certainly more explicit about their collective identity as a Catholic civic community than Londoners were about theirs as a Protestant one, but even without confessional triumphalism Londoners could express a sense of civic pride and identity that was rooted in a sense of the geographical and physical entity they inhabited.

3   'Lamentable pinfoulds of the deaths of men': parish churchyards and churchyard burial

In the medieval and early modern city, the dead were everywhere; unlike today, they were neither out of sight nor out of mind. Their place was among the living. They occupied important spaces in the urban map, in the parish churches and churchyards that were the focus of the local community, as well as in the ritual calendar. The living recognised and to a great extent honoured the claims of the dead to such a space and seem to have been willing to maintain a dialogue with them. Important aspects of the spatial constraints on burial were the impact of population pressure on land values, and the large number of activities for which open spaces such as churchyards might be used. The dead had to share their space with other dead, with generations of burials past and future, and to give room to the rites associated with burial, but churches and churchyards also teemed with the activities of the living, domestic, commercial, communal, and ceremonial, as well as religious.

Places of burial were scattered across the city. Pre-Reformation London had more than a hundred parishes, and Paris over forty. The majority of parishes buried both inside the church and outside in a nearby parish churchyard. In addition each city had more than a score of religious houses that accepted bodies for burial. Paris had a major burial place that served the whole community and in some sense helped to create its identity, the churchyard of the Innocents, while London had St Paul's churchyard with a more limited but still significant role. Within the spaces assigned for burial, there were further distinctions: churchyard or church, or some intermediate location such as porch or cloister; in the public area of the church, or in a chapel or vault assigned to a particular group; in a tomb or marked grave, or in the open and undifferentiated spaces of church and churchyard. Over the city as a whole, and within parishes and churches, there was a broad correlation between burial location and social importance. Élites secured burial in the topographical and spiritual heart of the community, in the best and holiest parts of the church; those on the margins of society were buried in places peripheral to the parish or even to the urban entity. For many, there was no actual choice to be made, since

cost and availability determined what they could have, but the discriminations made by the few exemplify a vision of centrality and marginality in society that was applied also to the place of burial. Both cities
opened new burial spaces in the sixteenth and seventeenth centuries,
mostly in peripheral areas, either to take the overflow from central burial
spaces or to accommodate newly defined communities, and the more
specialised uses of these new spaces extended the centrality/marginality
paradigm and underlined growing social and cultural divisions in urban
society.[1]

In general it is true to say that churchyard burial involved the rights
and interests of the majority of the community, who expected to use the
space in both life and death. Burials in churchyards were subject to rules
which, though they might be hallowed by traditional observation, were
essentially imposed in the interests of control and management. Most of
those who were buried there had little or no say in making the rules, and
limited influence over their operation. Churches, whether they belonged
to the parish community or to a religious order, were a privileged location
where most of the socially powerful obtained burial. These individuals
participated in the government of parish and city and were able to exert
a good deal of control over the manner and location of their own burials,
though church burial was obviously subject to great practical constraints.
The distinction was not absolute, however: the cemetery of the Innocents
in Paris attracted élite burials, attended by rituals and commemorated
in monuments and epitaphs, as well as the mass burials of the poorer
sort. Several parishes in London had no churchyard, and so attempted
to accommodate almost all the burial population within the church. The
relationship between church and churchyard burial was always a locally
variable and chronologically shifting one, affected by the character and
size of the parish's population, the size and spatial layout of the church,
and by local actions to modify church or churchyard.

This and the following three chapters consider the spaces occupied by
the dead in early modern London and Paris, in churchyards and cemeteries and inside parish and conventual churches. All four chapters deal with
the tension between the needs of the living and those of the dead, and
the ways in which this tension was resolved or deflected. Although burial
practice in churchyards and inside churches was affected by the same

---

[1] See V. Harding, '"And one more may be laid there": the location of burials in early
modern London', *London Journal* 14 (1989), 112–29; V. Harding, 'Burial choice and
burial location in later medieval London', in S. R. Bassett (ed.), *Death in towns. Urban
responses to the dying and the dead, 100–1600* (Leicester, 1992), pp. 119–35; V. Harding,
'Burial on the margin: distance and discrimination in the early modern city', in M. Cox
(ed.), *Grave concerns: death and burial in England, 1700–1850* (York, 1998), pp. 54–64.

range of concerns – availability of space, questions of safety, decency, hygiene, and the competition between private interest and public utility or resource – the specific issues often took a very different form. In each case the physical–geographical setting was crucial; in each case, also, the dead population had different characteristics. However, the accounts of burial in different places build on one another, as important issues, such as the treatment of disturbed remains, and the ways in which they were resolved, are first explored in one setting and then inform the discussion of burial in other places.

The majority of the dead, in both early modern London and Paris, were buried in open churchyards. In London these were predominantly the churchyards of the parish churches, though St Paul's and the new church-yards took a certain proportion. In Paris, parish churchyards were also important, but the central cemetery of the Innocents played a very signifi-cant part, both for ordinary Parisians dying at home and for the numerous dead buried from the Hôtel-Dieu. Because of these differences, and the individualities of particular parishes, it is necessary to tell separate sto-ries of churchyard burial in the two cities. This chapter, therefore, gives an account of burial in the London parish churchyards, followed by a similarly structured account for Paris. However, several common themes emerge: the physical limitations of the ancient spaces, the competition with other uses of those spaces, and the need to deal with an increas-ing problem either by finding new sites or through the management of burial.

Parish churchyards in London

London comprised more than a hundred parochial communities before the Reformation. At least eighty-five to ninety of these parishes had some churchyard, but the classic image of a church set freestanding within a surrounding churchyard was rarely true of London. Most city churches were hemmed in by buildings, with a small graveyard on perhaps one or two sides. By the late middle ages, some churches had been extended over formerly open burial ground; some had never had any adjacent burial space; others had no churchyard at all. There were a number of detached parochial churchyards, lying within the parish bounds but not adjoining the church. In the period between the Black Death and the Reformation several parishes were able to extend their burial space by enlarging their churchyards or acquiring new ones, often by gift or devise, while land val-ues were low and space relatively cheap. But in no case were churchyards spacious or ample: few can have been more than a few square metres in extent.[2]

The suppression of the chantries in 1548 initiated a reorganisation of lands and investments by guilds and companies, and also by parishes.[3] By this date, though London's great early modern population growth had already begun, its future scale was beyond imagining, and in several cases churchyard space was transferred to other uses, often it seems to compensate for the loss of parish revenue from chantry endowments. Parish authorities were under pressure to use open space around the church or in the churchyard to meet other needs of the parochial community. Building onto the churchyard was often the only way of enlarging the church for worship, arguably as high a priority as burial, or of providing for other community needs such as storage for parish goods and coals for the poor, accommodation for parish clergy or employees, and such facilities as schoolrooms.[4] The authorities also had to consider the needs of the living poor, and the possible advantages of building houses for rent or to house poor parishioners on or around their churchyard, even though this might encroach on scarce burial space. A number of parishes built houses or shops over some of their burial space in the sixteenth and seventeenth centuries.[5] They must have decided that the value of such an investment to the parish was greater than the sacrifice of space, and in London, where the cost of poor relief was constantly rising, they may well have been right. As with judgements on the best way to manage burials and allocate space, however, considerations other than pure utility may have weighed with them. Building or buying houses may have offered opportunities for business or patronage, and controlling their allocation, whether at concessionary rents or otherwise, brought similar rewards.

It cannot, however, have been long before parishes realised that the demand for burial space seriously limited their options for disposing of

---

[2] See Lobel, *The city of London*, map and gazetteer, for the setting of London parish churches and churchyards prior to the Reformation. For examples of churches extended over their own churchyards, St Pancras Soper Lane; with no adjacent churchyard, St Gabriel Fenchurch; with no parochial churchyard at all, St Mary Colechurch; with an additional detached churchyard, St Magnus; with enlarged adjacent churchyard space, St Mary le Bow. Further details on St Mary le Bow, St Mary Colechurch, and St Pancras are in Keene and Harding, *Historical gazetteer of London before the Great Fire*, 1, *Cheapside*, properties 104/0, 105/0, and 145/0.

[3] See Kitching, *The London and Middlesex chantry certificate*.

[4] W. H. Overall (ed.), *The accounts of the churchwardens of the parish of St Michael Cornhill, 1456–1608* (London, 1871), pp. 88–103; Keene and Harding, *Historical gazetteer, Cheapside*, nos. 11/4, 104/0, 104/4, and 145/0; GL, MS 9531/13, pt. 1, ff. 90v–92; GL, MS 3016/1, pp. 60, 174, 301, 368; GL, MS 6554/1, f. 124.

[5] E.g. Overall, *Accounts of St Michael Cornhill*, pp. 88–103; GL MS 6554/1, passim.

churchyard ground for other uses, and that they must manage their space carefully and, where possible, obtain additional space. Population growth was greatest within the walls in the sixteenth century and in the spreading suburbs in the seventeenth. New churchyards could be formed within the walls in the sixteenth century in space formerly belonging to religious houses or precincts, such as the former churchyard of the Pappey fraternity, which the parish of St Martin Outwich acquired in 1538–40, or the Dean's garden in St Martin le Grand, obtained by the parish of St Leonard Foster Lane in 1579.[6] Though population growth was increasing, pressure on space was somewhat less in the suburbs, and several parishes in the extramural wards of the city were able to buy or acquire open ground. Not all acquisitions are documented, but the majority of those that are were in suburban parishes, and in the seventeenth century, when growth and mortality were accelerating there. St Bride Fleet Street acquired a new churchyard by donation and agreement in 1610; St Sepulchre, outside Newgate, consecrated a new churchyard in 1612, St Botolph without Aldgate did so in 1615, and St Botolph without Bishopsgate in 1617. The latter was already discussing acquiring more ground by 1622.[7] St Dunstan in the West consecrated the west part of its new churchyard in Fetter Lane in June 1625, perhaps an early response to the plague of that year; Stepney parish urgently sought new burial space after that epidemic.[8] St Margaret Westminster consecrated new ground in 1611, 1620, and 1627.[9] St Giles Cripplegate added a third churchyard in 1662, and considered the possibility of obtaining more ground, so that they could stop burying in one of the other churchyards for at least ten years.[10]

In the early seventeenth century some waste space outside the walls near the city's ditches and watercourses was still available, and this was what was exploited by St Bride's (near Fleet ditch), St Sepulchre, St Bartholomew the Great, St Giles Cripplegate, and St Botolph Bishopsgate.[11] The suburban churchyards, especially the new ones, were much larger than the intramural ones could possibly be. St Olave Silver Street, a small parish just within the walls, consecrated a new churchyard of about 170 m^2,

[6] GL, MS 6842, f. 52; GL, MS 9531/13, pt. 1, ff. 90v–91.

[7] GL, MS 9531/13, pt. 2, ff. 394v–395, 397–8, 400v–401, 407v–408; GL, MS 4526/1, ff. 16, 22.

[8] GL, MS 2968/2, ff. 288; G. W. Hill and W. H. Frere (eds.), *Memorials of Stepney parish. That is to say the vestry Minutes from 1579 to 1662* (Guildford, 1890–1), pp. 109, 111.

[9] J. Nichols, *Illustrations of the manners and expences of antient times in England, in the fifteenth, sixteenth, and seventeenth centuries, deduced from the accompts of churchwardens and other authentic documents collected from various parts of the kingdom, with explanatory notes* (London, 1797), pp. 29, 32, 36.

[10] GL, MS 6048/1, ff. 7, 8v, 9, 10, 15.

[11] GL, MS 9531/13, pt. 2, ff. 394v–395, 397–8, 407v–408; N. Moore, *The history of St Bartholomew's Hospital*, 2 vols. (London, 1918), vol. II, pp. 261–3, plan facing p. 260.

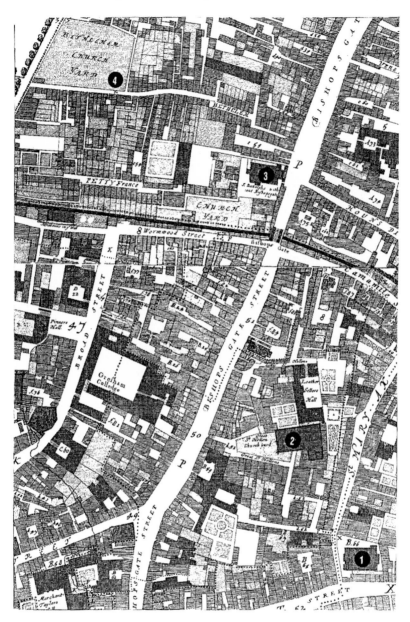

3 Churches and churchyards in seventeenth-century London: detail from Ogilby and Morgan's map of 1676, showing (1) St Andrew Undershaft, (2) St Helen Bishopsgate, (3) St Botolph Bishopsgate, and (4) the New Churchyard ('Bethlehem church yard') (London, Guildhall Library).

in 1612, but the new churchyard of St Bride's was about 1,100 m^2; St Sepulchre's about 1,350 m^2; St Botolph Aldgate's about 1,300 m^2; St Botolph Bishopsgate's 1617 acquisition about 630 m^2.[12] As well as being more spacious, these new churchyards were also more exclusively devoted to the uses of burial. They were intended to be walled and gated, and in most cases probably were. Often somewhat isolated from the centre of parish activity, they were less liable, at least at first, to be used as thoroughfares or to private appropriation than city-centre churchyards. However, the temptation for the parish to let some of the new space out for secular uses was often irresistible, and reclaiming it, or preventing further encroachment, could prove troublesome. It is also clear that they were seen as less desirable burial spaces than the older, more centrally located churchyards. St Botolph Bishopsgate noted in 1620 that 'the greater part of the parishioners are unwilling to bury their dead' in the new churchyard by the town ditch, 'lately procured ... to their great charge', and decided to counter this by raising the price of burial in the old churchyard.[13] Other parishes also discriminated between new and old or 'upper' and 'lower' churchyards.[14]

London churchyards were neither secluded nor quiet. Apart from the frequent business of burial itself, and rituals connected with the church and parish community, they were the scene of much purely secular activity. Much of the business concerning churchyards noted in parish records has nothing to do with burial, and gives no impression of a particularly reverent attitude towards the space. For reasons of London's historic development, several older churchyards served as thoroughfares, linking public streets and giving access to private houses as well as to churches. Private and public could easily become blurred in these circumstances. The alley gate to the churchyard of St Christopher le Stocks was locked every night with a spring lock after 1508, for security, but the 'dwellers in the churchyard' were given keys to it.[15] The privately owned cellar under the church of All Hallows Honey Lane, accessed from the churchyard by a trapdoor on the south side of the church, was used by its owners or tenants for storage of coal and salt; occupants of houses surrounding the churchyard of St Mary le Bow had rights of way over the churchyard, with front doors and cellar doors opening onto it.[16] In 1583, Mr Killigrew of

---

[12] GL, MS 9531/13, pt. 2, ff. 394v–395, 397–9, 400v–401, 407v–408. These areas are rough estimates from the linear dimensions given (in imperial measurements) in the grants or confirmations.

[13] GL, MS 4526/1, f. 15.

[14] LPL, CM VII/94; GL (Printed Books), Broadsides 12.79, 4.2.

[15] E. Freshfield (ed.), *Minutes of the vestry meetings and other records of the parish of St Christopher le Stocks in the city of London* (London, 1886), p. 70.

[16] Keene and Harding, *Historical gazetteer, Cheapside*, nos. 11/0, 11/8, 104/0, 104/9–14.

the parish of St Margaret Lothbury negotiated with the vestry for a 'way of ease' through the churchyard to pass to a house and garden he had recently acquired. He promised not to carry horse-straw or hay through the yard, and assured the parish that 'he dothe respeckt more the worthiness and reverensing the plac, then to have yt mad comon ore abussyde'. Nevertheless, some thirty-five years later either he or his successor of the same name was 'much discontent' with the parish for refusing him permission to extend his house into the churchyard, and insisting that he take up the foundation he had already laid.[17]

The inhabitants of houses adjoining or overlooking churchyards treated them as a space they could use for their own purposes. They made illegal windows and doors into churchyards, and their own paving, building, and sheds encroached onto the space needed for burials. Domestic activities such as laundry and poultry-keeping spilled out into the consecrated ground.[18] More noxious practices included industrial processes such as cloth-stretching, metal-casting, and brickmaking, and churchyards were also used for dumping unwanted refuse of various kinds.[19] The city churchyards were probably mostly too small and confined to offer sufficient space for the games and activities that so disturbed provincial churchards,[20] but the churchyard at St Margaret Westminster, as an open space adjoining a central focus of political activity, was used to place scaffolds or public seating for a number of state occasions in the mid-seventeenth century, including Cromwell's funeral and the coronation of Charles II. It was also used to accommodate Scottish prisoners taken at the battle of Worcester, after which it required considerable rehabilitation.[21] Perhaps for similar reasons, the vestries of St Bride and St Giles Cripplegate made orders in the 1650s banning military training in their churchyards.[22]

Although they preserved valuable open space in the city, few London churchyards could have been the green oases that the later romanticisation of death and burial would suggest, or indeed that the disused churchyards now constitute. Most must have been hard-surfaced, either paved or sanded or gravelled, or a mixture, with stone slabs set in gravelling,

[17] E. Freshfield (ed.), *The vestry minute book of the parish of St Margaret Lothbury in the city of London, 1571–1677* (London, 1887), pp. 14–15, 42, 50.

[18] GL MS 3016/1, pp. 17, 124, 166–7, 482; GL MS 6554/1, ff. 36, 51v, 156, 158r–v; GL MS 9583/1, ff. 19, 30; GL MS 6554/1, f. 114; GL, MS 6048/1, f. 18v; Overall, *Accounts of St Michael Cornhill*, pp. 239, 241, 246; Freshfield, *Vestry minute book of St Margaret Lothbury*, p. 16.

[19] GL MS 3016/1, pp. 40, 364; GL MS 9583/1, f. 19; J. V. Kitto (ed.), *St Martin in the Fields: the accounts of the churchwardens, 1525–1603* (London, 1901), p. 125.

[20] D. Dymond, 'God's disputed acre', *Journal of Ecclesiastical History* 50 (1999), 464–97.

[21] Nichols, *Illustrations*, pp. 58–60, 63–4.

[22] GL, MS 6554/1, f. 157; GL, MS 6048/1, f. 2.

and possibly also bare earth.[23] Some churchyards were referred to as 'the green churchyard', suggesting that they contained some plants, perhaps grass, and certainly a number had trees.[24] The most verdant city-centre churchyard may well have been at St Helen Bishopsgate. This was larger than the average intramural churchyard, and in the late sixteenth century there was enough grass there to need regular mowing. The parish register, listing the locations of churchyard burials in the early seventeenth century, mentions a great grass plot and a little green grass plot. Also growing there were willows, two great sycamore trees, a great ash tree, a little ash tree, a plum tree, a cherry tree, a gooseberry tree, a vine, a sweetbriar, and a rose tree. In this case it does appear that local residents saw the green space as an amenity in itself: in 1607 a parishioner was buried 'in the churchyard... where the cross stood, in which place she made a garden'.[25]

Where possible, churchyards were enclosed with walls, fences, or even a mud wall.[26] A few parishes had what they called cloisters, probably a modest bit of arcading round one or more sides of the enclosed space, probably paved, and more highly valued – or at least priced – as a location for burial than the open churchyard.[27] Several medieval churchyards are known to have had crosses, which were mostly removed at the Reformation.[28] Parish celebrations and observations naturally made use of churchyards. Several parish records refer to a 'processional way',[29] but in most cases it is doubtful that this was more than the path from the street to the church door. More secular assemblies used churchyards too: London's annual wardmotes probably took place in the most convenient

---

[23] E.g. GL, MS 4457/1, f. 88r–v; GL, MS 2968/1, f. 21; Nichols, *Illustrations*, p. 35; C. Burgess (ed.), *The church records of St Andrew Hubbard Eastcheap, c. 1450–c.1570* (London Record Society 34, 1999), p. 162; Overall, *Accounts of St Michael Cornhill*, pp. 223–4.

[24] E.g. H. Littlehales (ed.), *Medieval records of a London city church, A.D. 1420–1559* [St Mary at Hill] (London: Early English Text Society original series, 125, 128, 1904–5), pp. 370, 403, 41; Burgess, *Church records of St Andrew Hubbard*, p. 7; GL, MS 4887, p. 47; GL, MS 4570/1, ff. 11v, 45v, 77.

[25] GL, MS 6836, pp. 31–2, 39–40, 54–5, 55–6, 56–7, 58, 59, 62–3, 272; GL, MS 6831/1, burials from c. 1600–1625 passim, and entry for 10 February 1606/7. See Plate 3, p. 51.

[26] Gates, walls and fences are mentioned in many churchwardens' accounts: see e.g. GL, MS 4457/1, ff. 87v–92; GL, MS 593/1, f. 5.

[27] E.g. Overall, *Accounts of St Michael Cornhill*, pp. 74, 81. The word could be used in misleading ways, however: at All Hallows Honey Lane the cellar under the church was known as 'the cloister' when burial took place there from 1613: Keene and Harding, *Historical gazetteer*, Cheapside, no. 11/0; GL, MS 5022, f. 118; *Registers of All Hallows Honey Lane* (Harl. Soc. 44), p. 267.

[28] Prockter and Taylor, *The A to Z of Elizabethan London*, shows several crosses c. 1550. For others, see GL, MS 2968/1, f. 83; Littlehales, *Medieval records of a London city church*, p. 300; GL, MS 9171/8, f. 202; GL, MS 4570/1, f. 87v; GL, MS 1432/1, f. 101v; Overall, *Accounts of St Michael Cornhill*, p. 99.

[29] E.g. Overall, *Accounts of St Michael Cornhill*, p. 248.

parish churchyard. Although the use of churchyards by the community for these kinds of collective purposes posed some problems of order, and might be thought to compromise the sacred nature of the space, in another sense such use validated and confirmed the churchyard as the traditional property of the whole community, living and dead. As a special kind of public domain, churchyards could lend sanction to collective activities that took place there.

The prime reason for setting aside churchyards, however, was to accommodate the bodies of the dead. Paradoxically, although the Protestant Reformation challenged the belief that holiness could have a physical location, and that association with specific places conferred spiritual benefit, there is little evidence for a changed perception of spatial priorities in relation to burial. Later sixteenth- and seventeenth-century Londoners were as keen to be buried in traditional places as their Catholic predecessors. Even though the churchyard was the home for the dead of modest status, individuals showed attachment to older rather than newer churchyards, even when this caused real environmental problems, and cared about the precise location of graves. Those who had charge of churchyards had therefore to find a way of managing the demand for burial that would satisfy sensibilities and individual preferences, while still meeting the need for speedy and safe disposal of increasing numbers. In most cases we can only infer attitudes and assumptions from actions, but the evidence suggests that a set of common responses to the problem evolved, exploiting a range of expedients and increasingly refined distinctions.

The great majority of Londoners buried within their parish were interred in the churchyard, though the actual proportion must have varied by parish, according to the space available, and the social composition of the living population. Before the institution of burial registration in 1538, we normally only know about the burials for which some payment was made to the parish, for space or accompanying rituals.[30] At St Dunstan in the East, between 1498 and 1502, only three people paid for burial in church, while thirty were buried in the Pardon churchyard.[31] At St Martin in the Fields, there were at least forty-five funerals in 1531–3, but only four of these paid for graves in church.[32] Other parishes record

---

[30] One exception is the parish of St Andrew Holborn, for which the lightwardens' account for 1477–8 survives (BL, Harl. Roll H 28). This has twenty-nine entries presumably referring to burials (including ten to children), and two years' minds or anniversaries. It seems plausible that this total represents all the burials in the parish that year. C. Barron and J. Roscoe, 'The medieval parish church of St Andrew Holborn', *London Topographical Record* 24 (1980), 55–9.

[31] GL, MS 4887. St Dunstan's had at least two churchyards, and burial in the second of these was perhaps free, so the number of churchyard burials was probably even higher.

[32] Kitto, *St Martin in the Fields: the accounts of the churchwardens*, pp. 21–5.

only church burials, but when these can be compared with totals from the early registers, it is clear that they represented only a small proportion of the total, and that the remainder of the dead must have been buried in the churchyard.[33] Several parish registers in the later sixteenth and seventeenth centuries give details of some places of burial, but it is rare for all burials to be located; it is more likely that details would be omitted for a churchyard burial. However, where full details do exist, churchyard burials normally outnumber burials in church, often by a long way. At St Pancras Soper Lane, between 1557 and 1560, twenty-one out of thirty-nine people were said to have been buried in the churchyard and only eight were certainly buried in the church.[34] At St Helen Bishopsgate, between 1630 and 1658, at least 453 out of 767 people were buried in the churchyard, or around 60 per cent. At St Michael Cornhill, in the 1650s (when there may be some under-recording of deaths), the proportion of located burials taking place in churchyard and cloister was just over 51 per cent. Proportions would vary from year to year, however, and when there were more deaths, a higher proportion were buried in the churchyard. Both St Helen's and St Michael's were large churches, and relatively well provided with burial space inside and out for the twenty-five to forty burials they handled each year; neither needed to send bodies outside the parish for burial.[35] In the extramural and suburban parishes the proportion of churchyard burials must have been far higher. Parishes which were burying 200–400 bodies a year by the 1650s, such as the extramural city parishes of St Bride Fleet Street and St Dunstan in the West, can only have accommodated a small fraction of these inside their churches. At St Bride's, forty-one bodies were buried in the month of January 1665 (long before the beginning of the plague epidemic), but only two of these appear to have been buried in the church and one in the vault. The remainder were buried in the upper and lower churchyards ('above' and 'below').[36]

Burial in one's parish churchyard was normally one of the cheapest options, as well as the most convenient, and the burial population of such places therefore included most of the poorer and less powerful in society. But parish churchyard burial was not exclusively for the poor: the numbers involved indicate that many of middling status were also buried there. There was a long medieval tradition of lay burial in churchyards,

[33] Overall, *Accounts of St Michael Cornhill*, pp. 74, 81; *Registers of St Michael Cornhill* (Harl. Soc. 7), pp. 178–9.

[34] *Registers of St Pancras Soper Lane* (Harl. Soc. 44), pp. 286–7.

[35] *Registers of St Helen Bishopsgate* (Harl. Soc. 31), pp. 293–307; *Registers of St Michael Cornhill*, pp. 246–9.

[36] GL, MS 10345; GL, MS 6540/1; GL, MS 6570/1, item 62.

and indeed the secular élite had only obtained the privilege of burial in church in relatively recent times. A crude way of categorising medieval and early modern Londoners in an approximation of wealth and social standing is into those who made no will; those who made a will leaving movable goods but no real estate; those citizens who made wills leaving real property in the city; and those individuals, some élite citizens and gentry, who made wills disposing of real property outside as well as inside the city of London.[37] Almost all of those in the first category, those adults who made no will, and their dependants, who together comprised the great majority of Londoners, would have been buried in their parish churchyards. In the later middle ages, churchyard burial was also the expressed choice of about 40 per cent of those in the second category, for themselves and their wives.[38] A much smaller proportion of property-owning citizens – about 20 per cent – chose churchyard burial in the same period, and very few if any of the fourth group did so.[39] In the later sixteenth and seventeenth centuries it became less common to use the will to specify the place of burial, but the express choice of churchyard burial declined even more.[40] This could be the product of variation in several factors (the personal wealth of testators, testamentary practice, the cost of church burial, the availability of space), but it could also suggest that more Londoners of a moderate social and economic level were aspiring to church burial. Where there are cases of an individual expressly choosing churchyard burial in the later seventeenth century, this may be a reflection of an idiosyncratic perspective on the whole process.[41]

Few registers give adequate detail of both the deceased person and his/her place of burial for socio-economic correlation to be feasible, but the register of St Helen Bishopsgate offers some insights. Between 1640 and 1658, 322 people were buried in the churchyard and 203 in the church; only seven were buried outside the parish. Some occupational

---

[37] Registers of wills (movables) proved in the Archdeaconry and Commissary Courts are in GL. Those proved in the Bishop's Consistory Court are in the London Metropolitan Archive; early sixteenth-century wills from this series are printed as I. Darlington (ed.), *London Consistory Court wills, 1492–1547* (London, 1967). Citizens' wills proved in the court of Husting are in CLRO; calendared by R. R. Sharpe, *Calendar of wills proved and enrolled in the Court of Husting, 1258–1688*, 2 vols. (London, 1889–90). Prerogative Court of Canterbury wills (PRO, PROB 11) are available both in the Public Record Office, Kew, and in the Family Records Centre, Clerkenwell.

[38] Based on the sources used in Harding, 'Burial choice and burial location', pp. 121–7.

[39] Based on calculations in an unpublished paper presented by W. Kellaway to the Seminar in Medieval London History, Institute of Historical Research.

[40] See Harding, 'And one more', table 1, p. 114.

[41] E.g. PRO, PROB 11/353, f. 65; GL, MS 9171/23, f. 20; *The diary of John Evelyn*, ed. J. Bowle (Oxford, 1985), p. 301.

or status description is given for most of the dead, more consistently for church burials than for churchyard ones. As is to be expected, between a third and a half of all burials were identifiable as infants and children, but they seem to have been buried where older members of their families were. In this sample, esquires, gentlemen, merchants, and mercers and their family members were buried in the church; so too were a number of family members of skinners, haberdashers, and leathersellers. Some more of these last, and most merchant tailors, clothworkers, and drapers and their families were buried in the churchyard. Almost all those from artisanal crafts – carpenters, masons, bricklayers, plumbers, plasterers, joiners, shoemakers, brushmakers, weavers, and their families – were buried in the churchyard. All those recorded as 'poor', or as pensioner, almsman or almswoman, all but one servant, and all foundlings and parish children were also buried in the churchyard.[42] The occupational makeup of the local community varied considerably across the city, with local concentrations of wealth and particular occupations, and different parishes could accommodate different proportions of their population in church or churchyard, but it is likely that this general pattern prevailed across London.

Members of the one nuclear family were normally buried in the same sort of place, regardless of age or status, but servants, despite their residence within the household, were more likely to be buried in the parish churchyard than in church. At St Stephen Walbrook, between 1614 and 1619, eleven servants were buried in the churchyard and only three in the church; at St Michael Cornhill, between 1653 and 1657, eight out of eleven servants were buried in the churchyard, and the other three in church, while in the same period thirty-eight children were buried in church and thirty-one in the churchyard or cloister.[43] There are several instances of householders burying a child and a servant in different places within a short space of time.[44] It is equally clear that those who had no family or friends to make decisions about their burial were much more likely to be buried in a churchyard. All four foundlings and three pensioners in this period in St Michael Cornhill were so buried, as were all three foundlings and a beggar found dead in the street in St Helen Bishopsgate. Even the notorious case of Job-raked-out-of-the-ashes, a newborn baby boy abandoned on a cinder-heap in St Helen's parish in 1612, on whose behalf a certain amount of self-righteous indignation was generated, was

[42] *Registers of St Helen Bishopsgate*, pp. 293–307.
[43] *Registers of St Stephen Walbrook* (Harl. Soc. 49), pp. 89–90; *Registers of St Michael Cornhill*, pp. 246–9.
[44] E.g. *Registers of St Pancras Soper Lane*, pp. 296 (Richard Brooke's servant and son), 298 (John Parker's daughter and servant), 302 (Sir Thomas Soames' son and servant).

buried in a corner of the churchyard.[45] Only where the parish had no churchyard were foundlings and dead strangers at all likely to be buried in church, and such parishes often developed a practice of transporting the poor to an extraparochial churchyard.[46]

The total cost of burial normally included a fee for the grave site itself, paid to the churchwardens and usually listed as 'breaking the ground' or for a 'pit' or 'laystall'; a fee to the priest for his participation in the service; and a fee to the clerk and sexton for participating in the service and for actually digging the grave. One of the earliest statements of the latter dates from 1499, at St Mary at Hill, where the clerk was paid 2s. for making a grave in the church, 8d. for a 'man's pit' in the Pardon churchyard or the great churchyard, and 4d. for a child's. The practice of charging for a grave site in the church was well established in London by the early years of the sixteenth century, but churchwardens did not normally charge for the ground for a grave in the churchyard at this time, though the clerk or sexton was paid for digging the grave.[47] Over the course of the next century, most parishes began to charge for churchyard burial, and these charges, like those for burial in church, increased in level and complexity, though it always remained the cheapest option within the parish.[48]

A significant distinction came in with the increasing use of coffins for churchyard as well as church burial. Many burials in church up to the mid-sixteenth century were not coffined, and nor were most churchyard burials for probably another half-century at least.[49] It is unusual to find references to coffin burial in London churchyards before the later six-teenth century, though the parish of St Dunstan in the West charged 12d. for a woman's grave in the churchyard in 1553–4 'because she was coffined'.[50] In 1592, however, London parishes were charging from noth-ing to 3s. for the ground for an uncoffined churchyard burial and from 4d. to 5s. for a coffined one.[51] In 1593, during a plague epidemic but clearly with an eye to the future, the vestry of St Dunstan in the East noted that

---

[45] *Registers of St Michael Cornhill*, pp. 246–9; *Registers of St Helen Bishopsgate*, pp. 293–307; GL, MS 6831/1 (St Helen's paper burial register), entry for 2 September 1612; A. Munday et al., *The Survey of London ... begun first by the Paines and Industry of Iohn Stow, in the yeere 1598 ... And now completely finished by the study and labour of A.M., H.D. and others, this present yeere 1633* (London, 1633), pp. 180–1.

[46] Cf. below, and Harding, 'And one more', p. 123.

[47] Littlehales, *Medieval records of a London city church*, p. 231. Cf. BL, MS Harl. 2252, f. 163v; Overall, *Accounts of St Michael Cornhill*, pp. 223–4; GL, MS 4956/2 , f. 7; GL, MS 6842, f. 3.

[48] LPL, CM IX/45.

[49] In these cases, the body would be completely wrapped in a winding sheet. Late medieval illuminations show the corpse wrapped and tied in a kind of parcel, so that the human shape is discernible but no flesh is visible: R. S. Wieck, *Painted prayers. The book of hours in medieval and renaissance art* (New York, 1997), pp. 120, 126, 128–31.

[50] GL, MS 2968/1, f. 159v.   [51] LPL, CM IX/45.

'multitudes . . . more than in former times hath been accustomed' had of late been buried in coffins in the churchyards, making it 'very likely that in short time there would be either very scant or no buriall at all to be had'. Since 'the said coffins are a great hindrance, and speciallie to the poor of the said parish', they agreed to raise the charge for coffin burial in the churchyards to 6s. 8d. for adults and 3s. 4d. for children.[52] The trend continued, however, and it is probable that the majority of burials in single graves in London churchyards were coffined by the early to mid-seventeenth century. Most of the recorded burials (which may not include the poorest) at St Botolph Aldgate were uncoffined in the 1580s, but coffined by c. 1610. More than half the churchyard burials at St Dunstan in the West in 1623–4 were coffined.[53] There are some grounds for considering this a fashion that spread from the top down, since it was initially associated with church burial and with the prolonged burial rites of the élite. Certainly it appears that the choice of coffined burial could be read as a signal of ability and willingness to pay a higher level of charges across the board.[54] To take a single parish as an example of the general picture, at St Andrew Undershaft in 1612 the fees for an adult burial in the churchyard in a coffin were 2s. to the parson, 1s. to the clerk, and 6d. to the sexton; an uncoffined one would pay 1s. 4d., 1s., and 4d. to the same persons respectively.[55]

Obviously, uncoffined burials took up less space both in the short and long term, as did the burials of children, so some price differential was justified, but equally clearly churchwardens were ready to use pricing generally as a means of distributing demand between church and one or more churchyards, and sometimes to achieve other ends. At St Botolph Bishopsgate, the new parish churchyard opened in 1617 did not prove popular with parishioners, who still preferred the old or upper churchyard. In 1620, therefore, the vestry decided to increase the parson's, clerk's, and sexton's duties for burials in the latter to the level charged for a church burial and to double the parish's charge for churchyard ground there, 'which order is not made for the augmentation of the duties but to cause them more willingly to bury their dead in the lower churchyard'.[56] Local circumstances varied so much that it is impossible to establish for certain when and by how much burial charges rose in the seventeenth century overall, though St Giles Cripplegate did publish two sets of rates in

[52] GL, MS 4887, f. 145v.

[53] GL, MS 9235/2, passim; GL, MS 2968/2, ff. 218–26. Stephen Weston asked in 1617 to be buried in the churchyard of St Sepulchre 'only in a winding-sheet without any coffin', but an explicit request of this kind was unusual: GL, MS 9171/23, f. 20.

[54] LPL, CM IX/45.   [55] LPL, CM VII/94.

[56] GL, MS 9531/13, pt. 2, ff. 383–384v, 407v–408; GL, MS 4526/1, facing f. 15. It is not clear whether the charges were in practice applied.

1644 and 1664, showing that the minimum cost of burial in the cheapest
location (the upper churchyards) had been raised over that period from
1s. 10d. to 2s. 6d., and in the next cheapest, the lower churchyard, from
5s. to 6s. 6d.[57] Nor is it clear whether there was a price gradient across the
metropolis: the inner parishes, with less space but a wealthier population
could perhaps charge more, but equally had less need to do so, dealing
with a few dozen deaths a year, while the large suburban parishes, despite the high mortality rates they had to cope with, could not set prices
that their poor population could not afford. In any case, despite their
readiness to set formal schedules of prices, vestries and churchwardens
recognised that not everyone would be able to pay even this much, and
that many burials would have to be free or subsidised. At St Bride in
1624, a complex statement of charges concluded 'Item, for such as are so
poor they be not able to pay duties, allowance be made ... according to
the churchwardens' discretion'. It seems that half or more of all burials
in the parish by the 1660s were excused from paying any fees.[58]

Although churchyards offered more liberty than the interior of the
church, where burial locations had to be very carefully monitored, the
space still had to be managed. It may have been easier for the churchwardens to do this since the majority of people they were dealing with
were of less importance and status than those who were buried in church;
they were also paying less, and so perhaps were less likely or able to resist
direction. Both testamentary choices and burial registers contribute to an
impression that churchyard burial was not closely regimented from above
in the sixteenth century. Before c. 1550, willmakers asked for a range of
churchyard locations, indicating that they perceived the space as differentiated, and valued it accordingly, but also that they were confident that
they could secure a particular site. Several said that they wished to be
buried near a spouse, but others asked for a specific place: near the cross,
'ayenst the high altar in the procession way', 'at the aulter end', before the
vase containing holy water.[59] Choices of specific places in churchyards
declined sharply in the later sixteenth century, along with the testamentary choice of churchyard burial.[60] But if churchyard burial was thereafter

---

[57] GL (Printed Books), Broadsides 12.79, 4.2.

[58] GL, MS 9531/13, pt. 2, ff. 372v–373v; GL, MS 10345; MS 6540/1; MS 6570/1, item 62.

[59] In the churchyard, near the cross: William Marcham, merchant haberdasher, St John
Zachary, 1520 (GL, MS 9171/9, f. 166); between the cross and the church: William
Hopkynson, tailor, St Dunstan, 1520 (ibid., f. 169v); 'ayenst the high altar in the
procession way': Margaret Tynwynter, St Bride, 1520 (ibid., f. 149v); 'at the aulter
end': Nicholas Bagge, All Hallows Barking, 1541 (GL, MS 9171/11, f. 50); before the
vase containing holy water: John Cotson, goldsmith, St Benet, 1500 (GL, MS 9171/8,
f. 203).

[60] Harding, 'And one more', p. 114. Only one testator out of fifty wills sampled for 1560
specified the location within a churchyard; none did so in similar samples from 1580 and

being directed by the churchwardens or the clerk and sexton, it still seems to have reflected individual associations or preferences. At St Helen's in the early seventeenth century bodies were buried singly in more than a dozen different places, identified in relation to parts of the church, trees, or other features. Burying family members near one another also suggests that affective associations were important in churchyard burial, as in church: Margaret daughter of William Warren was buried in 1600 near where her brother had been buried seven years earlier; Edward son of George Tedder was buried in 1603 'close before the pumpe at his father's feet'.[61] And at St Botolph Bishopsgate in 1620, as noted above, parishioners so strongly preferred the old churchyard to the new that the vestry tried to shift the pattern of demand by loading the charges in favour of the latter.[62]

Though most churchyard graves must have been unmarked, there are some references to slabs and stones, which may have helped both to locate a preferred family burial spot and to organise the space more generally. Churchyard space was not as subject to privatisation as the interior of the church, but individuals still sought to mark and memorialise their place of burial. John Cotson, goldsmith, was buried in the churchyard of St Benet in 1500, but requested his brother to fix a small marble stone, with images and writing, to the churchyard wall in his memory.[63] In 1541, Richard Branche, citizen and skinner, asked to be buried in the churchyard of All Hallows Staining, as near as possible to the monument (which he may well have erected) where the bones of his mother and children rested.[64] The appearance of large altar tombs in churchyards, sometimes covering private vaults, appears to have been a fairly late development. Such a concession was made by St Bride's parish to Joseph Holden in 1657: the site was in the parish's north churchyard, near his own house, and he had already buried several of his children there. At his own cost he made it into a vault, and laid a monument or gravestone over it. The parish was careful to restrict the future use of the vault, and to reserve its right to recover the vault if Holden or his descendants failed to maintain it.[65]

Evidence for forward planning the layout of burials in churchyards is rare, though there was concern about accommodation, and more efforts

1600: GL, MS 9051/2, ff. 282v–305; GL, MS 9051/4, ff. 185v–222; GL, MS 9051/5, ff. 149–84.

[61] GL, MS 6831/1, entries for 1600–3 passim; cf. *Registers of St Helen Bishopsgate*, pp. 263, 265.

[62] GL, MS 4526/1, f. 15.

[63] GL, MS 9171/8, f. 203. There were four parishes dedicated to St Benet, and it is not clear which one this was.

[64] GL, MS 9171/11, f. 63v.   [65] GL MS 6554/1, ff. 181, 188.

were made in the seventeenth century.[66] Despite its efforts to encourage burial elsewhere, the parish of St Botolph Bishopsgate reported in 1622 that its upper churchyard was 'buried so full that convenient ground can hardly be found for the burial of a child'.[67] Some areas had to be kept clear for access: the vestry at St Stephen Coleman Street forbade the clerk to allow any pit or grave to be made in the procession way 'without great need', though St Michael Cornhill reserved the right to bury in the procession way 'if need be'.[68] An attempt to plan the layout of future burials was made at Stepney early in 1625 (almost certainly before there was any hint of that year's plague epidemic). The vestry decided in April 'because of the inconvenience of multiplying burials in certain places near the church, to the annoyance of the parish and the danger of future infection', to order that all graves be dug on the north side of the church, 'beginning at the Elms and so westward', and not coming nearer than seventeen yards from the church. When that side was full, graves were to be dug on the south side 'ranging west by the mud wall'. Within three months, however, plague mortality forced them to amend this order, to allow burial within seven yards of the church.[69]

The norm in London, both before and after the Reformation, appears to have been burial in single graves. What changed over time was the increasing density of burial, and the way in which the remains of earlier burials were treated. Graves were dug by the clerk and sexton – a combined office – in the later middle ages, and by the sexton or someone referred to as a gravemaker or gravedigger in the early modern period. As indicated above, he was paid a fee for digging the grave, equal to or greater than a day's wage for a labourer in the early sixteenth century, but proportionately less later. This suggests that it was at least a day's work for one man to dig a grave, since the clerk or sexton also received a regular if minimal wage; possibly he subcontracted or employed an assistant.[70] At St Bride Fleet Street, there was both a sexton and a gravemaker. The former took half the fees for burial in church, because he had to clear up afterwards, but the gravemaker had the profits of all churchyard burials. In the same parish, in the plague of 1665, the vestry agreed to give the gravemaker 'something extraordinary for his pains', to reward

[66] E.g. *Registers of St Pancras Soper Lane*, p. 294; *Registers of St Helen Bishopsgate*, pp. 288–90.

[67] GL MS 4526/1, f. 15; GL, MSS 4515/1–3. Possibly the clerk kept more detailed notes which have not survived: at St Botolph Aldgate, a nearby parish with similar problems, the laconic registers (GL, MSS 9221–3) are supplemented for some periods by the detailed parish clerks' memorandum books: cf. GL, MS 9223, which contains both formal register entries for *c.* 1593–1606, and memoranda from *c.* 1614.

[68] GL, MS 4456, pp. 154–5; Overall, *Accounts of the parish of St Michael Cornhill*, p. 248.

[69] Hill and Frere, *Memorials of Stepney parish*, p. 105.

[70] C. Pendrill, *Old parish life in London* (London, 1937), p. 122.

and encourage him to dig the graves deep; later they employed extra labourers at 2s. a day.[71] Graves were dug large enough to take the current interment, but may have been relatively shallow by modern standards. In *c*. 1542 the parish of St Stephen Coleman ordered its sexton to bury adults 4 ft deep and children 3 ft, to avoid 'corrupt heyers'; the requirement to dig graves at least 6 ft deep appears to have been instituted by the plague orders of 1582.[72] Some early medieval grave pits were lined with chalk or charcoal, but there is no evidence of such practices in the early modern period. Churchwardens bought lime and sand for necessary work on church burials, but these were probably used for mortar and bedding floor slabs and tiles, rather than to fill the graves to promote either decay or preservation.[73]

No burial was secure against future disturbance, usually for further burial on the same site. Even in the early medieval churchyard of St Nicholas Shambles, most of the interments had been disturbed by later burials in the same ground.[74] By the later middle ages several of London's parishes had charnels. How they were used remains unclear: although in Paris churchyard ground was later systematically managed, with older graves being regularly opened and emptied to make way for more burials, it seems probable that London parish charnels were the product of a more casual process, in which the sexton collected bones disturbed by later burials and stored them appropriately.[75] There appears to have been a comprehensive clearance at St Dunstan in the West in 1516–17, when fifty-nine loads of earth were carted away from the churchyard and charnel house, and the sexton was paid for two days' work removing bones from the charnel house, prior to rebuilding it and the vestry.[76] Such charnels were probably cleared at the Reformation, when the notion of bones as sacred relics and an encouragement to intercessory prayer was suppressed, and the practice of respectfully storing them was discontinued; the parish of St Alphege took down its charnel house in 1547.[77] This does appear to mark a break with tradition, but the accumulation of bones in the ground still presented a practical problem. Many parishes seem to have left them in the earth, cutting through them or clearing them aside to make room for a new interment. In the 1630s, St Bride's gravemaker complained that he had been obliged to dig up a corpse he had only

[71] GL, MS 6554/1, ff. 186v, 276, 289v.
[72] GL, MS 4456, p. 148; CLRO, Journal 21, ff. 284v–286v.
[73] E.g. Overall, *Accounts of St Michael Cornhill*, pp. 50, 84.
[74] W. White, *Skeletal remains from the cemetery of St Nicholas Shambles, city of London* (London, 1988).
[75] Harding, 'Burial choice and burial location', p. 128.
[76] GL, MS 2968/1, ff. 4–5v, 79.   [77] GL, MS 1432/1, f. 96.

recently buried, for lack of space for a new burial.[78] Archaeological evidence supports this: at St Benet Sherehog, some 250 post-Fire burials in single graves intercut and truncated one another, though the sequence remained fairly clear.[79] Some parishes attempted more systematic clearances. St Margaret Westminster in 1616 had a large pit (some $31\,\mathrm{m}^3$) dug to rebury bones from the churchyard, while St Peter Paul's Wharf has references to burial 'by the bones' in 1612, possibly indicating a similar pit or store.[80] A large store of disarticulated bones found at St Bride's church in the 1950s could be the remains of a medieval bone store, or the result of some later churchyard clearance.[81] John Aubrey claimed that 'our bones in consecrated ground never lie quiet: and in London once in ten yeares (or thereabout) the Earth is carried to the Dung-wharf', whence it would presumably be removed by boat along with other city rubbish. However, although such clearances may have taken place on some occasions, neither archaeological nor documentary evidence supports the idea that it was a common practice.[82]

Although churchyard burial was normally based on single graves, these were often used for more than one body, either within a short period or over time. In some cases the practice seems have been intentional. At St Helen's, Elizabeth Pistor was buried in the churchyard on 26 December 1651, and Anne Smith, a pensioner, 'in the grave upon Elizabeth Pistor' on 25 February 1652. William Gaskin, a poor man of the Leathersellers' Company, was buried in the north part of the churchyard on 30 November 1653, and Grace Buck, a parish pensioner 'upon William Gaskin' on 27 January 1654. These were dependent individuals, and probably this doubling-up was to save the parish both money and space.[83] The still more pragmatic practice of opening large pits and filling them with bodies over the space of some days or weeks was only adopted in London in time of epidemic, and popular response to it, vividly evoked by Dekker and Defoe, indicates that it was regarded with fear and distaste. Parishes reacted conservatively to the burial crisis of a plague epidemic,

---

[78] GL, MS 9583/1, item 19.

[79] MoLAS site reference ONE 94. All the bodies were coffined, though coffin preservation was very poor; some furniture, plates, and handles survived. See A. Miles, 'Number One Poultry: post Great Fire burial ground, London' (post-excavation assessment and updated project design, MoLAS, November 1997).

[80] Nichols, *Illustrations*, p. 31; *Registers of St Peter Paul's Wharf* (Harl. Soc. 41), entries for 23 January and 19 September 1612.

[81] G. Milne, *St Bride's church, London. Archaeological research 1952–60 and 1992–5* (London, 1997).

[82] *Aubrey's Brief Lives*, ed. O. L. Dick (London, 1958), p. civ. I thank Ralph Houlbrooke for drawing my attention to Aubrey's statement.

[83] *Registers of St Helen Bishopsgate*, pp. 200–301.

continuing normal burial practice for as long as possible and only using new expedients under extreme pressure.[84]

The very severe mortality of the 1550s influenza epidemic and the 1563 plague fell heavily on the city-centre parishes, and there was certainly anxiety about the capacity of the churchyards to cope with it: 'the common churchyards of the city being very small for the most part were so pestered with dead bodies that there was no room left for any burial if the same [epidemic] should any longer have endured'.[85] It is not certain whether burial in mass graves was used or not at this time; the creation of the New Churchyard, in response to this anxiety, may have relieved the problem for the epidemics of the 1580s and 1590s.[86] There is literary evidence for mass burial in pits in the 1603 and 1625 epidemics, and considerable documentary evidence for the expedient in 1665. Balmford mentioned 'open graves where sundry are buried together', and Dekker wrote of 'an hundred hungry graves' each to be daily filled with sixty bodies, in 1603.[87] In 1625 'they are compelled to dig Graves like little cellers, piling up forty or fifty in a Pit'.[88] Many of these large pits were in existing parish churchyards, dug on the vestry's order when the need for burial space became critical. In the 1665 plague, this moment occurred at different times in different parishes. The first pits were dug at St Dunstan in the West and St Bride's in August. A second pit was dug at St Bride's in early September and perhaps a third in late September, with more work in mid-October.[89] At St Botolph Aldgate a number of pits were dug in August, but the 'great pit' in the churchyard, which came to contain over a thousand bodies, received its first corpse on 6 September, according to Defoe's account. 'Some blamed the churchwardens for suffering such a frightful thing ... but time made it appear the churchwardens knew the condition of the parish better than they did': within a fortnight it had been filled up with 1,114 bodies.[90] It seems likely that most, perhaps all, of the larger suburban parishes of London ended by burying their plague dead in mass graves, but that the smaller city-centre parishes did not need to do so.[91]

[84] V. Harding, 'Burial of the plague dead', pp. 53–64.

[85] CLRO, Journal 19, f. 180.   [86] See below, pp. 95–6.

[87] J. Balmford, *A Short Dialogue concerning the Plagues Infection* (London, 1603), p. 32, quoted by Slack, 'Metropolitan government', p. 75; Thomas Dekker, *The wonderful year* (1603), in F. P. Wilson (ed.), *The Plague Pamphlets of Thomas Dekker* (Oxford, 1925), pp. 28–9.

[88] Dekker, *A rod for run-awaies* (1625), in Wilson, *Plague Pamphlets*, pp. 158–9.

[89] GL MS 2968/4, 16 August 1665; GL MS 6552/1b, not paginated; GL, MS 6554/1, f. 289v.

[90] D. Defoe, *Journal of the plague year* (Harmondsworth, 1987), pp. 77–8; cf. GL, MS 9235/2 part 2, ff. 491v–492.

[91] Cf. Harding, 'Burial of the plague dead', pp. 53–64.

The main motive for digging mass graves was obviously to accommodate the maximum number of corpses in a small space, but the parishes
may also have been driven to it to save money. They were shouldering the
massive financial burden of supporting 'visited' families, watching houses,
searching and reporting the dead, and by the height of the epidemic the
great majority of families could make no contribution to the cost of burial.
At St Bride's, the clerk was instructed to take the usual fees from 'the persons visited that are able to pay', but received fees from only 254 of the
1,491 burials in August, September, and October.[92] Though the pits were
expensive to dig, taking several days' labour, they were cheap to fill, while
individual graves and interments would have been more costly, even had
space been available. Parishes that had been heavily affected by plague
found it necessary to rehabilitate their churchyards afterwards. After the
epidemic of 1625, St Margaret Westminster bought 272 loads of gravel for
their churchyard; Stepney parish ordered their churchyard to be earthed
over with sand and gravel 'for prevention of such noysome sents as may
arise from the graves and bodies there buried'. Stepney's vestry agreed
that they urgently needed to acquire a new place of burial, since the old
one 'will affoord no more convenient place of Buriall without danger of
infection by reasone of the noysomeness of the ground there so opened
by reason of so many bodies formerly enterred there'.[93] Soon after the
epidemic was over, however, parishes reverted to burying in single graves,
and as far as possible in traditional churchyards.

Responses to plague mortality underline the resistance of parish vestries
to new burial practices, no doubt reflecting the conservatism of parishioners. This is an important theme in the history of early modern burial,
and it is striking how little difference the Reformation had made to the attachment to traditional places of burial. Indeed, with the abandonment of
charnelling, the planned removal and storage of bones from the ground,
the dead of modest status appear to have been able to exert a stronger claim
to occupy communal space in perpetuity in post-Reformation London.
This was not necessarily a principled decision on the part of civic or ecclesiastical authorities; it seems more likely to be the result of failure to
find an acceptable framework and justification for a more robustly pragmatic approach. The Great Fire of 1666 allowed some revision of burial
within the city, since many churches were not rebuilt and some of their
sites became available for burial for the new united ecclesiastical parishes,
and this may have relieved overcrowding for some time, especially as the

---

[92] GL, MS 6570/1, items 62–9; GL, MS 6540/1; GL, MS 6554/1, f. 275v.
[93] Nichols, *Illustrations*, p. 35; Hill and Frere, *Memorials of Stepney parish*, pp. 109, 111.

city-centre population declined.[94] London's city churchyards remained in use for nearly two centuries more, though the situation became increasingly difficult in the inner suburbs. At some point, probably in the eighteenth century, the pressure of numbers was such that deep pits, filled with stacks of coffined burials, were the only possible response. By the early nineteenth century the overcrowded and dangerously unhealthy state of the churchyards was seen as a scandal, provoking polemic in various forms against 'the unwise and revolting custom of inhuming the dead in the midst of the living', but the proposal to close them entirely was still met with a storm of protest.[95]

Parish churchyards in Paris

Although it is not possible to investigate churchyard burial in Paris in anything like the detail that is available for London, it is clear that it shared many of the same characteristics and problems: ancient, cramped churchyards in the centre of the city, usually adjoining the parish church, heavily used for burials, particularly by the poorer members of the community; serious competition for use of the space with other needs and interests; a pressing need to find new burial spaces or practices, restrained by the desire for burial in traditional locations. One major difference between London and Paris was that in the latter the pressure on parish churchyard burial was relieved by the availability of the Innocents and of other large churchyards for the burial of the poor and outcast. Hospitalisation often intervened between sickness and death, at least by the mid-seventeenth century, and usually determined the burial options of those who died there. Likewise, since so many died in the hospitals of the Hôtel-Dieu and Saint-Louis during plague years, and, by the mid-seventeenth century, of other causes, so that their burials became the responsibility of the institutions, the parishes from which they had come had a much lighter burden than they might otherwise have had. The burial of the vagrant poor and others dying in the street was the responsibility in London of

---

[94] T. F. Reddaway, *The rebuilding of London after the Great Fire* (London, 1940); cf. Miles, 'Number One Poultry'.

[95] G. A. Walker, *Gatherings from graveyards, particularly those of London, with a concise history of the modes of interment among different Nations from the earliest periods and a detail of the dangerous and fatal results produced by the unwise and revolting custom of inhuming the dead in the midst of the living* (London, 1839); *Report from the Select Committee on the improvement of the health of towns* (Parl. Papers 1842 (X), no. 327; J. Saunders, 'London burials', in C. Knight (ed.), *London*, 6 vols. (London, 1841–4), vol. IV, pp. 161–74; Mrs Basil Holmes, *The London burial grounds. Notes on their history from the earliest times to the present day* (London, 1896), pp. 206–25. The issue was publicised by Charles Dickens in *Bleak House* (1853).

the parish in which they were found, but in Paris it fell to the religious of Sainte-Catherine. They were charged with collecting and shrouding the bodies of those killed, drowned, or dying in prison, and with burying them in their part of the Innocents.[96] The practices of digging mass graves, and of exhuming and charnelling the remains, also suggest a different, and in some ways more considered, response to the problem.[97]

The evolution of the parishes of Paris, significantly different from the history of London, and their relationship to large civic cemeteries in the early middle ages, meant that most of the small parishes on the Ile de la Cité, and some larger ones on the right bank, had no churchyard of their own.[98] Most of these parishes are known to have buried within the church at some time, and some had vaults and/or *charniers* in which burial took place, but individuals who did not wish or could not afford to be buried there were normally sent to the Innocents, where all these parishes had burial rights. The large right-bank parishes of Saint-Jacques-de-la-Boucherie, Saint-Germain-l'Auxerrois and Saint-Eustache had burial rights at the Innocents, though the latter two also had cemeteries of their own.[99] In addition, some individuals from almost every other parish in Paris chose burial at the Innocents, so the pressure on the parish churchyards was less than it might have been, and several parishes were free from direct responsibility for maintaining and managing a burial space. All the left-bank parishes, however, and most of the right-bank parishes, did have churchyards, and had the same problems of rationing space and resolving conflicting demands on it as were experienced in London. The rebuilding of the parish church, or the addition of side chapels, both quite common in the sixteenth and seventeenth centuries, often encroached on outside burial space. The churches of Saint-Merry and Saint-Sulpice were enlarged at the expense of their churchyards; the parish of Saint-André-des-Arts built houses on part of its churchyard.[100] The parish of Saint-Gervais encouraged parishioners to subscribe to building a range of lateral chapels, and in addition rebuilt the arcade of *charniers neufs*, with accommodation for the clergy above, in the early seventeenth century,

---

[96] J. Hillairet, *Les 200 cimetières* du vieux Paris (Paris, 1958), p. 25. Cf. AN, L 571, no. 2 (papers of Saint-Germain-l'Auxerrois): 'aux Dames de Sainte-Catherine lesquelles...sont tenues de Ensevelir les corps thuees noyes et prisonniers'.

[97] Cf. Thibaut-Payen, *Les morts, l'église, et l'état*, pp. 35–6, 78–92.

[98] Friedmann, *Paris, ses rues, ses paroisses*; Hillairet, *Les 200 cimetières*, pp. 39–57. Cf. Pillorget, *Paris sous les premiers Bourbons*, pp. 85–8.

[99] See below, chapter 4, and M. Foisil, 'Les attitudes devant la mort au XVIIIe siècle: sépultures et suppressions de sépultures dans le cimetière parisien des Saints-Innocents', *Revue Historique* 251 (1974), 307.

[100] Hillairet, *Les 200 cimetières*, pp. 41, 93; *Commission municipale du vieux Paris, année 1904. Procès-verbaux* (Paris, 1905), p. 31.

but admitted in the eighteenth that these works had reduced the space available for burial.[101]

The growing need for burial space was recognised, and parishes could seek the authority of an order of Parlement for compulsory purchase of the desired land, on the grounds of 'la necessité publique, absolue, et morale'.[102] As in London, it was the peripheral parishes that saw the greatest population growth and spread, and therefore these that acquired more churchyard ground. Saint-Laurent in the northern suburbs built over its churchyard but replaced it in 1622 with another, larger one to the north; Saint-Médard in the south enlarged its churchyard in 1542 and 1644; Saint-Sulpice in the faubourg Saint-Germain acquired new churchyards in 1562 and 1664.[103] Sainte-Marguérite, originally a private burial chapel in the faubourg Saint-Antoine, became a succursal to the parish of Saint-Paul in 1634 (they reported together in the Etat des Baptêmes from 1670 as 'Saint-Paul et Sainte-Marguérite son annexe'), and opened a large churchyard in 1637.[104] Somewhat surprisingly, there appears to have been little difficulty about transferring ground that had been used for burial to secular uses, though episcopal approval was probably necessary.[105] In the fourteenth century the old churchyard of Saint-Jean-en-Grève had been made into a marketplace, and only replaced some sixty years later with a new churchyard, the 'cimetière vert' or 'neuf'. In the sixteenth century Saint-Eustache sold part of its large cemetery in the rue du Bouloi, to help finance the rebuilding of the church. In 1634 the parish sold the rest to Chancellor Pierre Séguier, then extending his hotel nearby; a new site was bought adjoining the rue Montmartre. The churchyard of Saint-Benoît on the left bank was closed in 1614 to give accommodation to the Collège Royal, and a new space nearby became the churchyard. While the first part of the churchyard of Saint-Eustache to be sold may not have contained any recent burials – it was said to be larger than needed by the parish – all the other transfers, and most of the building encroachments, must have included ground that had been used for interment.[106] Possibly the ground was cleared in advance, since exhumation and charnelling were acceptable practices. When part of the cemetery of the Innocents was cut off in 1669 for the

[101] Hillairet, *Les 200 cimetières*, pp. 64–8; AN, LL 746, f. IIIr–v; AN, LL 756, ff. 44v–48, 320–331v; AN, S 3359, dossier 1 (response to inquiry, 1763).

[102] Thibaut-Payen, *Les morts, l'église, et l'état*, p. 84.

[103] Hillairet, *Les 200 cimetières*, pp. 68–9, 84–6.

[104] Hillairet, *Les 200 cimetières*, pp. 137–41; *Commission municipale du vieux Paris*, pp. 55–118.

[105] Thibaut-Payen, *Les morts, l'église, et l'état*, p. 86.

[106] Hillairet, *Les 200 cimetières*, pp. 87–9, 98, 110–19; Thibaut-Payen, *Les morts, l'église, et l'état*, p. 86.

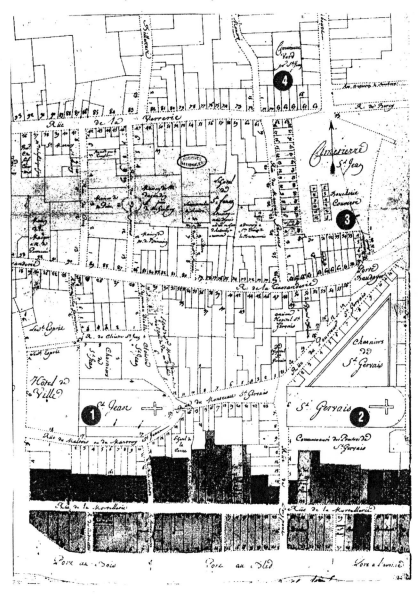

4 Churches and churchyards in eighteenth-century Paris: detail from a contemporary plan, showing (1) Saint-Jean-en-Grève and (2) Saint-Gervais, each with their adjacent *charniers*, and (3) the Cimetière Saint-Jean and (4) the Cimetière Vert of Saint-Jean-en-Grève (Paris, Archives Nationales, N[III] Seine, 421, no. 5).

enlargement of the rue de la Ferronerie, earth and bones were cleared from that area and taken to Saint-Nicolas-des-Champs; bones from part of the churchyard of Saint-Sulpice, closed in 1680 and sold to help re-build the church, were transferred in 1701 to another of the parish's churchyards.[107]

The most evocative source for the character and use of the churchyards of Paris in the Ancien Régime is the series of depositions in response to the *arrêt* of Parlement, 12 March 1763, requiring depositions from all *commissaires des quartiers* as to the state of their cemeteries, and the same from each parish vestry.[108] While, clearly, customs, burial practices, sen-sibilities, and indeed the spaces themselves could have changed consid-erably since the 1670s, in the absence of a mass of informative parish records, like those for London, this source still offers some insight into seventeenth-century conditions and problems. The city-centre church-yards were usually small, and surrounded by buildings, which must often have been three or four stories high. In the eighteenth century the inhabi-tants around the churchyard of Saint-Gervais complained that the 'mau-vaise odeur' of the burials was concentrated by the height of the church and the buildings.[109] The suburban churchyards were larger, though they also had to accommodate a much larger population. Eighteenth-century estimates of churchyard size may be of varying reliability, but while Saint-Jean-en-Grève's *cimetière vert*, of *c*. 440 m², or Saint-Séverin's two church-yards totalling 680 m² were generous for the inner city, those of Saint-Paul in the eastern suburb, and Saint-Laurent in the Villeneuve, both neared 3,000 m².[110] Saint-Laurent was, however, burying around 1,200 bod-ies a year in the 1670s, while Saint-Séverin buried fewer than 500 and Saint-Jean-en-Grève fewer than 350.[111]

A frequent feature of both urban and suburban churchyards was a *charnier*, usually to be interpreted not primarily as a charnel-house but as a kind of arcaded gallery, similar to that at the Innocents, perhaps also with bone storage above, and the location for private and family grave sites and epitaphs. Some of the *charnier* at Saint-Séverin, built in the fifteenth century, survives, though part was destroyed in 1673 for other building.[112] Saint-Gervais built a row of *charniers* in 1475 after the style of the cemetery of the Innocents, and rebuilt the arcades as the *charniers*

---

[107] Hillairet, *Les 200 cimetières*, pp. 90–8.

[108] BN, MSS Joly de Fleury 1207, 1208; much used by Hillairet, *Les 200 cimetières*, passim, and his appendix 2, pp. 382–3, which lists the area of some cemeteries now disappeared.

[109] AN, S 3359.

[110] Approximate figures, based on the returns to the inquiry of 1763, and cited by Hillairet, *Les 200 cimetières*, pp. 60, 68, 77, 88.

[111] See appendix 2.   [112] Hillairet, *Les 200 cimetières*, pp. 61–2.

neufs, in 1603.[113] Saint-Jean-en-Grève, which had a detached churchyard, built galleries and a cloister by the church *c*. 1570, and then a small burial area with *charniers*. The latter was said in 1672 to be over-used and a cause of infection.[114] Saint-Laurent rebuilt its *charniers* in 1630. These structures offered accommodation for a range of uses as well as burial: Saint-Gervais had a room for parish officers over its *charniers*, before building more accommodation for parish clergy there in 1626; Saint-Benoît also had a gallery of *charniers* with clergy houses over.[115] Saint-Jean-en-Grève used a room over its *charniers* as a parish assembly room in 1672, and in the eighteenth century the *charniers* at Sainte-Marguérite were used as a space for catechising and instructing children.[116] Tombs, shrines, crosses, and other objects of devotion also figured in Parisian urban cemeteries, and as in pre-Reformation London they were the focus of parish liturgical practices and collective celebrations. Tenants of Saint-Jean-en-Grève were bound to keep open and clean the alley leading to the *cimetière vert*, for the parish's regular procession.[117]

A contemporary painting of the cemetery of the Innocents depicts part of this large space as green grass and part as bare earth.[118] Smaller churchyards were perhaps too heavily used to support grass, though the term '*cimetière vert*' suggests that this was possible. Other vegetation is occasionally mentioned: there was a fig tree in the churchyard of Saint-Paul in the mid-sixteenth century, cut down in the mid-seventeenth, and the churchyard of Saint-Benoît on the left bank was referred to as the *cimetière des acacias* before its closure in 1614.[119] Despite the environmental problems caused by inner-city burial, neighbours of churchyards valued their access to or view over the open space, and there was a continuous battle with the parish authorities to restrict their use. While Parisians may not have used their churchyards for threshing wheat, pasturing animals, or playing *jeux de paume* or *boules*, as apparently happened in the nearby countryside,[120] there were many more urban problems. At Saint-Jean-en-Grève, the children and scholars of charity played games in the *charniers*, damaging the glass and lead of the church. The gates were locked to prevent this, but illicit rendezvous still continued, and the parishioners also objected

[113] AN, S 3359 (loose paper in bundle); AN, LL 746, f. IIIr–v; Hillairet, *Les 200 cimetières*, p. 65.
[114] AN, LL 663/10, f. 5; AN, LL 797, f. 21v.   [115] Hillairet, *Les 200 cimetières*, pp. 68, 81.
[116] AN, LL 797, f. 13; *Commission municipale du vieux Paris*, pp. 68–70, citing BN, MS Joly de Fleury 1208.
[117] Cf. AN, LL 746, ff. 152–3; AN, S 3402, unnumbered dossier (Saint-Jean-en-Grève, processions).
[118] Plate 6; reproduced in colour in Babelon, *Paris au XVIe siècle*, plate facing p. 392.
[119] Hillairet, *Les 200 cimetières*, pp. 33, 78, 81.
[120] Thibaut-Payen, *Les morts, l'église, et l'état*, pp. 88–90.

to the locking-up because it prevented their access to the chapel of the sacrament.[121] The parish of Saint-Gervais petitioned in 1473 for permission to acquire the property around its churchyard (granted in 1475), then occupied by shops and dwellings of poor people. They claimed that having the poor overlooking the churchyard generated 'plusieurs immondices' in the churchyard and nearby, and deterred noble persons from frequenting the churchyard and raising [? tombs] there, as in other churchyards in Paris.[122] The parish of Saint-Jean-en-Grève ordered some tenants overlooking their churchyard to block their windows in the early sixteenth century, but also allowed some other views to continue. A tenant who was later granted the right to make windows and views through a party wall had to promise not to throw dung or water into the churchyard.[123] This clearly remained a problem for all churchwardens, and was taken over as a matter of public order by the police in the late seventeenth century. In 1700 the widow Rance was punished for throwing ordure and 'matières fécales' from her windows into the churchyard of Sainte-Opportune, and all others were warned against it.[124] Less serious, but still an annoyance, was the question of laundry. The gravedigger at Saint-André-des-Arts was instructed to prevent any washing from being hung out in the churchyard, except the church linen, and the neighbours of the Innocents were also forbidden to air and clean their bedlinen and clothes there.[125]

It is hard to estimate the proportion, and numbers, of the population of Paris buried in the parish churchyards with any degree of accuracy, since the two main sources, wills and extracts from burial registers, are highly socially selective. These can give some information, especially when compared with the total burial figures from the 1670s, but the picture remains very impressionistic. The evidence surveyed by Pierre Chaunu's students and reported on in his *La mort à Paris* indicates that among members of the willmaking strata of society burial in a parish churchyard was a minority choice, though not a negligible one.[126] As in London, local differences of accommodation and tradition had a significant impact on practice in individual parishes: the proportions of willmakers choosing parish churchyard burial varied from less than 1 per cent in one sample to 40 per cent in another. A distinction should be made between inhabitants of those right-bank parishes with a right to be buried at the Innocents (among whom that was quite a popular option) and those of

---

[121] AN, LL 798, ff. 29, 30v, 35r–v.   [122] AN, LL 756, ff. 44v–48.
[123] AN, S 3405, dossier 4. The later grant was annulled by the crown.
[124] Delamare, *Traité de la police* (BN, MS Fr 21609), vol. IV, f. 237.
[125] AN, S 3311, f. ccclxix; AN, L 570, nos. 15, 22, 26.
[126] Chaunu, *La mort à Paris*, passim. See bibliography for a list of *mémoires de maîtrise* consulted in AN.

the left bank, where burial in the local parish churchyard was a more frequent choice.[127] The Innocents was both the actual parish churchyard for one tiny parish (reporting only twenty-three deaths in 1670), and the equivalent of a parish churchyard for several others, though it had a particular appeal, transcending what might otherwise be a predictable church/churchyard divide. Social differences between samples, however, could be skewing these figures, since the students who analysed their samples and burial choices by social class found that a higher proportion of *gens de métiers* chose cemeteries or *charniers*, but the social comparability of different samples was not formally tested.[128] In any case, as Chaunu observed, the sample of testators in no way matched the stratification of Parisian society proposed by Roland Mousnier. Some 70 per cent of the late seventeenth-century testators came from the top 30 per cent of society – clerics, nobles, officeholders, merchants and *honorables*, with some skilled craftsmen; the lower 70 per cent of society (artisans, shopkeepers, wage-earners, servants) wrote only 30 per cent of the wills.[129]

Among willmakers, any appearance of change over time, in the balance of preference between church and churchyard burial, could well be produced by either the geographical location or the social character of the samples being studied at different periods. Chaunu states that church burial became more popular in the second half of the sixteenth century and in the seventeenth, but that churchyard burial (or indifference to the place of burial) was more important in the eighteenth.[130] However, the geographical balance of the samples shifted from left bank to right bank between the later sixteenth and the later seventeenth centuries, and also became more suburban, and possibly less aristocratic, as the city grew; this could have been enough in itself to reshape the overall profile of burial choice.[131] The antiquaries' extracts from the burial registers confirm that, for the strata of society in which they were interested, church rather than churchyard burial was the norm. Only a very small percentage of the recorded burials at Saint-André-des-Arts, Saint-Jean-en-Grève, and Saint-Gervais (6–8 per cent) were in parish churchyards, but recorded

---

[127] Of de Rot's left-bank sample (Etude 33, 1539–53) 40 per cent chose the parish churchyard or charnel, and 6 per cent the Innocents; of Rossignol's right-bank sample (Etudes 24, 54, 1561–1600), only 1 per cent chose the parish churchyard, but 41 per cent chose the Innocents: AN, *mémoires de maîtrise*.

[128] In de Rot's sample, 40 per cent of the whole sample, but 71 per cent of *gens de métiers*, chose the parish churchyard. A similar social bias is visible in Chaunu's table, based on the *mémoire de maîtrise* of Michèle Massucco: Chaunu, *La mort à Paris*, pp. 321, 486–7, though this does not distinguish between parish churchyards and the Innocents.

[129] Chaunu, *La mort à Paris*, pp. 393–4. Cf. R. Mousnier, *La stratification sociale à Paris aux XVIIe et XVIIIe siècles. L'échantillon de 1634, 1635, 1636* (Paris, 1976).

[130] Chaunu, *La mort à Paris*, pp. 321–2.   [131] Ibid., pp. 393–7, 518–20.

burials were 10 per cent or less of the total.[132] It seems likely that not more than 10 per cent of the city's population was buried in church; if that were so, many parishes, especially the suburban ones, would have been burying hundreds if not over a thousand bodies a year in their church-yard. In 1670, the parish of Saint-Sulpice buried 1,676 in all, Saint-Paul and Sainte-Marguérite buried 1,517, Saint-Nicolas-des-Champs 1,423, Saint-Laurent 1,202. Some of the 1,621 and 930 buried by Saint-Eustache and Saint-Germain-l'Auxerrois respectively would have gone to the Innocents, but they would still have been accommodating a very large number in their own churchyards.[133]

Wills and burial register extracts also give some clue as to the charac-ter of the burial population of the parish churchyards. As noted above, several of Chaunu's students reported a higher proportion of those from the lower to middling layers in society (artisans, *gens de métiers*, etc.) choosing burial in the parish churchyard.[134] One suggested that essen-tially the churchyard was not a choice, but the place one went if one had no means to go elsewhere, and calculated that seventeen out of eighteen in her sample who chose churchyard burial left estates of less than 150 *écus*.[135] This impression is borne out by the parish register material. In the right-bank parishes of Saint-Jean-en-Grève and Saint-Gervais, nobles, es-quires, lords, and officeholders and members of their families made up fewer than half of the hundred persons buried in the churchyards; the rest included several *honorables hommes* and *bourgeois de Paris*, merchants (of wine, silk, grain) and craftsmen (dyers, cordwainers, coopers, an iron-monger, a painter, a feathermonger, a mason) and their dependants.[136] At Saint-André-des-Arts, a parish dominated by officeholders, *noblesse de robe*, and lawyers, several of each of these were buried in the church-yard, as were merchants and bourgeois, and most of the small number of craftsmen noted in the extracts.[137] These extracts are very heavily biased in favour of the upper ranks of society: wage-earners, labourers, servants, and the very poor were not represented at all, but must have made up the greater part of the churchyards' population. In 1763 the churchwar-dens of Saint-Gervais said that almost all burials in the churchyard (over 400 in the last year to Easter) were in fact convoys of charity.[138] The

[132] BN, MS Fr. 32589 (Saint-André-des-Arts, 1550–1670; 104 out of 1628 entries); MS Fr. 32588 (Saint-Jean-en-Grève, 1623–32: 15 out of 211 entries); MS Fr. 32838 (Saint-Gervais, 1639–70, 85 out of 1,036 entries).

[133] Calculations from Etat des Baptêmes, BN (Réserve), LK[7] 6745.

[134] Chanterac, Genin, de Rot: AN, *mémoires de maîtrise*.

[135] Martin: AN, *mémoire de maîtrise*, p. 34.

[136] BN, MS Fr. 32588 (Saint-Jean-en-Grève, 1623–32); BN, MS Fr. 32838 (Saint-Gervais, 1639–70).

[137] BN, MS Fr. 32589 (Saint-André-des-Arts, 1550–1670).   [138] AN, S 3359.

low desirability of churchyard burial, in the eyes of the socially superior, is underlined by the fact that at least three of the notables buried in
the churchyard of Saint-André-des-Arts were only interred there because
they died of plague.[139]

Burial in a parish churchyard was nevertheless a positive choice for
some, though reasons varied. As in London, affective and familial association with the place of burial was strong. Thirty-six per cent of those
choosing churchyard burial in one will sample mentioned their wish to
be near a 'proche'.[140] The parish of Saint-Jean-en-Grève, claiming burial
rights in the churchyard of Saint-Gervais in 1563, said that some parishioners wished to be buried there 'ayans encore memoire de la sepulture de
leur famille audit cimetiere'.[141] Claude le Gay, three times widow, from
the rue Saint-Denis, 'bourgeoise sans doute' according to Chaunu, asked
in 1634 to be buried in the churchyard of Saint-Nicolas-des-Champs
where the bodies of her late husbands lay.[142] Associations of this kind also
surface in the desire of Parisian Huguenots for parish burial; though they
may not have wished for burial in church, and certainly wanted to bury
according to their own rites, they were still keen to share the traditional
space of the urban dead, where their own ancestors were buried, claiming it in terms of natural right. But this was unacceptable to Catholics,
who saw their presence as pollution, endangering the Christian community. Attempts to bury Huguenots in parish churchyards were resisted, at
times with physical force, or by subsequent degrading exhumation, and
the churchyards grudgingly conceded by the various edicts of pacification were new, peripheral, and non-parochial.[143] The exclusion of the
Huguenot dead from parish churchyards is underlined by their separate
listing (under the heading 'de la religion pretendue reformée') after the
parochial totals in the Etat des Baptêmes from 1670.[144]

It was certainly cheaper to be buried in a churchyard than in a church,
and this could have been an important consideration for some. At Saint-
André-des-Arts, those who were being buried in the churchyard could
choose which palls, hangings, and attendants they wished to hire, rather
than being obliged to take one of the better sets, required for a burial
in church.[145] Presumably in an attempt to deter those who could afford church burial from taking a cheaper alternative, the vestry of Saint-
Gervais ordered in 1709 that anyone who by will or otherwise actively
chose churchyard burial should pay a fee equivalent to half that due for

[139] BN, MS Fr. 32589, entries for 5 November 1580, 15 September 1591, 1 July 1628.
[140] Carré, *mémoire de maîtrise*.   [141] AN, LL 663, ff. 19–21.
[142] Chaunu, *La mort à Paris*, pp. 505–7.
[143] Thibaut-Payen, *Les morts, l'église et l'état*, pp. 157–68.
[144] BN (Réserve), LK[7] 6745; see appendix 2.   [145] AN, LL 687, f. 183r, no. 259.

opening the ground in the church (30 *livres* for a wooden coffin); for the rest, the ground in the churchyard was free.[146] The choice of churchyard as an exhibition of humility, however, was probably only ever that of a tiny minority, and may have focused more on the churchyards specifically of the poor rather than parish churchyards.[147] It may also be associated with an emerging 'hygienic' perspective in the eighteenth century, a desire to separate decay from the celebration of the holy mysteries.[148]

Burial in Paris, as in London, was priced according to location and the number and quality of services and accessories required. Fewer lists of prices and alternatives survive, and apparently none for early dates, but those that do, from the mid- and later seventeenth century, suggest a similar hierarchy of desirable locations, and a similar tendency to rate other costs (hire of ornaments and hangings, ringing of bells) according to the status or cost of the burial place chosen. However, as in London, there was little consistency from one parish to another in the actual level of charges, or in some of the fine distinctions made. At Saint-Jean-en-Grève in 1670, while church burial cost at least 12 *livres* for an adult, opening the ground in the *charniers* cost only 7 *livres*, in the new churchyard around the *charniers* 5 *livres*, and in the *cimetière vert*, the detached churchyard in the rue de la Verrerie, 3 *livres*. The poor, whether dependent on the parish's charity or not, paid nothing for the ground for burial in the churchyards. The gravedigger received a similarly graded fee for digging the grave, delivering the trestles, hearse, and palls, and fetching the body. For a burial in church he received 5 *livres*, in the *charniers* 4 *livres*, in the new churchyard 3 *livres*, and in the *cimetière vert*, 50 *sous*. For children's graves he was paid half these rates; for paupers and charity burials he received nothing.[149] Very similar distinctions are recorded at Saint-Gervais in 1675 and Saint-André-des-Arts in 1687.[150]

Perhaps as a result of the complex evolution of the Parisian parishes, in which ecclesiastical lordship and filial relationships played a large part,[151] the issue of churchyard burial rights, and therefore control of the use of the space, was often very complicated. The most famous case is the cemetery of the Innocents, where the parish of les Saints-Innocents itself had the right to bury its own dead in the cemetery but had no control of other burials and no claim to ownership of the ground. Several other parishes had the right to bury there, but paid burial fees to the proprietors of the

---

[146] AN, LL 752, ff. 60–62v.

[147] See below, chapter 4; cf. also the case of *noble homme* Simon le Telier, regent in the faculty of medicine, who chose by will to be buried in the cemetery of the Incurables (BN, MS Fr. 32589, entry for 19 November 1644).

[148] Thibaut-Payen, *Les morts, l'église, et l'état*, pp. 35–6.

[149] BN, MS Fr. 21609, vol. IV, f. 37.   [150] AN, L 651/2; AN, LL 687, f. 183r, no. 259.

[151] See chapter 2; cf. Friedmann, *Paris, ses rues et ses paroisses*.

soil, the dean and chapter of Saint-Germain-l'Auxerrois. These in turn acknowledged the burial rights of the Hôtel-Dieu and the religious of Sainte-Catherine in part of the ground.[152] Parish churchyards could be literally contested spaces. The parish of Saint-Gervais resorted to both negotiation and litigation to assert control over its churchyard. In 1521 the parish agreed with the master and sisters of an adjoining hospital or Hôtel-Dieu (not the main city hospital of that name), that the latter would renounce their claims to make graves for themselves and their domestics in the churchyards and *charniers* of Saint-Gervais, and to take fees for burial there, in return for a space in the church being granted for the burial of the religious, and a plot in the *charniers* for the domestics. The churchwardens of Saint-Gervais in turn renounced their claim that the hospital was bound under the ancient agreement to launder the church's linen, and conceded a rent of 20 *livres* per annum.[153] In the later sixteenth century the churchwardens of Saint-Gervais also resisted the claim of the parishioners of Saint-Jean-en-Grève to burial rights in their churchyard. The parish of Saint-Jean had originally been part of the parish of Saint-Gervais, and the parishioners of Saint-Jean claimed they could bury in the churchyard without needing permission from the parish or attendance by the *curé* of Saint-Gervais. The latter, for his part, was prepared to accept bodies for burial, but not to allow another priest to officiate at burials in his churchyard. Several sentences of the Châtelet and appeals failed to clarify the position, though it seems that very few cases were actually at issue, and the dispute may simply have faded out. The parishioners of Saint-Jean continued to make their Palm Sunday procession into the churchyard of Saint-Gervais in the late seventeenth century.[154]

Parishes in Paris employed gravediggers (*fossoyeurs*), who, like the London clerks and sextons, were responsible for a range of tasks related to the management of burial, and also for assistance at services, bellringing, etc. The *fossoyeur* of Saint-Gervais agreed to perform forty articles of agreement on his appointment in 1572, in return for his wages of 60 *livres tournois*.[155] At Saint-André-des-Arts, the *fossoyeur* was bound to notify the parish clerk of any forthcoming interment, so that the latter could negotiate over services and attendance, and he (the *fossoyeur*) also delivered a memorandum of all burials and their location, in church or churchyard, every Sunday to the churchwarden responsible.[156] The

---

[152] See chapter 4, below.
[153] AN, LL 746, ff. 152–3. The parish source refers to the hospital as the Hôtel-Dieu or hospital, but presumably it was the hospital of Saint-Gervais or Sainte-Anastase: Hillairet, *Les 200 cimetières*, p. 64.
[154] AN, L 663, ff. 19–21.
[155] AN, LL 746, f. 164. Unfortunately the articles are not listed.
[156] AN, LL 687, f. 184v.

fossoyeur was responsible for delivering the coffin or trestles and the pall and candlesticks for the vigil to the house of the deceased, returning to collect the body, and taking it to the place of interment, as well as digging and covering the grave itself.[157] Churchwardens may have set rules and fees about church and churchyard burial, but it must have been the *fossoyeurs* who in practice made important decisions about graves and pits, since they had the most intimate knowledge of the graveyards themselves, gained in some cases by service over many years.[158]

Churchyards in Paris contained both individual, marked graves, often in the arcades or *charniers* encircling the ground, and areas of unmarked and probably mass burial in the centre. In this way they topically inverted the centre/margin paradigm which broadly structured the location of burial, in that the best places were round the edges; the churchyard was defined by its periphery, not its centre. As noted above, several parishes, especially suburban ones, were burying well over a thousand bodies a year in their churchyards by 1670. Some were in single graves, but many must have been in pits. The expedient of digging large pits in which numbers of shrouded but uncoffined bodies were buried is one of the most difficult features of churchyard burial to establish and date precisely, at least as regards its normal use in parish churchyards. It was certainly the case in the middle of the eighteenth century, when most parishes used mass graves, opening one or two a year, and leaving them open for longer in winter than in summer, but it is not clear whether it was regularly practised, outside the Innocents and other large-scale cemeteries, in the seventeenth century or earlier. Hillairet, the historian of Paris's churchyards, simply states that burial in the parish churchyards 'se faisait en fosse commune' but gives no source or date for this, nor any indication that the practice is likely to have had a complex evolution.[159] Parish records are in any case sparse but, at least in the parishes studied particularly for this work (Saint-André-des-Arts, Saint-Jean-en-Grève, Saint-Gervais), they make no mention of digging mass graves within the period to 1670, though it is true that these were moderate-sized parishes. By 1763, Saint-Gervais had a well-established system of rotating burials in some forty *fosses communes*, using two or three a year so that they did not need to be opened in less than twelve or thirteen years, but the churchwardens offered no opinion as to when this practice began, though they said there had been burial in the churchyard since time immemorial.[160] However, given the numbers buried in some parishes by the end of the period considered here, it seems very probable that

---

[157] AN, L 651/2; AN, L 663 (unnumbered papers); AN, LL 687, f. 184v; AN, LL 752, f. 61v; AN, LL 805, p. 255.
[158] Cf. AN, LL 797, f. 21v; AN, L 663.   [159] Hillairet, *Les 200 cimetières*, p. 12.
[160] BN, MSS Joly de Fleury 1207, 1208; AN, S 3359.

some kind of conscious management strategy was in place. Even if mass graves of the later kind were not universally found, there was certainly crowding of burial, reopening of graves, and disturbance of burials for other, more secular, purposes. When Saint-André-des-Arts decided to build two houses in their churchyard in 1641, to accommodate the *curé* and choir priests, they agreed to remove the bones to another part of the cemetery.[161]

Epidemics, in Paris as in London, increased overall mortality and also the pressure on parish churchyards, but such crises may well have been handled with greater resolution. It was common for those suffering the disease to go, or be taken, to the Hôtel-Dieu, the plague hospital of Saint-Louis, or one of the special isolation hospitals set up in tents or sheds outside the city, from which the dead would be buried in an extramural cemetery.[162] Attempts to compel all the sick, and even those suspected, to go to a hospital, cannot have been totally effective, even when backed up by force, as it appears they were; some must have died at home and probably been buried locally. In 1580 the guards at the city gates were ordered to prevent the entry into the city of people sick with plague, and to ensure that they went to the tents and other places to receive them; at the same time they were told to stop anyone bringing bodies into the city to be buried, and see that these were taken to the cemeteries 'plus proches des fauxbourgs de la ville'.[163] Whether this means that the suburban parish churchyards had to take more of the dead from the inner city is not clear. There certainly was some burial of plague victims in city parish churchyards. Only six of the deaths in the parish register extracts for Saint-André-des-Arts were said to be from plague (*peste* or *contagion*), but all were buried in the churchyard. The burial of the Dame de Corbrin was annotated 'a cause de laquelle maladie elle ne fut point enterré en l'eglise aupres de son mary ainsy quelle l'avoit ordonné'. At least one was buried in an identifiable grave, since he was exhumed some months later and buried in his ancestors' chapel.[164] A police order of 1627, addressed to the *fossoyeurs* of Paris, forbade them to accept bodies for burial at night, although night burial had been practised since 1596, because such a practice was dangerous to public security, allowing crimes and murders to evade detection. This again suggests that parish burial was continuing during the epidemic.[165]

[161] AN, S 3309/9.
[162] See below for the Hôtel-Dieu; Fosseyeux, 'Les épidémies de peste à Paris'; C. Hohl, 'Les épidémies et leurs consequences sur l'organisation des hôpitaux au XVIe siècle à Paris', *Bulletin de la Société de l'Histoire de Paris et Ile de France* 89 (1962), 33–6.
[163] Fosseyeux, 'Les épidémies de peste à Paris', p. 118.
[164] BN, MS Fr. 32589, entries for 9 August 1562, 5 November 1580, 15 September 1591, 1 and 3 July 1628.
[165] Fosseyeux, 'Les épidémies de peste à Paris', p. 139.

In Paris, as in London, burial in city-centre churchyards continued well after the period covered in this study. Agitation against the practice began earlier, in the mid-eighteenth century, and appears to have been taken up as an issue in the conflict between enlightened and religious perspectives. Burial in church came under attack first, but anxieties about churchyards soon surfaced. The problem of the smells and infection produced by frequent burial was made worse by the people's habit of throwing *immondices*, urine, and excrement into the churchyards. The church shared in the desire to maintain the dignity and propriety of this consecrated space, and to exclude profane uses, but was reluctant to speak against urban burial as such. Various ways of improving the situation were suggested in 1738,[166] but by the 1760s arguments for banning the practice altogether were being made. The principal case made against it was its impact on health: 'la malheureuse coutume d'enterrer les morts au milieu des vivans, de faire de nos villes de vastes cimetieres, etoient funeste a l'espece humaine . . . Une partie des maladies qui afflige les hommes, qui corromp leur sang, et produit des fievres putrides, revient de ce que nous respirons un air infecté d'exhalaisons cadavreuses'. A particular Parisian scandal led to an enquiry in 1763, followed by an order banning burial in city churchyards in 1765, in favour of creating suburban cemeteries, but this order – 'un reglement si precieux, si sage' – was largely ignored.[167] The curés of Paris fought the idea, claiming that there was no evidence that the health of those who lived around the churchyards suffered. More crucially, they argued that the remedy would cause more problems than it solved, and that in particular by distancing the dead from the living it would destroy respect for them, 'blesse le culte religieux des funerailles', and undermine religion – in a century in which there had been many attacks on religion and doctrine from materialists.[168] Both sides used highly emotive language, and in the event the resistance of the clergy, and the real difficulties of implementing the elaborate schemes that had been suggested, deferred effective action, except in the case of the Innocents, until the Revolution.[169]

Despite the divergence of Catholic and Protestant eschatologies, there were many common features to the development of parish churchyards in early modern London and Paris, including conflicts over access, increased

---

[166] BN, MS Joly de Fleury 1317, ff. 50–9.   [167] BN, MS Joly de Fleury 1207, ff. 7–12.
[168] Ibid., ff. 15–21.
[169] Foisil, 'Sépultures et suppressions de sépultures'; J. McManners, *Death and the Enlightenment. Changing attitudes to death among Christians and unbelievers in eighteenth-century France* (Oxford, 1981; paperback edn. 1985), pp. 303–19.

pressure on space, the creation of new sites, and popular reluctance to accept any move away from traditional locations. In both cities, parish churchyards played an important part in the development of an idea of a public as well as a communal or collective interest in urban space. They were key sites for the confrontation between the needs of the living and the dead. The conflicts and contests played out there on the whole concerned local interests and issues, at least until anxieties about hygiene and safety came to the fore in the eighteenth century. The older parish churchyards were strongly identified with the traditional centre of communal activities, of which burial of the community's dead was only one. Although they accommodated large numbers of dead, mostly from the poorer strata of society, the personal element in the interaction between living and dead remained strong. Identifiable individuals (clerk, sexton, *fossoyeur*, usually long-serving employees of the parish) were responsible for order and for carrying out the policies of vestry or *fabrique*. Likewise it was named and knowable neighbours and tenants who invaded the space, obstructed the parish's intentions, and asserted private interests against the public or pragmatic. Churchwardens and *marguilliers* had to accommodate and compromise with members of the community over a range of claims to churchyard space, and we can see them working out rules and negotiating their implementation. They seem to have been reluctant to give any interest absolute priority, at least until forced to do so by the pressure of mortality. Any anxieties that were expressed about this close cohabitation of living and dead were usually in terms of natural rather than supernatural dangers, but even these could be ignored or overridden by the need for speedy disposal of the dead. Both cities seem to have endeavoured to maintain the fiction of permanent and peaceful burial, either just by ignoring the reality of disturbance or by endowing the process of charnelling with spiritual value.

Nevertheless there were changes as well as continuities, and differences as well as similarities. Over the sixteenth and seventeenth centuries the numbers and acreage of the parish churchyards increased, but at the expense of the close spatial and psychological connection between the congregation of living worshippers and the dead. More churchyards were opened, mostly towards the periphery of the city, since this was where population growth was strongest, but also where for a while some land remained available. Compared with the rich density of traditional uses and associations of the older churchyards, these new burial spaces must have seemed undifferentiated and lacking in meaning, and there was clearly some reluctance to use them, overcome in due course by the pressure of numbers on space. There must over time have been an increasing depersonalisation of the dead, as more of them were despatched to these distant and non-traditional spaces. London practice, which did not resort to mass burial in this period except in epidemics (and then against the strength of popular feeling), may have remained a more sensitive and personal business, compared with Parisian churchyard burial.

4   Innocents and outcasts: civic and non-parochial churchyards

If the appearance and use of the parish churchyards of London and Paris demonstrated the tension between the needs of the living and those of the dead largely at the level of the local community, the central churchyards added another factor, the sense of the civic community and identity, to this interplay of forces. The non-parochial churchyards were also meant as overflow and last-resort burial places, especially in epidemics, so other parties – municipal, police, governmental – took an interest. There were important differences, however, between the role and image of St Paul's churchyard in London, and of the Innocents in Paris: the former was more strongly identified with the activities of the living community, almost incidentally serving as a burial place for the dead, while the latter gained its special meaning from the sense of generations of Parisians buried there, visibly present in the bones piled high in the attics of the surrounding *charniers*. In a period of religious tension and conflict, the Innocents came to symbolise the identity of Christian, Catholic Paris, and became the focus of sectarian activity. In some ways these identities as community symbols, whether civic or religious, became clearer as the cemetery function of the spaces declined, as it did over the early modern period. The opening of new extramural and distant churchyards reduced the need to bury in these central ones (and also called into question assumptions about the spatial relationship between living and dead), but did not undermine their role in the imagining of the city. The proposed closure of the Innocents in the eighteenth century, and the opposition to it, can be read as a clash between a traditionalist, Catholic clergy and an 'enlightened' professional or intellectual interest, but it also tapped deep reserves of popular feeling about a location that was infused with meaning and affective associations. As in the preceding chapter, the history of particular spaces in London and Paris is so distinctive that it is necessary to treat them separately, even though, as will appear, there were important common themes in their development and use.

London: St Paul's churchyard

St Paul's cathedral and the churchyard outside it formed what was probably the most significant of London's topographical foci in the middle ages. The churchyard had been the meeting place of the city's early medieval folkmoot or communal assembly, and also allegedly for the muster of armed citizens; the Midsummer Watch collected there before its procession round the city, and royal and civic processions terminated there.[1] In the later middle ages the churchyard retained some of that significance, as a location for public oratory and for official sermonising, and also at times as a focal point of disorder.[2] Stow's account of the enclosure of the precinct between the twelfth and fourteenth centuries implies that the churchyard once surrounded the cathedral, but that different parts were claimed for different uses: the east for the folkmoot assembly, the west for military assemblies.[3] A reconstruction of the precinct in the sixteenth and seventeenth centuries by Peter Blayney shows that, by that time, much of it had been filled with houses and offices of the bishop, dean and chapter, petty canons, and other ecclesiastical administration. Most of the space to the south of the cathedral was occupied by building; the bishop's palace filled the north-west corner of the precinct, and St Paul's School and other buildings lined the eastern enclosure. The churchyard proper lay to the north-east of the cathedral, with a gate opening to Cheapside. This, known as the north churchyard, the great churchyard, or Paul's Cross churchyard, contained the pulpit or Paul's Cross, and was where most burial took place. The great churchyard was surrounded by small tenements, along the cathedral walls and inside the north and east precinct walls; among these were a charnel vault and chapel, on the north side, and Holmes College, against the cathedral. There was also a belltower in the north-east corner, pulled down in the reign of Henry VIII. To the west of the cathedral's north transept was a separate, smaller churchyard, surrounded by a cloister, and known as the Pardon Churchyard.[4] 'About this Cloyster was artificially and richly painted the dance of *Machabray*, or dance of death, commonly called the dance of *Pauls*: the like whereof was painted about S. *Innocents* cloyster at Paris in France.'[5]

[1] John Stow, *A Survey of London* (1603), ed. C. L. Kingsford, 2 vols. (Oxford, 1908; rev. edn, 1968), vol. I, pp. 102, 325; Brooke and Keir, *London 800–1216*, pp. 154, 249.

[2] R. Bird, *The turbulent London of Richard II* (London, 1949), pp. 68, 82.

[3] Stow, *Survey*, vol. I, pp. 328–9.

[4] P. W. M. Blayney, *The bookshops in Paul's Cross churchyard* (London, 1990), pp 3–5. Christopher Wilson (personal communication) corrects Blayney's location of the Pardon Churchyard to west rather than north of the north transept.

[5] Stow, *Survey*, vol. I, p. 327.

The great churchyard was an accessible and permeable space, which accommodated two main kinds of activity in addition to its function as a burial place. The first was public and partly symbolic, the second commercial. Because of the site's identification with the city as a community, as in the memory of the folkmoot, events at St Paul's were deemed to have a special publicity. To address a congregation from Paul's Cross pulpit in the churchyard was to address the city, and through it the nation: Papal Bulls were read there, and both Protestant and Catholic Reformations were preached there. Wolsey pronounced anathema on Luther from a platform in the churchyard in 1521, and finished with burning his works; Tyndale's Testament and Coverdale's Bible were burned there in 1546. In the seventeenth century printed works deemed 'popish' were burned there. The presence of stationers and booksellers trading in the churchyard may have made these demonstrations of control of the press especially pointed.[6] Control of the pulpit at St Paul's was an extremely important part of the ecclesiastical policy of both Tudor and Stuart monarchs, and the selection, approval, or dismissal of preachers was a great matter. Several present and future bishops preached there, as did other prominent preachers of the time, subject to episcopal or archiepiscopal approval.[7] The presence of the Lord Mayor and aldermen of London, and often also their ladies, at these sermons reinforced the sense that these occasions represented the establishment.[8] It was also an important site for demonstrating the power of the state, not on the whole by punishment of dissenters but by their submission. Numerous recanting heretics did their penance at St Paul's in the Reformation years; in one instance Cranmer insisted that the man recant his error, which had been 'so greatly spread abroad in this realm', not in a parish church but at St Paul's 'when most people might be present'.[9] The fact that these acts took place in the presence of the dead, of the bones of the faithful, may have added to their significance. Heretics were not usually burned in St Paul's churchyard, though their books were, but the open area at the west end of the cathedral was occasionally used for executions, such as the Guy Fawkes conspirators, and the Leveller Robert Lockyer in 1649.[10]

[6] S. Brigden, *London and the Reformation* (Oxford, 1989), pp. 151–2, 339; M. MacLure, *Register of sermons preached at Paul's Cross, 1534–1642* (Ottawa, 1989), p. 27; N. E. McClure (ed.), *The letters of John Chamberlain*, 2 vols. (Philadelphia, 1939), vol. I, pp. 202, 214; vol. II, p. 313.

[7] MacLure, *Sermons preached at Paul's Cross*, passim and esp. p. 138.

[8] E.g. ibid., p. 72. See plate 5.

[9] MacLure, *Sermons preached at Paul's Cross*, pp. 22–8, 37–9, 55.

[10] W. S. Simpson, *Gleanings from old St Paul's* (London, 1889), pp. 140–1, 145–9. For Lockyer's funeral, see below, chapter 9.

5   St Paul's churchyard, 1616. An imagined scene, looking south, in
which a sermon is being preached from the pulpit (demolished in 1643)
to James I and Anne of Denmark. The painting was one of a pair drawing
attention to the cathedral's need for restoration; it shows the houses
built up against the transepts, and the generally secular aspect of the
churchyard. Engraving, undated (eighteenth-century) from an original
seventeenth-century painting (London, Guildhall Library).

Given the public nature of the space, its situation in the commercial heart of the city, close to the important marketplaces of Cheapside and the Newgate Shambles, and the fact that many urban parish churchyards were invaded by commercial activity, it is not surprising that trading of various kinds spilled over into St Paul's churchyard. A proclamation of 1554–5 against people leading horses or other beasts, or carrying vessels, baskets, bread, beer, flesh, fruit, fish, fardels of stuff, wood, billets, or faggots through the cathedral, indicates the extent to which the area was regarded as a thoroughfare.[11] The cathedral was a meeting place for craftsmen and potential employers, but the churchyard and environs became known especially for the stationers selling writing materials, books and prints.[12] A significant cluster of stationers can be found there in 1523, and during the second half of the sixteenth century St Paul's churchyard became 'the unrivalled centre of retailing bookselling in London'. By the mid-seventeenth century virtually every one of the tenements surrounding the churchyard was, or had been, a bookshop. Around 1650, following the dissolution of the cathedral chapter by the Long Parliament, the space of the former Pardon Churchyard was built over with a block of twelve buildings, three storeys high, soon occupied by booksellers.[13] At about the same time, the city's rulers moved the Cheapside herb market into the churchyard, to relieve congestion in the streets, though they may also have been emphasising the secularisation of formerly sacred space. The restoration of king, episcopacy, and chapter in 1660, however, obliged the market to return to the street.[14] The effect of all this passage and commercial activity must have been to degrade and secularise the churchyard. Latimer drew attention to its insanitary condition in 1552,[15] and a contemporary poem castigated the sheds and houses

> suche as ioyne to paul's against her will,
> that have impaired her strength by vaults and cellars,
> to make more room for buyers and for sellers...
> are they not accursed that did yeeld
> to make God's courts a merchandizing field...?

and asked if there was

[11] W. S. Simpson, *St Paul's Cathedral and old city life: illustrations of civil and cathedral life from the 13th to the 16th centuries* (London, 1894), pp. 85–6.

[12] Stow, *Survey*, vol. I, pp. 81, 329; ibid. vol. II, p. 281.

[13] Blayney, *The bookshops in Paul's Cross churchyard*, pp. 5, 19, 81–9. cf. A. Johns, *The nature of the book. Print and knowledge in the making* (Chicago and London, 1998), esp. ch. 2, pp. 58–186.

[14] Stow, *Survey*, vol. I, pp. 329–30; B. R. Masters, *The public markets of the city of London surveyed by William Leybourn in 1677* (London, 1974), p. 15.

[15] MacLure, *Sermons preached at Paul's Cross*, p. 33.

No easement but against the temple walls?
No other place to p–e or make Laystalls?[16]

Despite these uses, St Paul's cathedral and its churchyards also accommodated a good number of burials, though no full burial register survives
before the eighteenth century.[17] There was some distinction between the
smaller Pardon Churchyard enclosed by the cloister on the north side of
the cathedral, and the great churchyard. Stow notes that 'many persons,
some of worship, and others of honour' had been buried in the Pardon
Churchyard, though he named only Thomas More, dean (d. 1421).[18]
A fifteenth-century memorandum stated that the vergers were to keep
the churchyard clean, especially for processions, and to dig the graves
for fees fixed by statute. It also stated that only those wearing the habit
of the church should be buried in the cemetery.[19] However, while the
Pardon churchyard did serve as a burial place for the cathedral's minor staff and domestics, and may have been attractive to other clerics,[20]
burial there was not exclusively reserved for clergy. In 1525–6 the chamberlain recorded the receipt of 6s. 8d. for the burial of one Agnes, and of
the servant of Master Middleton, *in cimiterio venio*.[21] Similar sums were
received for burial there in 1535–6 from a Dr Lee and 'a certain haberdasher', and again in 1548–9 from the wives of John Holyman and John
Reynes.[22] The cloister and Dance of Death round the Pardon Churchyard were demolished in 1549, but the name survived. Part of the area
became a garden, but there may still have been burials in the remaining
ground, until it was built over in *c.* 1650.[23]

The great churchyard to the north-east of the cathedral was the burial
ground of first resort for some parishes and of choice for some individuals; it was not, however, the prime burial place of the civic community.
In the later middle ages, a small number of testators asked for burial in St
Paul's churchyard (probably meaning the great churchyard). It was the
most popular alternative to parish burial among those who expressed a
choice in their wills, but it was still very much a minority choice. Many of
those choosing burial there came from parishes immediately adjoining or
very close to the precinct, at least two of which had little or no burial accommodation outside the church. These parishes may have seen St Paul's

[16] Quoted in Simpson, *St Paul's Cathedral and old city life*, pp. 195–200.
[17] GL, MS 25741.   [18] Stow, *Survey*, vol. II, p. 327.
[19] Simpson, *Gleanings from old St Paul's*, pp. 81–2.
[20] London Metropolitan Archive, Consistory Court wills, 10.
[21] GL, MS 25634, f. 28v.
[22] GL, MS 25635, f. 3; GL, MS 25636 (not foliated). Later accounts in this series record
only burials in the crypt.
[23] Blayney, *The bookshops in Paul's Cross churchyard*, pp. 4, 81–9.

as one of their 'natural' or traditional burial places, perhaps because of simple proximity, perhaps because of some memory or custom surviving from an earlier era when St Paul's claimed extensive burial rights. Several burials came to St Paul's from parishes elsewhere in the city which apparently had no churchyards, and some individuals seem to have chosen it because relatives already lay there.[24] Despite the paucity of references, there must have been a large number of burials in the great churchyard over time, to justify the charnel. Possibly this served other parishes in the city as well, though there is no tradition of this, and several parishes, as noted above, had their own charnels. Stow claimed to know 'by report of him who paid for the carriage' that when the charnel was closed and cleared in 1549 more than a thousand cartloads of bones were taken to Finsbury Fields. After the closure the charnel chapel was rebuilt as shops and tenements.[25]

In the early modern period, St Paul's churchyard did not attract the burials of the civic élite, despite Stow's reference to 'honour' and 'worship'. Possibly it was only the Pardon Churchyard that had that special cachet, and with the destruction of the cloister and the Dance of Death, the attraction ceased. None of the aldermen and officeholders whose funerals are recorded by Henry Machyn between 1550 and 1563 were buried in St Paul's churchyard.[26] After the Reformation, the explicit choice of burial in St Paul's churchyard virtually disappeared.[27] The cathedral itself still retained importance as a place of celebration and burial, but most Londoners seem by this date to have focused their attention and loyalties more closely on their parishes. In fact the character of burial in St Paul's churchyard shifted, and several parishes evidently looked on it as a burial resource inferior in desirability to their own church and churchyard. All Hallows Honey Lane buried twenty-six individuals at St Paul's between 1554 and 1577, twenty-two of whom were servants and one a stranger.[28] Burials at St Paul's from the nearby parish of All Hallows Bread Street in the sixteenth century included servants, inmates or temporary residents, almsmen of the Salters' Company, paupers, and nameless strangers dying in the street. This parish appears to have taken lower fees for burials at St Paul's than its customary charges for burial in the church.[29] St Margaret

---

[24] Harding, 'Burial choice and burial location', p. 123; GL, MS 9171/8, ff. 218v, 219v.

[25] Stow, *Survey*, vol. I, p. 330; Blayney, *The bookshops in Paul's Cross churchyard*, p. 5.

[26] Stow, *Survey*, vol. I, p. 327; Machyn, *Diary*, passim. The only burial there he notes is that of Mrs Hunt, a (?skinner's) widow, in 1561: ibid., p. 255.

[27] No London willmaker, in samples of fifty wills at twenty-year intervals from 1540 to 1660, chose burial there, but by the seventeenth century only a minority were expressing a choice in their wills in any case: Harding, 'And one more', p. 114.

[28] *Registers of All Hallows Honey Lane*, pp. 258–61.

[29] *Registers of All Hallows Bread Street* (Harl. Soc. 43), pp. 160–7.

Moses, also nearby, buried some servants, pensioners, and strangers in St Paul's churchyard in the late sixteenth and early seventeenth centuries.[30]

Several parishes turned to St Paul's to accommodate their increased number of dead in time of epidemic, though it is not clear whether this was encouraged or merely tolerated by the authorities. The practice evidently had medieval roots: Henry Inssher, goldsmith, said in his will of 1500 that he wished to be buried in St Paul's churchyard if he died 'at the tyme of this sykenesse, or elles where it shall please owr Lord to dispose'.[31] The elevated mortality of the 1550s brought extra burials from All Hallows Bread Street, as did the plague of 1563.[32] All Hallows Honey Lane buried eleven bodies there in the plague of 1563, and another four alleged plague victims between 1564 and 1577.[33] St Margaret Moses buried twenty-nine out of thirty dying between July and October 1625 at St Paul's, though in normal years it buried fewer than half its dead there.[34] A report by the city's surveyors in 1654 opposed the idea of building on some void ground at the west end of the cathedral, since in time of plague 'it hath bene a very usuall buriallplase for the ease of the Citty when other bureing plase hath been opresed with dead corpses'.[35] By this time, however, the New Churchyard outside Bishopsgate (discussed below) had for many parishes taken on the function of overflow churchyard, both for the socially marginal and for plague victims. At the same time as he founded the New Churchyard in 1569, Lord Mayor Sir Thomas Rowe erected a building in St Paul's churchyard for people to hear the sermons there. These two benefactions were surely linked in what appears to be a conscious plan to reclaim the cathedral churchyard for godly observance; the burial of the dead was no longer seen as a guarantee of, or even an aid to, the sanctity of the location.[36]

In 1582 the then Lord Mayor asked the Privy Council to approve an order restraining parishes with churchyards of their own from burying at St Paul's. Burials had been so numerous, and in such shallow graves, that 'scarcely any graves could be made without corpses being laid open'; parishes that had been 'pestering of the churchyard' were henceforth to use the new burial place provided by Rowe, or to make or buy new spaces for themselves. The order affected ten parishes; thirteen others, with no churchyards, were allowed to continue burying at St Paul's, and the order was also not meant to prevent anyone of 'honour or worship' being buried

[30] *Registers of St Margaret Moses* (Harl. Soc. 42), pp. 66–74.
[31] GL, MS 9171/8, f. 200v.   [32] *Registers of All Hallows Bread Street*, pp. 159–61.
[33] *Registers of All Hallows Honey Lane*, pp. 258–61.
[34] *Registers of St Margaret Moses*, pp. 79–80.
[35] Simpson, *Gleanings from old St Paul's*, pp. 150–1. Cf. *Calendar of State Papers Domestic, 1654*, pp. 141–3.
[36] CLRO, Journal 19, f. 180 (proclamation founding the New Churchyard); ibid. f. 214b (1570) mentions both enterprises together.

there.[37] All Hallows Honey Lane, which must have been one of the ten 'restrained' parishes, significantly reduced its use of St Paul's.[38] Some other parishes without churchyards continued to bury there occasionally, especially, as noted above, people of modest status and in plague years.[39] The secular takeover of the churchyard by booksellers, and by a market in the Interregnum, seems to have transformed perception of the space, and it is not clear whether any burial was going on there in the 1660s, before the destruction of the cathedral and the long process of its rebuilding effectively put a stop to the practice. The loss of city-centre population after the Fire and the creation of new burial grounds on the sites of destroyed churches may also have offered parishioners of the city centre a more acceptable alternative to the extramural burial grounds.

The new London churchyards

The new churchyards of early modern London were the result of civic or sectional initiatives, and their evolving use reflects a shift in attitudes to burial in the metropolis and in its social meaning. While the sixteenth-century New Churchyard's creation represented a municipal intervention, an act of individual and collective foresight and forward planning on behalf of the whole civic community, in practice the way the site came to be used exemplified the increasing ideological and social polarisation of the population. The late seventeenth-century cemeteries took this further, with the development of new burial places for self-defined communities.

The context of the new creations, however, was the previous loss of a considerable burial resource in the shape of the monastic churchyards, and especially that at St Mary Spital, a hospital on the northern fringe of the medieval city. Probably all the London convents accepted some bodies for burial from the outside community; two major houses, the Charterhouse and the abbey of St Mary Graces by the Tower were founded after the Black Death on sites opened for burial during the epidemic.[40] Recent excavations at St Mary Spital indicate that its graveyard must have been used by a much larger community than that of the hospital.[41] The remains

---

[37] W. H. and H. C. Overall, *Analytical index to the series of records known as the Remembrancia preserved among the archives of the City of London, A.D. 1579–1664* (London, 1878), nos. I. 331, 343.

[38] *Registers of All Hallows Honey Lane*, pp. 262–3.

[39] *Registers of St Vedast Foster Lane* (Harl. Soc. 30), pp. 142–4, 173; *Registers of St Margaret Moses*, pp. 74–83; *Registers of All Hallows Bread Street*, pp. 181–2.

[40] Stow, *Survey*, vol. I, p. 124; vol. II, p. 81.

[41] For what follows, on the current (1999–2000) excavations at St Mary Spital, I am grateful to Barney Sloane and Chris Thomas, of the Museum of London Archaeology Service, for information and comment.

of over 11,000 interments had been excavated by the spring of 2001. Dating of the remains has yet to be confirmed, but even over a 300-year span – longer, probably, than the cemetery was in use – these numbers would represent a living population much larger than the hospital inmates and visitors alone. What is striking is that there is so little in the documentary record to indicate that St Mary Spital was a major place of burial in medieval London. Wills as well as parish records focus on parochial burial, and in only three wills proved in the Commissary or Archdeaconry Courts of London did individuals request burial in the churchyard,[42] though several more, including servants of the hospital, individuals staying there or in the precinct, and parishioners of nearby St Botolph Bishopsgate, asked for burial in the hospital church.[43] However, the existence of a charnel chapel in the churchyard in 1380 presupposes a significant volume of burials in the cemetery. How the chapel was used is not yet clear; it may have been essentially a mortuary chapel, also used to retain and sanctify the disturbed bones from past burials, rather than a formal ossuary for deliberately exhumed and retrieved bones. It seems to have attracted some burials to its vicinity, including William Eynsham, pepperer, whom Stow identifies as the builder or founder of the chapel.[44] The concentration of references around 1390–1400 may suggest that the charnel chapel had an immediate but perhaps shortlived popularity with Londoners of middling and upper status, but further documentary evidence for burial at St Mary Spital is needed, to establish its significance among the burial options of medieval Londoners and the part it played in perceptions of the issue. A single reference, to the removal in 1512 of eight loads of earth from the churchyard of St Martin Outwich to St Mary Spital, may imply that the site was seen as a place to dispose of the remains of the dead, not one where those remains would necessarily secure a positive value.[45]

St Mary Spital was exceptional among London's medieval hospitals in the number of burials there, but not in its association with the burial of the poor. There may well have been a notion that hospital burial bestowed some of the benefits of burial in a conventual churchyard, but those who died in a hospital's care and were buried by its charity are usually identified as poor. St Bartholomew's Hospital at first shared burial space with the adjacent priory, but by 1224 the prior and convent had set aside a separate burial ground for the poor of the hospital, and also the brethren. In

---

[42] GL, MS 9171/1, ff. 440v, 466; MS 9171/3, f. 126v.
[43] GL, MS 9171/2, ff. 116, 301, 350v; GL, MS 9171/3, ff. 20, 149; GL, MS 9171/4, f. 49; GL, MS 9171/5, ff. 79v, 193v, 223v, 366; GL, MS 9171/8, ff. 8v, 199v, 205v, 246v.
[44] Sharpe, *Calendar of wills proved and enrolled in the Court of Husting*, vol. II, pp. 313–14; Stow, *Survey*, vol. I, p. 167.
[45] GL MS 6842, p. 15.

1373 Archbishop Sudbury granted a cemetery to the hospital on the understanding that the poor of the hospital would no longer be buried in the priory's churchyard. A mid sixteenth-century reference to the purchase of linen for the burial of poor people, and the early seventeenth-century maps showing the churchyard for 'the poore of the hospitall', indicate that this identification continued.[46] The number of dead from the hospital in the sixteenth and seventeenth centuries is not known: the so-called 'death books', though mandated in the seventeenth century, do not begin until 1762, and it seems unlikely that the modest totals of dead recorded in the Bills of Mortality for the parish of St Bartholomew the Less include all the dead from the hospital.[47] The number may not in fact have been very great – Sir William Petty contrasted the better care of the London hospitals with the Parisian ones in the later seventeenth century, and as late as 1758 the hospital only buried 318 people compared with 7,182 'cured and discharged'.[48] However, the partial identification of extra-parochial burial with anonymity and poverty is important, since it helped to colour attitudes to new early modern churchyards. Individuals who died and were buried, 'after much charge in their illness', in hospital cemeteries, may often have been vagrant or unsettled, and had in any case already lost their connection with fixed household and parish, such a central part of early modern identity.

The New Churchyard on the north-eastern fringe of the city was the first of the early modern non-parochial churchyards. It was established in 1569, six years after the plague of 1563. Fearing that space in the churchyards of the city might be insufficient if such an epidemic happened again, the mayor and aldermen decided to establish a new burial ground 'before the time of necessity requireth it'. They chose a site of about 1 acre (0.4 ha) already belonging to the City, at the time let as a tenterground, adjoining the north-east side of Moorfields, part of the lands of Bethlehem Hospital. The plot was walled in at the expense of Sir Thomas Rowe, then Lord Mayor, and the level of the ground was raised by dumping rubbish from around the city.[49] Rowe's wife was buried there,

---

[46] E. A. Webb, *The records of St Bartholomew's Priory and of the church and parish of St Bartholomew the Great, West Smithfield*, 2 vols. (London, 1921), vol. I, pp. 188–91; Moore, *The history of St Bartholomew's Hospital*, vol. II, pp. 263, 277, plate facing, p. 260.

[47] V. C. Medvei and J. L. Thornton (eds.), *The royal hospital of St Bartholomew, 1123–1973* (London, 1974), p. 303; *Bills of Mortality*. Cf. W. Maitland, *The history and survey of London from its foundation to the present time*, 2 vols. (London, 1756), vol. II, pp. 740–1, on the omission of hospital dead from the Bills in the eighteenth century.

[48] Petty, 'Two essays in political arithmetick', pp. 508, 510–11; Moore, *The history of St Bartholomew's Hospital*, vol. II, p. 867. In 1758, the parish of St Bartholomew the Less reported sixteen deaths, that of St Bartholomew the Great, twenty-five: *Bills of Mortality*.

[49] CLRO, Journal 19, ff. 180, 180v; Repertory 16, ff. 476v, 491v, 492, 505; Letterbook V, ff. 237, 274b. Cf. CLRO, Comptroller's City Lands Plan 270. The site is shown

though he himself was buried at Hackney in 1570.[50] It is clear that this new location was meant to be integrated into the city's burial traditions and practices, in part replacing St Paul's churchyard. A pulpit was built in the churchyard and an annual sermon endowed, which the mayor and aldermen were expected to attend. This never rivalled the St Paul's or St Mary Spital sermons, however, and it is not known how long it continued. Payments for the sermon are recorded in the City's Chamber Accounts for 1584–6, and Strype refers to a particularly good sermon given there in 1584.[51] In 1586 Peter Symonds of the parish of All Hallows Lombard Street left money for sixty penny white loaves for distribution at the New Churchyard after the Whitsun sermon.[52] Within a short time, however, the churchyard's characteristics of low cost and non-parochiality combined with its peripheral location to make it the place of burial for individuals who were seen as marginal to or excluded from the community. Its proximity to Bethlehem, the city's hospital for the insane, may well have influenced its image, and indeed the identities blurred so that by the seventeenth century it was often referred to as 'Bethlehem churchyard'.[53] Those parishes that were short of space used it to bury some of their poorer inhabitants, especially servants, strangers, and inmates. Suicides and nonconformists, who in different ways excluded themselves from the moral community of the established church, were often buried there, as were the unclaimed bodies of prisoners who died at Newgate. Inevitably also it received a heavy charge of plague victims.[54]

Use of the New Churchyard, like use of St Paul's, varied from parish to parish, according to the local pressure on space. Some parishes seem to have had no need to use it, others only in time of plague, but as noted above, several parishes that had customarily buried a number of bodies at St Paul's had begun to use the New Churchyard by the end of the sixteenth

as 'Bethlehem Church yard' on Ogilby and Morgan's map of 1676: Hyde, Fisher, and Cline, *The A to Z of Restoration London*, spreads 17, 18.

[50] Stow, *Survey*, vol. I, p. 165; A. B. Beaven, *The aldermen of the city of London, temp. Henry III–1908*, 2 vols. (London, 1908, 1913), vol. II, p. 35.

[51] B. R. Masters (ed.), *Chamber accounts of the sixteenth century* (London, 1984), pp. 97, 237; John Strype, *A Survey of the cities of London and Westminster . . . written at First in the year MDXCVIII by John Stow . . . now lately corrected, improved and very much enlarged . . . by John Strype*, 2 vols. (London, 1720), vol. I, bk. 2, pp. 95–6.

[52] *The endowed charities of the city of London, reprinted . . . from 17 reports of the Commissioners for inquiring concerning charities* (London, 1829), p. 46. By 1820 the loaves were given away on Whitsun morning to poor people of the parish of St Botolph Bishopsgate 'at a place now forming the garden of a house, at the corner of Spinningwheel Alley, Moorfields, which was, it is said, formerly a burial ground': ibid.

[53] The site is so named on Ogilby and Morgan's map of 1676: Hyde, Fisher, and Cline, *The A to Z of Restoration London*, spreads 17, 18. See Plate 3, p. 51.

[54] For further discussion of these issues, cf. Harding, 'And one more', pp. 119–20; Harding, 'Burial on the margin', p. 60.

century. Others turned to it increasingly in the seventeenth century.[55] The cost of burial to the individual was based on fees for ground and services; the cost to the parishes included the opportunity cost of filling up their own space. For all these, the New Churchyard could offer significant savings. Supposedly, no fee was due for burial there, except 6d. to the gravedigger, though in 1641 Katherine Chidley complained that burial at 'Bedlam, which is the cheapest place that I know' still incurred charges for bearers, gravediggers, and ground, and also at least a shilling for the priest.[56] Notwithstanding this complaint, burial there was cheaper than elsewhere. Although in most cases the minister's fees are not known, at St Mary Colechurch he only took 1s. for accompanying a corpse to the New Churchyard, compared with 4s. for burying one in the church.[57] All Hallows Honey Lane charged parishioners 3s. for an adult and 20d. for a child buried in the New Churchyard in the early seventeenth century, compared with 6s. 4d. or more for burial in the parish churchyard. Even this much might be beyond the means of the poor: in 1611 the parish clerk noted regretfully against the burial of William Harrice's son in the New Churchyard 'he is a poore man & the duties is 20d. wch is loste'.[58] Other parishes waived fees entirely: 'For Dorcas daughter of Henrie Evan, New Churchyard, 00. 00. 00'.[59] The vestry of Holy Trinity Minories mandated its churchwardens to pay the cost of making the grave there '[if the] friends of the party deceased be poor or not able to pay'. This was the complement to its declared policy of sending all burials there except 'ancient dwellers being head of a house', who could still be buried in the parish.[60] Lower fees encouraged householders to bury servants and dependants in the New Churchyard. Twenty-two of the thirty-eight servants dying in the parish of St Margaret Moses between 1636 and 1666 were buried there, as were most of the Drapers' almsmen and almswomen from the parish of St Olave Hart Street.[61] Several parishes also buried there at least some of the foundlings and stranger paupers for whom they found themselves responsible, such as 'a foundlin, unchrissened', 'a poor weoman that was found deade in Mr Wrothes entrie', 'a poore

---

[55] E.g. St Vedast from the 1640s: *Registers of St Vedast Foster Lane*, pp. 173–89.

[56] CLRO, Repertory 16, f. 492; Chidley's complaint quoted in Cressy, *Birth, marriage, and death*, p. 457.

[57] GL, MS 66, f. 14.

[58] *Registers of All Hallows Honey Lane*, pp. 266–7. The fees noted in the register are not consistent, however, and do not match the rates noted at the end of the original volume: GL, MS 5022, f. 118.

[59] E.g. GL, MS 818/1, for 1621.

[60] LPL, MS 3390, f. 101v. I thank Martha Carlin for this reference.

[61] *Registers of St Margaret Moses*, pp. 83–93; *Registers of St Olave Hart Street* (Harl. Soc. 46), pp. 141–209.

cuntryman that dyed suddanely in Savage Yard (whose name wee know not)'.[62]

Not all those buried in the New Churchyard were poor, and it had clearly not been Rowe's intention that it should become an outcast burial place. It seems likely that it was choice that brought at least five members of the respectable Norrington family of All Hallows Honey Lane to be buried there between 1587 and 1615, some or all of them in a grave near Lady Rowe's.[63] Thomas Eaton, citizen and draper, asked for burial there in 1599, where his father, mother 'and diverse of my kindred' had already been buried.[64] Several more individuals, of sufficent substance to make a will, requested burial there in the seventeenth century, and funerals were not necessarily minimalist.[65] Because it was not attached to a parish church, the New Churchyard seems to have been attractive to the small but significant number of semi-separatists and advanced Protestants in later sixteenth- and early seventeenth-century London. The Scottish minister James Lawson was buried there in 1584, and in 1590 the court of High Commission acted to curb its use by irregular or dissenting congregations from across the city.[66] Thomas Eaton, mentioned above, was the brother of John Eaton, 'preacher of Godes worde', and left remembrances to 'my good frendes' the preachers Thomas Barber, Stephen Egerton, and Thomas Redrich.[67] James Tassard of St Botolph Aldgate, silkweaver, who in 1618 requested burial in the New Churchyard near his wife, may well have belonged to a French Protestant immigrant family, and the Dutchmen buried from several parishes may likewise have belonged to a stranger church.[68] The executed Leveller Robert Lockyer was buried there in 1649, with an impressively well-attended funeral procession.[69]

Though undoubtedly important in keeping the city's burial problem under control, the New Churchyard was not a final solution. London's

---

[62] *Registers of St Vedast Foster Lane*, p. 178; *Registers of St Peter Cornhill*, (Harl. Soc. 1), p. 170; *Registers of St Olave Hart Street*, p. 195.

[63] *Registers of All Hallows Honey Lane*, pp. 263, 266–8. The register of St Pancras Soper Lane, p. 292, mentions the burial place in the New Churchyard of 'M. Norrington citoyen ancien et grave'.

[64] PRO, PROB 11/95, f. 6.

[65] PRO, PROB 11/95, f. 61v; GL, MS 9051/8, f. 339; GL, MS 9171/31, f. 28; A. G. B. Atkinson, *St Botolph Aldgate, the story of a city parish* (London, 1898), p. 126.

[66] P. Collinson, *The Elizabethan Puritan movement* (London, 1967), p. 371.

[67] PRO, PROB 11/95, f. 6; for Barber, Egerton, and Redrich, see Collinson, *The Elizabethan Puritan movement*, pp. 370–1; P. Seaver, *The Puritan lectureships. The politics of religious dissent, 1560–1662* (Stanford, 1970), passim.

[68] GL, MS 9051/6, f. 13v; *Registers of St Vedast Foster Lane*, pp. 141–2; *Registers of St Peter Paul's Wharf*, p. 212; *Registers of St Margaret Moses*, p. 85.

[69] I. Gentles, 'Political funerals during the English Revolution', in S. Porter (ed.), *London and the Civil War* (London, 1996), pp. 219–20. See also below, chapter 9.

burial total mounted year by year, and the recurrence of plague epidemics in the late sixteenth and early seventeenth centuries seems to have stimulated a fresh attempt, in 1604, to find more space. The Court of Aldermen appointed a committee to 'find out some fit and convenient place in or near this city to be a burial place for the dead', and to report back.[70] Nothing more is heard of this, however, and in the 1610s and 1620s several of the larger suburban parishes turned their attention to finding new parochial grounds. The increasing suburbanisation of plague in the seventeenth century, and the long respite from serious epidemics between 1636 and 1665, may have allowed the city's governors to close their eyes to the problem, but in 1665 they were again confronted by it. Over-use of the New Churchyard in that epidemic produced a new crisis of accommodation. The 'noisome stenches arising from the great number of dead' buried there, together with the plea from many parishes that their own churchyards were now full, forced the mayor and aldermen to look for new accommodation. On 6 September 1665 they deputed one of their number to treat with the city's tenant of Finsbury Fields, to the north of the city, to obtain a piece of ground there for burial 'during this present visitation'. Their intention was that it be 'speedily set out and prepared for a burial place', and 'the new burial place in Bunhill Fields' had been walled by 19 October, though the gates were not finished until 1666. It seems probable that it was in use almost immediately; at any rate, the keeper of the New Churchyard, formerly so hard-pressed, was able to stop digging pits and return to burying in single graves before the end of the epidemic.[71] References in some parish registers to burials in 'the new ground' from September 1665 could be either to this ground or to new parochial grounds.[72]

This burial ground subsequently became the famous dissenters' ground, Bunhill Fields. It is clear that the nonconformist congregations of the Civil War and Commonwealth period were submerged, but not suppressed, by the Restoration, and that they resisted reincorporation into the Anglican communion. Strype noted in 1720 that, since the plague of 1665, Bunhill Fields 'hath been chosen by the dissenters from the Church of England for interring their friends and relations, without having the office of burial appointed by the Book of Common Prayer said at their graves'. Early inscriptions give some account of those buried

[70] CLRO, Repertory 26 pt. 2, f. 388v.

[71] Defoe, *Plague Year*, p. 240; CLRO, Repertory 70, ff. 153v, 155v–6; Strype, *Survey*, vol. II, bk. 4, p. 54; Maitland, *The history and survey of London*, vol. II, p. 1370. The tradition that it was not used in the 1665 plague appears to derive from Maitland, but Strype does not say this. The site is shown as 'Church Yard' in 1676: Hyde, Fisher, and Cline, *A to Z of Restoration London*, spread 6.

[72] E.g. *Registers of St Martin Orgar* (Harl. Soc. 68), pp. 123–4.

there: one of the earliest records the burial of the son of an Anabaptist minister in 1669, another (1672) makes reference to 'prisoners and oppressors'. Several nonconformist ministers were buried there in the late seventeenth century.[73] George Fox had encouraged Quakers to 'stand against the Superstisious Idolizing of those places Caled holy grownd', and the Quakers had difficulty in burying as they wished; the parish of St Anne Aldersgate intervened, on warrant from the Lord Mayor, to preempt a Quaker burial from being accompanied 'in way of Triumph' in 1664.[74] The Quakers acquired a burial ground for themselves in 1661 close to the subsequent site of Bunhill Fields; in the late seventeenth or early eighteenth century they used another near St Bartholomew the Great.[75]

It is estimated that 40–50,000 French Huguenots came to Britain in the later seventeenth century, before and especially after the revocation of the Edict of Nantes in 1685. The majority of them settled in London, establishing churches and congregations in the northern and western suburbs, though some assimilated with the Anglican community, as in eighteenth-century Spitalfields.[76] Another distinctive group were the Jews, who returned to England from the later 1650s, and who had established a sizeable community in the north-west of the city by 1695.[77] These developments, together with the toleration of English Protestant dissent, multiplied the number of burial sites in London. By the 1680s and 1690s the city parish of St Dionis Backchurch was recording burials in its own church and yard and also at 'Bethlem' (the New Churchyard), 'the Quakers' ground', 'the Swedes church', 'the Jewes burial place', and 'Tindells ground by Bunhill fields'.[78] By the mid-eighteenth century, Maitland acknowledged that the Bills of Mortality, based on returns from

[73] Strype, *Survey*, vol. II, bk. 4, pp. 54–9. Cf. [Corporation of London] *Bunhill Fields Burial Ground: proceedings in reference to its preservation, with the inscriptions on the tombs* (London, 1867).

[74] Quoted in G. Stock, 'Quaker burial: doctrine and practice', in Cox (ed.), *Grave concerns*, pp. 129–43; W. McMurray, *The records of two city parishes: a collection of documents illustrative of the history of SS Anne and Agnes, Aldersgate, and St John Zachary, London* (London, 1925), p. 101. At least one Quaker was buried in the New Churchyard, in early 1660: ibid., p. 326.

[75] Holmes, *The London burial grounds*, pp. 141–2; Webb, *Records of St Bartholomew's Priory*, vol. I, p. 191.

[76] R. D. Gwynn, *Huguenot heritage. the history and contribution of the Huguenots in Britain* (London, 1985), pp. 35–8, 91–109; T. Molleson and M. Cox, with A. H. Waldron and D. Whitaker, *The Spitalfields project*, vol. II: *The anthropology. The middling sort* (York, 1993), pp. 3–7.

[77] A. S. Diamond, 'The community of the resettlement, 1656–84', *Jewish Historical Society of England, Miscellany* pt. 6 (1962), 73–141; A. P. Arnold, 'A list of Jews and their households in London, extracted from the census lists of 1695', *Jewish Historical Society of England, Transactions* 24 (1970–3), 134–50.

[78] *Registers of St Dionis Backchurch* (Harl. Soc. 3), pp. 252–60.

the Anglican parishes, were quite inadequate to capture the full annual total of burials in London.[79]

Paris: the cemetery of the Innocents

The greatest difference between London and Paris, in terms of burial accommodation, was the existence of a popular central burial place, the cimetière des Innocents, associated with the city rather than the cathedral, though controlled by a religious foundation. The churchyard of the Innocents played a prominent part in the mythology of Parisian identity. Death and the macabre were an essential part of its image, graphically expressed in the fifteenth-century Danse Macabre that decorated the arcade or cloister around the cemetery. Stories and images abounded: the soil was said to have come from the Holy Land; it was said to have the property of consuming bodies buried there within in nine days, or even within twenty-four hours.[80] Even if this was a myth, the Innocents received a huge number of burials and in the fullness of time did transform them into its other major feature, the bones that filled the attic charnel over the arcade that surrounded the space. Although it was in a literal sense a piece of private or institutional property (it belonged to the dean and chapter of Saint-Germain-l'Auxerrois, the hospital of Sainte-Catherine, and the Hôtel-Dieu, who controlled and took the profits from all burials there according to a complex allocation), and although a significant part of it was given over to private burials, it was still viewed as a public or common resource, 'le cimetière de toutes les paroisses de la cité'.[81] It was a major public open space in the early modern city and had an important role in the conflicts of the later sixteenth century.

Originally peripheral to the post-Roman city, the cemetery of the Innocents had by the late middle ages long been included within the enceinte. It lay on the right bank, next to the marketplace of les Halles, from which it was separated by an enclosure in 1186.[82] The cemetery occupied a rectangle stretching from the rue Saint-Denis in the east to les Halles and the rue de la Lingerie in the west, with the rue aux Fers to the north and the rue de la Ferronerie to the south. Estimates of its size vary from 1,450 to 2,000 *toises* (fathoms) or some 5,500 to 7,500 m^2,

---

[79] Maitland, *The history and survey of London*, vol II, pp. 736–46; cf. D. M. George, *London life in the eighteenth century* (London, 1925; republished Harmondsworth, 1966), p. 35 and n. 1.

[80] Ariès, *Hour of our death*, p. 360.   [81] BN, MS Joly de Fleury 1207, f. 155.

[82] Except where otherwise stated, this description is based on T. J. H. Hoffbauer, *Paris à travers les ages*, 2 vols. (new edn, annotated by P. Payen Appenzeller; Paris, 1982), vol. I, pp. 354–83; Hillairet, *Les 200 cimetières*, pp. 23–38. Cf. also H. Couzy, 'L'église des Saints-Innocents à Paris', *Bulletin Monumental* 130 (1972), 279–303.

either before or after the loss of a large section, up to a quarter of the total acreage, for the widening of the rue de la Ferronerie in 1669–70.[83] There were two pedestrian gates and three for carts, all in theory closed at night. The parish church of les Saints-Innocents occupied most of the northeast corner of the rectangle, and adjacent to it was the Fontaine des Innocents, erected in 1549, at the angle of the rue aux Fers and the rue Saint-Denis.[84] Early modern representations of the cemetery highlight the contrast between the open space of the centre, dotted with a few tombs and monuments, and the arcades round the periphery. A strip at the west end of the open churchyard, known as the *parterre*, was marked off by a ditch: this was where the Hôtel-Dieu buried their dead. The open ground contained a pulpit, a medieval tower or turret known as la tour Notre-Dame des Bois, and several crosses; there were also evidently several table-topped tombs. The surrounding walls were lined with arcades known as the *charniers*, the bays of which were mostly given over to family shrines, with a more substantial structure housing chapels of the Orgemont and Villeroy families built out from the western arcade.[85] These arcades were probably built individually, for reasons of private devotion and public benefit, but within a short enough period to form an architecturally homogeneous sequence. The east and west arcades were open to form cloisters or promenades; those on the north seem to have been made up of single bays giving only onto the churchyard. All round they were roofed with an attic storey, in which exhumed bones were stored. This storey was open under the eaves, and had open skylights or dormers, to allow air to circulate, and the piled-up skulls and bones were clearly visible. Bones had been stored in this way since at least the late fourteenth century, and it remained one of the most remarked features of the Innocents: 'Que d'os l'un sur autre entassez!'; 'tant d'ossemens de trépassés que c'est chose incréable'.[86] The other major feature was the Danse Macabre, painted in 1424–5 along ten arcades of the south wall, known as the Charnier des Lingères. The Parisian Danse, a series of tableaux and verses, seems to have been remarkable and influential in the fifteenth century. It was recorded in a woodcut representation printed in

---

[83] 1,450 *toises*: BN, MS Joly de Fleury 1207, f. 164; 1,775 *toises*: plan of 1756, cited in Hoffbauer, *Paris à travers les ages*, vol. I, p. 358; 1,800 *toises*: Hillairet, *Les 200 cimetières*, pp. 25–8; 2,000 *toises*: AN, L 571/3, mid-18th century *mémoire* concerning the cemetery and its use. Pillorget, *Paris sous les premiers Bourbons*, p. 196, gives 7,200 m².

[84] For the Fontaine des Innocents see D. Thomson, *Renaissance Paris* (Berkeley, 1972), pp. 77–9.

[85] Cf. the sixteenth-century painting of the Innocents in plate 6, and the careful reconstructions in Hoffbauer, *Paris à travers les ages*, vol. I, plates I, II, V.

[86] Claude le Petit and Gilles Corrozet, cited by Hoffbauer, *Paris à travers les ages*, vol. I, pp. 355, 357.

6   The cemetery of the Innocents in the later sixteenth century, looking east toward the parish church. The *charniers* or arcades around the
sides are topped by an open storey in which skulls and bones were
stored. Painting, attributed to Jacob Grimer (1526–89) (Paris, Musée
Carnavalet. Photothèque des Musées de la ville de Paris).

1484[87] and apparently inspired a number of others, including the Dance
of Death at St Paul's in London (though their degree of similarity is not
known). It is not clear how easily visible it was by the seventeenth century,

[87] Reproduced in Abbé V. Dufour, *La danse macabre des Saints-Innocents à Paris* (Paris,
1874).

when the number of monuments and epitaphs in the *charniers* must have accumulated,[88] but it does not seem by then to have been held in high account. The historian Sauval referred to its 'vers ridicules' under the heading 'Peintures et tapisseries inutiles'.[89] No antiquary seems to have taken special note of it in anticipation of its destruction in 1669, when the south wall and *charnier* were pulled down to widen the rue de la Ferronerie, site of Henri IV's assassination in 1610.

The Innocents, like St Paul's churchyard, was invaded by many other users, which may have compromised its air of sanctity but reinforced its place in the city's social life and culture. It was a large open space in a densely crowded city, and located next to the city's main market complex, so such invasion was almost inevitable. Police orders of the seventeenth century deplored the passage of watercarriers and basketmen through the cemetery 'comme ci c'estoit une rue ou halle publique', and also noted the activities of traders such as mercers, linendrapers, fruitsellers, and sellers of biscuits and spice bread. Others were condemned for using the space to practise their trade of stretching and shearing cloths.[90] The *charnier* of the Innocents was a well-known location for the unlettered to find a scribe or letter-writer.[91] The chapter of Saint-Germain-l'Auxerrois licensed the sale of images and devotional works, but obtained orders against other traders, in particular the so-called *secrétaires de Saint-Innocent* who hired out their scrivening services there, apparently using the table-topped tombs as desks.[92] Legitimate and illegitimate trading merged with other kinds of commerce and disorderly behaviour; idlers and suspicious characters lingered in the churchyard. In the fourteenth century, 'the cemetery itself was a meeting place for prostitutes, profiteers, vagabonds, and idlers of every description. It was also a place where all sorts of con-men lay in wait for gullible victims', and thieves disposed of stolen goods.[93] In the sixteenth century, the presence of unlicensed scriveners, with all the possibilities of forged and fraudulent documentation, may have been a particular anxiety, as were the opportunities for illicit rendezvous and unsanctioned contracts. People urinated and deposited ordure in the Innocents; children and servants played games there, breaking glass and damaging monuments.[94] The *fossoyeur* of Saint-Germain-l'Auxerrois was ordered in 1605 to control the activities of the living, if he could not find a sergeant to arrest ill-doers; he was also

[88] AN, MS L 571/1, 'Estat des charniers du cimetiere des Saints Innocens', *c.* 1599.
[89] Cited by Hoffbauer, *Paris à travers les ages*, vol. I, p. 383.
[90] AN, L 570/15, 18, 22.   [91] Hoffbauer, *Paris à travers les ages*, vol. I, p. 372.
[92] AN, L 570/15, 18, 22, 44; AN, L 571/15.
[93] B. Geremek, *The margins of society in late medieval Paris* (Cambridge, 1987), p. 86.
[94] AN, LL 798, f. 29r–v; AN, L 570, no. 15. Cf. Brièle, *Collection de documents*, vol. I, p. 166.

responsible for closing the gates of the cemetery, at 9 or 10 at night in the summer, after calling out a suitable warning.[95] Although the irreligious nature of these activities in a consecrated place of sepulture was disturbing enough, uncontrolled public access also exposed monuments and graves to deliberate desecration and plunder. Despite the curfew order of 1605 just cited, in 1620 the *fossoyeur* reported a number of thefts of brass plates and destruction of marble tablets, which he blamed in part on the negligence of those supposed to lock up the gates.[96] Disorders continued, however, both commercial and criminal. The perception that the Innocents gave space to or encouraged scandalous and unsuitable activities may well have contributed to the other pressures for its closure in the eighteenth century.[97] Cemeteries often function as centres of market transaction, and sometimes become marketplaces in actuality. The creation of a market on the old cemetery of Saint-Jean-en-Grève was cited, in a *mémoire* of the mid-eighteenth century, as a precedent for closing the Innocents and replacing it with a market, and in fact the herb market of the rue de la Ferronerie was transferred there after the cemetery's closure in 1786.[98]

The Innocents had always been a centre for public gathering and collective witness, as for example the mass attendance, said to be five or six thousand daily, at the preaching of the Franciscan Friar Richard in 1429, against the English occupation, or the 12,500 children who formed a procession there in 1449.[99] It is striking how significant a part the cemetery played in the Parisian drama of Reformation and Counter-Reform. As a central public space in the city it was important, of course, but it was highly charged with symbolic meaning. It was seen by Parisians, whose numberless ancestors had been buried or charnelled there, as embodying their identity and history – most specifically, after the beginning of religious conflict, their Catholic history. The cemetery was on several occasions the scene of the expression of Catholic fervour in the later sixteenth century. In 1559, churchgoers rioted against a supposed Lutheran; in 1562 and 1564, attempts were made to exhume and despoil Protestant corpses buried there. The churchyard was overlooked by the Croix de Gastine, a monument erected on the site of the demolished house of a Protestant family, and 'an important symbol of the religious hatreds of

---

[95] AN, L 570/15; AN, LL 758, ff. 109r–v.   [96] AN, L 570, no. 16.

[97] Hoffbauer, *Paris à travers les ages*, vol. I, p. 357; Foisil, 'Les attitudes devant la mort au XVIIIe siècle'. Cf. C. Métayer, *Au tombeau des secrets. Les écrivains publics du Paris populaire. Cimetière des Saints-Innocents, XVIe–XVIIIe siècles* (Paris, 2001).

[98] AN, L 571/3; Hoffbauer, *Paris à travers les ages*, vol. I, p. 363.

[99] C. Beaune (ed.), *Journal d'un bourgeois de Paris* (Paris, 1990), pp. 253, 412, 441, 444; G. L. Thompson, *Paris and its people under English rule: the Anglo-Burgundian regime, 1420–36* (Oxford, 1991), pp. 109, 181.

the Parisian populace'. The cross became the centre of controversy and violent resistance when the authorities attempted to remove it to the Innocents in 1571, as part of the peace process.[100] The legend of the hawthorn that bloomed there on St Bartholomew's day in 1572 enhanced the cemetery's reputation with an apparently miraculous witness, a sign, it was said, of divine approval of the massacre.[101] The processions of children that followed soon after the assassination of the duke and cardinal of Guise in 1588 included the cemetery of the Innocents in one of their circuits, and there may have been an intentional allusion to the biblical Massacre of the Innocents and messages of martyrdom.[102] Less exceptionally, the Innocents, like some other churchyards, was also the place where the militia of the *quartier*, and sometimes other troops, could muster.[103] However, since one of the features of the disturbances of the Wars of Religion was the assumption of police powers by vigilante groups and voluntary militias, this also reinforced its identity as a centre of Catholic activism.

Alongside these other activities, the cemetery accommodated an enormous number of burials. Control of burial was at times contested between the three proprietors of the churchyard, each of whom had a different interest. According to a judgment of 1371/2, the rights of *fossoyage* (the right to employ a gravedigger, make graves, license the erection of epitaphs, and take the fees for this) belonged to the collegiate church of Saint-Germain-l'Auxerrois for dead from the parishes of Saint-Germain, Saint-Eustache, and Saint-Sauveur; to the hospital of Sainte-Catherine for the dead for whom it was responsible (from the street, the river, and the prisons) and those of the parish of Saint-Jacques-de-la-Boucherie; to the Hôtel-Dieu for its own dead and those of the parishes of Saint-Christophe and Sainte-Marine on the Ile de la Cité, whom it buried in its own section of the churchyard. The parish of les Saints-Innocents could employ a gravedigger and bury its own dead, but had no other claim over the ground. Fees for burials of individuals from other parishes in Paris were divided between the dean and chapter of Saint-Germain-l'Auxerrois and the religious of Sainte-Catherine.[104] Not surprisingly, the questions of propriety, possession, rights, and licence to use were often in dispute.

---

[100] Babelon, *Paris au XVIe siècle*, pp. 229, 433, 442, 445, 451, 478; Diefendorf, *Beneath the cross*, pp. 53, 62, 73, 84; L. Mouton, 'L'affaire de la Croix de Gastine', *Bulletin de la Société de l'Histoire de Paris et Ile de France* 56 (1929), 102–13.

[101] Hoffbauer, *Paris à travers les ages*, vol. I, p. 356.

[102] Pierre de l'Estoile, *Journal de l'Estoile pour le regne de Henri III*, ed. L. R. Lefèvre (Paris, 1943), pp. 612, 614.

[103] Pillorget and Viguerie, 'Les quartiers de Paris au XVIIe et XVIIIe siècles', p. 255; Hoffbauer, *Paris à travers les ages*, vol. I, p. 356.

[104] BN, MS Joly de Fleury 1317, ff. 8–10. An explicit account of rights and fees is given in AN, L 571/2, dating from the sixteenth or seventeenth century.

The principal was that of ultimate control: whether Sainte-Catherine had any rights, for example to permit or deny the erection of epitaphs, apart from its share of the fees, and whether the Hôtel-Dieu owned absolutely that part of the churchyard, the *parterre*, in which it buried its dead, or only occupied it. Most of these were resolved in Saint-Germain's favour.[105] By the eighteenth century the chapter of Notre-Dame, which had succeeded to the rights of the chapter of Saint-Germain-l'Auxerrois, was said to draw '[un] profit immense' from the burial fees at the Innocents.[106]

The varied origins of the dead buried at the Innocents, and the division of control of burial between several parties, mean that it is impossible to calculate the actual number buried there in any year within the period covered by this study. Madeleine Foisil has estimated that some 1,800 bodies were buried there every year in the second decade of the eighteenth century.[107] Since the population of Paris was probably not significantly greater in the early eighteenth century than in the 1670s, this figure could plausibly apply to the earlier period.[108] A mid-eighteenth century *mémoire* estimated annual burials at 2,000, and also implied that a similar number had been buried there before the reduction in size of the cemetery in 1669–70.[109] If true, this would suggest that some 10 per cent of the population of Paris was normally buried there, even after the opening of new burial grounds outside the city such as Clamart.

Although those buried at the Innocents in the eighteenth century came from many parishes in Paris, there was a strong bias for historic and geographical reasons. The largest numbers of fee-paying burials in 1715 (the basis for Foisil's calculations) came from the parishes of Saint-Eustache and Saint-Germain-l'Auxerrois (*c*. 380 and 300 respectively).[110] Some 710 adults and 223 children from Saint-Eustache, Saint-Germain, and Sainte-Opportune together were buried there in 1730.[111] The other parishes which made use of it from time to time included Saint-Jacques-de-la-Boucherie, Saint-Merry, Saint-Josse, Saint-Leu–Saint-Gilles, Saint-Pierre-des-Arcis, Saint-Germain-le-Vieux, Saint-Louis-du-Louvre, Saint-Pierre-aux-Boeufs, Sainte-Madeleine (en la Cité), Saint-Christophe, Sainte-Marine, and Sainte-Croix.[112] For several of

---

[105] Cf. AN, L 570/28, 29, 30, 30 bis, 31, 32 (early eighteenth-century depositions and counter-claims).

[106] AN, L 570/32, p. 7.   [107] Foisil, 'Les attitudes devant la mort', p. 307.

[108] D. Roche, *The people of Paris, an essay in popular culture in the 18th century* (Berkeley, 1987), p. 20, accepts an approximate population total for Paris for the whole period 1680–1715 of 500,000. Cf. Bertillon, *Des recensements de la population*, pp. 11–15 (tables based on Etat des Baptêmes from 1670).

[109] AN, L 571/3.   [110] Foisil, 'Les attitudes devant la mort', p. 307.

[111] AN, L 571/4.

[112] Foisil, 'Les attitudes devant la mort', p. 307.

these parishes, the Innocents was the only churchyard available to them, though probably all had some vault or space for burial in their church.[113] All of these were right-bank or Cité parishes, and a similar bias is seen in the choice of burial by testament in the sixteenth and seventeenth centuries; burial at the Innocents was much less popular with inhabitants of the left bank.[114] Only twenty-seven people out of the 1,636 noted in the antiquaries' extracts from the burial registers of Saint-André-des-Arts were buried at the Innocents between 1550 and 1670. One of these was buried in the church, at least one in the *charniers*, others in the cemetery. Four members of the Mandat family were buried there, two others were said to be buried with their ancestors, and one with his father.[115] Burial at the Innocents was clearly a positive choice for a few, often perhaps because of family associations, and private grave sites suitable for persons of standing were available. Most surviving records of individual burials and monuments focus on the upper end of the social spectrum, but in addition to identifying some noble individuals they also suggest a good proportion of merchants and *bourgeois*. A register for 1668 of the *fossoyeur* of Saint-Germain (who collected fees from some burials, but not from charity burials or from the Hôtel-Dieu) gives the occupations of 256 people buried there. These appear to be much more representative of society as a whole. There was a preponderance of *gens de métiers* and artisans (60 per cent), merchants and *bourgeois* (22 per cent), and servants (10 per cent).[116] Chaunu detected 'une désaffection…à l'égard des Saints-Innocents' developing in the eighteenth century, and references from that period appear to stress its low status. It was said to serve for the burial of the poor and other persons of a mediocre fortune from the parishes of Saint-Germain-l'Auxerrois, Saint-Eustache, the Innocents itself, and the parishes of the Cité.[117] Sainte-Madeleine en la Cité associated choice of the Innocents with a particular attitude to death and burial: those who 'par esprit d'humilité' did not wish to be buried in the church's vault would be buried at the Innocents.[118]

Notwithstanding its long-established rights of burial at the Innocents, the Hôtel-Dieu buried only a small proportion of its dead there in the early eighteenth century (some 230 out of *c.* 3,500 per annum). The majority of the hospital's dead had been buried at Clamart since 1673, and

---

[113] See BN, MS Joly de Fleury 1207, 1208 (*mémoires* and depositions concerning burial in Paris, *c.* 1765).

[114] AN, *mémoires de maîtrise*: Martin and de Rot (left-bank parishes); Blanc, Delaporte, Rossignol (right-bank parishes). Cf. also Cessole and Landier, who do not give precise figures.

[115] BN, MS Fr. 32589.

[116] AN, H^5 3816 (2), analysed by Foisil, 'Les attitudes devant la mort', pp. 313–14.

[117] Chaunu, *La mort à Paris*, p. 322; AN, L 571/3.

[118] See BN, MS Joly de Fleury 1207, 1208.

at la Trinité before then.[119] The hospital bought two coffins or biers to carry the dead to the Innocents in 1517,[120] but other references suggest that those who were buried from the hospital at the Innocents were probably among the better-off, individuals who had made an actual choice, by will or otherwise, and were prepared to pay for it. Laurent le Maire, native of Arras, dying at the Hôtel-Dieu in 1647, left the hospital 50 *livres* in recognition of their services and assistance, and asked for burial at the Innocents with a *service entier* at the Hôtel-Dieu, the costs of his burial to be paid before other legacies were distributed. Other testators from the Hôtel-Dieu similarly requested burial at the Innocents and left the hospital money for masses, services, and burial costs.[121] They may have chosen the Innocents because they were strangers to Paris, because of the Hôtel-Dieu's long identification with the Innocents, or perhaps on account of 'la dépense modique de ce transport'.[122] In addition to those who made some kind of choice, however, the Innocents received a significant number of bodies for charitable burial. There were an estimated 400 *convois de charité* a year to the Innocents in the early eighteenth century, probably sent only by the parishes with formal burial rights there. The dead buried by Sainte-Catherine, estimated at 150–200 per annum at this time, could have come from all over Paris, since they comprised the bodies found in the streets, retrieved from the river, or dying in the prisons.[123]

Burial at the Innocents was therefore a matter of choice for some individuals as well as one of convenience for some institutions and parishes needing inexpensive space to bury their poor. Many of those choosing burial there from the right bank and city parishes must have had a family grave or site in mind. Although such monuments could only be set up with permission of the proprietor (Saint-Germain-l'Auxerrois for the greater part of the cemetery, the Hôtel-Dieu for its section),[124] they effectively privatised part of the burial space. A report on the *charniers* in c. 1599 refers to several vacant bays of the *charniers* as available to be let ('propres a bailler') and lists prominent graves and inscriptions in the other *charniers* and the persons now responsible for them. For 'la tumbe des Crocquantz', for example, in the fourteenth *charnier* along the rue de la Ferronerie, 'Ce fait addresser a Monsieur Gobelin, rue neufve Saint Mederic'.[125] Monuments in the centre of the churchyard

[119] Foisil, 'Les attitudes', pp. 309, 312; see below.
[120] Brièle and Husson, *Inventaire-sommaire*, vol. II, p. 184.
[121] Archives de l'Assistance Publique, cat. 6358 (layette 330, liasse 1413(1)), register of testaments at the Hôtel-Dieu, ff. 6, 12v–13, 39v, 46v.
[122] AN, L 571/3.   [124] Foisil, 'Les attitudes', p. 310.
[124] Cf. AN, L 571/5, 7 (bundles of such permissions granted by Saint-Germain-l'Auxerrois, 1411–1651).
[125] AN, L 571/1.

also appear to have focused family burials.[126] Epitaphs and tablets were added and amended to record later burials, and some families seem to have buried members over several generations. Twelve of the Lhuillier family, dying between 1468 and 1668, were so commemorated;[127] the heirs and executors of Jehan Luillier, *conseiller du roi*, paid 45 *livres tournois* in 1537 for permission to put a tomb over his grave.[128] The chapels of the Orgemont and Villeroy families presumably represent a more advanced privatisation. When the south *charnier* was demolished in 1669, the bones, tombs, monuments, epitaphs, and inscriptions from there were transferred to the other *charniers*, as far as possible with the assent of those whose families were buried there.[129]

As in parish churchyards, burial in tombs and *charniers* was more highly prized than burial in the open churchyard. In 1546 coffined burial in the part of the churchyard belonging to Saint-Germain-l'Auxerrois cost 17 *sous* 6 *deniers*, with a surcharge of 35 *sous* for burial in the *charniers*; later in the sixteenth or seventeenth century churchyard burial was 35 *sous* and burial 'soubz tumbe ou charnier' 52 *sous* 6 *deniers tournois*.[130] Burial in the Hôtel-Dieu's section of the churchyard in 1587 cost 52 *sous* 6 *deniers tournois* for a *fosse à coffre* and 5 *sous* for a burial *sans bière*.[131] By the early eighteenth century the prices for opening the ground had been raised to 18 *livres* in the main *charniers* and 25 *livres* in the *petit charnier de la Vierge* (with a reduction if there were no tomb-slab to be lifted); 'les sepultures de familles', perhaps because of some earlier payment or concession, paid 12 *livres*. Although these burials were the best recorded, both as interments and memorials, they represented only a very small proportion of burials at the Innocents. An early eighteenth-century *mémoire*, opposing the new list of charges for private burials, noted that burials in the churchyard were far more common, and that of 200 burials barely six would be in the chapels or *charniers*. Burial in the open churchyard cost 3 *livres* 10 *sous* for those who had ordained it by will, and 2 *livres* 10 *sous* for 'les enterremens ordinaires'. One part of the churchyard, before the chapel of the Virgin, was made more expensive, at 6 *livres*, 'vue les frequents sepultures dont les corps pourroient causer infection'.[132] The contrast between the private family grave or tomb and ordinary burial was as marked as the price. In the later sixteenth or seventeenth century, burials of 'corps nudz et sans coffre ou biere' would cost 5 *sous tournois* (of

[126] AN, L 570/16.   [127] AN, LL 434/B (Epitaphier), pp. 2–4; cf. AN, L 571/5.
[128] Brièle, *Collection de documents*, vol. II, p. 262.
[129] AN, L 570/26.   [130] AN, L 570/11; AN, L 571/2.
[131] Brièle, *Collection de documents*, vol. IV, pp. 30–1; Brièle and Husson, *Inventaire-sommaire*, vol. II, pp. 192, 201, 206–7, 220.
[132] AN, L 570/31, 33.

which 2 *sous* went to the gravedigger), compared with 35 *sous* for a 'fosse à coffre'.[133]

By the early eighteenth century, burials at 3 *livres* 10 *sous* and less were all in one mass grave, the *fosse commune*, whether ordained by will, coffined, or not.[134] This practice was still somewhat disorganised at that time, 'sans aucun ordre dans la distribution des fosses'. In 1738 it was recommended that a plan be made of the churchyard, so that mass graves could be dug in succession according to a pattern. It was also recommended that only one *fosse commune* be kept open at a time, instead of the three currently used (one for the dead from the Hôtel-Dieu, one for adults of the parishes, and one for children).[135] There may also have been small or large graves opened by the gravedigger of the parish of les Saints-Innocents, and it is not clear if the dead buried by Sainte-Catherine had a separate pit. If the system of mass graves was not well organised in the early eighteenth century, it is likely that it was even less so in earlier periods. Five large pits were opened at the Innocents in the epidemic of 1418, each for some 600 corpses, apparently laid in layers of thirty to forty bodies like sides of bacon ('arrangés comme lards').[136] How soon it became the norm is not known; Ariès suggests by the end of the fifteenth century.[137] However, most of the descriptions of the *fosses communes* at the Innocents date from the eighteenth century, and explicit references in the sixteenth and seventeenth centuries are hard to find. The sixteenth-century Flemish painting of the cemetery shows one interment underway in a single grave, and a second such being dug or cleared, but nothing that can be interpreted as a mass burial pit. Although this is not necessarily a faithful representation of the Innocents, it seems unlikely that such a striking feature would have been omitted if it had been visible.[138] However, the storage of bones, noted from the end of the fourteenth century, suggests that charnelling practices associated with re-use of the ground were already accepted. There were bequests in aid of specific *charniers* 'pour y mettre les ossemens des loyaux trepassez', or for 'les ossemens de tous les trepassez qui ont eté ou seront enterrés au cimetiere'.[139] The *fossoyeurs* of Saint-Germain and the Hôtel-Dieu were charged with collecting and storing the bones in the *charniers*.[140] At a later date it appears both that small bones were left in the soil (it was suggested that sieving it would be advantageous), and that large amounts of bones were reburied

[133] AN, L 571/2.   [134] AN, L 570/31, 33.

[135] BN, MS Joly de Fleury 1317, ff. 50–9.   [136] *Journal d'un bourgeois de Paris*, pp. 133–4.

[137] Ariès, *The hour of our death*, p. 57.

[138] See plate 6.   [139] Hoffbauer, *Paris à travers les ages*, vol. I, p. 367.

[140] AN, L 570/11; Brièle, *Collection de documents*, vol. IV, pp. 30–1.

at either end of the large gutter or *rigole*.[141] At the cemetery's clearance
in 1785–7, the ground was excavated to a depth of 6 ft in some places,
and 197 *toises* (*c.* 1,460 m^3) of bones and earth removed, though much
still remained.[142] However, though it may appear brutal, exhumation and
charnelling of remains was a practice sanctified by time, and very impor-
tantly it allowed for a reinterpretation of the meaning of the remains of
the dead. Bones became safe and even sacred relics. Stored in the charnels, they satisfied the need to value and respect the dead, and to feel
their continuing presence in the community.

Probably at least four *fossoyeurs* operated in the churchyard at one
time, one each for the burials under the jurisdictions of Saint-Germain-
l'Auxerrois, the hospital of Sainte-Catherine, the Hôtel-Dieu, and the
parish of les Saints-Innocents. The frequent recapitulation of the different areas and rights in the churchyard suggests that confrontations on
the ground, as well as litigation, may have been common.[143] Nor was
burial there wholly secure. In 1509 the *fossoyeur* of the Innocents was
condemned for having exhumed and sold the lead coffin of a burial that
had taken place some two years previously, and in 1620 the *fossoyeur*
of Saint-Germain deposed that persons unknown had broken or stolen
numerous epitaphs of marble or bronze.[144] Multiple burials and exhuma-
tions brought up quantities of bones, not all of which were safely stored in
the charnels. Scattered bones are shown in contemporary representations
of the churchyard; Rabelais averred that the beggars used the bones as
fuel for fires 'to warm their bottoms'.[145] One of the most macabre stories about the Innocents dates from June 1590, when the siege of Paris
had been under way for some months and the citizens were starving. An
emergency committee is reported to have endorsed a suggestion that the
charnelled bones from the Innocents could be ground up to make a kind
of flour for those who had no grain. Bread made from 'the bones of our
fathers' was apparently available in mid-August, but the experiment was
hardly a success: those who ate it soon died.[146]

The smells and the fear of infection from the high level of burials at
the Innocents certainly caused concern in the sixteenth and seventeenth
centuries, and in the eighteenth there were prolonged and eventually

[141] BN, MS Joly de Fleury 1317, ff. 50–9.

[142] Hoffbauer, *Paris à travers les ages*, vol. I, p. 363; Hillairet, *Les 200 cimetières*, pp. 35–8, 303.

[143] AN, L 570/4, 11; Brièle, *Collection de documents*, vol. IV, pp. 30–1; AN, LL 758.

[144] AN, L 570/16, 41.

[145] See Plate 6, p. 103, above; Hoffbauer, *Paris à travers les ages*, vol. I, p. 355; Ariès, *The hour of our death*, pp. 59–60.

[146] N. L. Roelker (ed.), *The Paris of Henry of Navarre, as seen by Pierre de l'Estoile. Selections from his mémoires-journaux* (Cambridge, Mass., 1958), pp. 188, 192.

successful efforts to close it down. In 1738, when there was as yet no clamour for closure, numerous possible remedies and reorganisations were suggested, including renewing the soil by exchange with the suburban cemetery at Porcherons.[147] The 1763 inquiry into the churchyards of Paris and the attempt to ban burial in the city centre were in part spurred by anxieties over the Innocents. 'On ne peut pas penser sans frémir qu'il existe dans le sein meme de cette capitale . . . un espace rétréci et entouré de maisons dans lequel il n'est ouvert par année qu'une fosse commune'. 'Ce gouffre de corruption . . . se nomme Le cimetiere des Innocens'. The open pits were said to exhale 'l'odeur la plus infectée et la plus propre a ruine aux habitans des maisons voisines'. However, there was strong opposition from interested parties, especially the *curés* of Paris, who raised both practical and moral objections, and in practice only the Innocents was closed before the Revolution.[148] Burial there was banned by *arrêt* of Parlement in 1780, and the cemetery and *charniers* cleared – a massive and gruesome task – in 1785–7.[149]

The Hôtel-Dieu and its cemeteries at la Trinité and Clamart

While the Innocents was the principal common cemetery in medieval Paris, it had been supplemented from an early date by one at la Trinité. The hospital of la Trinité, a hostel or overnight asylum in the rue Saint-Denis – perhaps to that extent similar to St Mary Spital in London – had its own adjoining cemetery, to which in 1350 was added one for the plague dead of the Hôtel-Dieu, which seems to have acted as the receiver of sick and dead from all over Paris in that crisis. At a later date the cemetery was said to measure 1,180 *toises* (*c.* 4,500 m^2), smaller than the Innocents and still, like the Innocents, inside the city walls.[150] The Hôtel-Dieu continued to use this burying ground, especially in times of crisis, and sent 9,224 bodies there in the years 1416–18, when plague and factional warfare racked the capital.[151] Four large pits were dug at la Trinité in 1418, each to take some 600 bodies.[152] Several hundred bodies a year were transported from the Hôtel-Dieu to la Trinité in the

[147] BN, MS Joly de Fleury 1317, ff. 50–9.
[148] BN, MS Joly de Fleury 1207, ff. 7–12, 164, 5–21.
[149] Foisil, 'Les attitudes', pp. 303–30; Hillairet, *Les 200 cimetières*, pp. 35–8.
[150] Hillairet, *Les 200 cimetières*, pp. 248–9.
[151] C. Jéhanno, 'Les comptes de l'Hôtel-Dieu de Paris au Moyen Age. Documents pour servir à l'histoire économique et sociale', *Etudes et documents (Comité pour l'histoire économique et financière)* 9 (1997), 512.
[152] *Journal d'un bourgeois de Paris*, p. 134.

mid-fifteenth century, including over 700 in the plague year of 1466.[153] Although figures do not appear to have survived for the later fifteenth and most of the sixteenth centuries, it is clear that the Hôtel-Dieu continued to make heavy use of the cemetery at la Trinité. *Charniers* and a chapel were made or repaired there in 1512, and in the same year a large pit of 137 *toises* (*c*. 1,010 m^3) was dug.[154] Plague increased the pressure on the cemetery, and in 1531, during the epidemic of 1529–33, arrangements were made by the Bureau de Ville to buy land at la Grenelle to bury the plague dead.[155] This may also have influenced the thinking of the Hôtel-Dieu, which in 1532 considered acquiring land from the abbey of Saint-Victor for a burial ground for its poor, since transporting bodies to la Trinité was 'fort long et pénible'.[156] Burial at la Trinité was banned in 1554–5, again during plague, and the Bureau de Ville and the Hôtel-Dieu were forced to consider other alternatives. In 1557 the Ile Maquerelle upstream of the Cité was proposed, but rejected because the site was liable to flooding in summer and to icing in winter, and would have necessitated opening the city's gates at night to allow access. The Bureau de Ville ruled that the burial ground should remain where it was, if possible enlarged by taking in the nearby Cour de Meaux.[157]

Burial at la Trinité continued, therefore. To a significant extent it appears to have been the pragmatic mass burial of those too poor to make their own arrangements, and who had indeed resigned control over their own bodies to the hospital before death. In 1587 the *fossoyeur* at la Trinité was paid 2 *écus sol* (= 4 *livres*) for digging several large pits, each for 700 to 800 corpses.[158] The Hôtel-Dieu was responsible for burying thousands of dead in the crisis years of the 1590s, presumably because large numbers of starving and sick Parisians came to the hospital to die. In 1593 and 1594 it paid for the transport of 357 and 247 bodies to la Trinité, but in 1595 this rose to 1,230, in 1596 to 7,100, and stayed at nearly 2,000 in 1597 and 1598. The figure of 1,051 in 1599 may reflect a return to a new normality.[159] Figures for the numbers of dead transported from the Hôtel-Dieu to la Trinité survive for most years between 1609 and 1628. Between 1609 and 1620 these ranged from 1,087 to 2,065, averaging 1,380 per annum. For most of the 1620s they were much higher,

[153] Jéhanno, 'Les comptes de l'Hôtel-Dieu', p. 512.

[154] Brièle and Husson, *Inventaire-sommaire*, vol. II, p. 182.

[155] *RDBVP*, vol. II, p. 135.

[156] Archives de l'Assistance Publique, no. 6382 (Registres de l'Hôtel-Dieu, 1531–45), f. 10v.

[157] Brièle and Husson, *Inventaire-sommaire*, vol. II, pp. 21, 101; *RDBVP*, vol. IV, pp. 382, 402, 457, 466, 475–6; cf. Hillairet, *Les 200 cimetières*, p. 248.

[158] Brièle, *Collection de documents*, vol. II, pp. 179, 259, 260; vol. IV, p. 32; Brièle and Husson, *Inventaire-sommaire*, vol. II, pp. 193, 200.

[159] Brièle, *Collection de documents*, vol. IV, pp. 48, 50, 53, 56, 59, 61.

owing to a long-running outbreak of plague from 1622 to 1632. Numbers climbed from 1,789 in 1622 to 5,665 in 1627 before falling back to 2,680 in 1628.[160] This year-to-year variation must reflect fluctuations in the health and welfare status of poorer Parisians, but the figures also probably indicate a growing trend for them to seek support, or at least a last shelter, from the Hôtel-Dieu. No figures survive for the middle third of the seventeenth century, but by the early 1670s between 3,000 and 4,000 people were dying in the Hôtel-Dieu each year (and up to twice this in bad years in the later 1670s).[161] It is likely therefore that numbers buried at la Trinité increased through the century, with very large numbers during plague epidemics. This increase no doubt contributed to the pressure to supplement or replace la Trinité with another burial ground. Nothing had come of the earlier attempts to move the burying ground elsewhere, but the urgency of finding a solution increased in the 1660s, with the approach of plague in 1668 and the proposed reduction in size of the Innocents. The Hôtel-Dieu began to enquire into ownership and burial rights in the cemetery, and accepted the need to move elsewhere in 1670; in 1672 it acquired land at Clamart in the southern faubourg Saint-Marcel and began burying there in 1673. The cemetery at la Trinité was discontinued, except for a small part, in 1678.[162]

Much less has been written about the appearance and use of la Trinité than the Innocents, though as is clear from the preceding it was very heavily used, and burial in *fosses communes* was common there from the sixteenth century at least. It was significantly smaller than the Innocents, so exhumation and some form of bone storage must have been practised.[163] While the cemetery was less in the public eye, and less likely to attract market and trading activities (and incur police censure) than the Innocents, it may also have been less well managed. There was anxiety over a long period about its ill effects on the children of the hospital of la Trinité, and complaints were made in 1660 that the gravedigger was failing to cover corpses adequately.[164] The distance from the hospital, the fact that transport took place at night, and perhaps the low status of the dead themselves, made the business of their transport and burial more liable to malpractice, cases of theft of as well as from bodies being noted. In 1626 certain *emballeurs* of the Hôtel-Dieu were sacked for selling a corpse to a surgeon. They had shrouded the corpse and put it in the

---

[160] Brièle and Husson, *Inventaire-sommaire*, vol. II, pp. 216–23.
[161] Etat des Baptêmes, BN (Réserve), LK[7] 6745.
[162] Brièle and Husson, *Inventaire-sommaire*, vol. II, pp. 22–3, 117–19, 122–3; Brièle, *Collection de documents*, vol. I, pp. 138, 178, 190; Hillairet, *Les 200 cimetières*, p. 249.
[163] Hillairet, *Les 200 cimetières*, pp. 248–9.
[164] Brièle, *Collection de documents*, vol. I, p. 190; Brièle and Husson, *Inventaire-sommaire*, vol. II, p. 117.

cart to be taken to la Trinité, but by arrangement they stopped just outside the hospital gate and handed over the body.[165] The dead from the
Hôtel-Dieu were taken to the burial ground fairly unceremoniously,
shrouded but not coffined, on a bier, cart, or *chariot*. By the early seventeenth century the carts must have been carrying six or more, but even
so, in 1656 and 1659, some *emballeurs* were reprimanded for failing to
take the corpses before they began to putrefy. Nor was the shrouding
adequate: Mlle de Montpensier's carriage was involved in a collision with
the dead cart in 1652, and she recorded a frisson of fear at the thought
of being touched by one of the hands or feet that stuck out from the cart.
However, the procedure was not quite without ceremony. The cart was
accompanied by an ecclesiastic carrying a cross, and by two lit torches
in summer, or two large lanterns (*fallotz*) in winter. The carts continued, with a rather longer journey, after Clamart replaced la Trinité as
the burial ground for the Hôtel-Dieu in 1673. The new cemetery does
not appear to have been any better managed than the old, though it was
much more spacious, and within a few years there were complaints of
grave-robbing, smells, and other disorders.[166]

Although la Trinité was taking a significant proportion of all Parisian
burials in the sixteenth and seventeenth centuries, especially in plague
years, it never appears to have rivalled the Innocents in popular perception as the poor cemetery of Paris. It caught the attention of some, such
as the M. Duval who requested burial there in 1550 'avec les pauvres de
l'Hôtel-Dieu où il espère finir ses jours',[167] but such choices were rare,
and it may well have been that la Trinité's association first with plague
burial, and then with Huguenot burial, made it less attractive even to
the ostentatiously humble. Huguenots were allowed burial there according to the Edict of Amboise (1563), in a designated space distant from
the hospital's chapel, but still under the special conditions applying to
Protestants.[168] As in London, the space allotted to religious separatists
was marginal and mingled them with the poor and diseased, and even
so was not secure. The gravedigger was accused in 1659 of despoiling
Huguenot corpses of their shrouds and even their shirts, and of selling
the bodies to the surgeons.[169] The increasing pressure on Protestants in

[165] Brièle and Husson, *Inventaire-sommaire*, vol. II, p. 107.
[166] Ibid., vol. II, pp. 23, 107, 110, 113, 115, 118; Brièle, *Collection de documents*, vol. I,
pp. 92, 119, 190, 220; vol. III, pp. 179, 259; vol. IV, pp. 44, 46, 48, 50; Hillairet,
Les 200 cimetières, pp. 23–38, 245–9; Bernard, *The emerging city*, pp. 188–90. Mlle de
Montpensier's adventure is noted in M. Fosseyeux, *L'Hôtel-Dieu de Paris au XVIIe et
XVIIIe siècles* (Paris, 1912), p. 248n.
[167] Quoted in du Rot, *mémoire de maitrise*, p. 187.
[168] Hillairet, *Les 200 cimetières*, pp. 249, 265–6; Pillorget, *Paris sous les premiers Bourbons*,
pp. 196–7.
[169] Brièle, *Collection de documents*, vol. I, p. 138.

the later seventeenth century led the hospital to challenge their rights to burial at la Trinité in 1662.[170] An attempt was made to integrate the cemetery into the ceremonial round of Catholic Paris, and perhaps to eliminate the taint of Protestantism, in 1652, when an All Saints procession from the Hôtel-Dieu to the cemetery was instituted. This failed, at least from the church's point of view, and was called off in 1659: the procession was said to cause public scandal through the noise and irreverence of the *menu peuple* who attended; it had become an opportunity for boys and girls to meet, rather than one for increasing devotion.[171]

The non-parochial cemeteries of London and Paris made a major contribution both to the management of the burial problem in both cities, and also to the culture of burial. In different ways they represented a civic identity that transcended the parochial, and in some senses undermined it. The Innocents certainly acted as a focus for Parisian and Catholic loyalties at a time of extreme stress, reinforced by its association with the Hôtel-Dieu, a symbolic and practical manifestation of the city as a charitable community. It is interesting how completely it eclipsed la Trinité in this, being perceived as the burial place of the poor of Paris, even though the latter took as many if not more bodies, especially in years of crisis. Though there may have been 'désaffection' in the eighteenth century, support for the Innocents remained strong up till its closure, perhaps partly because consciousness of the identity and use of la Trinité was so repressed. St Paul's churchyard and the Innocents both exemplify the struggle for open space in the early modern city; private interests and commercial pressures invaded and finally triumphed over the spiritual traditions of the sites. In Paris, it was necessary to invoke an enlightened discourse of hygiene and public health to overcome the traditional attachment to the Innocents, which was encouraged by those with a significant investment in the ideas it represented: historic tradition, religious piety, Catholicism, and the established role of the church in society. The failure of St Paul's churchyard to maintain its medieval status as a place of 'honour and worship' for burial may reflect the uneasy relationship of Londoners with the ceremonial and episcopalian aspects of Anglicanism; the parochial focus was preferred by many, but a number subscribed to an alternative tradition of dissent and congregationalism which supported the development of other non-parochial burial grounds. Burial in St Paul's churchyard seems to have declined without dispute or conflict over the seventeenth century, and its other users took over. Bunhill Fields became one of the most significant sites in the nonconformist memory, contributing to the identity of that community over time, but weakening

[170] Ibid., vol. I, pp. 138, 154.   [171] Ibid., vol. I, p. 158.

the sense of local identity and attachment to the parish characteristic of medieval and Reformation London.

At the same time, these peripheral graveyards, extensively used for the burial of the poor and outcast, including religious separatists, fitted with the model of centrality and marginality which informed patterns of burial location in local communities. Extramural or truly suburban, they placed the socially marginal or excluded on the margins of the civic community. However, their increasing use in the later seventeenth century suggests that the simultaneously integrated and multifocal character of the medieval and early modern city was breaking down; burial distinctions by place could not be fully maintained. The result was a city that was both more disintegrated and more globalised. That there was still resistance to such a development, and to its implied reduction of valued distinctions, is shown by the vigorous hostility to burial reform in eighteenth-century Paris. According to the *curés*, the people's cry, in response to the magistracy's attempts to close the city churchyards and enforce burial outside the city, was 'Le parlement nous assimilent aux Huguenots, on nous envoye a la voirie'.[172] The future, however, lay in the direction already signalled by municipal intervention in sixteenth- and seventeenth-century London, and by the magistracy of pre-Revolutionary Paris: the closure of city-centre burial sites, and the creation, as a public work, of cemeteries on the outskirts of cities. The proper place for the dead moved further and further from the heart of the city.

[172] BN, MS Joly de Fleury 1207, ff. 15–21. The cry had a double reference to refuse collection (*la voirie*) and to the cemetery of foreign Protestants in the chemin de la Voirie (present-day rue René-Boulanger, 10e: Hillairet, *Les 200 cimetières*, p. 269).

5 'Making churches charnel houses': the constraints of church burial

In the early modern western Christian world, the élite among the dead received many of the attentions paid to the élite among the living. In the short term they were watched and waited on, dressed, wrapped, given protection and shelter, and treated with respect; in the longer term they secured permanent shelter under a roof and inside a noteworthy building. Physical and spiritual protection went together. Most religious services and sacraments took place in enclosed, indoor spaces, and the most significant and prestigious place for any individual to be buried was in a church, a chapel, or a mausoleum. Those who could, sought to place the bodies of themselves and their families within a sanctified space and locale of worship, to establish a permanent association between themselves and the ongoing activity of the church. Nor did this change with the Reformation: though some Protestant reformers opposed the reverencing of the dead body, very few, in practice, rejected church burial.[1] While concern was voiced in some quarters over the practice of burying within a building (which certainly demanded attention both to the management of space and to hygiene and safety), in general in this period it was widely accepted as normal. It seems to have been taken for granted that anyone who could afford it would choose church burial, and there are very few cases where powerful individuals deliberately chose an alternative. The widely shared desire for church burial came into conflict, however, with the communal or public interest of the living, for whom churches served many social as well as religious purposes, and this led to a complicated balancing of demands and priorities. The major questions to be resolved were the terms of access to this privileged space, and the negotiation of competing demands made by powerful individuals and interests. Local

---

[1] Though see A. Spicer, '"Rest of their bones": fear of death and reformed burial practices', in W. G. Naphy and P. Roberts (eds.), *Fear in early modern society* (Manchester: Manchester University Press, 1997), pp. 167–83; A. Spicer, '"Defyle not Christ's kirke with your carrion": burial and the development of burial aisles in post-Reformation Scotland', in Gordon and Marshall (eds.), *The place of the dead*, pp. 149–69.

conditions sometimes permitted the burial in church of some people of middling or even modest status, but on the whole those buried inside a church comprised the élite of the parish, the city, and the national community. In pre-Reformation London, and in Paris throughout the period, some of these were buried in a conventual church, chosen for reasons of local, family, or devotional association; members of the nobility also had the option of being transported for burial in a church or chapel on their provincial estate. The majority of burials in churches, however, took place in parish churches.

Although burial space within churches was a very limited resource, those who obtained burial there made larger and more lasting claims on it than those who were buried in churchyards.[2] They were more likely to be able to secure undisturbed burial, to commemorate themselves with visible monuments, and to ensure their own immortality by endowing services, sermons, and distributions in perpetuity. Up to a point those seeking church burial were supplicants, requesting the favour of accommodation in a privileged place that belonged to a community, and subject to the decisions and direction of the representatives of the congregation. The more powerful, however, were able to exercise a greater degree of control. They took steps to shape the physical setting in which their bodies would lie, and to direct the liturgical performances around the site, and in the process did much to transform the church from a space of collective worship and action to one that served to memorialise individuals and individual families.

This chapter and the next deal with these two aspects of church burial. In this chapter we see the church and congregation in charge, setting priorities and rationing space, responding to changing fashions, such as coffin burial, but preserving, at least to some extent, the collective spatial resource of the church. In chapter 6, the private interest of individual and family takes over, reconfiguring the space to meet private needs and preferences. Whereas the preceding chapters treated churchyard burial in London and Paris separately and consecutively, because of major differences between locations and the sources available for study, the comparison of church burial in the two cities is better served by a more integrated discussion. Individual and local variations in resources and conditions are still important, but church burial in both cities was subject to similar constraints and anxieties, and these similarities make the divergences more striking.

---

[2] There are similarities between this situation and the one that developed in nineteenth-century cemeteries, where individuals and families sought private concessions in a communal setting: T. A. Kselman, *Death and the afterlife in modern France* (Princeton, 1993), esp. pp. 165–221.

Getting into the church

The importance of relics to the early Christian church, and their role in conversion and the establishment of centres of cult, had profound implications for attitudes to the dead bodies of the faithful. Relics were the magnet that drew burials into towns and churches from rural, pagan sites.[3] Once they had been allowed in, it was not possible to keep the ordinary dead at a distance. Early church councils, from at least the sixth century, legislated against burials inside churches, and the prohibition was frequently repeated, but these repetitions seem merely to confirm that the practice was continuing. The canons concerning burial left a loophole, by permitting the burial in church of distinguished ecclesiastics and some loyal and devoted lay members of the congregation.[4] These undoubtedly included founders and major donors; from this it was a relatively short step to allowing the burial of lesser benefactors. More and more of the dead crept into churches from the early middle ages, as the notion of 'benefactor' was stretched to include 'contributor', and finally anyone who made a donation or payment for the place of burial. By the later middle ages it may have been desire for proximity to the site of the celebration of the mass, rather than to the relics of the saints, that motivated the faithful, but the attraction was at least as strong. At several different moments there were more strenuous efforts to end the practice, but the representatives of religious and parish communities were at best ambivalent, since church burials brought in revenue, encouraged endowments, and enhanced the status and often the appearance of the church itself.

If early churches were often founded to secure burial sites for their benefactors, funding enlargements, rebuildings and additions to existing churches could offer similar opportunities, with the added advantage of harnessing the gratitude and intercession of an existing congregation to the benefactor's own benefit. Richard Whittington, three times mayor of London, refounded the parish church of St Michael Paternoster in 1409/10 as a collegiate church with a chantry for himself, his wife, their parents, and others. He was buried there on his death in 1423. The college was staffed with five secular priests, two clerks, and four choristers, but the church remained a parish church, with 213 communicants in 1548.[5] Other late medieval Londoners made lesser donations to their own churches but still secured a prominent burial place. John Barton,

---

[3] P. J. Geary, *Living with the dead in the Middle Ages* (Ithaca, 1994), pp. 30–45.
[4] Ariès, *The hour of our death*, pp. 47–8, 50.
[5] *VCH London*, vol. I, pp. 578–80; J. Imray, *The charity of Richard Whittington. A history of the trust administered by the Mercers' Company* (London, 1968), pp. 9–10, 31–3; Kitching (ed.), *London and Middlesex chantry certificate*, p. 96.

mercer, contributed to the rebuilding of St Michael Bassishaw, 'as appeareth by his marke placed throughout the whole roofe of the quier and middle Ile of the church' and was buried in the choir. Ralph Austrie, fishmonger and mayor, re-roofed and glazed the church of St Martin in the Vintry, and was buried there with his two wives and other members of his family; Richard Shore, one of the sheriffs of London in 1505 'was a great benefactor in his life', and when he died left £20 to the church of St Mary Woolchurch to build a west porch, where he was buried.[6] Nicolas Flamel, 'fort généreux', endowed numerous charitable objects but left the residue of his goods to Saint-Jacques-de-la-Boucherie, where he was buried in 1417 'under the flagstones', that is, presumably, in the body of the church.[7]

For those who were not able or willing to be major benefactors or virtual founders, 'the only effect of the canonical prohibitions . . . was to make the customary practice of burial in church subject to the payment of a fee'.[8] The question of the legitimacy of mortuary demands and fees for funeral services and places of burial exercised canon lawyers and at times incensed the laity. While early medieval ecclesiastical authority forbade demanding anything on the occasion of burial, whether for the grant of a place of burial, or for the accompanying office, the Lateran Council of 1215 approved the 'laudable custom' of making offerings on this occasion, and declared this obligatory in future.[9] With this sanction, the clergy were able to accept payment for their participation in funeral services; it also effectively legitimised the taking of fees for burial places in, and later outside, churches. Wills and parish records from London show that over the later fifteenth century the informal practice of making a testamentary bequest or benefaction to the parish church to secure a burial space there evolved into formal and fixed charges for burial in particular places. By the mid-sixteenth century, most parishes were charging a standard sum – normally 6s. 8d. for an adult – for 'breaking the ground' in church, and some had begun to elaborate a list of charges according to location.[10] Comparable records do not survive from such an early date for Paris, but the principles of charging for a place in the church, and of differential pricing according to location, were well established by the late seventeenth century, and probably very much earlier.[11] Opposition was still voiced, however, in both Protestant and Catholic confessions, to the sale of burial space. Sir Henry Spelman (d. 1641) contended it had been prohibited under canon law, and that these canons had not been

---

[6] Stow, *Survey*, vol. II, pp. 243, 289, 248, 227.

[7] Hillairet, *Les 200 cimetières*, p. 46.   [8] Ariès, *The hour of our death*, p. 50.

[9] R. Naz, *Dictionnaire du droit canonique*, 7 vols. (Paris 1935–65), vol. V (1953), p. 926.

[10] Harding, 'Burial choice and burial location', pp. 125–6, 129–31.

[11] AN, L 651/2.

abolished by the Reformation, so that it remained 'a horrible and simo-niacal act, and in no way justified by long continuance'.[12] The French jurist and Oratorian Thomassin noted that burial in church was granted to lay people 'as a reward for their prayers and donations', a situation that at least potentially gave rise to simony.[13] Nevertheless the practice was too firmly established to be shaken by such criticism, and indeed the idea that burial space, in all kinds of location, is a commodity with a monetary value is now unquestioned.

Although the Protestant Reformation included a strand of thought opposed to elaborate burial ceremonies and to the idea of favoured places, this was not widely shared, and London churches continued to be the burial place of choice for almost all who could afford it, with a geography of desirability that reproduced the pre-Reformation one.[14] The coun-cils of the Counter-Reformation also tried to oppose the custom and return to the ancient law, but were hampered by the demands of hon-our and piety. They continued to permit the burial within churches of 'those who by their nobility, actions and merit have distinguished them-selves in the service of God'.[15] Parisian churches remained prime burial locations and, like those in London, became filled with the monuments and tombs of the laity. The early eighteenth century saw renewed op-position to church burial on both sides of the Channel, invoking the legal and historical arguments but also, as noted above, hostile to what was perceived as the commodification of burial through the selling of spaces. A new hygienic discourse began to emerge, and anxieties were heightened by the reappearance of plague in Mediterranean France in 1720. Thomas Lewis argued in 1721 against the 'indecent and danger-ous' custom of burying in churches: 'it is an undoubted truth, that the corruption of dead bodies interred in churches may be communicated to the living'. The practice was not justified by its long Christian tradi-tion, which had been 'begun thro' pride, improv'd by superstition, and encourag'd for lucre'.[16] The bishop of Rouen issued an order in 1721 against excessive burial in church, which he said kept the faithful at a distance on account of their fear of infection, though he still allowed the

---

[12] Sir Henry Spelman, *De sepultura*, in *The English works of Sir Henry Spelman* (London, 1723), p. 179.

[13] L. Thomassin, *Ancienne et nouvelle discipline de l'église, touchant les Bénéfices et les Bénéficiers*, 3 vols. (Paris, 1725), quoted by Ariès, *Hour of our death*, p. 50.

[14] The strong attack on church burial by the clergy of other reformed communities clearly met with much opposition: Spicer, '"Rest of their bones"', pp. 167–83.

[15] Ariès, *The hour of our death*, pp. 47–8.

[16] [Thomas Lewis], *Seasonable considerations on the indecent and dangerous custom of burying in churches and church-yards, with remarkable observations, historical and philosophical, proving that the custom is not only contrary to the practice of the Ancients but fatal in case of infection* (London, 1721), pp. 6, 56.

burial of substantial benefactors (paying at least 30 *livres* for burial in the nave of a town church).[17] Thomassin blamed the laity for 'the vain and ridiculous pride that seeks to distinguish itself even by its place of burial', while the Abbé Porée, in his *Lettres sur la sépulture dans les églises* (1745) spoke of 'pestilential vapours'.[18] A memorandum of 1738 noted that the 'odeur pendant la putrefaction des corps' was worse in churches than in churchyards, and was not always contained even by sealed tombs; the church of Saint-Germain-l'Auxerrois was specially mentioned.[19] However, resistance and custom were strong. Although the (London) Fifty New Churches Act of 1711 determined that there should be no intramural burial in the new churches, there was burial in intramural vaults within a few years.[20] The *curés* of Paris, and some of the churchwardens, strongly opposed the idea of closing the churches and city-centre churchyards to burial in the mid-eighteenth century, on the grounds that it would undermine the devotion of the population, and also that the loss of burial fees would impoverish the church. They noted that burial in churches was still going on in London, a city as populous as Paris.[21] The question of burial in Paris was directly addressed after the Revolution, when the churches were closed, the churchyards emptied, and further burial within the city was banned, even though, in the event, this merely transferred many of the issues about location, status, and privatisation to the new scene of the cemetery.[22] When similar concerns were voiced about 'the unwise and revolting custom of inhuming the dead in the midst of the living' in mid-nineteenth-century London, there was still local and popular resistance to the proposed closure of the city churches to burial.[23]

Hierarchies of space: convents, churches, chancels

By the early sixteenth century, in addition to their numerous parish churches, both cities were richly supplied with convents, friaries, and hospitals, of old and recent foundation, all of which at some time or

[17] A copy of this order is in BN, MS Joly de Fleury 1317, f. 34, along with other eighteenth-century papers on the issue of city burial.

[18] Thomassin, *Ancienne et nouvelle discipline de l'église* (1725), quoted by Ariès, *The hour of our death*, p. 50; Abbé Ch.-G. Porée, *Lettres sur la sépulture dans les églises* (1745), pp. 5–8, 30, quoted in McManners, *Death and the Enlightenment*, p. 306.

[19] BN, MS Joly de Fleury 1317, ff. 50–9.

[20] M. Port, *The commissions for building fifty new churches. The minute books, 1711–27, a calendar* (London Record Society 23, 1986), pp. xiv, xx, xxi, no. 114; cf. J. Reeve and M. Adams, *The Spitalfields project*, vol. I, *The archaeology: across the Styx* (York, 1993).

[21] BN, MS Joly de Fleury 1207, ff. 15–21; BN, MS Joly de Fleury 1208, ff. 194–201v.

[22] Kselman, *Death and the afterlife in modern France*, pp. 171, 177, 182–99.

[23] Walker, *Gatherings from graveyards*; Saunders, 'London burials', pp. 161–74. Cf. Harding, 'Burial on the margin', pp. 54–64.

other attracted burials. Conventual burial was always a minority choice, however, and usually restricted to certain categories. Lay burials in convents tended to be either those of precinct inhabitants and lay servants of the house, or of nobility and royalty. Only 10 per cent of a sample of (mostly male) London testators of middling rank between 1480 and 1540 chose conventual burial, and fewer than 20 per cent of a sample of male testators, and 6 per cent of female, in Paris between 1550 and 1600.[24]

The most noteworthy and popular London houses were the priories of Austin Canons at St Bartholomew Smithfield and Holy Trinity Aldgate, the four major friaries, Greyfriars, Blackfriars, Austin Friars, and Whitefriars, and the convent of Poor Clares or Minoresses. The mendicant orders encouraged laymen to choose burial with them, offering them an active intercessory environment, and their success at attracting burials and bequests earned them the hostility of the London parish clergy in the early fourteenth century. Even though the numbers involved were quite small, if this meant that the bodies and bequests of richer parishioners were being attracted away from the parish churches, the city rectors had some cause for complaint.[25] The Austin Friars, an international order, attracted burials of alien merchants who died in London, as did the hospital of St Anthony of Vienne. The house or hospital of St Thomas of Acre in Cheapside attracted both Italians and Londoners, especially members of the prestigious Mercers' Company, whose hall lay nearby and who had an aisle chapel within the conventual church.[26] All of these burial options were eliminated at the Reformation, with the exception of St Thomas of Acre: the Mercers took over its premises and thereafter used the conventual church as their own chapel, converting the separate chapel they had recently built on Cheapside into lettable shops. Mercers' Chapel remained a significant location for the burial of mercers and parishioners of St Mary Colechurch.[27] A few other conventual churches also gained a new ecclesiastical identity: the Greyfriars church became the church of the new parish of Christchurch Newgate Street; the chancel, crossing, and transepts of the priory church of St Bartholomew became the parish church of St Bartholomew the Great; the chapel of Elsing Spital became the parish church of St Alphege. The church of Austin Friars became, in due course, the Dutch church of the immigrant Protestant

---

[24] From the samples analysed in Harding, 'Burial choice and burial location', pp. 122–4; Chaunu, *La mort à Paris*, p. 436.

[25] F. M. Powicke and C. R. Cheney, *Councils and synods with other documents relating to the English church*, vol. II: *1205–1313*, pt. 2 (Oxford, 1964), pp. 1255–63; *VCH London*, vol. I, pp. 200–1.

[26] Harding, 'Burial choice and burial location', p. 124.

[27] Keene and Harding, *Historical gazetteer of London before the Great Fire*, 1, *Cheapside*, nos. 105/0, 105/18. Cf. GL, MS 4438 (register of St Mary Colechurch).

congregation. Others, however, were converted to secular uses or demolished altogether.[28]

Paris had its friaries of Jacobins, Cordeliers, Augustins, and Carmes, and an array of other houses, old and new, that continued to attract burial. The Jacobins and Cordeliers obtained a number of royal corpses and body parts from the middle ages onwards, as well as members of officeholding and university families. Other houses accepting bodies for burial included the Billettes, the Blancs-Manteaux, and the Celestins; in the seventeenth century the Jesuits, also with a strong mission to the laity, began to attract burials, to the dismay and detriment of the parish clergy.[29] Choice of burial in a convent was primarily a question of religious or family affiliation, sometimes overriding more predictable choices. François le Picart, doctor of theology in the University of Paris and dean of Saint-Germain-l'Auxerrois, chose to be buried at the convent of the Blancs-Manteaux, where his parents already lay.[30] Certain houses had special prestige. The Celestins had numerous burials and tombs of distinction, including the hearts of Louis XII, Henri II, François II, Charles IX, François duke of Anjou, and Catherine de Medici; the comte de Brissac was buried there with lavish honours in 1569.[31] The duc de Joyeuse was buried at the convent of the Grands Augustins on the left bank in 1588, after a service attended by the king and queens.[32] Conventual churches often had a strong pull on nearby residents. The Grands Augustins was also a popular place of burial for leading parishioners of Saint-André-des-Arts, within whose parish the convent lay. Ninety-eight burials at the Augustins, often after a service at Saint-André, are noted in the antiquaries' extracts from the burial register of the parish. Some families seem to have established a tradition of burial there: eleven members of the family of Charles de Paris, *maître-patissier* on the pont Saint-Michel, were buried at the Grands Augustins between 1608 and 1637. Twenty-seven others from Saint-André-des-Arts were buried in the church of the Cordeliers, also nearby, though not within the bounds of the parish.[33] On the whole, though, *bourgeois de Paris*, municipal and government officeholders, and most minor *noblesse de robe* chose to be buried in parish churches.

---

[28] See Harben, *Dictionary of London*.

[29] For a full account of the Parisian religious houses in which lay burials took place, see Hillairet, *Les 200 cimetières*. Cf. Thibaut-Payen, *Les morts, l'église, et l'état*, pp. 38–52; Golden, *The godly rebellion*, pp. 106–7.

[30] *RDBVP*, vol. IV, pp. 450–1; L. J. Taylor, *Heresy and orthodoxy in sixteenth-century Paris. François le Picart and the beginnings of the Catholic Reformation* (Studies in Medieval and Reformation Thought, vol. LXXVII, Leiden, 1999), pp. 25–6, 213.

[31] Hillairet, *Les 200 cimetières*, pp. 190–4; *RDBVP*, vol. VI, pp. 111–14.

[32] Hillairet, *Les 200 cimetières*, pp. 188–9; *RDBVP*, vol. IX, pp. 104–6.

[33] BN, MS Fr. 32589.

There was rivalry between the houses accepting lay burials and the parishes from which they came. It was generally accepted that an individual was entitled to designate his or her own place of burial, but it was also acknowledged to be reasonable that the parish should receive some compensation for a burial taken elsewhere, for the loss of revenues, offerings, and perhaps also prestige. The Blancs-Manteaux were bound by an agreement of 1330 to pay 12 *livres parisis* or 15 *livres tournois* to the parish of Saint-Jean-en-Grève in lieu of the funeral offerings of any parishioner choosing to be buried at the convent; the body was to be taken first to the parish church, and then to the convent. Similarly the house of the Carmes Billettes, in the same parish, acknowledged the rights of the parish, agreeing to share the offerings (of wax, bread, etc.), while claiming full rights over their own domestics. The religious of Sainte-Croix de la Bretonnerie, however, contested the obligation that bodies should go first to the church of Saint-Jean-en-Grève, and obtained an *arrêt* of Parlement to this effect in 1648.[34] This was only one episode in an ongoing and acrimonious dispute between the regular and the parish clergy over burial rights in the seventeenth century, involving confrontations, 'convois furtifs et vexatoires', affrays, and litigation; one case, concerning the Minimes, took seventeen years to resolve.[35]

Even when the church of burial had been agreed, there were still important decisions to be made. All churches are highly ordered spaces, according to a particular set of meanings and values, which are articulated both in architectural forms and divisions and in liturgical activities. Burial practices both contributed to the ordering of space within the church and were affected by it. The burial environment of a church differed from that of a churchyard and even cloisters and *charniers* in being more exclusively dedicated to sacred uses, perhaps, but it was not free from rival claims. 'The development of the tomb [in the middle ages] was... tied up with the emergence of a certain politics of space: those seeking burial had to compete for space in buildings which, unlike mausolea, were not necessarily planned as specialized burial sites.'[36] In general the medieval hierarchy of desirable location was common to cathedrals, conventual churches, and parish churches. The best places were near an altar where mass was celebrated, whether in the main church or in a chapel. Spaces farther away were less valued, but it was always better to be inside the church than outside it. In the parishes, this hierarchy

---

[34] AN, L 663, ff. 29–36.
[35] Thibaut-Payen, *Les morts, l'église, et l'état*, pp. 48–50; Golden, *The godly rebellion*, pp. 106–8.
[36] P. Binski, *Medieval death, ritual and representation* (London, 1996), p. 74.

was manifested in the practice of charging different sums for burial in different places. 'What was first a Donation, afterwards became a price; what was first a gift, was then a demand; and a rate was afterwards made according to the dignity of persons or the site of the ground.'[37] As early as 1456 the wardens of St Michael Cornhill were charging 6s. 8d. for burial in the church and 3s. 4d. for burial in the vault. In 1524 the parish of St Mary at Hill set out a table of its burial charges, in which the ground for burial in the two chapels cost 13s. 4d., in the cross aisle before the choir door 10s., and elsewhere in the church 6s. 8d.[38] Most parishes did not put a price on the ground in the chancel, which was the right of the rector, but in the few parishes where they did it seems to have been at least as much as the most expensive place in the rest of the church.[39]

Not all parishes differentiated between spaces in church as early or as precisely as this, but similar hierarchies did exist in many other London and Paris churches in the later sixteenth and seventeenth centuries. These might be expressed in great detail, reflecting the layout of the individual building: urban churches were constrained and often irregular in form, with a range of aisles, chapels, and vaults. St Helen Bishopsgate in London decided in 1565 that burial between Sir Thomas Gresham's pew and the vestry door should cost 15s., between the steps and the choir door 10s., and in the rest of the body of the church 6s. 8d.; later records refer to the two latter spaces as 'the ten-shilling ground' and 'the noble ground'.[40] All Hallows the Great in London in 1622 priced five locations within the church: the chancel (fees at the discretion of the rector), the Lady Chapel in the south aisle (13s. 4d.), St Katherine's chapel in the north aisle (10s.), 'any other part of the church' (6s. 8d.), and 'Mr Campion's vault' (6s. 8d.).[41] The list of fees for Saint-Gervais in Paris in 1675 mentions the choir, the chapel of the Communion, 'autres chapelles', the church, and the *charniers* and cemetery. Saint-André-des-Arts and Saint-Jean-en-Grève also distinguished between the choir and the body of the church.[42] Some parish registers note the location of individual burials, partly as a

---

[37] [Thomas Lewis], *Seasonable considerations on the indecent and dangerous custom of burying in churches and church-yards*, p. 51.

[38] Overall, *Accounts of the churchwardens of St Michael Cornhill*, p. 88; Littlehales, *Medieval records of a London city church*, pp. 319–20.

[39] At St Bride Fleet Street in 1624, where the parsonage was leased by the parish, the ground in the middle aisle of the chancel was rated at 40s., the two side aisles of the chancel 20s., and the body of the church 20s.: GL, MS 9531/13, pt. 2, ff. 372v–373v.

[40] GL, MS 6836, p. 272; *Registers of St Helen Bishopsgate*, pp. 286, 288, 292. A noble was a gold coin worth 6s. 8d.

[41] GL, MS 9531/13, pt. 2, ff. 377v–378v.

[42] AN, L 651/2 (Saint-Gervais, 1675); AN, LL 687, ff. 183r–184 (Saint-André-des-Arts, 1687); AN, LL 805, pp. 253–5 (Saint-Jean-en-Grève, 1716).

memorandum of the availability of space, but partly to keep a check of the fees due to the parish.[43]

A key feature of differential pricing by location was the parallel evolution of a set of rates for funeral services and accoutrements that was often tied to the place of burial. The clerk and sexton or the *fossoyeur* often received a larger fee for burials in church, according to the place chosen, and not simply on account of the greater difficulty of making graves in the church. The clerk's fee for participating at a burial in St Andrew Undershaft in London ranged from 4s. 8d., when the deceased had a grave in the high choir, down to 20d., for a grave in the body of the church; the sexton's fee ranged likewise from 2s. to 20d.[44] Anyone who was buried in church was expected, and in time required, to have a larger number or better quality of accessories and attendants, for each of which a higher price was payable. If one chose one of the better places, one must have the better, and more expensive, accessories, and conversely, in some cases, one could only have the better accessories if one chose burial in the church. The vestry of Saint-André-des-Arts decreed in 1687 that anyone buried in church must also hire a pall and silverware, and have bells rung; if he or she chose 'la grosse sonnerie', the better hangings and the full range of silverware must also be hired.[45] These charges were a relatively minor part of the cost of a grand funeral, but the principle, of increasing charges for other services in line with the cost of the place of burial, contributed to the process of commodifying burial and all its attributes. It also perhaps supported the identification of the dead, as represented by their executors and families, as consumers or customers, entitled to demand a certain kind of treatment in return for their contributions.

Anyone who specified a burial place within a church must have been aware of the hierarchy of pricing, but wishes were expressed in a variety of ways. The range of choices made seems to have been similar in London and Paris, except that in the latter private chapels figured largely. Although the place of burial would be, in each case, a compromise between several different options and motivations, some patterns emerge, within the limits of testamentary convention. An important but minority choice, in pre-Reformation London and in early modern Paris, was for a place defined by its religious associations. In one Paris sample from the mid-sixteenth century, just under half said precisely where they wanted to be buried, but less than a quarter of these chose 'devotionally'. The majority of these chose a site of Marian devotion – an image, a statue, or a chapel of Notre-Dame.[46] In another such sample, seven chose to

---

[43] E.g., GL, MS 9223.   [44] LPL, CM VII/94.   [45] AN, LL 687, ff. 183r–184.
[46] Chaunu, *La mort à Paris*, pp. 325–6, citing the *mémoire de maîtrise* of M. Massucco.

be buried in the choir or before the high altar, seven near a cross or crucifix (in church or churchyard), and eleven near an image or object of Marian devotion.[47] The vestry of Saint-Gervais refused to allot the chapel of the Virgin as a private family burial chapel, as burial there was apparently a popular request.[48] Marian dedications are less common in pre-Reformation London wills, though they do occur, and the designation of a location for religious reasons in general was less common than choosing burial near a family member or other associate. A few in both London and Paris chose their place of burial in words that indicate that they envisaged themselves after death as continuing participants in the worship of the church: 'in St Sepulchre's where I am parishioner, at my pew door there'; 'in the churche of the Mynoresse withoute Algate of London, in the litle chapell before the mydille of the aultar ther by my pue wherin I was wonte to knele and her my devine service'. Others perhaps imagined the liturgical circuit of the church: 'in the choir before the first steps going to the high altar of the church', 'in the church of St John by the holy water stock on the south side'.[49] There was increased devotion to the Sacrament and the Communion in Counter-Reformation Paris, resulting in the building of several dedicated chapels which became the foci of devotional observance. The epitaph of Claude d'Aubray, buried in Saint-André-des-Arts in 1609, noted his full and singular devotion to the body of Our Lord, and his deathbed desire to be buried near the chapel of the Holy Sacrament, so that he might obtain mercy through the prayers of the faithful worshipping there, and rise again with them in glory.[50]

References to saints' altars and images obviously disappeared from London wills after the mid-sixteenth century, but there were still requests for burial in the chancel, which remained a location of high status and price; others also chose to be buried 'at the side of the pew where I used to sit'.[51] It is difficult to tell whether this choice was exactly a devotional one, since it had other implications as well. At this date, seating in the parish church was not normally assigned permanently, but reviewed at intervals to reflect the changing fortunes and life-cycles of the parishioners. Pew assignment gave a visible, spatial form to a hierarchy of status, implying the existence of a collective or consensus view of the social pyramid;

---

[47] G. du Rot, *mémoire de maîtrise* , pp. 192–4.
[48] L. Brochard, *Saint-Gervais. Histoire du monument* (Paris, 1938), pp. 120–1, 349.
[49] E.g. GL, MS 9171/9, ff. 149, 170, 175, 178.
[50] E. Raunié, *Epitaphier du vieux Paris. Recueil général des inscriptions funéraires des églises, couvents, collèges, hospices, cimetières et charniers depuis le moyen âge jusqu'à la fin du XVIIIe siècle*, 13 vols. (Paris, 1890–), vol. I (1890), p. 16.
[51] E.g. GL, MS 9051/4, f. 197v.

contests over placement attest the importance people attached to it.[52] Probably only those who had achieved a satisfactory recognition of their personal status in the parish pewing would choose to be buried under their pew, but to do so was to stake a perpetual claim to a place achieved in a dynamic process. It also entailed a conspicuous expenditure of money and effort. The parish of St Mary Colechurch ruled that 'those that are buried under any of the pews in the church shall be at the charge of taking them down and setting them up in the same good order they find'.[53]

In both London and Paris it was most common, if requesting a specific place for one's own burial, to cite the grave of a particular person. Given that most willmakers in London were either male householders or widows, it is not surprising that spouses were the most frequently chosen neighbours there, both inside and outside churches. In a sample of fifty wills proved in London in 1500, five widows (out of seven in the sample) asked to be buried 'nigh the place whereas my late husband lyeth buried', or words to that effect. Seven men chose to be buried where their late wives were; one asked for burial by his late wife's pew door, another by his wife's pew. When a man's wife had predeceased him, it is likely that he had chosen her burial site in the first place, with the expectation of being buried there himself. The other graves identified were of a brother, a father, a cousin, and a master.[54] Similar choices continued to be made in London in the later sixteenth and seventeenth centuries, though the proportion specifying any location (other than choosing church rather than churchyard) declined over the period.[55] The 1500 sample included six priests; after the Reformation, the number of these declined, and they were as likely now to be married as any other adult male. In Paris there was a similar predilection for burial near spouses, though the samples cannot be exactly comparable, since more women, including married women, made wills, and the numbers of clergy, necessarily celibate, continued or indeed grew.[56] One important development over the period was the increase, discussed in chapter 6, in family tombs (in both London and Paris) and private chapels and burial vaults (in Paris especially). This obviously affected both assumptions and desires about burial location, and the way in which they were expressed: to ask for burial in a particular tomb or chapel was to ask for burial both in a known place and

---

[52] *VCH London*, vol. I, p. 320. The vestry minute book of St Mary Colechurch contains twenty-six versions of 'the order of sitting as appointed by churchwardens and other ancient parishioners' from 1613 to 1661: GL, MS 64. Disputes over placement are illustrated in GL, MS 3016/1 (vestry minutes of St Dunstan in the West), pp. 272, 275, 295, 380, 423, 524.

[53] GL, MS 66, f. 14.   [54] GL, MS 9171/8, ff. 200–19.

[55] Cf. Harding, 'And one more', p. 114.   [56] Chaunu, *La mort à Paris*, pp. 325–6.

near relatives, with the expectation that other relatives would be buried there subsequently. It may also have been felt unnecessary to express any wish in the will if there was known to be a conjugal or familial tomb ready.

The church burial population

As chapter 3 has already shown, the dead who were buried in a church were usually of higher status than those buried in a churchyard, the élite of the parish and local community. Church burial was always a minority option, though the social bias of willmaking makes it appear more important than in statistical terms it really was. The Parisian parish register extracts are themselves a socially biased sample; London parish registers, while recording almost all burials, are more likely to identify church burials as such, and London churchwardens' accounts usually deal only with the burials for which fees were received.

For many London parishes at least, there was only a small handful of burials in church every year in the early sixteenth century. Many of the small parishes of the city centre buried fewer than twenty a year even by the mid-seventeenth.[57] Most of the registers for the very large suburban parishes do not give the locations of burials, but sometimes other sources can help. Churchwardens' accounts for St Martin in the Fields for the later sixteenth century list two or three payments of 6s. 8d. 'for breaking the ground' (i.e. for a grave in the church) for every hundred burials; there were only about three burials a year in the church in the large parish of St Botolph Bishopsgate in the same period.[58] The parish clerk's detailed memorandum books for St Botolph Aldgate for the early seventeenth century likewise suggest that not more than 4–5 per cent of burials in or from that parish were in the church.[59] In some of the larger, wealthy city parishes, as the period progressed, numbers may have increased, but usually remained in the minority. Two hundred and three (39 per cent) of the 510 people whose deaths were recorded in St Helen's parish between 1640 and 1658 were buried in the church.[60] Parishes without churchyards necessarily buried a larger proportion of their dead in the church, even when, as in the case of St Mary Colechurch, the church stood not on natural ground but on vaults which were in private occupation. Between 1600 and 1628, the parish register records 241 deaths, of which 141 (59 per cent) were buried in the church; sixty-one were buried in the New Churchyard outside Bishopsgate, fifteen in the nearby Mercers' Chapel,

[57] See above, chapter 2.
[58] Kitto, *St Martin in the Fields, accounts of the churchwardens*, passim; GL, MS 4524/1.
[59] GL, MS 9223.   [60] *Registers of St Helen Bishopsgate*, pp. 286–95.

and the remainder in other parishes.[61] Comparable statistics for Paris do not exist. The will samples of Chaunu's students only corroborate that a high proportion of willmakers sought burial in church, not how many of the population at large were buried there, but they can throw some light on the social composition of that group. Of a sample of 199 wills made between 1550 and 1599, the proportions choosing church and churchyard burial were about equal, though nearly three-quarters of the latter were choosing the Innocents, which included many private and high-status grave sites. The 'church burial population' of this sample was made up of 8 per cent clergy, 30 per cent nobles, 47 per cent *honorables* and *bourgeois de Paris*, and up to 12 per cent from the middling and lower third estate.[62]

The social composition of the living population of each parish or locality obviously determined the size and character of its 'élite'. The parish of St Helen Bishopsgate in the city of London lay near to the Royal Exchange and other sites of mercantile importance. Of 101 individuals buried in the church between 1630 and 1642, all but eight are identified by occupation or status (of themselves or of the head of their household). Thirty-one came from seventeen merchant households; eight others appeared to follow mercantile occupations; eleven were gentlemen or from a gentry or knightly household. Few retailers and craftsmen (carpenters, chandlers, pewterers, and even merchant tailors) were buried in the church.[63] The parish of Saint-André-des-Arts in Paris, just across the river from the Palais de Justice and the Parlement, but also near to the Sorbonne, had a population of magistrates and ministers, some of great wealth and standing.[64] At least 50 per cent of those known to have been buried in the church between 1550 and 1670 came from families of *avocats* (mostly in the parlement of Paris), *procureurs*, *conseillers*, or *secrétaires du roi*, or those who held office or title from the crown. A small number were doctors of medicine or members of the faculty of medicine, and there were a few clerics, but only a handful were merchants and/or *bourgeois de Paris*, or from their families. Similarly, the 133 *nobles* (including lawyers, *parlementaires*, and officeholders, or their families) greatly outnumbered the fourteen *honorables*, in this perhaps untypical parish.[65] A note of contributors to

[61] GL, MS 4438. I am grateful to Jean Imray, former archivist of the Mercers' Company, for drawing my attention to this register.

[62] Chaunu, *La mort à Paris*, pp. 319–21, 325, table pp. 486–7, citing the *mémoire de maîtrise* of M. Massucco.

[63] *Registers of St Helen Bishopsgate*, pp. 286–95. See above, chapter 3.

[64] Babelon, *Paris au XVIe siècle*, p. 245.

[65] Based on an analysis of 1,083 individuals said to have been buried at Saint-André-des-Arts (excluding those buried in the churchyard), in BN, MS Fr. 32589. For a discussion of the royal household, courts, and governments offices in Paris, and their members, see Pillorget, *Paris sous les premiers Bourbons*, pp. 46–59.

the rebuilding of the church in 1613 indicates the relative wealth and importance of different occupational groups. Fourteen advocates and twenty other legal or clerical professionals (*conseillers, procureurs, greffiers*) contributed, several of them 100 *livres* or more. Five *bourgeois*, one merchant, and seven craftsmen or tradesmen made donations, the largest of which was 36 *livres*.[66]

Opening church burial to benefactors, however defined, could also undermine notions of burial as an element of community. The laity who were buried in conventual churches were perhaps accepted as honorary members of those communities on account of their benefactions, and sometimes took minor orders or a habit as a sign of this. But the majority almost certainly did not, and it must therefore have been very striking that the most sacred spaces within the precincts of the religious orders contained many monuments to secular dignitaries. In the same spirit, parishes recognised that individuals who were not a regular part of the congregation might wish to be buried in their church. This was uncommon before the Reformation in London, when those choosing burial outside their parish church or churchyard usually opted for a religious house. Only one person from a sample of 450 London willmakers between 1380 and 1540 chose burial in another parish, while eighty-two chose burial in a conventual church or St Paul's churchyard.[67] Most of the earliest (fifteenth- and early sixteenth-century) accounts and statements of burial fees make no special reference to the burial of strangers; the exception is St Michael Cornhill, where in 1521 the vestry agreed that 'for all strangers that is buried in the church or in the churchyard or in any place belonging to the church, being no parishioner, that then the clerks to take the best they can with good reason and conscience'. Recognising that the category included passers-through and lodgers, and that not all strangers were wealthy outsiders, they added cautiously 'so that ther be awghte to be had'.[68]

In the later sixteenth century this situation changed, perhaps partly as a result of the loss of the option of conventual burial, more probably as the size, and the geographical and social mobility, of London's population increased. 'Stranger' had a number of meanings in early modern London, including alien birth or nationality, but in parish records it usually means non-parishioner, either a local resident who was in theory temporary or

---

[66] AN, LL 686, ff. 14–16.

[67] Harding, 'Burial choice and burial location', p. 122. The collegiate church of St Michael Paternoster – somewhere between a parish church and a conventual one – attracted several burials of mayors and aldermen, perhaps because of its association with Richard Whittington: Clive Burgess, personal communication.

[68] Overall, *Accounts of churchwardens of the parish of St Michael Cornhill*, p. 223.

unsettled, or someone who was a resident member of another parish. Local but temporary residents might reasonably look to their parish of present residence for burial; the second group could buy their way into it from outside. In doing so they were of course asserting a kind of community through association – past residence, connections with family or friends – but one that was voluntary and individualistic, rather than the inclusive and 'natural' community of the co-resident parish congregation. At first this seems to have been accepted cautiously: at St Helen's in 1563, the vestry ruled that nobody 'not of this parish and not departing this world within the parish' should be buried in the church or churchyard except with the consent of the parishioners at the vestry.[69] By the later sixteenth century, many London parishes were accepting the bodies of strangers for burial in church. These may have been visitors to London, like Thomas Grysold, gentleman, of Tamworth, Staffordshire, who was buried in the church of All Hallows Bread Street in 1599: 'he died here in London... and for because some of his Frends were buried here before, his desire was to be buried here'. Likewise, later the same year, the same parish allowed the burial of Mr William Gibson, who 'dwelt in Kent, and died in Cheapside at a friend's house, who was the son of Mr William Gibson of this parish, and his desire was to be buried by his father'.[70] Others were Londoners who wished to maintain a past personal or family association, such as Daniel Ensor, living in the parish of St Mary Colechurch, who in his will of 1610 requested burial in the church of St Helen Bishopsgate near his uncle John Robinson, or the letter writer John Chamberlain, resident in St Mary Aldermanbury, who wanted to be buried in the church of St Olave Old Jewry, where he was born and christened and where his father, mother, brother, 'and other frendes' were buried.[71] Other 'strangers' recorded in burial registers must have included non-settled residents of the parish, lodgers, or 'inmates', an increasingly numerous category in seventeenth-century London.

Acceptance into a burial community came at a price. This was not in itself unreasonable, since non-residents and lodgers would not have paid tithe or, possibly, church rates. Several parishes had schedules of fees approved in the 1620s, usually including words to the effect that 'all strangers, inmates, lodgers, and sojourners to pay double duties to all the particulars abovenamed'.[72] Exceptions could be made in particular

---

[69] GL, MS 6836, p. 268.   [70] *Registers of All Hallows Bread Street*, pp. 168–9.

[71] PRO, PROB 11/116, ff. 367r–v; *Registers of St Helen Bishopsgate*, p. 273; McClure (ed.), *Letters of John Chamberlain*, vol. II, pp. 632–5.

[72] GL, MS 9531/13, pt. 2, ff. 372v–373v, 378v, 383–384v, 385v–386v, 399v–400. St Anne Aldersgate said in 1633 that it did not charge double fees to strangers or sojourners: McMurray, *Records of two city parishes*, pp. 92–3.

cases, at the churchwardens' or vestry's discretion. The friends or executors of Barbara Johnson, 'being inmate', were charged 23s. 4d. for her burial at St Helen's in 1599, but in the same parish in 1602 Mrs Collyns, from Bucklersbury, was buried for 11s. 8d., 'which should be double dutyes by these auditors agreed upon single', perhaps because her mother had been buried in the same place.[73] Being a stranger did not exclude one from a good location, if one could afford it. St Bride Fleet Street listed the price for strangers' burials in the church (20s.), in the side aisle of the chancel (30s.), and in the middle aisle of the chancel (£3), indicating that even the most prestigious places were for sale.[74] At St Stephen Walbrook, Andrew Backcliffe, stranger, and his son were buried in the middle of the north aisle of the church; Richard Goldman, alderman of Norwich, was buried under the communion table; Elizabeth Thacham, widow and stranger, was buried in the chancel.[75] The parishes in the western suburb and Westminster, where gentry, nobility, court employees, and legal professionals lived, had an awkward problem, since these individuals might be recent incomers or part-time residents, technically strangers, but nevertheless so distinguished and powerful that their claims to burial space in the church could not be passed over.[76]

Traditions in Paris seem to have been rather different. The notion of parishioner versus stranger is rarely made explicit in the records of the parishes, in the way that it was in London, though there was a distinction in price in some parishes: Saint-André-des-Arts charged those 'non domicillies' 30 *livres* for burial in church (as opposed to 20 *livres* for parishioners), and also insisted that they hire the best hangings, hearsecloth, and bellringing.[77] More generally, there appears to have been less loyalty to the parish of residence, owing to a number of factors. Obviously, the practice of conventual burial could and did continue through the period, so that the 'devotional' choice might be in favour of a religious order or place of cult, but it also appears to have been more common than it was in London to choose burial in another parish church. The role of the Innocents, both a parish churchyard and a civic focus attracting burials from other parishes, was no doubt important in weakening the primacy of the parish of residence as the place of burial; so too was the historical development of the Parisian parochial structure, less territorially coherent and with filial relationships between certain parishes, so

[73] GL, MS 6836, ff. 60v–61, 65v; *Registers of St Helen Bishopsgate*, pp. 262, 264.
[74] GL, MS 9531/13, pt. 2, ff. 372v–373v.   [75] *Registers of St Stephen Walbrook*, pp. 89–91.
[76] J. F. Merritt, 'Religion, government and society in early modern Westminster, *c*. 1525–1625' (Unpublished Ph.D. thesis, University of London, 1992).
[77] AN, LL 687, f. 184.

that individuals might look to the mother church, rather than the daughter parish in which they lived, for their burial. Probably of greatest importance, though, was the strength of family ties and the consciousness of lineage among the Parisian élite. While London's civic élite experienced a rapid turnover, often lasting not more than three generations in the city, families in Paris's professional and municipal élites seem to have survived much longer. In the sixteenth century, 'the highest city offices were dominated by a small nucleus of interrelated families', who were markedly successful at gaining and retaining office within their lineages.[78] The practice of selling offices and status or resigning in favour of a designated other helped to consolidate and retain wealth and position in the hands of a limited group, and their continued dependence on the circles of power and patronage associated with the royal government kept them in Paris, even when they acquired rural estates. A long-lived Paris-based élite established tombs and chapels in parish and conventual churches to which their more scattered descendants returned for burial. It is likely that there was considerable movement of this kind, at least into the larger and wealthier parishes where traditions of family burial had been established. However, attachment to a family place of burial was presumably at the expense of attachment and commitment to the community of residence, if that was different, and suggests that the Parisian élite put family loyalties above local ties.

The development of tombs and chapels is discussed below, in chapter 6, but the practice of removing bodies from one parish for burial elsewhere is well attested even when the circumstances of an individual burial are not known. Ninety-four people (out of a total of 1,636 recorded) were taken from the parish of Saint-André-des-Arts for burial in one of twenty-six other parishes. The largest number (twenty-one) were buried at Saint-Séverin, close geographically and the dominant church on the left bank; twelve more were buried in other left-bank parish churches. Ten were buried in churches on the Ile de la Cité and forty-three on the right bank, including ten in Saint-Germain-l'Auxerrois and seven in Saint-Eustache. Where any motive can be identified, it was to be buried with family: four cases of burial 'avec ses ancêtres' were noted, and in twenty-six cases the individual shared a family name with at least one other person taken there from Saint-André-des-Arts. Similarly, at least 200 of those buried in the church of Saint-André between 1550 and 1670 had been brought in from other parishes. They came from twenty-four other Parisian parishes and fourteen places outside Paris, but as before the left-bank parishes were important: twenty came from each of Saint-Séverin and Saint-Sulpice,

---

[78] Diefendorf, *Paris city councillors*, esp. pp. 33–42.

nineteen from Saint-Cosme, and ten from Saint-Benoît.[79] Some of these transported bodies may simply have been parishioners who happened to die away from home, but the great majority were residents of other places who were brought to Saint-André to be buried with parents, other ancestors, or family. They included M. Séguier, *prévôt de Paris*, marquis de Saint-Brisson, who died in 'sa paroisse' of Saint-Jean-en-Grève in 1653 but was buried in the chapel of the Séguier family in Saint-André-des-Arts.[80] The individuals recorded reflect the antiquaries' genealogical interests, so the picture is skewed, but it is clear that several families maintained an interest in burial at Saint-André after they had moved away, and that descendants and connections shared in this. At least half of those brought to Saint-André for burial shared a family name or descent with others formerly or currently resident in the parish.[81] In 1763 members of the du Tillet family, who had long since left the parish, said that they maintained the same attachment to the parish church, and to their family chapel in it, as had their ancestors who were resident there.[82]

Managing burial in church

In accepting burials within their churches, the vestrymen of the London and Paris parishes found themselves faced with conflicting demands. They needed to balance the demand for burial space against the requirements of the liturgy and worship, to accommodate burials within an enclosed space without creating an intolerable environmental problem, to make the best use of space and yet treat the process of burial with proper respect, and to satisfy the demands of present and future parishioners without offending the families of those who had already obtained burial there. Of fundamental importance to the outcome of these conflicts was the fact that the members of the vestries were themselves part of the parish élite, from the class normally buried in church. As vestrymen, they were inclined to protect their interests as prospective consumers of burial space. They were certainly not prepared to oppose burial in church on principle, both because of the money it brought in to the parish, and because they themselves hoped to be buried there. One London parish where vestrymen explicitly favoured themselves was St Bride Fleet Street. For burial in two out of three named locations in the church (the side

---

[79] BN, MS Fr. 32589.   [80] Ibid., 9 October 1653.

[81] Ibid. Precise figures would be impossible to calculate, given the selective nature of the source. My estimate is based on noting surnames, married women's maiden names, and mother's maiden names, as well as phrases such as 'avec ses majeurs', and the antiquaries' marginal notes linking individuals.

[82] AN, L 632/40.

aisles of the chancel, and the body of the church) churchwardens and
'such as have borne office' paid 15s. and 10s. respectively, while those
who had not so served paid 20s. for either. The distinction was carried
through to the audible signal of status, the peal of bells, which cost 4s.
for an officeholder, past or present, and 8s. for all others, while the great
bell was only to be tolled for officeholders and other parishioners and
strangers 'of good ability'.[83] In Paris, the *marguilliers* of Saint-André-des-
Arts exempted themselves and the priests and beadles of the church from
charges for opening the ground and for bells and the hire of hangings and
silverware; almost all the grantees and proprietors of private chapels in
Saint-Gervais, highly desirable sites of burial, had been *marguilliers*.[84]

However, while parish officers were on the whole socially and politically
superior to those who were buried in churchyards, and could deal with
the issues of burial there with some pragmatism, they were not necessarily in such a position of authority in relation to the general constituency
of those who would be buried in church. Clerks, sextons, and *fossoyeurs*,
though of modest status themselves, may have wielded quite a lot of influence over the burials of the very modest, but could hardly be admitted
to do so in respect of those buried in church. It was also true of churchwardens, who as the officers of the parish made decisions about burials as
they happened, as opposed to the vestry who made policy. The working
churchwardens or *marguilliers comptables* were usually men of solid standing in their parishes, but outranked in authority by the members of the
vestry or *fabrique* and in status by notable and *noble* parishioners. When
it came to burials in church, therefore, in both London and Paris, it is
likely that vestries and churchwardens would have found their control of
the process compromised by the power, importance, and special interests
of some of those seeking burial there.

The first issue facing vestries and churchwardens was how physically
to accommodate all those who asked for burial in the church. The policy
of charging higher fees for a grave (and the accompanying services and
accoutrements) in church must have helped to keep the numbers down
to some extent, but it could at most reduce, not halt, the flow. Practical
measures, such as the sparing use of space, and diligent noting of the
location of burials, helped to make the most of what space there was.
Implementing these measures would not necessarily generate records of
a permanent nature, but a few London parish clerks used their registers
to record locations in great detail, with memoranda of space still available. The register of St Helen Bishopsgate, around 1600, records burial

[83] GL, MS 9531/13, pt. 2, ff. 372v–373v.
[84] AN, LL 687, f. 184v; Brochard, *Saint-Gervais. Histoire du monument*, pp. 136–7.

locations with such details as 'in the middest of the ile before the par-
dondore, [his] feete lyeth even with Mr Robinson's head, being vj tyles
in bredth distance', while other parish clerks noted, for example, 'that
rome is full but closse to the pues side under the stone [there is] rome'.[85]
Provision might be made for later use of the same grave pit: the clerk of
St Clement Eastcheap noted in 1623 that William Momforde was buried
'very deepe, so that one may bee laid in the same grave', and that one
was buried 'upon Mrs Robinson before buried in the same grave and one
more may bee laid there'.[86]

'Burial in church' could have several different physical realities. In its
simplest form it meant interment, with or without a coffin, in natural
ground under the floor of the church. The words 'pit' and 'laystall', and
the phrase 'for breaking the ground', commonly used in London churchwardens' accounts for graves and gravemaking, imply the excavation of
natural ground for burial, even though the phrase 'I remit my body to
the earth from whence it came', used in wills, cannot always be taken
literally.[87] Bodies buried in earth under the church floor could be expected to decompose in a reasonable time, allowing re-use of the space
after moving or removing any bones. A variant of simple interment was
to be placed, probably coffined, in a narrow vault or lined grave dug
into the ground, in which decomposition, and hence reduction in mass,
could also be expected to occur, if more slowly.[88] These were probably the
commonest and most practical implementations of the idea. The London
churchwardens' accounts contain frequent references to covering, tiling,
or paving graves, and to purchases of lime, sand and mortar; sometimes
also graves were filled up with earth.[89]

Coffins, an item of conspicuous consumption, and one that displays
wealth and the power to waste, were most likely to be used by those being
buried, more expensively, in church.[90] Even here, though, they were far

---

[85] *Registers of St Helen Bishopsgate*, p. 263; *Registers of St Olave Hart Street*, p. 144.

[86] *Registers of St Clement Eastcheap*, p. 175.

[87] See e.g. Overall, *Accounts of the churchwardens of St Michael Cornhill*, pp. 223–4, for 'takyng up of the stone', 'makyng of the pytt', 'brekeing the grounde', and 'laynge doune the stone', 1521. For 'I remit my body to the earth', cf. Harding, 'And one more', p. 114.

[88] C. Daniell, *Death and burial in medieval England* (London, 1997), notes that rates of decomposition, with and without coffins, are very variable. A sealed coffin may arrest the process, but an unsealed one, or one that itself rots or collapses, will not. Coffins may disintegrate completely, leaving no trace but a stain in the soil or a few coffin nails: pp. 119–21, 162–4.

[89] E.g. GL, MS 6836, ff. 1v–2, 24, 51, 56.

[90] John Aubrey noted that Sir William Davenant, buried at Westminster Abbey in 1668, had a walnut coffin, 'the finest that ever [his informant] sawe', but this was clearly exceptional, and surely intentionally showy: *Aubrey's Brief Lives*, pp. 85–8.

from universal in the first half of the sixteenth century.[91] For uncoffined burials, parishes and fraternities lent hearses and coffins, to serve for the vigil, transport, and funeral, retrieving them before the interment. Parish accounts and inventories contain many references to these coffins.[92] But some were already being buried in their own coffins: in 1540–1 a coffined burial in the church of St Mary Woolnoth was charged 10s., and one not coffined 6s. 8d.[93] The distinction must have been made because a coffined burial took up more space and for longer, but it was soon replaced by the expectation that all church burials would and should be coffined. The vestry of St Helen Bishopsgate decided in 1563 that none should be buried in church unless coffined in wood, and a review of London burial fees in *c*. 1592 implies that coffined burial in church was the norm, since it distinguishes between coffined and uncoffined burials in churchyards but not in churches.[94]

But 'burial in church' could also mean being stored, in a coffin, in spaces in the walls or under the floor, in which there was no contact with the earth. This was necessarily so for churches which stood over cellars or vaults, not on natural ground, such as St Mary Colechurch and All Hallows Honey Lane, but it applied to vault burials as well. In such cases the process of decay was contained within the coffin, and it is difficult to see how re-use of these locations could be accomplished inoffensively. Where proper burial vaults were established, in which several coffins could be stacked, the aim was clearly not to allow decay and re-use of space but to preserve indefinitely, in a durable shell, the mortal remains.[95] At St Mary Colechurch there were four or five burials a year in the church in the early seventeenth century, with more in plague years. The clerk listed burials in numerous sites, such as 'in the churche by the longe pewe under the lofte', 'in the darke entrie at the further ende on the churche side', 'in the churche under the lofte in the seconde place upon Mrs Gibson' or even 'at the foote of Mr Foster lieing in the 4 place from the north waulle at the 24 pew on the north sied close besied Mr Phillips'. All of these coffins must have been fitted into spaces in the walls or

[91] Katherine Bracy, widow, was buried in the church of St Nicholas Shambles in 1543, in a winding-sheet that cost 20d.: *Consistory Court Wills*, 178.

[92] GL, MS 2968/1, ff. 105 ff (1533–4), 159 ff (1553–4); Overall, *Churchwardens' accounts of St Michael Cornhill*, p. 112.

[93] GL MS 1002/1A, f. 6v. Gittings notes that church burials in her provincial samples were often but not invariably coffined: *Death, burial and the individual*, p. 115.

[94] GL, MS 6836, p. 268; LPL, CM IX/45.

[95] Cf. Litten, *English way of death*, pp. 195–226; Reeve and Adams, *The Spitalfields project*, vol. I: *The archaeology*.

between the floor of the church and the ceiling of the tavern below it.[96] The size, shape, and material of coffins thus came to be very important. The gabled or 'peaked' coffin may have been the predominant medieval form, but in increasingly crowded churches it was inconvenient and wasteful of space, and it seems to have been replaced by flat-lidded coffins rather earlier in London than elsewhere in England.[97] The vestry of St Mary Colechurch determined in 1615 that 'none shall be buried in our church in a ridged coffin but in a square flat coffin, which may be no hindrance to the burial of two corps in one grave if need be'.[98] Stepney parish also ruled in 1629 that only flat coffins should be used in church.[99] The chronology in Paris is less clear, but vestries shared the same pre-occupations: at Saint-André-des-Arts in 1687, the gravedigger was paid 4 *livres* for handling an ordinary six-foot coffin, but 5 *livres* for those 'faicts en dome'.[100]

The increase in the use of coffins has been attributed to 'an increased sensitivity towards human decomposition...a growing concept of the self and its individuality'.[101] It did at least disguise the reality of the post-mortem body, for burial both inside and outside churches, but there may be different interpretations of this. Denise Leveson requested in 1560 that her body be 'not seared [= cered, or wrapped in a waxed shroud] but enclosed after a convenient manner in a coffin of boards' before being buried in the middle aisle of St Andrew Undershaft, but it is not clear whether she saw the coffin as more or less likely to preserve and protect her corpse.[102] Coffin burial could not in any case guarantee that the body would remain undisturbed, nor could it promise exclusive use of space. In the short term coffined burials would be doubled up, as noted above; in the longer term most wooden coffins would decay. Pepys' report of his conversation with the sexton, when he went to discuss his brother's burial in the church of St Bride Fleet Street, drives home the point: 'see how a man's tombes are at the mercy of such a fellow, that for 6d. he would (as his own words were) "I will justle them together but I will make room for him" – speaking of the fullness of the middle Isle where he was to lie'. Pepys' brother was certainly coffined and so no doubt were the earlier burials on the site.[103]

---

[96] GL, MS 4438, entries for 4 and 14 Jan. 1622/3, 6 Jan. 1623/4, 5 May 1626.
[97] Litten, *English way of death*, pp. 88–99. Litten suggests that the gable-lidded coffin gave way to the flat-lidded type around 1660–75, but it was clearly recognised as inconvenient earlier than that in London.
[98] GL, MS 66, f. 14.   [99] Hill and Frere, *Memorials of Stepney parish*, p. 130.
[100] AN, LL 687, ff. 183r–184.   [101] Gittings, *Death, burial and the individual*, p. 114.
[102] PRO, PROB 11/43, f. 463.
[103] S. Pepys, *The Diary of Samuel Pepys 1660–69*, ed. R. Latham and W. Matthews, 11 vols., (London, 1970–83), vol. V, pp. 87, 90.

Though rarer than wooden coffins, lead coffins were occasionally used before the start of the period, and probably quite widely by the end. At first they were of the 'anthropoid' type, closely wrapping or modelling the corpse they contained; these leaden forms may well have been enclosed in wooden box coffins for burial.[104] As with wooden coffins, the increasing use of lead probably represented a trickle-down or emulation effect, starting with royalty and the nobility, whose prolonged funeral ceremonies necessitated an effective preservative measure.[105] One élite Parisian testator of the early seventeenth century specified a lead coffin because of fears that the 'mauvaise odeur' of the corpse would otherwise deter those ordained to transport it from doing so.[106] Lead coffins were much more expensive than wooden ones, and formed part of a lavish and ostentatious approach to the funeral as a whole. Sir Nicholas Bacon, Lord Keeper, was buried at St Paul's in 1578 in a lead coffin costing £5 4s. 9d. inside an elm shell costing only 15s.[107] But lead coffins also had a larger implication for views of the body after death: a sealed lead coffin could preserve the body inside it indefinitely, arresting the endogenous process of decay, or at least concealing it from the observer.[108] Binski points to the relationship between effigies (especially tomb sculptures, but perhaps also including funeral effigies), which deny decay, and *transi* tombs, which reveal or represent it.[109] The use of anthropoid lead coffins, which simultaneously model the body's natural form and counter its expected, natural fate, could add a further dimension to this. The subsequent popularity of the lead box coffin, reproducing the standard wooden form, also has interesting implications. Such coffins, used in vault and chapel burials, were not lost to sight, but could be expected to be seen after deposition, when the vaults were opened to admit further coffins of the same kind. Though the bodily form of the anthropoid coffin was lost, the body inside a box coffin was increasingly carefully preserved, dressed, and presented, as in sleep, creating an image of the dead as hidden but unchanging.[110]

---

[104] Litten, *English way of death*, pp. 90–5. Sir Richard Whittington (d. 1423) was said to have been buried in a 'Leaden sheet': Stow, *Survey*, vol. I, p. 243. Two lead coffins of this type, probably of the seventeenth century, from Mercers' Chapel, are preserved in the Museum of London. See plate 7.

[105] Cf. Gittings, *Death, burial and the individual*, p. 216; Paul S. Fritz, 'From "public" to "private": the royal funerals in England, 1500–1830', in Whaley (ed.), *Mirrors of mortality*, pp. 61–79.

[106] Cited in P. Landier, *mémoire de maîtrise*, p. 40.

[107] Bodl. MS Ashmole 836, pp. 21–36.

[108] Cf. Daniell, *Death and burial in medieval England*, pp. 119–20.

[109] Binski, *Medieval death*, p. 149.

[110] Litten, *English way of death*, chs. 4 and 5, pp. 57–118; Reeve and Adams, *The Spitalfields project*, vol. I: *The archaeology*; R. Janaway, 'An introductory guide to textiles from 18th and 19th century burials', in Cox (ed.), *Grave concerns*, pp. 17–32.

Leaden Coffin discovered on the 22 June 1808 in a Vault
in the Chancel of S.t Helens Church.
Length 6 feet 4 Inches, Width 2 feet 2 Inches . —
Publish'd 22 July 1808 by R.Wilkinson N.o 58 Cornhill

7 Anthropoid lead coffin of Alderman Sir John Spencer, clothworker,
former Lord Mayor (d. 1610), as found in 1808, in a vault in the church
of St Helen Bishopsgate. Anonymous drawing, 1808 (London, Guildhall Library).

Corpses wrapped or coffined in lead posed several major problems. Their weight and bulk made them awkward to handle; Parisian *fossoyeurs* were paid more for doing so.[111] More significant, however, was the fact that lead coffins were permanent and irreducible, a continuing material presence in the ground or vault. If wooden coffins were a compromise between short-term decency and long-term dissolution, lead coffins guaranteed the former at the expense of the latter. The Londoner who in 1580 willed that his body 'be wrapped in lead and buried in the church of All Hallows the Great at the side of the pew where I used to sit' was precluding the possibility of other burials in that spot at any time in the foreseeable future.[112] For this reason, several churches either banned the use of lead coffins for burial in the generality of the church, or charged double for allowing it. The vestry of Saint-André-des-Arts in 1625 decreed that lead coffins could only be used for burial by those who had chapels or vaults, 'attendu l'incommodité qui est causée par lesdites cercueils de plomb'.[113] There may also have been a counter-cultural opposition to their use, seeing them as a symbol of self-importance, an attempt to impose a permanent substitute 'body' on the community. In his will made in 1651, the *curé* of Saint-Gervais expressly forbade that he be buried in a lead coffin, asking for burial in the choir of the church 'sans pompe ceremonye ny aulcune tanture'.[114] The added expense must also have deterred some. Lead coffins could not in any case absolutely guarantee bodily safety: the *fossoyeur* of the Innocents was prosecuted for stealing a lead coffin in 1509, and in 1601 the gravemakers of St Dunstan in the West were charged with opening a grave in the church at night, and taking up and selling a lead coffin, together with an hourglass, a handkerchief, and a garland of flowers.[115] But these must have been exceptional incidents, and given that wooden coffins were certainly no defence against disturbance, even in church, lead coffins may have seemed increasingly attractive to most people. They became common, and possibly nearly universal, for vault burial in the later seventeenth and eighteenth centuries; in Britain the use of lead coffins for intramural burial was made mandatory in 1813.[116]

The examination of burial in church has raised a number of new issues. Though only available to a minority of the population, it was nevertheless an important area of contest, negotiation, and development which

---

[111] AN, LL 687, f. 185.   [112] GL, MS 9051/4, f. 197v.

[113] AN, LL 686, ff. 64v–65; AN, LL 805, pp. 253–5.

[114] Brochard, *Saint-Gervais. Histoire du monument*, pp. 359–62.

[115] AN, 570/4, no. 4; GL MS 3016/1, p. 40.

[116] M. Cox, *Life and death in Spitalfields, 1700–1850* (York, 1996), pp. 99–101.

brings out many of the concerns of this study. It had a long history, as a privilege won from a reluctant clergy but claimed over the centuries by an increasingly large number of people, and it continued to be desired even when, in England, the religious rationale that had justified it was undermined. Parish churches were places of memory and affective association as well as cult, and these remained strong motives for seeking burial there. Those wishing for burial in church were seeking to locate themselves in the heart of the community, to express a continuing membership of the congregation, and in part to benefit from the accumulation of spiritual merit in that location.[117] To some extent they repaid this by their bequests and donations, and Howard Colvin believes that the concession of burial rights was mutually beneficial,[118] but the balance was probably unequal. Vestries had a somewhat ambivalent attitude towards church burial, recognising it as a source of income and prestige but also as the progressive alienation of an important and finite resource; they could not wholly reconcile their personal interest in allowing the practice to continue with their official responsibility to limit its impact.

Church burial also highlights the interaction of two important themes: the hierarchy of space, and its translation into price. The spaces of churches were divided visibly and invisibly, and imbued with meanings and associations. There was a shared sense of a hierarchy of desirability for spiritual reasons of different spaces, but over time this was submerged in a more obvious and easily apprehended hierarchy of social desirability. At the same time, the complex criteria of status and eligibility for church burial, based on traditional ideas of community membership and entitlement, began to give way to pragmatic distinctions of wealth; strangers were welcome, if and because they paid a high price. Burial space, like so many other features of the early modern city, did in effect become a commodity that could be bought and sold. The growing use of lead coffins and preservative measures, by extending the physical existence of the dead, increased the difficulties faced by the vestries and emphasised the conflict between the private interest and the public, as well as between the interests of the dead and of the living.

[117] See above, pp. 127–9.
[118] H. M. Colvin, *Architecture and the afterlife* (London, 1991), p. 192.

6 'A fine and private place': burial chapels, vaults, and tombs

The original justification for being buried in church was that proximity to holy things and activities conferred spiritual benefits. Over time, it came to seem that an important aspect of securing these benefits was drawing attention to the fact of burial and protecting the individual grave site against future disturbance. By the early modern period, it had long been the case that a small number of people had been able to do this, obtaining church burial for themselves, and ensuring identification and commemoration with tombs and monuments. However, as populations grew and the practice spread more widely socially, it began to transform the idea of the church as a public or communally owned space. In a certain sense all those who asked for burial in church were claiming for themselves alone a portion of a space in which the whole community had rights and interests. But as first wooden coffins, then lead ones, and private burial vaults, became more common, the claim made by the dead became more substantial and more long-lasting. Effectively, certain areas of churches became private domains. The increasing numbers of large funeral monuments also made a permanent claim to space, and to the attention of succeeding generations. The meaning of vaults and monuments was continually reactivated as they were used, amended, or repaired by later generations. Equally, even when the physical space taken was minimal, those who were buried in church were still affecting the use of the larger space when they placed stones and epitaphs calling on the attention of other users of the church. Funeral services and the repeated performance of masses, anniversaries, and chantries, exploited the sanctified environment of the church for the benefit of particular individuals. Although such services could augment and enrich the parish's worship, by subsidising the numbers of clerical staff and the elaboration of music and liturgical accompaniments, they also allowed individual interests to shape collective practices. Where memorial services were said over the grave of the donor, claims to space, time, and attention reinforced one another.

The urban setting was undoubtedly important to the way church burial and monumental commemoration developed in London and Paris. It was a fertile field for competitive display and conspicuous consumption. The élite population's anxieties about status and the fragility of worldly success could be partly assuaged by material commemoration; their political, economic, and social rivalries found one outlet in the construction of personal and family tombs and chapels. Wealth, access to high-quality craftsmanship, and a taste for symbolic display, allowed such commemoration to take elaborate and durable monumental form. Growing urban populations, high mortality rates, and the limited opportunity for structural expansion of church buildings intensified the pressure on and competition for space. The world at large was constantly reminded of the élite dead and their continuing physical presence and action among and upon the living, and it may be seen as another way in which a social élite could secure power and privilege to themselves. The effects that this competition for space and attention had on the traditional space of the church attracted adverse comment from a number of contemporaries.

Chapels

The building, enlargement, and restoration of parish churches were always projects in which both private and collective interests played a part. Similarly, the addition or assignment of chapels was part of a complicated bargaining between the individual and the community. Paul Binski notes the private and 'inherently anti-communal' nature of chantry chapels in the middle ages, especially perhaps cage chapels, located within a larger space but literally fencing off a private enclosure.[1] In medieval London and Paris, chapels dedicated to particular cults or saints had been added to or created within the structures of the parish churches, supported by endowments and by the devotion of individuals and confraternities.[2] The loss of many of the buildings limits our appreciation of the appearance and impact of these chapels, but in many cases their foundation and use are quite well documented.

There were numerous chantry endowments, fraternities, and dedicated altars in medieval London churches, but there may not have been very many structurally distinct private chapels.[3] The surviving church of St Helen Bishopsgate has two such chapels, dating from the late

---

[1] Binski, *Medieval death*, p. 120.

[2] *VCH London*, vol. I, pp. 213–15; B. Plongeron, *Le diocèse de Paris*, vol. I: *Des origines à la Révolution* (Histoire des diocèses de France, XX, Paris, 1987), pp. 192–7.

[3] Cf. *VCH London*, vol. I, pp. 205–7; Kitching, *The London and Middlesex chantry certificate of 1548*; C. M. Barron, 'The parish fraternities of medieval London', in C. M. Barron and C. Harper-Bill (eds.), *The church in pre-Reformation society. Essays in honour of F. R. H. du Boulay* (Woodbridge, 1985), pp. 13–37.

fourteenth century, dedicated to the Holy Ghost and St Mary.[4] Among others documented but not surviving was a chapel of St Stephen, 'made and ordeyned' by William Cambridge on the north part of the church of St Mary at Hill, where he was buried in 1431.[5] Stow reports that Sir William Capel, mayor (d. 1509), built a chapel on the south side of St Bartholomew the Little, where he and Sir Giles Capel were buried; Sir James Yarford, mayor (d. 1527), was buried 'under a fayre Tombe with his Ladie in a speciall chappell by him builded, on the North side of the Quire' of St Michael Bassishaw. Sir Hugh Brice, goldsmith, however, who built a charnel chapel at St Mary Woolnoth, was buried in the body of the church in 1496.[6] Constraints on space may have been one reason for the rarity of separate chapels; the considerable cost another. Stow's account highlights the élite status of founders, and it may be that only the increasingly wealthy merchants of London could support such expense. After the Reformation, with the abolition of chantries, private masses, and services for the dead, there was less reason – certainly no theological justification – for building or maintaining private burial chapels, though there are instances in other parts of the country.[7] The communal, devotional impulse to improve and beautify parish churches also weakened, though there was perhaps more of this than has been acknowledged hitherto.[8]

A major feature of parish worship and burial practice in early modern Paris, however, was the proliferation of private chapels, assigned to individual families or interests, and used by them as private burial spaces. The parish community, or its representatives, pursued the objective of enlarging and adorning the church by conceding spaces and rights over them to wealthy individuals, or by encouraging the latter to build new chapels opening into the church. This was not, to begin with, very different from medieval practice, but promoted on a larger scale it came to reshape the churches both physically and as experienced spaces. The aim of the exercise, from the would-be proprietor's point of view, was to secure a burial place for himself or herself and his or her family, in a place associated with the performance of dedicated commemorative services. Such was the case of Jacques Mercade, 'premier sommelier du corps du roy', and his wife, Jehanne Chanteprime, who founded a chapel in the church of Saint-Gervais at the end of the fifteenth century. He and some of their

[4] RCHM, *City of London*, pp. 19–20.
[5] Littlehales, *Medieval records of a London city church*, p. 14.
[6] Stow, *Survey*, vol. I, pp. 185, 205, 289.
[7] Examples of chapels of the nobility and gentry are illustrated in Litten, *English way of death*, pp. 185, 191. See also Spicer, '"Defyle not Christ's kirke with your carrion"', pp. 149–69.
[8] J. F. Merritt, 'Puritans, Laudians, and the phenomenon of church-building in Jacobean London', *Historical Journal* 41.4 (1998), 935–60.

children were buried there, and she, in 1500, came to a formal agreement with the parish over the chapel's use. It was to remain forever to the memory of the benefactors and their descendants, who were to keep a key for access to the chapel, and could have services said, be buried there, and make devotional *tableaux* and so on as necessary for their devotions, without interference. The sum paid for this grant is not recorded, but the chapel was to be repaired at the parish's expense thereafter.[9]

One of the best-documented sequences of chapel foundations is at Saint-André-des-Arts, where an eighteenth-century enquiry into the present-day proprietorship of the chapels produced a mass of reports and depositions.[10] Several chapels had been founded in the church before 1500, but the number and probably the aesthetic and architectural importance of the chapels increased significantly in the sixteenth and seventeenth centuries. By the mid-eighteenth century the church, originally a simple rectangle, had eighteen or nineteen chapels forming a row of cells along the south and north sides. Most of these had been assigned to families for burial and the performance of commemorative services. The majority dated structurally from the sixteenth and seventeenth centuries; some had been built *ab initio* by the families, others taken over and their repair or rebuilding subsidised.[11] One of the earliest recorded concessions of this sequence dates from 1518, when Olivier Alligret came to the parish assembly and offered 500 *livres tournois* to finish building the second chapel begun in the church by the side of the rue des Deux Portes, in return for the grant of 'siège et sépulture' there for himself, his wife, and successors. The assembly debated and agreed to the offer and Alligret expressed his gratitude. The chapel was to be lockable, and Alligret could erect a tomb there where he and his family could be buried without paying anything further to the vestry. He was buried there in 1532, his wife in 1548.[12] Similarly, in 1522 the parish accepted an offer from Mathieu Chartier, *avocat en parlement*, of 200 *livres tournois* to finish constructing a chapel 'which otherwise would not be completed', to be granted to him, his wife, family, and heirs in perpetuity. Chartier was to furnish the chapel, making seating, burials, etc. as he wished. He also endowed two weekly masses there, to be followed by the anthems and prayers *de profundis, inclina*, and *fidelium* (part of the liturgy of the dead), and with sprinkling of holy water over the graves of any buried in the chapel. He and his wife Jeanne Brinon subsequently endowed other

[9] AN, LL 756, ff. 272–274v.
[10] AN, L 631–3, S 3308–10, S* 3311, S* 3312.
[11] J. Lebeuf, *Histoire de la ville et de tout le diocèse de Paris*, 3 vols. (new edn. by H. Cocheris, Paris, 1863–7), vol. III (1867), pp. 28–35, 275–83.
[12] AN, L 632/42.

services there, and both were buried there, she in 1554 and he in 1559.[13] Enthusiasm remained high, and demand for private chapels exceeded supply. In the late sixteenth century the la Guesle and Ysambert families both claimed possession of the chapel of Saint-Laurent, founded by Yves Cautel in 1538. The dispute took some years to resolve, but in 1605 the la Guesle accepted the parish's offer of the chapel of Saint-Pierre instead, leaving the Ysambert in possession of the chapel of Saint-Laurent.[14]

In the early seventeenth century, the parish wished to enlarge the church but could not afford to do so at its own cost. The vestry called a meeting of the parishioners in 1617, and they decided to grant a chapel to whomever would give most for the building. *Noble homme* Claude Gallard, notary, and his wife Marguerite Mandat were the winners of this competition, offering 5,000 *livres* in cash and 300 *livres* in goods. The churchwardens agreed to build a chapel 13 ft long by 6 ft wide, matching the design and materials of the adjoining chapel of the Chartier family. Under the chapel was to be built a vault (*cave voutée*) for the burial of Gallard, his wife, and their heirs and assigns; no other person was to have a claim to burial there. The chapel was to belong to Gallard and his successors, so they could hear service in the church and have masses said in the chapel whenever they wished. It was to be enclosed with a balustrade or closure that would allow those outside to see the priest celebrating mass.[15] In the same year M. du Tillet offered 5,000 *livres* and an annual rent of 20 *livres* for a chapel to be built for him.[16] A different arrangement, but with a similar result, was made in 1618 with the Guillon family, who paid 160 *livres tournois* to the vestry but undertook to pay for the building work themselves, employing a named mason and agreeing to match the dimensions of the Chartier chapel and other building specifications. They were to be entitled to place their arms inside and outside the chapel, and to have exclusive rights to its use for services and burial.[17]

Almost all the chapels in Saint-André-des-Arts were assigned in this way, and the parish was not unique in this enterprise. A similar pattern of patronage, negotiation, and concession was used to expand the church of Saint-Gervais in two main phases in the sixteenth and seventeenth centuries. Unable to rebuild the church all at once, the vestry decided to 'dilate' it, extending its wall outwards into the churchyard by building or conceding the right to build chapels.[18] Christophe de Carmone requested

[13] AN, L 632/27–8.
[14] AN, L 633/6, 8; AN, LL 686, pt. 1, f. 49r (no. 62), ff. 50r–51 (no. 63).
[15] AN, L 632/1.   [16] AN, LL 686, pt. 2, f. 46r (no. 118), f. 58v (no. 135).
[17] AN, L 632/16.
[18] This enlargement, in a private interest, was of course at the expense of the larger communal interest in the churchyard space. See above, chapter 3.

the first of these, the chapel of the Madeleine, in 1500, and was himself buried there after its completion in 1507. His descendants claimed exclusive burial rights there from 1609.[19] In the seventeenth century a new line of private chapels, sometimes referred to as *charniers* (emphasising their mortuary purpose), was built along the north side of the church to cover tombs and secure burial vaults for a number of families; a number of 'lateral' chapels were fitted within the bays of the church structure. Patrons undertook to enclose and furnish the chapels and were allowed to excavate vaults for burial. Not every request was granted, or granted in full: the chapel of the Virgin was apparently sought after for private burial, but not conceded, and although the *ligueur* Pierre Acarie obtained the adjoining chapel of Notre-Dame de Souffrance in 1590, he had to continue to allow others access.[20] Saint-Jean-en-Grève likewise had at least thirteen chapels by 1690, most of which were assigned to families and used by them for burial.[21]

Chapel-building was a visible demonstration of devotion and the desire to multiply altars and masses: it may be significant that the parishes of Saint-André-des-Arts and Saint-Gervais were prominent centres of Catholic fervour and political action in the sixteenth century. The *curé* of Saint-André-des-Arts, Christophe Aubry, was a vocal and inflammatory preacher, strongly hostile to conciliation and the *politiques*, an opinion shared by Simon Vigor, who preached at Saint-Gervais. The parish of Saint-Gervais housed several *ligueurs* and the church was the centre of a cult of the Sacrament.[22] But in early modern Paris, as in Renaissance Florence, 'a chapel such as this was more than just a place of burial. In a society where several hundred rich and intensely competitive families lived in narrow streets . . . the need to express their corporate identity was strong.'[23] Those who obtained chapels were families of distinction, usually in municipal or royal service, obviously wealthy and concerned to establish or maintain a dynastic identity. Despite the expressions of deference and gratitude on the part of the concessionaries, they were also members of the group with which they negotiated: almost all the proprietors of chapels in Saint-Gervais had served as *marguilliers*, including four members of the Poussepin family in the sixteenth and seventeenth centuries.[24] Pierre Acarie was *marguillier* at the time he obtained the grant

[19] Brochard, *Saint-Gervais. Histoire du monument*, pp. 38–47, 114–15, 345–6.
[20] Ibid., pp. 48–56, 61–88, 100–50. For Acarie, cf. AN, LL 746, f. 165.
[21] AN, L 663/10, ff. 8–16.
[22] Roelker, *Paris of Henry of Navarre*, pp. 185–260, passim; Diefendorf, *Beneath the cross*, pp. 33, 45, 155.
[23] Colvin, *Architecture and the afterlife*, pp. 190–1 (referring to Florence).
[24] Brochard, *Saint-Gervais. Histoire du monument*, pp. 136–7, 138–9.

of the chapel of Notre-Dame de Souffrance for the burial of his mother.[25] The association of family and location went both backwards and forwards from the date of foundation, as the remains of ancestors, perhaps of a less-distinguished generation, were translated into new chapels or vaults. When *noble homme* François de Guillon was buried in his recently founded chapel in Saint-André-des-Arts in 1623, his father's body, buried elsewhere in the church some time before, was lifted and placed in the same vault.[26] Bodies were also moved from parish to parish, as when the Bourlon family, in 1600, had 'les corps et ossements' of their ancestors transported from the Innocents into their chapel in Saint-Eustache.[27] The rights to chapels were granted in perpetuity, and descended through the families and their collaterals, sometimes over several generations. In 1613 Louise d'Aligret, daughter and sole heir of François Aligret, principal heir and eldest son of Olivier Alligret, granted the 'chapelle des Aligrets' in Saint-André-des-Arts to Jerome de Montholon, *ecuyer*, and Renée de Florette his wife, probably Louise's daughter. Louise herself was buried in the Aligret chapel in 1615, though the Montholons soon after built another chapel which may have become their main place of burial.[28] At least eighteen people were buried in the chapel of the Chartiers between 1554 and 1624. One was a grandson of Mathieu Chartier; several others came from the collateral Buyer family. One of these was brought from the parish of Saint-Séverin, another from Saint-Paul.[29]

The fact that grants of this kind detracted from public control and use of the church, and that therefore the public interest was involved, was acknowledged in the procedures adopted and the language in which the concessions were recorded. The needs of the parish, and 'la commodité publique' of church enlargement were often cited in explanation, and the grantees expressed gratitude for 'l'honneur que on luy faisoit'.[30] It was thought important to consult the parish in general, to obtain their sanction. Seventy-one parishioners of Saint-Gervais were present at the meeting in 1500 that debated and approved Christophe de Carmone's offer to endow one of the new chapels, which he made 'for the love and devotion he has to the said church of which he was and is a parishioner, and for the augmentation of the chapels and buildings'.[31] In the eighteenth century, when the vestry of Saint-André-des-Arts was reviewing the present state of the chapels and their ownership, they took pains to defend the practice

[25] AN, LL 746, f. 165.   [26] BN, MS Fr. 32589, entries for 15 and 16 November 1623.
[27] AN, LL 434B, p. 79.
[28] AN, L 632/42, L 633/7; BN, MS Fr. 32589, entry for 19 October 1615.
[29] BN, MS Fr. 32589.   [30] AN, L 632/1, 42.
[31] Ibid.; Brochard, *Saint-Gervais. Histoire de la paroisse*, pp. 179–80; AN, LL 756, ff. 320–324v, 324v–327v, 327v–331v.

of such perpetual grants, which were neither 'vicious' nor the result of bad administration, it being natural for the parish to mark its gratitude to its benefactors in such a way. The present enquiry, they said, was primarily to identify those presently responsible for the charges attached to such foundations, and only secondarily to assert the parish's right to enter and re-grant the chapels if the perpetual grant had been annulled by the extinction of the persons to whose profit it was made.[32]

Nevertheless, as a result of repeated grants of this kind, an increasing proportion of the actual space of the church was made over to private uses. Whatever the arguments in favour of the practice from the point of view of the parish – a larger and more beautiful church, an augmented liturgical round, the engagement of powerful families as patrons – it emphasised and perhaps even furthered the stratification of Parisian society by class and lineage. The extreme pragmatism with which the majority were buried, in *fosses communes*, regularly emptied for re-use, contrasts starkly with the privilege of private, secure burial and long-term commemoration enjoyed by the few.

Private vaults

The Parisian chapels would have contained both tombs and monuments on the main level, and access to a burial vault. Julian Litten suggests that there were four main types of intramural burial vault in England between 1650 and 1850: 'the large dynastic vaults, either beneath a sidechapel or aisle, more usually associated with noble families; the family vaults, often not much more than a double- or triple-width brick-lined grave with its own barrelled roof, usually for the landed gentry; the single-width brick-lined grave, capped off by a ledger stone, a superior version of the family grave, patronized by the professional classes'; and the large private and parish vaults of the eighteenth century.[33] When the Parisian records speak of *caves*, as in 'la cave de la chapelle de M Chartier', 'mis en ladite cave', they are probably implying vaults of the first or second kinds. Burials are noted in *caves* in at least seven chapels in Saint-André-des-Arts,[34] but it is not always clear from the burial register extracts whether the coffin finally rested in the chapel itself or in the vault underneath it. The numbers involved suggest that the latter must have been more common. At least twenty members of the Le Clerc family were said to be buried in the chapel of Saint-Claude and Saint-Nicolas and in the chapel of

---

[32] AN, L 633/7, un-numbered papers.   [33] Litten, *English way of death*, pp. 207, 211.

[34] BN, MS Fr. 32589, Chartier (13 May 1583); Galoppe (3 December 1618); Guillon (15 November 1623); Joly (11 August 1631); Montholon (14 April 1632 and many subsequently); Saint-Laurent (7 December 1643); Thou (23 January 1646).

the Eight Hours (probably an alternative name for the same) between 1550 and 1650, and it seems likely that most were actually placed in a vault below it.[35] On the other hand, the 'sepulture ou tumbe' of Jacques Cottier stood in front of the altar in his chapel; prayers were said over the grave (*fosse*) of the widow of Jehan Bemon or Brinon in the chapel of Saint-Loy.[36]

Since all these vault burials must have been coffined, the process was more one of storage than literal inhumation or interment, though the word *inhumé* continued to be used. Lead coffins were probably increasingly common, if not universal. The regulations for fees at Saint-André-des-Arts priced the *fossoyeur*'s labour for moving a *bière de plomb* from the choir of the church (where the main funeral service would be said) into a chapel at 30 *sous*; he was also paid 5 *livres* for opening and replacing the tomb or *pierre de sépulture* in a chapel.[37] At Saint-Gervais in 1709 the *fossoyeur* was paid 15 *livres* 'pour la dessente du cercueil de plomb, ouverture de la cave et retablissement, chargement de carrosse et ais de plomb et autres choses necessaires'.[38] In the eighteenth century the vault of the chapel of the Trinity, of the Galoppe family, in Saint-André-des-Arts, was found to contain twenty lead coffins, including three small ones, and several others crushed or in pieces.[39]

Although the main aim of founding a chapel was to connect a family burial site with the performance of liturgical services for the benefit of those buried there, there were some cases where vaults and chapels were not physically linked. In Saint-Jean-en-Grève, the Montmagny family held the chapel of Saint-Nicolas, to the right of the choir, but access to their burial vault was behind the high altar near the sacristy. A black marble stone, with rings inset, covered the entrance to the vault; on it were engraved the names of six members of the family buried there at different times from 1525 to 1610.[40] Others wished or could afford to establish vaults only. Elizabeth Damours, widow of Michel de Lauzon, was refused permission in 1615 to make the vault (*cave* or *caveau*) she wanted in Saint-André-des-Arts, to contain the bodies of her husband, daughter, son-in-law, and in due course herself. The parish refused out of concern for the foundations of the church, and because the sum offered was too small to offset the costs and 'l'incommodité du publicq'. She was, however, able to endow a daily mass at an altar in the church, and three anniversary masses, and to place an epitaph to that effect. By the time of her own death in 1631 she had also evidently secured a burial vault as she had originally wished, though this may have been smaller than a chapel

[35] Ibid., passim.   [36] AN, LL 692, ff. 4–5, 28.
[37] AN LL 687 [f. 186] no. 259 (June 1687).   [38] AN, LL 752, f. 61v.
[39] AN, L 632/41.   [40] AN, L 663/6.

vault, closer to Litten's 'brick-lined grave', since no further burials there are noted.[41]

In post-Reformation London, it was also possible to establish a family burial vault or site, but since prayers and services for the dead had been abolished, there was no theological justification for linking this with an altar or chapel. Such vaults are likely to have conformed to Litten's second or third types, fairly limited in dimension. They were sometimes, but not invariably, structurally integral with the monuments or tombs commemorating the individual or family. William Kirwin, the Queen's master mason, may well have made his own 'comely alabaster tomb' in the midst of the church of St Helen Bishopsgate, as well as the vault in which he was buried in 1594. His second wife Magdalen joined him there in 1597; his son Benjamin, and five of Benjamin's children, were also buried in the vault.[42] Sir Julius Caesar Adelmare, Master of the Rolls, was buried in the same church in 1636, 'under Mr Williams' stone by the communion table'. In 1637 his widow was buried 'in the vault by her late husband', and, in all, five members of his household were buried in the same place. However, the altar tomb with a black marble slab on which Adelmare is commemorated appears to have been moved more than once.[43] Probably most London parish churches had one or more vaults of this kind, according to the wealth and numbers of the local élite, but although they focused family burials and excluded others, and were associated with monuments that made other claims on the congregation's attention and public space, they did not represent the same degree of privatisation as those in Paris. Nevertheless, their appropriation of a public resource was recognised in the terms and language of the negotiations for their grant. At St Helen Bishopsgate, the vestry in 1565 ordered that no 'vault or tombe' should be made in the church without composition with the churchwardens and parishioners.[44]

Vaults of this kind are distinct from Litten's fourth type, the vaults that parishes made or acquired for general use, subject to appropriate charges. There were several of these in early modern London churches, not all of them exclusively associated with burial. St Michael Cornhill allowed a vault under its south aisle to be used as a coal-house for some time before

[41] AN, LL 686 pt. 2, ff. 28v–29v (nos 98, 99); BN, MS Fr. 32589, entries for 4 November 1610, 20 December 1614, 30 January 1631.

[42] Munday et al., *Stow's Survey*, p. 180; *Registers of St Helen Bishopsgate*, pp. 260, 264, 269, 271, 280; RCHM *City of London*, p. 23; GL, MS 2480/2, p. 524.

[43] *Registers of St Helen Bishopsgate*, pp. 286, 288, 290; RCHM, *City of London*, p. 23 and pl. 127. It was presumably originally in the nave or chancel; according to J. E. Cox, *The annals of St Helen Bishopsgate* (London, 1876), p. 294, it was then in the south transept, but in 1929 it was in the nuns' choir: RCHM, *City of London*, p. 23.

[44] GL, MS 6836, f. 272.

reclaiming it for burial in 1589; All Hallows Honey Lane reclaimed the cellar under the whole church from its private lessee, and began to bury there in 1613, referring to it thereafter as 'the cloister'. In both these cases they probably excavated into the ground under the floor, rather than simply stacking coffins in the vault itself.[45]

Epitaphs and monuments

While any burial took up scarce space in church, tombs and monuments made a double claim, on space and attention. Gravestones, inscriptions, and epitaphs, if more limited in their demands on space, also claimed attention. Monuments and epitaphs represent a continuing effort to connect present and past, to attach the seemingly transient to the permanent, and also to assert individuality against the threat of personal annihilation. The presentation of images of those now dead as if they were alive is part of this, as are the allusions to remembrance and perpetuity. Apart from its possible role in protecting as well as marking the burial place of the deceased, the physical memorial had for the Catholic the aim of assisting his or her salvation by invoking prayer and intercession, as well as of securing a different kind of immortality for his or her personal identity. Both of these, however, necessitated an address to the living, using either a verbal or a visual medium or both. With the abolition of chantries and commemorative services in England, individuals who wished their names to be remembered had to find new ways of ensuring it. The endowment of charities, sermons, educational institutions, and almshouses was a continuation of pre-Reformation activity, when these good works had a salvatory aspect, though the scale and direction may have changed.[46] But of greater immediate significance was the construction of substantial and informative tombs and monuments, which increased in size and number in the later sixteenth and seventeenth centuries.

The iconography of medieval and post-medieval funerary monuments has been well explored, from a variety of perspectives, giving us both a good sense of the genre and a useful analytical framework.[47] Medieval

---

[45] Overall, *Churchwardens' accounts of the parish of St Michael Cornhill*, pp. 247–8; Keene and Harding, *Historical gazetteer of London before the Great Fire*, 1, *Cheapside*, no. 11/0; *Registers of All Hallows Honey Lane*, p. 267.

[46] W. K. Jordan, *The charities of London, 1480–1660. The aspirations and the achievements of the urban society* (London, 1960).

[47] See esp. E. Panofsky, *Tomb sculpture: its changing aspects from Ancient Egypt to Bernini* (London, 1964); Binski, *Medieval death*; N. Llewellyn, *The art of death: visual culture in the English death ritual c.1500–c.1800* (London, 1991); B. Cherry, 'New types of late medieval tombs in the London area', in L. M. Grant (ed.), *Medieval art, architecture, and archaeology in London* (London, British Archaeological Association Conference

tombs may have been something of a 'blurred genre . . . without any apparent system',[48] incorporating a collection of architectural motifs and structures, with allusions to classical forms like the sarcophagus and to early medieval ones like the canopied shrine, as well as figurative sculpture and verbal labelling or commentary. Early modern ones were also composite and varied, though arguably more coherent: 'interlocking sets' of 'signs [which] operate together to create the necessary effect'.[49] In both cases there were at any moment and in any location monuments of very different appearance and complexity, ranging from the plain slab or marker, using only words or symbols, or perhaps a simple picture, to the iconographically rich and physically imposing tomb or wall monument. As with funerals and also commemorative endowments, individuals had to tailor their ambitions to their resources, though strategies varied according to taste as well as wealth: the apparently humble and self-abnegating grave slab, intended to be walked on, could perhaps intrude into the consciousness of the visitor or worshipper as effectively as a more complex and elevated monumental tomb.

Medieval Londoners and Parisians seem to have shared the view that one of the principal aims of the monument, whatever form it took, was to create a link in the mind of the pious viewer between the name of the deceased and the responsibility of the Christian to pray for the salvation of others. Robert Garstang, grocer, of London ordered in 1460 that a new marble stone be placed over his body with his name and sign and the arms of his company, 'to have me in special memory'; William Turke, fishmonger, in 1480, asked his executors to provide 'a stone with a scripture thereon remembering my name and the names of my said wife and daughter Joan, to the intent to have our souls prayed for'.[50] A tablet in the *charniers* of the Innocents, dated 1433, exhorted

> Quiconque passe par cette loye
> je lui suplie quil me regarde
> prie dieu pour moy pense et voye
> et a son etat preigne garde.
> Cy git . . . [etc.]

The combination of the statement 'cy git' ('here lies') with the request 'prie dieu pour lui/elle' is the most common among the recorded monuments at the Innocents from the fifteenth and sixteenth centuries.[51] Other

Transactions, 1990), pp. 140–54. N. Llewellyn, *Funeral monuments in post-Reformation England* (Cambridge, 2000), appeared too late for full appreciation and reference in this chapter.

[48] Binski, *Medieval death*, p. 85.   [49] Llewellyn, *The art of death*, p. 115.
[50] GL, MS 9171/5, f. 297; GL, MS 9171/6, f. 300v.
[51] AN, LL 434/B, p. 127.

tropes were often incorporated, including the reminder to the reader to consider his or her own mortality, the *memento mori*, as above, though this too was frequently in the context of remembering the commemorated person's mortality ('as I am now...').

There is more useful work to be done on epitaphs and the use of verbal language in the dialogue between living and dead, in the way that there has been on testamentary discourse and visual language and symbolism.[52] Sixteenth- and seventeenth-century historians of London and Paris noted epitaphs as a significant source of information about the past and as a genre in themselves, but their studies tend to report the exceptional, the fulsome, and to ignore the brief and commonplace, and cannot safely be used to chart shifts in practice statistically.[53] There seems, however, to have been an expansion of the genre, to include more biographical detail, in both England and France, aiming to locate the deceased more fully in his or her social and temporal setting. The epitaph seems to have become more secular, both in its content and its purpose.[54] Raunié's study of Paris epitaphs avers that in the sixteenth century the primitive brevity of the medieval epitaph was succeeded by little pieces of eloquence, brief funeral orations; these in turn fell into excess, pretension, mannerism, before returning in the seventeenth century to their proper form as a simple and precise biographical document. Certainly he offers evidence for all these forms.[55] In England of course the explicit request on the gravestone for prayers virtually ceased with the Reformation, and in France, though such appeals continued, it seems to have become equally common to use less performative phrases such as 'may he rest in peace' or 'may God have mercy on his/her soul'.[56] Exhortations to prayer were aimed at the disinterested passer-by ('quiconcque passe', 'ô passant'); only a very careful analysis, for which there may not be sufficient material, could show whether appeals for prayers on tombs and tablets, addressed to passers-by, complement or replace endowments for commemorative services, which guaranteed prayers for payment. It would also be interesting to know how far such appeals correlate with the monument's expected visibility.

In French usage, *epitaphe* also often meant a tablet commemorating a foundation or endowment, not merely a reminder or biographical notice

---

[52] Cf. the forthcoming Harvard thesis of Scott Newstrom.

[53] Cf. Stow, *Survey*; Munday et al., *The Survey of London*; Strype, *Survey of London*; J. Weever, *Antient funeral monuments* [1631] (London, 1767); G. Corrozet and N. B[onfons], *Les antiquitiez, histoires, croniques et singularitez de la grande et excellente cité de Paris...Avec les fondations et bastiments des lieux: les sepulchres et epitaphes des princes, princesses et autres personnes illustres* (Paris, 1597).

[54] Cf. Llewellyn, *Art of death*, pp. 118–19.   [55] Raunié, *Epitaphier*, vol. I, p. vi, and passim.

[56] AN, LL 434/B, passim.

of the dead or a request for intercession. Such *epitaphes* were not necessarily attached to tombs or grave sites, but were displayed where they could be best seen, on walls or pillars, partly as a reminder of the commitment, since foundations were often negotiated and notarised as legal contracts. Thus when Nicole Habert founded two weekly masses in Saint-André-des-Arts in 1603, to be said at the altar of the chapel of Saint-Pierre where her late husband was buried, she was also granted permission to erect an *epitaphe* measuring 2.5 ft by 3.5 ft referring to the foundation, apparently outside the chapel.[57] In 1615 Mme de Lauzon founded a mass and other services to be said at a little altar in front of the choir, and was allowed to place an *epitaphe* over the door to the *trésor*. When the *trésor* itself was granted to another family in 1616, to be made into a private chapel, they were instructed to allow the Lauzon epitaph to remain. The epitaph itself, still visible in the eighteenth century, recorded that M. de Lauzon, his wife, and their daughter were buried before the altar of the Communion, at which Mme de Lauzon had founded a perpetual mass by arrangement with the churchwardens.[58] Other epitaphs were explicit about the contract they recorded: 'l'église de Saint André des Arcs est obligée de faire celebrer...', 'les marguilliers de l'oeuvre et fabricque de ceans sont tenuz de faire dire...'.[59] Because of the epitaph's necessary prominence, whether it referred to a foundation or drew attention to the name of a deceased person, the *marguilliers* had to give permission to put one up; at Saint-Jean-en-Grève, the *curé* also had to approve the wording.[60]

Both London and Paris once had a wealth of medieval and Renaissance parish churches, each of them containing numerous monuments and commemorations. Only a fraction of this number now survives physically in either city, but records made before destruction and loss can fill out the picture. In both cases there seems to have been a proliferation of funeral monuments and representations in the sixteenth and seventeenth centuries. The growth of population, the great wealth obtainable by successful merchants, professionals, and courtiers, a competitive and acquisitive society, perhaps an increasing consumerism and appreciation of display, all contributed to this. Nigel Llewellyn argues that the elaboration of funeral monuments in early modern England was needed to combat fragmentation, sustain social differentiation, and 'help the culture to survive',

---

[57] AN, L 633/6.

[58] AN, LL 686, pt. 2, f. 29r (no. 98), f. 30r (no. 99), f. 32v (no. 101), f. 37r (no. 109); AN, L 633/16–18; cf. Raunié, *Epitaphier*, vol. I, p. 17.

[59] Raunié, *Epitaphier*, vol. I, pp. 39, 64. In practice many such foundations were later reduced or consolidated, if the original endowment was no longer adequate.

[60] AN LL 687, f. 26r (no. 41); AN, LL 805, pp. 4–4 bis. One such tablet (unlocated but dating from 1620) is illustrated in Colvin, *Architecture and the afterlife*, p. 254.

and, as he shows, it was a rich and complex form, despite reformist anxieties about the use of images and figurative sculpture.[61] London was certainly a society that was experiencing constant challenges to its sense of stability, from mortality crises to social mobility and increased poverty, vagrancy, and geographical mobility; its continuously renewed élite asserted the permanence of their individual achievements and made perhaps exaggerated claims for themselves in their monumental commemorations. As the contemporary John Weever (1576–1632) noted, whereas in the past 'swelling titles, lofty inscriptions, or epitaphs, were prohibited to be inscribed, insculpted, or engraven upon the sepulchres of men of mean descent . . . [this] is not observed altogether in these times'. The tombs of 'a rich quondam tradesman, or griping usurer' could be 'so huge great that they take up the church'.[62] Metropolitan masons had easy access to fine materials, imported from the provinces and abroad, and the craftsmanship of skilled immigrants was also valued. London tombs could serve as a model for a wider society: Sir John Young (d. 1603) identified the tomb of London alderman Sir William Bonde in St Helen's church as a suitable 'patterne' for his own tomb in Bristol, though in the event a local mason produced something rather different.[63] While the need for continuity, restoration, and the maintenance of social differentiation was equally pressing in Paris, and was indeed surely increased by the crisis of confessional allegiance, it is possible that Parisians' continued access to liturgical forms of commemoration appeased their need for material representation in the public space. In the politics of space, the privatisation of much élite burial in chapels and conventual churches perhaps also reduced the competition for monumental display within the body of the church. Nevertheless, Raunié found records of nearly fifty tombs and commemorative tablets (excluding those just recording foundations) of the fifteenth to seventeenth centuries in the body of the church of Saint-André-des-Arts, and more than a hundred more in the chapels, many of them commemorating two or more persons.[64]

As with vaults, tombs annexed part of a public resource for private benefit, and the existence of a public interest was recognised in the negotiations about their erection. Stow says that Sir Thomas Gresham promised to build a steeple for St Helen's, 'in recompence of ground in their church filled up with his monument'.[65] In the early seventeenth

---

[61] Llewellyn, *The art of death*, pp. 104, 121–3.

[62] Weever, *Antient funeral monuments*, pp. xi–xii.

[63] Llewellyn, *Funeral monuments*, pp. 172–4, 193.

[64] Raunié, *Epitaphier*, vol. I, pp. 1–87.

[65] Stow, *Survey*, vol. I, pp. 171, 174. Apparently it was never built; the wooden cupola over the west front dates from the early eighteenth century: RCHM, *City of London*, p. 19.

century, the vestry of St Margaret Lothbury were uncertain whether to charge for permission to erect a tomb in the church: they allowed Lady Killigrew to make one 'according to her desire, and yf it pleased her to bestow any thinge upon the poore: at her pleasure', and that 'noe somme should be demanded of her for it'. However, a few years later, debating whether to allow Lady Stille to make a tomb for her late husband, Alderman Nicholas Stille, they noted that other parishes charged from 20 marks (£13 6s. 8d.) to £20 for such permission. In the event they agreed 'by erection of hands' to let her build the tomb for £13 6s. 8d., notwithstanding her 'assurance of bountie and liberalty towards the poor'.[66] Parisian chapel owners who had already made their contribution to the parish's funds were allowed to raise 'epitaphes tableaux et telles tumbes qui leur plaira'; others had to seek permission, and perhaps pay as well.[67]

Tombs could take three main forms: the freestanding tomb; the flat floor-slab; and the wall-fixed monument. The first, the *tombe levée* or *isolée*, made the largest claim, intruding into the circulation space, tending, as Weever said, to 'hinder the people from divine service'.[68] Only a very limited number of such tombs could be accommodated within the body of the average church. The most elaborate of these had a roof or canopy, sheltering kneeling or lying figures; others, roofless, had sculpted effigies or incised depictions; others took the form of a simple sarcophagus or altar-tomb.[69] The surviving London church of St Helen Bishopsgate has examples of all of these, dating from the later fifteenth century to the late seventeenth. There is a marble altar-tomb with a double-arched canopy and a recumbent effigy of Sir William Pickering (d. 1574); a tomb with effigies apparently of Sir John Crosby (d. 1476) and his wife; and at least three plainer sarcophagus-type or altar-tombs, to Sir Thomas Gresham (d. 1579), William Kirwin (d. 1594), and Julius Caesar Adelmare (d. 1636).[70] Other surviving London churches of this period also have examples, though tombs of this kind may be particularly liable to be moved when church interiors are remodelled. Descriptions of Parisian monuments and tombs are not always explicit; the 'grande tombe de pierre' of Martin Couvray in Saint-André-des-Arts could have been a plain sarcophagus or something more elaborate.[71] Anne du Drac clearly had something quite impressive in mind when she obtained permission in 1508 to erect over her husband's grave in the church of Saint-Gervais 'une grande tombe de pierre de marbre gravee a plusieurs personnages

[66] Freshfield, *Vestry minute book of the parish of St Margaret Lothbury*, pp. 41, 49.
[67] AN, LL 756, ff. 320–324v, 324v–327v, 327v–331v; AN, LL 746, f. 158.
[68] Weever, *Antient funeral monuments*, p. xii.   [69] Raunié, *Epitaphier*, vol. I, pp. xiii–xx.
[70] RCHM, *City of London*, pp. 23–4.   [71] Raunié, *Epitaphier*, vol. I, pp. 14–15.

et escript alentour au nom dudit defunct'.[72] The epitaph of Mathieu Chartier (d. 1559) somewhat disingenuously decried the 'vains honneurs' of the imposing architectural tomb, and renounced for himself 'des grands pilliers de marbre Parien, labourés d'ouvrage Phrygien' and the 'grand rang de colonnes', which gives some idea of what may have been found elsewhere.[73]

Limitation of space for freestanding tombs encouraged the development of the other types, and especially of the wall monument. This could achieve maximum visibility, by exploiting height combined with a richly articulated composition of sculptural and architectural forms; some examples were almost as three-dimensional as freestanding tombs.[74] The Spencer tomb (c. 1609) in St Helen Bishopsgate is effectively an altar-tomb against the wall, and has two full-size figures and one smaller one, obelisks, a wall canopy, and an entablature. It could perhaps qualify for Weever's category of 'huge great' (especially given Sir John Spencer's wealth and unpopularity), though it hardly rivals some of the tombs of the gentry or nobility in provincial churches.[75] Other wall monuments in London were more modest, hardly more than niches framed with pillars and pediment, with half-scale or smaller figures, or sometimes half-length figures or busts. The tomb (mausolée) of Jacques-Auguste de Thou (d. 1617) and his wives in the family chapel in Saint-André-des-Arts in Paris took the form of a heavily draped sarcophagus against the wall, flanked by kneeling figures. François de Montholon erected a tomb or wall monument of stone and marble in the same church in 1626, with busts of his father and grandfather of the same name, while Pierre Séguier (d. 1580) was commemorated with a mausolée enrichi of marble in a window or alcove, with his kneeling figure, fully armed, and inscriptions in French and Latin.[76] These large monuments suggest that some Parisians were, at best, slow to internalise Counter-Reformation opposition to 'insolence and arrogant pomp' and expressions of family pride.[77] Several wall monuments, in both London and Paris, were merely inscribed or painted tablets in architectural frames, though the latter could be elaborate. The wall monument of Claude Gallard (d. 1636) in Saint-André-des-Arts comprised a plaque of black marble with a Latin inscription, between Corinthian columns, with entablature, cherubs, weepers, and arms and

---

[72] AN, LL 746, f. 158.
[73] AN, L 632/32. This modesty was actually an inverted boast, since the epitaph claimed that such tombs were only needed for those whose name would otherwise be erased by death, not for such as the Chartiers whose virtues would live on their own.
[74] Raunié, Epitaphier, vol. I, pp. xiii–xx; Llewellyn, Art of death, pp. 114–20.
[75] RCHM, City of London, p. 24; cf. Llewellyn, Art of death, pp. 100–21.
[76] Raunié, Epitaphier, vol. I, pp. 35, 42–5, 57.
[77] Colvin, Architecture and the afterlife, p. 220.

ornaments. Heraldry figured largely in figurative and non-figurative monuments, and may indeed have been the most legible part of a small-scale wall monument.[78] Non-figurative tablets – including both *épitaphes proprement dites* and records of foundations and endowments – must have been the most common kind of monument or memorial, but seem to have been less often noticed by antiquaries and less often preserved if the church was remodelled or demolished.[79]

The floor-slab, whether incised stone or brass-inlaid, was more economical both in cost and space. Figurative brasses were popular in London in the later middle ages, but were much rarer after the mid-sixteenth century, though brass was apparently cheap and even mass-produced.[80] They may have fallen out of favour for artistic reasons, the stylistic limitations of the form, or perhaps for their traditional, and hence potentially superstitious, associations. Weever noted that many medieval brasses were defaced at the Reformation, the suspect wording 'cujus anime propitietur deus' being 'in many places scraped out of the brass', and surviving or recorded examples confirm this.[81] London parish churches are known to have sold brass from tomb-plates in the sixteenth century. St Dunstan in the West sold a marble stone, presumably for re-laying, to the executors of a deceased parishioner in 1538–9, and 'the pyctours of laton upon the said stone' to a marbler; St Andrew Undershaft sold a 'latten deske' and other latten scrap, weighing 2 cwt, in 1551–2.[82] Later sixteenth- and seventeenth-century brasses more commonly bore an inscription and arms, and sometimes domestic motifs and paraphernalia.[83] Floor-slabs in Parisian churches also underwent simplification, as pictorial decoration was reduced and finally all but eliminated; even the architectural frame, as well as the image of the deceased, disappeared by the second half of the seventeenth century.[84] Flat slabs could be multiplied until they covered most of the floor area, though in such cases they could hardly be marking discrete grave sites, unless the ground under the floor

---

[78] RCHM, *City of London*, plates 19–27; Raunié, *Epitaphier*, vol. I, pp. 12–87.

[79] Tombs of artistic merit or historical interest might be moved either to other churches or into museums: cf. the tombs from St Martin Outwich, transferred to St Helen Bishopsgate (RCHM, *City of London*, pp. 23–4); brasses and monumental sculpture in the Victoria and Albert Museum; monumental sculpture from Parisian churches in the Louvre, including the monument of Jacques-Auguste de Thou (d. 1617), from Saint-André-des-Arts, illustrated in Pillorget, *Paris sous les premiers Bourbons*, p. 361; *épitaphes* and tablets in the Musée Carnavalet.

[80] RCHM, *City of London*, pp. xxviii and passim. Cf. M. Norris, 'Later medieval monumental brasses: an urban funerary industry and its representation of death', in Bassett, *Death in towns*, pp. 184–209.

[81] Weever, *Antient funeral monuments*, epistle to the reader (unpaginated); GL, MS 1101 (drawings of brasses in St Helen Bishopsgate).

[82] GL, MS 2968/1, f. 93ff; Walters, *London churches at the Reformation*, pp. 151–160.

[83] RCHM, *City of London* (see index).   [84] Raunié, *Epitaphier*, vol. I, pp. xxv–xxvi.

had been honeycombed with individual vaults or brick-lined graves.[85] While this meant that a greater number of individuals could be memorialised in some way in the church, the proliferation of monuments and epitaphs must have limited the attention that would be paid to any one.

The privacy of élite burials in Paris, in a chapel or vault, or indeed in a conventual church, involved the apparent irony that the dead, secluded in this way, were separated from the larger community of the living and their possible intercession. It suggests an increased reliance on the efficacy of the sacrament itself, rather than the prayers of the laity, as a means to salvation. It also suggests a different approach to the idea and message of the monumental body. Graves and tombs in chapels were removed from the public gaze; the message of social importance was proclaimed by the existence of the chapel itself, and by markers external to it – arms and epitaphs – rather than by placing a large-scale representational monument in the public space. The chapels did in fact contain notable funerary monuments, but the imagery may have been directed rather at the few who would see it, focusing even more on individual qualities and family attributes. Since the proprietorship of a chapel conferred the right to erect whatever tombs and monuments were desired, and only the wealthy could afford one in any case, there were opportunities for lavish patronage and inventive design. The monuments in the chapels of Saint-André-des-Arts exceeded most of those in the body of the church, exploiting the wall space and orientation of the chapel enclosures to construct a remarkable array of images, using black, white, and coloured marble, portrait figures and busts, allegorical figures, emblems, armorial and architectural motifs, and grandiloquent epitaphs in Latin and French.[86] An epitaph in Latin – in London or Paris – is clearly a message addressed primarily to an educated élite.

Identity and affiliation

Funerary monuments use elements from a number of different sign systems to engage with the discourses of religion and salvation, and to make statements about social position, family, and lineage. Architectural forms and motifs, texts, pictorial or sculptured representation, heraldry, and ornaments with established symbolic significance, may all contribute to a complex message. As others have noted, the iconography and composition of early modern monuments became increasingly secular: the themes of mortality and morbidity declined and personality, family and position were more strongly emphasized.[87] But it would be wrong to infer from

---

[85] Cf. Litten, *English way of death*, p. 27.   [86] Raunié, *Epitaphier*, vol. I, pp. 1–87.
[87] Llewellyn, *Art of death*, pp. 115, 119.

this that religious devotion was necessarily declining in importance either in Protestant London or in Catholic Paris. As far as the individual is concerned, the monument is only one of a number of ways of expressing his or her identity and belief, and must be read in the context of declarations on the deathbed and in the will, funeral ceremonies, commemorative services, and charitable and pious dispositions. The place for an explicit statement of religious belief was the will preamble, even if, as we know, testamentary discourse was influenced by stylistic models and possible clerical intervention.[88] The funeral itself drew colleagues, associates, and neighbours into a collective performance that emphasised the deceased's position in the world he (or she) had just left. The monument, which was both visible and durable over a long period, highlighted identities that persisted over time: family and lineage, and the ranks or orders of a stable, hierarchical society. Several of these expressions, including the monument, may owe as much of their form and detail to the views of the surviving family and executors of the deceased as to any wishes the latter may have expressed.

It was certainly not uncommon for testators, in both London and Paris, to make some reference to a tomb, monument, or memorial, either already extant or to be erected. There are some cases where it seems certain that the deceased person planned or even built his or her monument. Dame Elizabeth Reed (d. 1531) asked to be buried in St John Zachary, 'in a tombe by me thereto ordeyned, which tombe doth serve at Esther tyme for the botom of the Sepulcre of our Lorde Jesu Criste'. This must have been an altar-tomb with a flat top, if it was to accommodate the Easter sepulchre, though it may have had a brass: Stow notes her 'fayre monument, her picture in habite of a widdow'. Her burial in St John Zachary was evidently a positive preference, since her late husband was buried at Charterhouse, and she herself was a 'sister' of the Crutched Friars. She planned her funeral with equal detail.[89] Sir Thomas Gresham is said to have prepared his own monument in his lifetime, though in his will of 1575 he simply bequeathed his body for burial in St Helen's parish 'in soche wysse as seame good by the discressione of my welbeloved wyffe'.[90]

---

[88] Cf. M. Zell, 'The use of religious preambles as a measure of religious belief in the sixteenth century', *Bulletin of the Institute of Historical Research* 50 (1977), 246–9; J. D. Alsop, 'Religious preambles in early modern English wills as formulae', *Journal of Ecclesiastical History* 40 (1989), 19–27; C. Burgess, 'Late medieval wills and pious convention: testamentary evidence reconsidered', in M. Hicks (ed.), *Profit, piety and the professions in later medieval England* (Gloucester, 1990), pp. 14–33; Chaunu, *La mort à Paris*, esp. pp. 288–329, 365–431.

[89] Stow, *Survey*, vol. I, p. 305; McMurray, *Records of two city parishes*, pp. 226–9.

[90] Stow, *Survey*, vol. I, p. 174; will printed in G. W. G. L. Gower, *Genealogy of the family of Gresham* (London, 1883), pp. 80–5.

Mr Guntar of St Michael Cornhill took the precaution in 1580 of getting the vestry's agreement that 'when God shall call him out of this present life' he should be buried under the tomb in the cloister.[91] Sir Julius Caesar Adelmare is said to have designed his own monument 'with its curious device and inscription', 'executed as we are informed by a Mr Walpole at a charge of £110'.[92] It is impossible now to know whether Chevalier Louis Bouchart's detailed instructions in 1568 for 'une tombe de pierre de liaiz' on which would be engraved his figure, fully armed, with a lion at his feet and the four evangelists, holding his arms, in the four corners of the slab, were in fact carried out.[93] Anthoine Vollart, *marchand bourgeois de Paris*, appears to have written and placed his own epitaph in the church of Saint-Eustache, under which he wished to be buried. In his will made in 1641/2 he described the copper plaque he had set up, combining notice of his parents, his sister (still living), and himself, his foundation of four grand obits in the church, and his bequest of money to buy vestments and plate.[94]

It was more common, though, for the deceased to depend on the diligence and discretion of others to erect a suitable monument. Quite often the survivor of a married couple would plan or set up a monument to both of them, expecting to be buried there in due course. Thus Millicent Herenden set up a monument to herself and her late husband Edward in the church of St Anne Aldersgate, and willed her own burial there in 1581; William Braynewoode of St Andrew Undershaft asked in 1586 for burial in the church in the same place where his wife was buried, and that 'the stone which I have there appointed shall be laid upon me'.[95] Suzanna du Lac, widow of Pierre Mauguin (d. 1627), placed an epitaph for him above his grave in the church of Saint-André-des-Arts, 'dum exspectat secum humari'.[96] The survivor was able to control what was represented or written, and though this was probably often unexceptionable (Suzanna du Lac recorded that she and her late husband had lived together sweetly and without argument for twenty-nine years), it may not always have been what the deceased had intended. John Morris asked in 1560 to be 'decently and comelie' buried in St Anne Aldersgate, either near his pew or else by his first wife; his second and surviving wife Thomasine, who presumably decided where the grave should be, herself chose to be buried

[91] Overall, *Churchwardens' accounts of St Michael Cornhill*, p. 239. 'Mr Phillippe Gunnter, a worthie man, & of ye age of iiij^{xx} & xij yeares' was buried on 5 March 1583, but the register does not say where: *Registers of St Michael Cornhill*, p. 198.

[92] Cox, *Annals of St Helen Bishopsgate*, p. 294.

[93] Cited in M. Rossignol, *mémoire de maîtrise*, p. 83.

[94] Chaunu, *La mort à Paris*, pp. 512–15.

[95] McMurray, *Records of two city parishes*, pp. 208, 311; GL, MS 9171/17, f. 16.

[96] Raunié, *Epitaphier*, vol. I, p. 26.

under the stone where he was buried, and to have 'graven in latine my picture with my iiij children'. It is not clear whether the first wife was in any way commemorated.[97] Children or other heirs might be left responsible for the monument, and, again, might emphasize aspects of character or identity that were flattering or pleasing to themselves: the laudatory verse on Sir Thomas Offley's monument contains the line 'Henry doth live, his father's heir, God grant him well to do'. They might also seek to draw attention to the piety or affection which had led them to erect the monument.[98]

Many testators left the erection of a monument to their executors' discretion, though this seems to have yielded a variety of responses. Sir Andrew Judd (d. 1558), who ordered his executors to set up a tomb or monument with a memorial of him upon his grave, is only commemorated by a small tablet fixed to the wall in St Helen Bishopsgate, with kneeling figures, in an architectural frame, perhaps less than he had hoped for.[99] Sir Thomas Offley (d. 1582), who asked for 'some convenient tomb . . . as my executors shall think meet' has 'the finest monument in the church' of St Andrew Undershaft, attributed to Gerard Johnson.[100] His brother Hugh Offley, alderman (d. 1594), asked to be buried in the vault where Sir Thomas Offley and his own first wife and children were buried, and instructed his executors (his son and brothers) to erect a monument nearby in remembrance of him. It does not, however, appear that they did so, though Hugh's widow, Dorothy Greswold (d. 1610) has an individual monument, on which he is just mentioned.[101] Equally, wishes might be fulfilled, but rather slowly: Philip Strelley (d. 1603) left £6 for a monument in the church of St John Zachary where he was buried, but the monument was not put up for twenty-five years, perhaps because of complications over other legacies.[102]

Tombs and monuments, once erected, remained significant sites, if not of cult, at least of piety, religious or familial. They normally offered the opportunity for other family members to be buried there, even if this was not a guaranteed and exclusive right, as it was with the private chapels in Paris. They had a part to play in the continuing dialogue between living and dead, allowing the dead to speak to the living and the living

[97] McMurray, *Records of two city parishes*, pp. 206–7.

[98] C. B. Boulter, *History of St Andrew Undershaft, St Mary Axe, in the City of London; with a description of the monuments and coloured glass therein* (London, 1935), pp. 95, 104. Cf. also McMurray, *Records of two city parishes*, pp. 314, 316.

[99] PRO, PROB 11/42a, f. 416v; RCHM, *City of London*, p. 23.

[100] PRO, PROB 11/64, f. 298; RCHM, *City of London*, p. 7. Boulter, *History of St Andrew Undershaft*, p. 104, attributes the tomb to Cornelius Cure, master mason. See jacket illustration.

[101] PRO, PROB 11/84, f. 294v; RCHM, *City of London*, p. 7.

[102] McMurray, *Records of two city parishes*, pp. 234, 314, 382.

to respond with action and observance. The message could be relayed to future generations, perhaps with additions, and indeed to pay explicit respect to the memory of those already long dead was to affirm one's own place in a tradition of remembrance. The tomb of William Kirwin, mason, in St Helen's commemorated his wife (d. 1592) and himself (d. 1594). His son Benjamin (d. 1621) was subsequently buried there, as were five of the latter's children, and text added to the inscription to this effect after Benjamin's death. In 1632 William's daughter Joyce Featly 'raised, repaired, and beautified' the monument, which with the passage of time had become 'somewhat defaced', and enclosed it with an iron paling; she also reglazed a window in the south aisle with her father's and husbands' arms.[103] She was buried 'in the vaulte of hir Father, William Kirwin' in 1637. The tomb was used as a location marker for burials for many years, though in 1670 it was referred to as 'the valte which formerly was Mr Kerwin's'.[104] Not all individuals placed an equal value on their progenitors' tombs: at the end of the seventeenth century, St Helen's reappropriated the vault in which Sir John Spencer had been buried, his descendant and heir the earl of Northampton 'taking no care for the repair of it'.[105]

Marked graves and monuments also played a part in liturgical commemoration, giving a focus to acts that reaffirmed the importance and continued effectiveness of the dead. Part of the point of seeking burial in church was to locate oneself in the middle of a community at worship; the Catholic sequence of funeral, trentals, month's mind (the commemorative service said a month after the death), and anniversary mass or obit initiated by an individual death merged with the ongoing cycle of daily chantry masses and the annual remembrance at All Souls. The chantry certificate for London of 1548 shows that most parish churches were maintaining several permanent chantry foundations and anniversaries, while wills demonstrate the even larger number of short-term foundations.[106] Obviously this focus of resources and observances ceased in England at this point, but over the next century and a half the Parisian churches accumulated great numbers of foundations. The personal aspect of commemoration, and the individual's perception of his or her place in the future, are complex issues, but in the context of burial it is clear that the performance of chantries and anniversaries incorporated

---

[103] GL, MS 2480/2 (MS volume of monumental inscriptions, 1910–19), p. 524, which also notes that the parish repaired and restored the monument in 1808; Strype, *Survey of London*, vol. I, bk. 2, p. 102.

[104] *Registers of St Helen Bishopsgate*, pp. 291, 314, 316.

[105] Cox, *Annals of St Helen Bishopsgate*, p. 114.

[106] Kitching, *London and Middlesex chantry certificate*; Sharpe, *Calendar of wills proved and enrolled in the Court of Husting*, vol. II, passim.

individual graves and tombs into a larger understanding of the space of the church. Chapels and graves were appointed as stages for liturgical performance, or became stations in the processional circulation round the church; they could also be specified as the locus of a distribution of goods or money. In making her tomb the pedestal for an Easter sepulchre in the church of St John Zachary in 1531, Dame Elizabeth Reed connected herself with one of the most dramatic and significant moments in the church's yearly observance.[107] Lady Packington (d. 1563) still wished to connect herself to that site, asking for burial 'at thende of high aulter wheras the sepultre was used moste commonly to stande', suggesting that its attraction and importance had not disappeared.[108]

Those who chose burial in the main part of the church certainly situated themselves in the middle of the liturgical round of the community. At Saint-André-des-Arts, immediately after the parish mass on Sundays, a low mass of the day was said at the high altar for the late Jehan Viole, *conseiller en parlement*, and his wife Ysabeau Taille, formerly wife of Réné de Beaulne, lieutenant of the *prévôt de Paris*. They were buried before the entry to the choir, and may have been imagined as viewers as well as beneficiaries of this rite. After this the chaplain was to go to to the tomb of Réné de Beaulne, which was in the nave of the church, in front of the image of Christ crucified, and repeat the prayers for the dead over the grave.[109] Within the same church at this time (1546), a low mass and/or a requiem mass was said daily for Jehan Bemon and his wife Jeanne Lhuillier, and Jean de Rameyes; the psalms and prayers *de profundis* and *fidelium* were said over their graves, and holy water was sprinkled there. Eleven other graves were similarly attended once a week, and several others once a year.[110] By the mid-seventeenth century the number of foundations had increased enormously: at least sixty-six obits, presumably including prayers over the grave, were being celebrated in the church, and there were many more commemorative low masses, requiem masses, and *saluts*, some of which also entailed psalms and prayers over the deceased's grave.[111] The proper maintenance of these foundations was a major concern for the parish, which kept much better records of them than of many other activities.

There was much less to keep the names of the dead alive in liturgical activity in post-Reformation London. One possibility was the endowment

[107] McMurray, *Records of two city parishes*, pp. 226–9; Stow, *Survey*, vol. I, p. 305. There are several fifteenth- and early sixteenth-century Easter sepulchre tombs in the London area: Cherry, 'New types of late medieval tombs in the London area', pp. 140–54.

[108] Llewellyn, *Funeral monuments*, p. 236, citing PRO, PROB 11/47, f. 73.

[109] AN, LL 692, f. 8r–v; Raunié, *Epitaphier*, vol. I, p. 20.

[110] AN, LL 692.   [111] AN, LL 691.

of sermons and charities, though the size and significance of this phenomenon remains controversial.[112] Sermons obviously were mostly given in church; tying distributions to church attendance was also a way of linking the act of benefaction with the general location of burial. Dame Anne Pemberton, who wanted a modest funeral in St John Zachary, nevertheless asked for a funeral sermon to be preached subsequently, at which seventy-one poor women were to be given 20s. each in lieu of a mourning gown, and 12d. each for a dinner. James Pecocke of St Anne Aldersgate left the parish a rent-charge to distribute 12d. in wheaten bread every week after the parish service or sermon, to the poor 'coming duly to heare Divine service and sermon'.[113] Other doles also required attendance at church, but few were focused on the grave or monument of the benefactor. It may therefore be that the prominence of funeral monuments in the churches of Tudor and Stuart London was a way of compensating for this loss of a physical focus for acts of pious remembrance. Monuments could still assert the ongoing importance and activity of the dead, even if they no longer featured in a liturgical reactivation of memory. They sometimes record benefactions and acts of generosity, either specifically or in general terms: Philip Strelley 'who gave to the poore of this parish 40s. for ever'; Simon Burton 'a good benifactor to the poore of this parish'; Sir Thomas Offley, 'in Stafford borne, whose liberalness the towne doth seme to know'.[114] A more subtle way of drawing attention to benefaction, while apparently discounting such a boast, appears in the epitaph of Sir James Pemberton:

> Marble, nor touch, nor alabaster can
> Reveale the worth of the long buried man;
> For oft we see men's goods, when they are gone,
> Doe pious deeds, when they themselves did none.
> Mine, while I lived, my goodnesse did expresse,
> Tis not inscriptions make them more or lesse.[115]

Contemporary commentators were certainly aware of the symbolic value of commemorative monuments. As well as enshrining the memory of the individual and his or her place in the social pyramid, monuments could also be taken to stand for the social and political order itself: permanence, tradition, an established religious orientation. Tombs and brasses were at risk in the fury of Reformation, especially in the reign of

---

[112] Jordan, *The charities of London, 1480–1660*; J. F. Hadwin, 'Deflating philanthropy', *Economic History Review* 2nd ser. 31 (1978), 105–17.

[113] McMurray, *Records of two city churches*, pp. 212, 235.

[114] Ibid., p. 314; Boulter, *History of St Andrew Undershaft*, pp. 95–6, 104–7.

[115] McMurray, *Records of two city churches*, p. 314.

Edward VI in England and the first religious war in France; destroying them assisted the people 'to discard the burden of history' and the traditional authority of the church.[116] Elizabeth in fact moved rapidly to restrain such desecrations, because of their explicit challenge to the understanding of genealogies and continuities,[117] and, as has been shown, London's ruling class, like royalty and the aristocracy, continued to spend on substantial monuments. John Stow, with his enthusiasm for uncovering and communicating the past, felt very strongly about the value of monuments, both as historical evidence but also as in themselves a kind of sacred bequest or charge laid by the dead on the living. His own monument, erected by his wife, notes that he 'practised the most careful diligence in reading the old monuments [and] with glory wrote the annals of England and a survey of the city of London', but in an explicit criticism of iconoclasts he omitted many recent monuments from his *Survey*. This may perhaps partly have been because he was less interested in modern works, but it was also, as he said, 'because those men have been defacers of the monuments of others, and so worthy to be deprived of that memory wherof they have injuriously robbed others'.[118] Stow's continuators made some attempt to amplify his record, and seventeenth-century writers like John Weever and William Dugdale took the systematic recording of monuments for granted as a part of the antiquary's task. Weever in particular, like Stow, saw monuments as key constructions in a moral universe, 'muniments . . . [that] did defend and fence the corps of the defunct' against both damage and oblivion.[119] He might criticise the citizens' fulsome epitaphs, but it is clear that they satisfied an aspiration that could not otherwise be met; concern with the salvation and immortality of the soul had mutated into a concern to ensure a metaphorical immortality in human memory.[120]

Reviewing the practice of burial by taking location as the primary category of analysis highlights the crucial importance of space and place to burial practices in the early modern city. The place where an individual was buried is a marker, as legible to historians as to his or her contemporaries, of the place of that individual in the community. Its significance worked on two levels: the geographical centrality or marginality

[116] Duffy, *Stripping of the altars*, pp. 494–5; D. McCullough, *Tudor church militant. Edward VI and the Protestant Reformation* (London, 1999), pp. 134–6; J. H. M. Salmon, *Society in crisis. France in the sixteenth century* (London, 1979), p. 137.

[117] D. Howarth, *Images of rule. Art and politics in the English Renaissance, 1485–1649* (London, 1997), pp. 153–4.

[118] Stow, *Survey*, vol. I, Introduction, p. xxxi.

[119] Weever, *Antient funeral monuments*, p. vi.

[120] Cf. Llewellyn, *The art of death*, pp. 101–21.

of location, which mapped a metaphorical centrality/marginality in social terms, and the institutional setting of burial in different places, which determined the range of issues and interests involved. Many of the varied spaces of early modern London and Paris were co-opted to serve the cities' need for burial accommodation. Conventual and parish churches, parish churchyards, old and new burial grounds for the civic community or for new self-identified communities, all provided sites for the dead to be buried but endowed these with a particular character or meaning.

The paradigm of centrality and marginality works best at the parish level. London and Paris were made up of clusters of parish communities each focused around the nucleus of the parish church. As has been shown, there was a hierarchy of desirable spaces within churches, with further distinctions being drawn between church and churchyards, between old and newer (and usually more distant) churchyards within the same parish, and between burial within the bounds of the parish and burial in a peripheral cemetery. This hierarchy of desirability was demonstrated by the choices made by individuals, for themselves and their dependants; most, it seems, chose as well as they could afford. Desirability was also reflected in the pricing policies of those in charge of particular burial spaces, which may have further enhanced the cachet of the more expensive locations. Other elements of attraction existed also, but tended to be linked to tradition (whether of the family or community), or devotion, and both of these reinforced the centripetal model. The result of this was, predictably, that the population of different burial locations within the parish was distinctive, sorted principally by social standing, with the wealthier élite in the better, more central locations and the poorer and weaker relegated to the periphery. Nevertheless this was a metaphor of complementarity: the meaning and value of central places depended on there being a periphery.

On a citywide scale, though there was an obvious contrast between the peripheral churchyards and those within the city, the gradient of desirability was not determined purely by geographical distance, but owed something to the perceived character of particular places. St Paul's churchyard was centrally located but proved to have a limited attraction, while la Trinité, within the walls of Paris, was clearly an outcast or marginal ground. The Innocents was not sited in the geographical centre of Paris, but it was both physically and emotionally at the heart of the right-bank Ville (and exercised a much weaker pull on Parisians of the left bank, at least as a place of burial). However, physical distancing or exclusion was strongly associated with moral exclusion. Suicides, heretics, and excommunicates were denied burial in consecrated ground; some traditions insisted that suicides should be buried in the roadway,

though it is not clear how far this happened in practice.[121] The home-
less poor and the dead of the hospitals were often buried in more re-
mote and non-parochial churchyards. The suburban locations of plague
pits and plague burial grounds, and the establishment of a Protestant
burial ground in the faubourg Saint-Germain, were a way of distancing
a polluting or dangerous presence. The combination of peripheral location with all its associations of moral marginality turned London's New
Churchyard from an amenity to a refuse burial ground within a couple of
generations. More generally, excluding certain categories from Christian
burial, as a way of marking the bounds of the community, came to have a
particular significance during religious conflict. Protestants were expelled
from Catholic burying places in Paris; Catholics were refused consecrated
burial in London.[122]

Burial always involved a complicated negotiation between interests,
not just between the living and the dead, but between the proprietors or
controllers of particular spaces and those wishing to obtain burial there,
for themselves or others. For the most part, burial space was under the
control of parish vestries and officers, acting on behalf of a larger community, but also at times with a class or group interest in mind. The terms
of their negotiations varied according to the place of burial in question.
They had most authority when dealing with the relatively modest claims
of those requiring burial in the churchyard, and least when negotiating
with powerful individuals seeking a more substantial share of the community's resource in the form of burial in church. The commitment of
the latter to church burial, and its potential for incorporation into a major statement of individuality and importance, cannot be doubted. There
were difficult issues to be resolved, and the success of local authorities
in balancing respect for traditions and sensibilities against practical considerations of space and hygiene, and in accommodating demands for
privileged treatment without alienating the unprivileged, was crucial to
the wellbeing of the local community. Watching them at work, analysing
the decisions they made in the management of burial, gives an insight
into their judgement of needs and priorities. They ended up by adopt-
ing the approach that best satisfied their assessment of the situation, but
there is some reason to think that this was a more responsive and inclusive compromise in London than in Paris. While there is certainly a
contrast in London between the unmarked and often shared graves of the

---

[121] Harding, 'And one more', p. 120. Several London cases show that an attempt was
made to reinclude the suicide in the community by demonstrating either repentance or
incapacity, in order to give him or her Christian burial: McMurray, *Records of two city
parishes*, pp. 84–5, 91–2.
[122] Cf. *VCH London*, vol. I, p. 327.

poor in distant churchyards and the secure, individualised spaces within churches allotted to the rich, the spectrum appears to have been wider in Paris. Here the contrast extended from carting the barely shrouded hospital dead to mass graves at la Trinité or later the even more distant Clamart, to guarding the coffined bodies of generations of individuals in private family chapels within parish churches. The tensions of this extreme contrast were perhaps increased by the fact that some at least of those gaining privileged resting places in the parish church had not been part of the living community at all, while important others from within the community preferred to seek burial elsewhere. The élite of Paris appear to have shown a greater withdrawal from an integrated parochial life, and resistance to incorporation in a civic universe.

If the geography of the city shaped burial practice, burial practice shaped the city, as physical and experienced space. The dead were buried in the midst of the living, and the space they occupied was incorporated into the secular circuits of the living city. Londoners and Parisians appear to have been relatively comfortable with the physical presence of the dead. It was especially easy when they could identify the dead as individuals, by epitaphs and monuments, or even by placing them in a liturgical round, but equally they do not seem to have found the sites of mass burial dangerous or repulsive. They were able to use burial grounds and churches for their own purposes, being prepared to respect, but not excessively to reverence, the place of the dead. Churchyards, as open areas, attracted much mundane activity; churches were required for the rituals of life as well as death. Places like St Paul's churchyard and the Innocents acted as nexuses in the circulations of commercial traffic, but they also drew citizens for important occasions of collective activity, figuring large in the the mental map of either city and in the emotional orientation of the city's inhabitants. Because burial was located in the heart of the city and the parish community, how to treat and respond to the dead was a question that could never be ignored. The evidence of the presence of the dead was a constant reminder that the living belonged to a world of spiritual as well as material values. And the setting of burial had an important impact on the rituals with which it was performed. Funeral ceremonies took place in a public space, open to the view, participation, and involvement of neighbours and even the passing crowd. They attracted attention, and were meant to do so; they relied on an audience to complete their meaning.

So far this study of burial practice has treated the living and the dead as if they were distinct and opposed categories, focusing on how the living responded to the demands that the dead made on them in the long term – for space, seclusion, protection, attention, respect – and how those demands themselves shaped the material environment of the living. However, all of the living will in due course join the category of the dead; all of the dead were once living. For all societies, the rituals accompanying an individual's transition from one state to the other are of great significance, designed to satisfy a practical imperative – the safe determination of the physical remains – and to meet the social, moral, emotional, and spiritual needs of the occasion. In urban societies, the first of these requirements has real urgency. Satisfying the latter may also be more pressing, as a society in flux has to deal with loss and interruption, though it also faces greater difficulties owing to high mortality rates: the strict observance of forms and rituals may at times have to be dispensed with, as epidemic experience shows.

If the *place* of burial remained of paramount and determining importance, funerals and the language of funeral ceremony had the potential to form a very powerful element in the social relations and mutual interactions of city-dwellers. Though it may have been more difficult to assert the importance of the eternal and transcendent against the pace and intensity of city life, the ritual gained added meaning from doing so. In pre-modern urban societies individuals were at greater personal risk of untimely death, and evidence of the death of others was all around them. Though daily totals varied by season and by year, in both London and Paris there must have been fifteen to twenty thousand burials every year in the later seventeenth century. An adult citizen would certainly attend a number of funerals over a period of years, and he or she would perforce notice many more. Even if in smaller parishes there might be only a few funerals in a month, the dense texture of the urban fabric and the close spacing of churches meant that all would have been aware of such events in parishes other than their own. In larger parishes funerals were a daily occurrence. The map of the city was traversed by frequent processions transporting bodies to churches or churchyards for services and interment; knells and peals filled the air. Normal civic activities were periodically suspended to allow larger civic or national funerals to take the stage.

Wills and parish records underline the importance attached to all parts of the funeral ritual, and indicate a considerable similarity of custom in London and Paris, following the shared Christian tradition, including the literary tradition of the Ars Moriendi. The major circumstantial differences are the smaller number of parish churches in Paris, which meant that burial communities were larger and perhaps more internally differentiated, and the greater frequency, at least as time went on, of family chapels within churches there. The major historical difference is of course the Reformation, and the institution of a reformed theology and practice in London, compared with a Counter-Reform ideology in Paris. Even with this, however, the continuities were considerable, and attitudes had much in common. Londoners certainly had to accept the Reformation's changes to liturgy and accompaniments, but interest in funeral practice remained vigorous and they were able to reshape and develop their traditions to maintain a sense of continuity and meaning. Parisians held strongly to the observance of tradition but similarly added new components and elaborated practices in response to a changing and challenging world.

Urban funerals shared the general liturgical framework of their time, but a great variety of additions, ecclesiastical and secular, was available to build a personal statement out of the event. The wealth of the two capitals, and perhaps an element of competition between their multiplicity of parishes, fraternities, and religious houses, made their inhabitants aware of a wider range of alternatives in burial ritual than their contemporaries in smaller communities. In both cities there were literate, articulate laymen and women ready to take an active part in their own and others' funeral arrangements, and to exploit the variety and richness of the urban church's resources. The city offered an almost unlimited range of supply for the material constituents and human participants of a funeral, and to that extent could encourage choice and display. It could also guarantee a large and appreciative audience for the performance. Contemporary Londoners and Parisians understood and valued this. The disposable wealth of the urban middling and upper classes allowed them to exploit these resources and opportunities for the occasion of the funeral. As with the choice of burial location and the design of memorials and epitaphs, it is not always easy to know whether it was the deceased person, or his or her heirs or executors, who was responsible for the programme of a particular event, but it must always have been a compromise between the desired, the affordable, the appropriate, and the feasible. However, 'the personalization and publicity of such burial was still a spiritual luxury';[1] we should remember that alongside this encouragement of display and discrimination, and perhaps adding to its impact, was the fact that most of the urban population were buried much more unceremoniously, and often almost anonymously.[2]

The next three chapters consider the funeral in early modern London and Paris from a number of different perspectives, though even these are not exhaustive. This chapter focuses on the individual, and looks at the funeral as an event scripted by its central participant, or by those to whom he or she had delegated that power. A common ceremony could be shaped into an expression of identity, affiliation, confession, and status. It also shows, however, that in responding to these demands for differ-ence, the church became involved in secular preoccupations with display and discrimination. Chapter 8 considers the constraints set by existing institutions, interests, and practices, and points to the professionalisation or commercialisation of funerals over the early modern period. It also ex-plores the ambivalence of attitudes towards funeral expense. The question of involvement and participation, and the construction of the funeral as a collective ritual in the urban context, is discussed in chapter 9. It is not, however, fully possible to separate the constituents of the funeral rit-ual into discrete 'liturgical', 'commercial', and 'social' elements; all these aspects interlocked, and all carried messages about status and social iden-tity. Anthropologists and social historians emphasize that death ritual is often co-opted for purposes of ideological and political domination, and it has, for example, been assigned an important role in the creation of a new social and theological order in Reformation and post-Reformation Germany.[3] Undoubtedly many aspects of the urban funerals considered here reflected and helped to inculcate the values of order, stability, and hierarchy, as well as affirming more explicitly devotional attachments, but power in urban societies is widely dispersed among groups and individu-als, and it is not clear that any single ideology – except in the broadest of definitions – dominated or controlled funeral performance. Despite con-siderable change over time, funerals remained complex rituals, in some aspects perhaps over-determined, in others no doubt failing to achieve their authors' ends. In particular, while there was collaboration between

---

[1] Ariès, *The hour of our death*, p. 207.

[2] Cf. Harding, 'Whose body?' Some examples used in this chapter are also discussed there.

[3] C. M. Koslofsky, *The Reformation of the dead. Death and ritual in early modern Germany, 1450–1700* (Basingstoke, 2000), pp. 6–8; cf. S. C. Karant-Nunn, *The Reformation of ritual. An interpretation of early modern Germany* (London, 1997), p. 192.

the church as provider and the laity as consumers of elements of funerary performance, there was also resistance to both the theological and the social discourses proposed by such performances. A wide variety of interests, aspirations, and constraints in practice shaped the funeral in early modern London and Paris.

Funeral liturgy and the evolution of practice

Over a long time, liturgical prescription and social custom combined to evolve a tradition of Christian burial. By the early sixteenth century, there was a widely accepted set of rites and practices associated with burial, which helped to satisfy the spiritual and emotional needs of the living.[4] The church specified what was essential in the way of service and ceremonial, but also offered extras and elaborations. Around the liturgical requirements there had also gathered a number of secular or semi-secular traditions, sanctioned but not prescribed by the church: the conduct of the deathbed, watching the corpse, the procession to bring it to church, bellringing, lights, the distribution of alms, and drinking and eating. Such elements have been described by Bob Scribner as 'paraliturgical celebrations' and by Susan Karant-Nunn as 'pararituals': 'all those ritualized social practices that were sometimes... only tenuously and initially perforce linked to ecclesiastical practice', taking their significance 'from life events rather than theological dictates'.[5] There could be important local or regional variations in practice, particularly in popular custom; there would also be very specific local differences in what was actually available, according to the staffing and equipment of the church and the spaces it could offer for burial. Many of the liturgical and secular elements could be varied or elaborated according to personal choice and means.

Several elements of the tradition of Christian burial were called into question by the Protestant Reformation. The fundamental change was the rejection of the doctrine of purgatory and the abandonment of the proposition that there could be any effective interaction between those in this world and those in the next. All prayers and acts of intercession for the dead in England were terminated by the Chantries Act of 1548. The cult

---

[4] G. Rowell, *The liturgy of Christian burial; an introductory survey of the historical development of Christian burial rites* (London, 1977); Duffy, *Stripping of the altars*, pp. 301–37, 369; J. Maltby, *Prayer book and people in Elizabethan and early Stuart England* (Cambridge, 1998), pp. 56–63. Cf. R. Dinn, 'Death and rebirth in medieval Bury St Edmunds', in Bassett (ed.), *Death in towns*, pp. 151–69.

[5] R. W. Scribner, 'Ritual and popular religion in Catholic Germany at the time of the Reformation', *Journal of Ecclesiastical History* 35 (1984), 53; Karant-Nunn, *The Reformation of ritual*, p. 193.

of saints and the veneration of relics and images, which had been criticised since the mid-1530s, were also eliminated, and by 1552 the sacrifice of the mass had been recast as a commemorative communion. These developments reflected the doctrine of justification by faith alone: no prayer, intercessor, image, or liturgical activity could affect the salvation of the individual, before or after his death. No multiplication of any of these could enhance his prospects. Taken to its logical conclusion, it meant that no place of burial, no elaboration of the order of service, was holier or more beneficial to the deceased than any other. By declaring that the living could do nothing for the dead, and vice versa, it challenged the reciprocity previously exemplified by testamentary benefactions and obligations.

This paradigm shift ought, perhaps, to have entailed a complete interruption to traditional funeral and burial practices. It should certainly have undermined some aspects, deplored by leading reformers, of the composite burial ritual discussed below. The fact that it did not do so completely seems to indicate that the rationale behind many practices associated with burial was not exclusively a spiritual one. Though there was certainly a Protestant discourse of simplicity and anti-ritual, many Protestant societies retained a good deal of traditional practice, if not of liturgy. German Lutheranism retained a degree of 'pomp and circumstance ... though without papist sacramentals': bells, black palls, mourning dress or emblems, the attendance of clergy and children all continued there.[6] Huguenots in Paris, though obviously requiring the use of a reformed liturgy, and eschewing some aspects of the funeral they deemed Catholic or superstitious, did not express indifference either to the fate of the body or to the ceremonials with which it was interred. Chaunu emphasises the continuities and similarities of Protestant and Catholic testamentary discourse. The two faiths shared a tradition of the *arts de mourir*, and of approaches to death, including the need to settle earthly responsibilities by willmaking. In one study of sixteenth-century Parisian wills, all the Protestant wills (10 per cent of the sample) dwelt on the theme of redemption, but so too did nearly 60 per cent of the Catholic ones, though the latter continued to invoke the Virgin and other saints as well. In another sample, 75 per cent of Protestants asked for pardon or mercy, but so did nearly 30 per cent of Catholics. Chaunu also suggests that a dualistic view of the body – as both the temple of the spirit and as an earthly shell, to be discarded – was common to both, and that some at least of the apparent differences of Huguenot testamentary provision for the place and style of burial resulted from their civil disabilities, and

[6] Karant-Nunn, *The Reformation of ritual*, p. 181.

perhaps a wish to avoid attention, and not from a real divergence from the tradition.[7] Many traditional or Catholic beliefs persisted in Protestant England, even in apparent strongholds of reformed thought. Elaborate ritual practices survived the Reformation, not just because they could find justification in Protestant theology, but because they served 'deeprooted social and familial needs'.[8]

What in fact happened to the English rite was that a few elements disappeared, while others gained in importance; some required new justification, while others were simply translated regardless of their original, possibly now discredited, rationale. Several factors contributed to this process of accommodation. As has often been noted, the English Reformation was piecemeal and sometimes reversed direction; reformed theology and liturgical practice moved haltingly towards ascendancy. Many of the reforms of Edward's reign had been signalled in the 1530s, though not enacted, and they had perhaps begun to influence the ways in which death and burial were approached. But of greater significance than the slow pace of change was the secular importance attached to many aspects of the funeral ceremony. It was surely this that ensured that post-Reformation funerals could be as complete a representation, as rich in ceremony, attendance, and decoration as their predecessors, even if they now lacked many of the liturgical options and a substantial clerical presence. The multiplicity and variability of detail, in reformed as in traditional practice, were an essential part of the strength of the ritual, allowing participants in this common rite to reaffirm the individuality of the deceased and his or her situation. At the same time, variation entailed discrimination and implied hierarchies of desirability. Meanings, especially of status, were associated with particular choices, and assumptions about the appropriate and normal began to inform decisions: 'my body to be buried in holy grave in such decent order as to the good discretion of my executors, meet and convenient for my estate and degree'.[9] Funerals became one of the ways in which wealth could, through various socially accepted forms of spending, be translated into status.

Deathbeds and burial intervals

Most prescriptions for deathbeds, and most accounts of funeral practice, assume the dying or dead person to be adult, at home, and at least potentially *compos mentis*. They also tend to assume that he, or less often

---

[7] Chaunu, *La mort à Paris*, pp. 249–60, 312, 319, 346.

[8] D. Cressy, 'Death and the social order: the funerary preferences of Elizabethan gentlemen', *Continuity and Change* 5 (1989), 99–119.

[9] PRO, PROB 11/38, f. 186.

explicitly she, had goods to leave and worldly as well as spiritual affairs to settle, and that willmaking would form an important part of the event. In reality, at least half of all urban deaths were of juveniles; many adults died accidentally, unprepared, away from home, or as vagrants or lodgers in a strange city. In mid-seventeenth-century Paris, up to a quarter of all deaths occurred in a hospital. Nevertheless the flourishing literature of prescription offered a set of customs for model circumstances; perhaps these could not always be observed, but they helped to establish norms and expectations that shaped practice more widely.[10]

Urban deathbeds may have had some distinctive features. Epidemic disease, especially plague, must often have disrupted or precluded the desired sequence of repentance, reconciliation, communion (for Catholics), and resignation. In Paris also there were long periods of civil unrest, if not open warfare, during which normal practices must have been jeopardised. In crowded urban dwellings, a private and peaceful death must have been hard to accomplish. On the other hand, there was perhaps no shortage of neighbours to assist, admonish, and afterwards bear witness.[11] In Paris even passers-by were drawn into deathbed scenes, according to an eighteenth-century commentator.[12] There ought at least to have been no delay in obtaining professional attendance, whether of notaries, attorneys, clerks, or clergy. This was obviously important, since many wills were written on the deathbed, whether or not the testator claimed to be sick in body; other deathbed wills were made verbally, and subsequently proved with the assistance of those who had been present.[13] The Hôtel-Dieu in Paris took seriously its responsibility to those dying there, the priests and chaplains witnessing deathbed testaments and their notarisation.[14] The small size of most parishes in both London and Paris, and the numbers of clergy, should have meant that no city-dweller dying at home need be without the services of a priest. Failure to obtain the Sacrament was more likely to be due to clerical negligence than distance or the difficulty of obtaining it.[15] The disposable wealth of some city-dwellers, and their freedom of testamentary disposition, could have

[10] Chaunu, *La mort à Paris*, pp. 274–87; R. A. Houlbrooke, 'The Puritan death-bed, c.1560–c.1660', in C. Durston and J. Eales (eds.), *The culture of English Puritanism, 1560–1700* (London, 1996), pp. 122–44, esp. pp. 130–1; Houlbrooke, *Death, religion and the family*, pp. 146–219.

[11] See the forthcoming London Ph.D. thesis of Danae Tankard.

[12] Restif de la Bretonne, cited by Chaunu, *La mort à Paris*, p. 347.

[13] Chaunu, *La mort à Paris*, p. 298; for London examples, see *Consistory Court Wills*, p. xv, and nos. 186, 188, 200 (nuncupative wills), and nos. 156, 158, 160, etc. (sickbed wills).

[14] Archives de L'Assistance Publique, register of testaments at the Hôtel-Dieu, cat. 6358 (layette 330, liasse 1413(1)), f. 6.

[15] But cf. Houlbrooke, *Death, religion and the family*, p. 153.

made the deathbed a more charged and contested scene, though here as elsewhere the spouse and immediate biological family were the principal players and beneficiaries.[16]

Few people had much choice about where they died, or the setting and attendance of the deathbed. Social and financial circumstances dictated the speed and style of the subsequent proceedings for the great majority. For some individuals, however, the precise form of the rituals following their own death was of great significance. Some of those who could afford to do so took pains to specify their performance in detail. This is apparent from both deathbed and 'precautionary' wills, but it seems that the approach of death could be an important stimulus. Forty wills out of 244 proved in the Consistory Court of London between 1514 and 1547 contain instructions about the funeral. Nine of the testators said they were sick, and several more were within a few days of death. Only one claimed to be 'in good helthe', and one other, a priest, dilated on the shortness of life and the possibility of sudden death.[17] In Paris, deathbed wills also formed a significant proportion of the whole, and there must also have been a number of sickbed wills written but not executed, owing to the patient's recovery. Jean Amery in 1571 expressed a precautionary sentiment also common in English wills ('considerant qu'il n'est rien plus certain que la mort et rien si incertain que le jour et l'heure d'icelle'), when he was already ill: 'et que dieu par ceste griefve maladie luy a pleu le visiter'. He still had time to make a full written testament.[18] In some of Chaunu's students' will samples, as many as 55, 60, or 75 per cent of wills were made 'gisant au lit malade', and in many cases death clearly ensued in fairly short order.[19] How well someone 'syke of bodye' could envisage and prescribe the ritual, and how far he or she may have been assisted or prompted by clerical or other attendants, is not clear, but some very detailed prescriptions do exist, for both London and Paris.

Joan Brytten of London (d. 1540) and Jeanne Passavent of Paris (d. 1582) were both widows of a middling or *bourgeoise* sort. The wills of both women specify the place of burial and the kind of service, itemising attendance, lights, ringing, distributions, and subsequent commemorations. They suggest that each woman, from her deathbed, envisaged her funeral as performance, centring on herself, with a cast moving in

[16] J. Murray, 'Kinship and friendship: the perception of family by clergy and laity in late medieval London', *Albion* 20.3 (1988), 376.

[17] *Consistory Court Wills*, passim, but esp. 32, 215. For further discussion of this, see V. Harding, 'Memento mori: la peur de l'agonie, de la mort et des morts à Londres au XVIIe siècle', *Histoire Urbaine* 2 (Dec. 2000), 39–57.

[18] Chaunu, *La mort à Paris*, p. 475.   [19] Ibid., pp. 188–9, 299.

a chosen setting according to her instructions.[20] These provisions are unusually comprehensive, but many sixteenth-century testators specified some aspect of their funeral.[21] Sir Cuthbert Buckle made his will when he was already 'diseased in body', only two days before he died on 30 June 1594, though he still invoked the stock phrase that 'death is most certain but the hour thereof altogether uncertain'. He may well have had a preliminary draft or an earlier will to work from, but his instructions – naming forty-six persons to whom mourning was to be given, and making other funeral bequests – indicate that scripting his own funeral and the distribution of remembrances was for him an important part of preparing for death.[22] Precise instructions of this kind became less common in seventeenth-century London wills, just as specification of the place of burial also waned, though they by no means disappeared.[23] It is hard to say whether their decline is due to either a more Puritan or a more secular view of the funeral ceremony. Arguably, since funeral ritual (and cost) was not itself declining, it simply reflects a move away from using the will to express such preferences; executors were trusted, and perhaps previously instructed, to do what was appropriate. In Paris, it appears that the majority continued to make some reference to their funeral; even if nearly half of a sample of 250 willmakers (1599–1653) left the arrangements to their executors, the mid-seventeenth century still marked 'un sommet dans le faste des convois'.[24] The pious preamble and the endowment of intercessory masses remained vigorous and widespread through the seventeenth century.[25]

From the moment of death, the inescapable course of physical decay impelled the sequence of actions and rituals. As far as can be ascertained, most bodies remained in the place of death until removed for interment. The registers of Saint-André-des-Arts often note the place of death ('mort en son hotel', 'mort en l'hotel de Thou', 'mort chez son frere Claude, logé en la rue Pavée') and this makes sense if this is where the funeral convoy started from.[26] More strikingly, when the baron de Thiers died

---

[20] See appendices 3, 4.   [21] *Consistory Court Wills*, passim.

[22] PRO, PROB 11/84, f. 87v; Bodl. MS Ashmole 818, f. 45.

[23] E.g. the will of John Juxon, senior, citizen, and merchant taylor, 1626 (PRO, PROB 11/150, f. 112), transcribed in K. Lindley and D. Scott (eds.), *The journal of Thomas Juxon, 1644–1647* (Camden 5th series 13, 1999) pp. 171–86. His son, Thomas Juxon, however, made no reference to his own funeral in his will of 1672 (PRO, PROB 11/340, f. 147): ibid., pp. 187–92.

[24] Chaunu, *La mort à Paris*, pp. 357–9.   [25] Ibid., pp. 365–431.

[26] BN, MS Fr. 32589, passim; cf. AN, L 510, microfilm no. 27. Some London parish registers also noted the dead person's origin or place of residence: see e.g. E. B. Jupp and R. Hovenden (eds.), *The registers of christenings, marriages and burials of the parish of Allhallows London Wall within the city of London, from the year of Our Lord 1559 to 1675* (London, 1878), pp. 88–135.

in a stranger's house after being attacked by enemies on his way home after supper, his body remained there for five days, before being removed to the family chapel in the parish church. It also appears that the convoy of Messire Jacques le Coigneux, *conseiller au Parlement*, started from the house of the linendraper on the pont Saint-Michel where he had died suddenly the previous night.[27] It looks as if it was felt impossible to transport the dead body of a notable individual except in a formal and ritualised manner. The vicar of the dean of Paris, who convoyed the bodies of deceased associates to burial, recorded the house, and often the room, in which death took place, and clearly expected to collect the body from that place.[28] This was also the case with the funeral convoys attended by the Bureau de Ville.[29] However, many poor people died in a space that was not their own and in which their bodies could not be permitted to stay. In Paris, the religious of Sainte-Catherine collected the dead from the streets and the river and buried them, probably mostly at the Innocents; the *emballeurs* of the Hôtel-Dieu were also rewarded for seeking and removing bodies from private houses and taking them to the Hôtel-Dieu, presumably for shrouding and a charity burial.[30] In London, the parish accepted responsibility for those found dead in the street, but the details of how such bodies were handled between death and burial are not clear.

In English practice, and in model circumstances, the body was washed after death, dressed at least in a shift, wrapped in a shroud or sheet, placed in a coffin or bier, and covered with a pall or cloth, ready for the watch.[31] The choice of burial place, and indeed the amount to be spent on the funeral, probably determined whether a burial was to be coffined or not, and whether wood or lead would be used, and few testators mentioned coffins in their wills.[32] Bodies that were to be buried without coffins would be completely wrapped, as the name suggests, in a winding-sheet.[33] In eighteenth-century Paris, the sisters of Charity supplied a shroud (*suaire*)

---

[27] BN, MS Fr. 32589, entries for 8 April 1565 and 18 Jan. 1623.

[28] AN, L 510, microfilm no. 27.

[29] E.g. *RDBVP*, vol. VIII, pp. 198–9, 352–4, 365–6, 502–3.

[30] Hillairet, *Les 200 cimetières*, p. 25; Brièle and Husson, *Inventaire-sommaire*, vol. II, p. 103. For discussion of the different treatment of 'personalised' and 'depersonalised' corpses in Paris, see Harding, 'Whose body?', pp. 171–6.

[31] Cressy, *Birth, marriage, and death*, pp. 425–32; Mr Tate, 'Of the Antiquity, Variety and Ceremonies of Funerals in England, [30 April 1600], in *A Collection of Curious Discourses written by eminent Antiquaries upon several heads in our English Antiquities, together with Mr Thomas Hearne's preface and appendix to the former edition*, 2 vols. (London, 1775), vol. I, p. 217. I thank Scott Newstrom for this reference. Cf. Chaunu, *La mort à Paris*, pp. 350–1, for the uncertainty of rituals around the corpse in Paris.

[32] One exception was Denise Leveson (d. 1560), who requested church burial and 'a coffin of boards': PRO, PROB 11/43, f. 463.

[33] Wieck, *Painted prayers*, pp. 120, 126, 128–31.

for pauper burials; it is not clear what happened earlier.[34] For burials of this kind, parishes and fraternities lent hearses and coffins, to serve for the vigil, transport, and funeral, retrieving them before the interment.[35] Shrouds for coffined burial could be looser and less completely concealing than those that wound a corpse; they served a different function and could be represented as more or less garment-like. John Donne and others are portrayed wearing shrouds that are closer to classical drapery, though still usually with the distinctive ties and knots of the real item.[36] Several writers have discussed the evolution of winding-sheets, shrouds, and corpse-clothes, and there is now some archaeological evidence for late seventeenth and early eighteenth-century practice in London. By that date, it was not uncommon to dress the corpse either in real clothes or in a simulacrum of them; it was also required (from 1678) that the shroud and other clothing be of wool.[37]

An important first step, for those of modest status who were not obliged to seek professional intervention, was to notify the sexton or gravedigger, so that a grave could be opened, and also to arrange the necessary equipment for the funeral. The authority for agreeing a grave space, fees, and other arrangements lay with the churchwardens, who were concerned to prevent private negotiations with gravedigger or priest.[38] In London the sexton delivered the parish's hearse-cloth to the house; he may also have brought a temporary coffin, for the watch or immediately before the removal of the body.[39] In Paris, too, the parish gravediggers were expected to deliver the pall, the bier or hearse, and trestles to the house where the dead person was, and bring them back with the body. An eighteenth-century gravedigger complained of having to go up to the fifth or sixth floors of some houses to collect bodies. The fact that these would have been the bodies of poorer persons, for whose burials he received less, added to his grievance.[40]

---

[34] AN, L 663. For the parish *charités*, see Bernard, *The emerging city*, pp. 142–5.

[35] The parish of St Dunstan in the West paid 20d. for a coffin in 1533–4, and probably owned at least two: GL MS 2968/1, ff. 105 ff (1533–4), 159 ff (1553–4). St Michael Cornhill mended its 'coffen that carrys the corsses to churche' in 1553–4: Overall, *Churchwardens' account of St Michael Cornhill*, p. 112.

[36] For examples see Litten, *English way of death*, pp. 67 (John Donne, 1632), 68 (Sir Geoffrey and Lady Palmer, 1674); Llewellyn, *Art of death*, pl. 30 (Lydia Dwight, *c.* 1674).

[37] Esp. Litten, *English way of death*, pp. 57–84. Cf. Janaway, 'An introductory guide to textiles from 18th and 19th century burials', pp. 17–32.

[38] E.g. GL, MS 3016/2, f. 5v (St Dunstan in the West, 1664); AN, L 651 (Saint-Gervais, 1675); AN, LL 687, ff. 183r–184 (Saint-André-des-Arts, 1687).

[39] See e.g. GL (printed books), Broadsides 12.79; Overall, *Churchwardens' accounts of St Michael Cornhill*, p. 112.

[40] AN, LL 805, p. 255; BN, MS Fr. 21609, f. 37; AN, L 663 (un-numbered 18C papers concerning charity burials at Saint-Jean-en-Grève).

Pre-modern burials were normally prompt, with a small number very delayed, and this was the case in both London and Paris. The pre-Reformation practice of reciting *placebo* with vespers the night before the funeral and a dirge and mass on the morrow implies at least a day's interval for most people. In many cases it may not have been much more, though there was a natural correlation between rank and length of time to burial; heraldic funerals clearly took days or even weeks to arrange.[41] Stephen Gardiner, bishop of Winchester, remained unburied for over three months, from 13 November 1555, when he died at Whitehall, to 24 February 1556, when he was buried in Winchester.[42] In the later sixteenth century, although there is little statistical evidence, burial on the same day was not unknown, and it seems likely that most intervals were short, though as the antiquary Tate wrote in 1600, 'Amongst us there is not any sett and determinate time how longe the corps should be kept, but as seemeth best to the friends of the deceased.'[43] In the city-centre parish of St Mary Woolnoth in the second half of the seventeenth century, 70 per cent of the dead had been buried by the end of the second day after death. As earlier, longer death–burial intervals correlate with higher rank: for such people, the problem of arranging a substantial funeral seems to have delayed the ceremony and interment.[44]

In Paris, even in a sample of higher social status from the parish of Saint-André-des-Arts, at least 75 per cent had been buried by the end of the second day after death. The modal burial date moved from the day of death in the mid-sixteenth century to the day after in the later sixteenth and seventeenth, but there is no indication that it was becoming common for burial to take more than three days. Moving a body around was likely to extend the interval, though not inevitably and not necessarily for long. Transport and burial on the same day were quite feasible.[45]

[41] Houlbrooke, *Death, religion and the family*, p. 259; Machyn, *Diary*, pp. 105–6, 111, 155, 170–1, 218–19, 268–9, 270–1, 306–7; *Collectanea topographica et genealogica*, vol. IV (London, 1837), pp. 382–4 (I thank Caroline Barron for this reference); BL, Add. MSS 71131/A–X.

[42] Machyn, *Diary*, pp. 96–7, 100–1.

[43] E.g *Register of St Pancras Soper Lane*, pp. 287–8; Tate, 'Of the Antiquity, Variety and Ceremonies of Funerals in England', p. 217.

[44] S. Porter, 'Death and burial in a London parish: St Mary Woolnoth, 1653–99', *London Journal* 8 (1982), 76–80.

[45] BN, MS Fr. 32589. The 597 cases with dates of death and burial are only 36 per cent of the total number of surviving register entries; and the entries are themselves selected from a larger whole, of which, at best, they probably make up not much more than 10 per cent; so the 597 cases may only be 3 to 4 per cent of the total of burials. Funerals of the poor are not represented at all. These would probably bring down the death–burial interval still further. There would be little reason for delay: no elaborate arrangements to be made, a common grave already open, not to mention the cramped living conditions of the poor and the unlikelihood of preservative measures. Cf. Harding, 'Whose body?', pp. 176–80.

Some burials, even of the great, happened in a remarkably short time. Dr François le Picart, dean of Saint-Germain-l'Auxerrois, died in the early hours of 17 September 1566. Within a few hours his body had been opened and the heart removed. The body was displayed in the courtyard of his *logis* that afternoon, and many came to view it. At about 5 o'clock it was taken into the church of Saint-Germain, and the heart buried; then the full funeral procession escorted the body to the church of the Blancs-Manteaux, where it was buried that evening. On the next day, the company reassembled for the *service* and funeral oration.[46] On the other hand, some funerals took weeks or even months. Long-distance convoys were largely confined to the highest groups in society – burial outside Paris was usually on the deceased's family estates – so in that respect too a long death–burial interval correlated with class.[47]

Liturgy, choice, and change

The individualisation of the funeral performance, whether specified by the deceased or by his or her executors, entailed a series of choices between possible alternatives. The first choice, usually made before death, and in many cases not a conscious choice at all, was the location of burial.[48] This decision was partly influenced by cost, but still more by association and affiliation. As we have seen, most people were buried in their parish of residence; a minority chose burial in some other location, either another parish, a conventual church or churchyard, or one of the civic or non-parochial churchyards. A substantial minority in right-bank Paris chose the Innocents. Of those buried in their parish, a few chose, and many more accepted, burial in the churchyard, but a small but important number chose burial in the church, sometimes specifying a particular site. The decision on location determined the physical setting of the funeral ceremonies, and by extension some of the attendant clerical personnel.[49] For those buried in private or family chapels, the setting may have been prepared over a longer period, and its appearance could certainly have been envisaged. The choice of location also framed the range of choices about service and accoutrements which could subsequently be made, since most of these were offered or managed by the representatives of the burial church itself. Although parishes were not competing with one another directly for burials, there was probably a spirit of fairly

---

[46] *RDBVP*, vol. II, pp. 450–1; cf. ibid., vol. V, pp. 54–5.

[47] E.g. BN, MS Fr. 32589, entries for 5 March 1645, 4 July 1616.

[48] According to Naz, *Dictionnaire du droit canonique*, only the deceased, not his heirs or family, may make this choice; it cannot be presumed: vol. V, p. 920.

[49] See chapter 9, pp. 236–8, below.

friendly rivalry and emulation between them as to the kinds and qualities of services they could provide for their parishioners. In pre-Reformation London and in Paris, parishes were also conscious that the convents, including the friaries, were in a more real sense their competitors in this field. As with the place of burial, increasing demand (in both numbers and quality) stimulated the management of supply: relying on the strength of personal wishes and the pressure to conform to expectations, the parish vestries offered a range of bells, hearse-cloths, hangings, and silverware.

The liturgical core of the Catholic funeral ceremonies was the trio known as *placebo*, *dirige*, and *requiem*. *Placebo*, or evensong for the dead, was recited in church the night before the funeral; *dirige* (alias dirge) or matins was usually said or sung the following day in the presence of the corpse, and was immediately followed by the requiem mass and interment. By the end of the middle ages some special votive masses were available to those who could afford it, in addition to the standard requiem.[50] The liturgical choices made in pre-Reformation London reflected personal devotions as well as an appreciation of display and drama, together with an awareness of cost. The primary distinction was between high and low *dirige*, and high and low mass. The 'high' versions entailed a larger cast and a longer performance, and hence greater expense: Sir James Taylor, priest, in 1519, apologising for the fact that 'my substance is no bettyr', asked his executor to ordain for him 'a lowe dirige and a masse of requiem becawse I have but smalle goodes'.[51] More ambitious choices, from testators in the same middling social stratum, were for a sung mass, or an additional sequence of five masses of the Five Wounds.[52] Up until the time of the Edwardian reforms, most London parishes had several chantry priests, chaplains and conducts, and some could probably put on an elaborate musical performance. St Michael Cornhill appointed a choirmaster in 1509, with detailed instructions as to his duties 'syngyng of pryksong and playnsong'.[53] The church of St Mary at Hill certainly had several singing priests at the Reformation, and apparently a local musical tradition. William Peyrson, a clerk there, in 1545 requested a mass and *dirige* by note 'accordyng to the use and custome of the sayd churche', for which each of the priests and clerks was to be paid 12d.[54]

---

[50] Duffy, *Stripping of the altars*, p. 369.   [51] *Consistory Court Wills*, 90.
[52] Ibid., 59, 85, 86, 102, 155.
[53] Overall, *Churchwardens' accounts of St Michael Cornhill*, pp. 1–2.
[54] *Consistory Court Wills*, 236; C. Burgess, 'Shaping the parish: St Mary at Hill, London, in the fifteenth century', in J. Blair and B. Golding (eds.), *The cloister and the world: essays in medieval history in honour of Barbara Harvey* (Oxford, 1996), pp. 248–50.

Wills and other accounts of funerals from London from the 1540s and 1550s indicate some confusion and inconsistency, and a great deal of variation from case to case. We can see a new theology of salvation: many wills omit the traditional request for intercession from the Virgin and the holy company of heaven (which both Joan Brytten and Jeanne Passavent invoked) and express a belief in the merits of Christ's blood and passion as the only source of redemption.[55] The endowment of chantries and commemorative services dwindled, to disappear under Edward. Liturgical variation was obviously curtailed by the Protestant prayerbooks, but the most obvious thing to go in the Edwardian reforms was the multiplication, in time or space, of liturgical celebration. Funerals were now commonly performed on a single day, and without either simultaneous services elsewhere or repeated services in the same place. The funeral was the end: it was not re-enacted, as in the annual obit, and the deceased was not taken as having any significant and ongoing relationship with the living. Benefactors' names were no longer kept on bederolls or recalled in beneficial masses.[56] Preference for a reformed liturgy was also occasionally expressed: Ralph Davenaunt in 1552 asked for the Parish Clerks to bring his body to the earth, 'singing such godly psalms in English before me as now be used for the dead'.[57] Henry Machyn, the London merchant taylor and memorialiser of city ceremonials in the 1550s, records the shifts over those years. His notes of Edwardian funerals are laconic, but mention sermons, and singing up to 1552. From the accession of Mary, the dirge and requiem mass were restored, with torches and candles.[58] He notes that several higher-status people such as aldermen had three successive masses on the day of burial, usually sung masses of the Trinity and Our Lady as well as the requiem.[59] Soon after Elizabeth's accession, though Catholic services did not cease immediately, Machyn begins to report funerals with 'nodur crosse nor prest, nor clarkes, but a sermon and after a salme of Davyd', or the presence of 'the nuw prychers in ther gowne lyke ley[men]' and prayers in English.[60]

The Elizabethan prayerbook, which governed Anglican funeral ritual until the Directory of Public Worship in 1645, eliminated lights and clerical processions, but left space for the 'personalisation' of the funeral with the accoutrements noted below, and the processions discussed in chapter 9. Bishops remained anxious that old practices continued to subvert the new, enquiring in 1560 whether parish clerks 'use to sing any

[55] E.g. *Consistory Court Wills*, 120, 206, 240.   [56] Duffy, *Stripping of the altars*, pp. 474–5.
[57] PRO, PROB 11/36, f. 11.   [58] E.g. Machyn, *Diary*, pp. 17, 43, 59.
[59] Ibid., pp. 99, 106, 110, 161, 167, 171.   [60] Ibid., pp. 179, 191, 193, 199.

number of psalms, dirge-like, at the burial of the dead?'[61] In the later sixteenth and seventeenth centuries, the choices available to those who wished to direct the spiritual character, as well as the material setting, of their funeral focused on preachers and sermons. Some merely left money that there should be a sermon; others named the preacher. Already quite common by the mid-sixteenth century, the genre, both preached and published, expanded considerably in the century after the Reformation.[62] It is probable that most Londoners of middling status and above had some kind of address at their funeral, most commonly given by the local minister or lecturer, but in some cases involving an invited outsider. In the 1660s the keen funeral-goer Richard Smyth noted the occasional absence of a sermon as if it were somewhat unusual.[63]

Though we should not underestimate the esteem with which conformist Anglicans regarded the liturgy of the prayerbook,[64] Puritan sympathies and observances, and a stronger resistance to funeral ceremony, were certainly present in London. Londoners were among those vocal in their opposition to Anglican ceremonial, including vestments, and many parishes showed their support for more advanced Protestantism by funding lectures, for which they often employed men of Puritan sympathies.[65] London was also a home for the early separatist churches. The New Churchyard offered a place of burial for members of irregular or dissenting congregations; an order of 1590 suggests that some funeral ceremonies there did not follow the Anglican prescription.[66] Londoners were also vocal in their opposition to the Laudian injunctions of the 1630s, which included full observance of the rituals and dress prescribed by the prayerbook. Possibly such sympathies lay behind the protest of the wife of Francis Jessop, who in 1636 attempted to bury her own daughter at St Katherine Creechurch without the services of the minister, and boycotted the service when he intervened.[67] The Directory of Public Worship of 1645 rejected the customs of kneeling, praying, and singing around

[61] W. H. Frere (ed.), *Visitation articles and injunctions of the period of the Reformation*, 3 vols. (London, 1910), vol. III, p. 91.

[62] Houlbrooke, *Death, religion and the family*, pp. 295–330.

[63] McMurray, *Records of two city parishes*, pp. 206, 207, 210, 214, 215, 232, 233, 235, 236, 237, 238, 326; Richard Smyth, *The Obituary of Richard Smyth, Secondary of the Poultry Compter, London, being a catalogue of all such persons as he knew in their life, extending from AD 1627 to AD 1674*, ed. H. Ellis (London, 1849), pp. 75, 84, 93, 97, 98.

[64] Maltby, *Prayer book and people*, esp. pp. 1–30.

[65] Cressy, *Birth, marriage and death*, pp. 403–9; Collinson, *The Elizabethan Puritan movement*, esp. pp. 84–91; Seaver, *The Puritan lectureships*.

[66] Collinson, *The Elizabethan Puritan movement*, pp. 370–1; M. Tolmie, *The triumph of the Saints. The separate churches of London, 1616–1649* (Cambridge, 1977). See above, pp. 95–8.

[67] Cressy, *Birth, marriage and death*, p. 405.

the corpse, but as Cressy has noted 'it lacked the disciplinary machinery to secure any kind of uniformity. Radicals could bury as they wished, while conservatives could continue as before'.[68] London in the 1640s and 1650s contained congregations that instituted the full Presbyterian structure, others that failed to do so, a few traditional Anglicans, and many independent or gathered congregations.[69] Almost certainly there was a variety of funeral practices, with only the most ritualistic observances being excluded. Testators continued to choose places of burial, to specify more than minimal burial costs, and to leave bequests to local poor for attendance. Churchwardens' accounts and vestry minutes, while they reflect responses to many contemporary developments, do not suggest any consistent changes in burial practice.[70] The parish of St Bartholomew Exchange continued to pay sums of between 10s. and about £1 2s. for the funerals of foundlings and pensioners through the 1650s, including payments to the bearers and for the cloth, and for wine and bread.[71] By this time also, however, the alternative approach was well established, and the separation of Quakers and other nonconformists from Anglican burial places and traditions was becoming marked.[72]

Catholic Paris continued to offer a wide range of liturgical choices, both in number and location and in specific devotion. The traditional funeral service and associated ritual of the middle ages were not undermined by changes in the sixteenth century. As Jeanne Passavent's will, typical of many, indicates, there was considerable continuity. The reform of ritual in 1614 simplified the formal requirements, and the second and third funeral masses were omitted, leaving only the mass of requiem; this change may not have been universally observed immediately, but appears to have been firmly established by the later seventeenth century.[73] Seventeenth-century Parisians seem to have concentrated more on the sequence of commemorative and intercessory masses beginning after the interment than on the liturgy of the funeral itself. There is indeed no consistent distinction, in the use of words such as *obsèques*, *pompe funèbre*, and *funerailles*, between services said at the time of burial and those held later or for someone dying and buried elsewhere.[74] It is not always easy to distinguish testamentary requests for masses at the time of the funeral

---

[68] Ibid., p. 416.   [69] Tai Liu, *Puritan London*, pp. 51–148.

[70] E.g. McMurray, *Records of two city parishes*, pp. 236–7, 337–47.

[71] E. Freshfield (ed.), *The account books of St Bartholomew Exchange in the city of London, 1596–1698* (London, 1895), pp. 141–66.

[72] Stock, 'Quaker burial: doctrine and practice', pp. 129–43. For an attempted Quaker burial in 1664, see McMurray, *Records of two city parishes*, pp. 101, 349.

[73] Ariès, *Hour of our death*, p. 178.

[74] Cf. R. Giesey, *The royal funeral ceremony in Renaissance France* (Geneva, 1960), p. 159, on the performance of obsequies without the body.

from the establishment of services of a more commemorative nature, but the majority of a sample of sixteenth-century testators, and a fairly large minority of seventeenth-century ones, used their wills to request specific numbers of masses. The proportion asking for more than sixty masses – implying a more extended period of commemoration – was small in the sixteenth century, but increased in the seventeenth.[75] Claude le Gay, widow, did not specify the service at her funeral in 1634, but asked for fifty low masses to be said in the church of her burial on the day of her death, or if not possible, on the morrow; she also asked for a total of five *services complets* to be sung in four other churches immediately after her death.[76] Nicolas Lambert, *conseiller du roi* and *sécretaire de ses finances*, was more explicit about his priorities in 1646. Conscious that the funeral (in the modern sense) centred on the physical body, which would soon be reduced to decay and dust, he asked that the *pompes funèbres* be carried out with the honour and modesty required by his condition as a miserable sinner. For the salvation of his soul, however, apart from the prayers and services that would be said at his burial, he specified two low masses for a year, in his parish church and a nearby convent.[77] Especially striking, by comparison with reformed practice in London, are the large numbers of priests involved in the liturgical life of the parish, and the continuing flourishing tradition of endowment for commemorative purposes. At Saint-Jean-en-Grève, Jeanne Passavent's parish, there were at least twenty-five new foundations of commemorative services between 1550 and 1600, and nearly fifty between 1600 and 1670. Some of these were just anniversary masses, some weekly or daily services, and not all were being fully maintained by the end of the seventeenth century, but the total is impressive.[78] Several parishes could only keep track of the sequence of services and commemorations that their priests were bound to perform by setting out a detailed programme organised by days of the week, month, and special dates.[79]

The concentration on longer-term intercession need not mean that Parisians lacked interest in the details of the services held at the time of interment, but the evidence does suggest that their concern focused on attendance and appearance rather than liturgical variety. The city churches were well staffed with priests and chaplains, whose attendance could be obtained for the appropriate payment, while the numerous religious communities in the city could supply additional personnel, often distinctively clad, representing a range of devotional associations. The lavishly baroque funeral preparations of a Parisian of relatively modest

---

[75] Chaunu, *La mort à Paris*, p. 410.   [76] Ibid., pp. 505–7.   [77] Ibid., pp. 515–16.
[78] AN, LL 805.   [79] E.g. AN, LL 691, 692 (Saint-André-des-Arts).

status, Raphael Bonnard, *marchand fripier*, in 1616, required the *curé* and forty priests of his parish church, and the attendance of members of the convents of the Augustins, the Cordeliers, the Jacobins, and the Carmes. His body was to be carried by brothers of the Caputs de Montaigu, and attended by children from the four hospitals of Saint-Esprit, la Trinité, the Enfants Rouges, and the Enfants de la Charité, all bearing torches.[80] Selection among the available religious, if usually on a more modest scale, clearly remained a significant and characteristic aspect of Parisian funerals, as it could no longer be in London. Pre-Reformation Londoners had called on parish clergy, children, and members of the religious orders to attend their funerals, but the number of religious personnel was sharply reduced by the Dissolution and the suppression of the chantries, whereas in Paris new orders and houses multiplied.[81] There may also have been a strong impulse on the part of devout testators to assert and exploit this particularly Catholic, Counter-Reformation, and Parisian feature of religious practice in their arrangements for interment and commemoration.

Lights, cloths, and bells

As has been noted, the liturgy formed only the core of a larger and more elaborate funeral performance. The Catholic rite was augmented by a number of 'paraliturgical rituals', many of which could be varied according to choice and means; even though some elements were eliminated from the reformed rite, it still allowed choice and the articulation of identity and status.

Almost inseparable from the sounds and gestures of the Catholic liturgy was the use of lights. Candles burned during funeral ceremonies, either placed around the hearse, in the hands of processionaries, or on the altar, 'an act with profound resonances', standing both for the illumination of Christ and as a form of prayer for the deceased.[82] In pre-Reformation London, churchwardens' accounts for wax, or separate lightwardens' accounts, suggest that every burial had some lights burning, either provided at the expense of the deceased or given of charity. The lightwardens' account for St Andrew Holborn for 1477–8 records the supply of lights for twenty-nine individuals (including ten children), probably all the deaths in the parish that year.[83] Other parishes recorded fewer payments, for larger or more numerous lights ('R of goodwife Cletherow for the ij

---

[80] Chaunu, *La mort à Paris*, p. 358, citing the research of Bruno de Cessole.
[81] E.g. *Consistory Court Wills*, 10, 39, 57, 59, 82, 143, 164, 215; Pillorget, *Paris sous les premiers Bourbons*, pp. 496–509; B. Plongeron, *Le diocèse de Paris*, vol. I: *Des origines à la Révolution* (Paris, 1987), pp. 230–4.
[82] Duffy, *Stripping of the altars*, pp. 361–2; cf. ibid., p. 147.
[83] Barron and Roscoe, 'The medieval parish church of St Andrew Holborn'.

standards in the choir for the waste at her husbands terment, 4d.'),[84] and probably supplied lights free for the poor. Some individuals provided lights for their own funerals but left what remained for the use of the parish. Richard Mylles in 1544 ordained six torches for his funeral; after his month's mind, two were to remain in his parish church of St Mary Colechurch, and two each to the nearby churches of St Sithe and St Stephen Walbrook, 'to be burnyd in the said churche to the honer and prayse of All myghty God'.[85] The practice also provided an opportunity to combine charity with religious observance, since poor men were often employed as lightbearers.[86]

Testators specified the number and kind of lights they wished to have or could afford. Joan Brytten had five children carrying 1-lb tapers, and more tapers before the cross; John Hudson, citizen and ironmonger, had four children holding tapers, but 'no torchis I will have'.[87] These were modest funerals in parish churches, and there are very few references in London churchwardens' accounts and the wills of the middling sort to more than six lights at a time. Belonging to a fraternity was a way of guaranteeing a better provision of light. The rules of the fraternity of St Fabian and St Sebastian in the church of St Botolph Aldersgate prescribed seven wax tapers each weighing 20 lbs, to be lit on feast days, and also to be set about the bodies of brethren who could not afford their own. Torches also were to be provided when any dead brother was brought into church. The fraternity of St Katherine in the same church had similar rules, but only provided five tapers; the fraternity of Holy Trinity kept both torches and tapers.[88] Craft guilds and companies likewise supported the burial of poor members. The Brewers' Company buried two almsmen in 1435–6: for one they paid 10d. 'for the hyre of ij taperes wt the wast and other smalcandell', while for the second they paid 10d. for two wax tapers, each of 4 lbs, and 14d. for 'the wast of torches wt the haldyng of the same'.[89] The number and resulting splendour of candles, tapers, torches, and standards could be multiplied almost indefinitely, and a grand funeral could have hundreds of lights. The sister of Clarenceux Herald was buried at the Savoy in 1556 with a hundred silver candlesticks, each with a half-pound candle, and twelve torches. This may have been exceptional, but the Catholic alderman Sir Thomas White buried his wife in March 1558 with 'a goodly herse of wax', four dozen torches, and 'ij grett whytt branchys'.[90]

---

[84] GL, MS 6842, f. 28.   [85] *Consistory Court Wills*, 215.   [86] Ibid., 59, 155.
[87] Ibid., 122, 85.
[88] P. Basing (ed.), *Parish fraternity register Fraternity of the Holy Trinity and SS. Fabian and Sebastian in the parish of St Botolph without Aldersgate* (London, 1982), pp. 139, 140, 103.
[89] GL, MS 5440, f. 269v. I thank Judith Bennett for this reference.
[90] Machyn, *Diary*, pp. 121, 167. Cf. pp. 47, 59, 99, 119.

Lights were one of the features of religious practice specifically targeted by the reformers. Lights before images were condemned as superstitious in 1538, as were rood-lights and the use of candles round corpses in the Injunctions of 1547.[91] London churches sold off their stocks of wax, and lightwardens closed their accounts.[92] The accounts of St Martin in the Fields record receipts and payments for lights consistently up to 1545–6, and again in the account starting at Christmas 1553, but not in between.[93] Machyn reports one funeral with torches in the reign of Edward VI, in June 1552, but this was an Italian ('Baptyst Borow the melener'), which may have been a reason for the exception. Torches and tapers were carried again at funerals throughout Mary's reign and in the first year of Elizabeth's. Machyn's last reference to torches appears to be the funeral of Lady Copley in Southwark in December 1559, 'with xx grett stayffe torchys bornyng', but before then, in October 1559, Lady Cobham had been buried in Kent with 'a goodly hers with-owtt wax'.[94] The Elizabethan Injunctions repeated those of 1547. Bishop Bentham of Coventry and Lichfield enjoined his clergy in 1565 'away with your lights at the burial of the dead', and Grindal in London must have taken a similar line.[95]

A lingering attachment to old forms, and an appreciation of their aesthetic quality, is suggested by the new tradition of honourable night burial, first much remarked in the early seventeenth century. It appears to have been an aristocratic innovation, drawing on Scottish practice and perhaps also on revulsion from the expense and formality of the heraldic funeral. Although it had not been hitherto a popular option in England, being associated with shameful burial, a number of the gentry and nobility in London chose night burial in the seventeenth century.[96] It obviously entailed the use of torchlight and candles, which may have been part of the attraction for some, but was also a cause of anxiety: 'I rather think it was brought up by papists which serve their turn by it in many ways.'[97] The occasional specification of daytime burial may therefore have been an expression of religious opposition to this practice.[98] Although night

[91] Duffy, *Stripping of the altars*, pp. 407, 451, 461.

[92] Walters, *London churches at the Reformation*, pp. 333, 415, 453, 481, 502.

[93] Kitto, *St Martin in the Fields, accounts of the churchwardens*, pp. 1–110, 151–78.

[94] Machyn, *Diary*, pp. 21, 43–177 passim, 179, 193, 194, 201, 213–14, 221.

[95] P. L. Hughes and J. F. Larkin (eds.), *Tudor royal Proclamations*, 3 vols. (New Haven, 1969), vol. III, *The later Tudors (1588–1603)*, pp. 122–4; Frere, *Visitation articles and injunctions of the period of the Reformation*, vol. III, p. 166.

[96] Houlbrooke, *Death, religion and the family*, pp. 272–5; Gittings, *Death, burial and the individual*, pp. 188–215, esp. p. 199; J. Woodward, *The theatre of death. The ritual management of royal funerals in Renaissance England* (Woodbridge, 1997), p. 141.

[97] McClure, *Letters of John Chamberlain*, vol. I, p. 578 (1615). Cf. Forbes, *Chronicle from Aldgate*, p. 30 (night burial of a recusant, 1617).

[98] E.g. GL, MS 9051/8, f. 353; McMurray, *Records of two city parishes*, p. 214.

burial revived the use of lights and torches, it seems likely that these were not supplied or purveyed by parish churches, as before, but by one of the private agencies increasingly involved in funeral provision.

Parisian practice with regard to lights seems to be similar to that in pre-Reformation London, in that it was shaped by personal choice, the need to make charitable provision, and the possibility of support from fraternities and guilds. Unlike London, of course, the use of lights as an element of the church's provision continued into the later sixteenth and seventeenth centuries, and may have been consciously encouraged. At the highest level, the number consumed was prodigious. The *chapelle ardente* for the service held in Notre-Dame for the queen of Spain in 1611 had 800 or 900 candles of half a pound each, and there were six great chandeliers with more large candles, and candles lining the choir and nave at one-foot intervals.[99] The cortège of Cardinal Richelieu in 1642 is said to have had over 2,000 candles and torches.[100] Lights had a very important part to play in later sixteenth- and seventeenth-century funeral convoys and processions, carried before or around the corpse, varying from a dozen to scores or even hundreds. One of the contributions made by the Bureau de Ville to honour colleagues and other notables was to provide torches, with the arms of the Ville, at their burials, from four for a *quartenier* to a dozen for an *échevin*.[101] At a more modest level, parishes hired out silver candlesticks for the vigil (up to twenty at Saint-André-des-Arts), and argued about who had charge of the waste wax from candles burning in the church.[102] Parisian citizens, like Londoners, often specified the number and kind of lights they wanted to be used: Jeanne Passavent had four dozen torches, each weighing 2 lbs; Raphael Bonnard had a dozen 1-lb torches carried by children, and at least an equal number carried by the religious who attended his convoy. Others, as in London, left it to their executors.[103] Lights were also maintained in particular memories on a more or less permanent basis in the church, as well as being used for anniversaries and chantry masses.

The use of hangings and hearse-cloths made an important contribution to the spectacle of the funeral. For noble and heraldic funerals, the church was hung with black, and in such cases there were usually also troops of soberly clad poor and mourners, but for most burials the hearse-cloth was the principal furnishing. London parishes owned cloths which they lent out for parishioners' funerals. Probably most had been gifts or bequests to the parish, some specifically recalling the donor's name: donating a cloth

---

[99] *RDBVP*, vol. XV, pp. 117–21.   [100] Chaunu, *La mort à Paris*, p. 357.
[101] See chapter 9, below.
[102] AN, LL 687, ff. 5v, 183v–184; cf. Thibaut-Payen, *Les morts, l'église, et l'état*, p. 69.
[103] AN, L 664, no. 6; Chaunu, *La mort à Paris*, pp. 358, 509.

of this kind was a pious work in itself, but also a way of ensuring notice and prayer from a funeral congregation in the future. Others belonged to parish fraternities. In 1555 the parish of St Dunstan in the West had four cloths, including one of green and gold velvet, one called 'Mrs Flaxton's hearsecloth', and two others kept by the sexton. Before the Reformation the wardens of St John's light in the church had been in charge of 'St John's hearsecloth'.[104]

These pre-Reformation hearse-cloths were often elaborate and beautiful. This is one area where London parishes were perhaps exceptionally well equipped, compared with other urban and rural parishes, having over the years accumulated donations from wealthy and pious parishioners, with access both to the imported fabrics and to the craftsmanship with which they were made.[105] The Edwardian inventories indicate, for example, that St Michael Cornhill had two fine hearse-cloths, one of purple velvet with images of gold, with a blue buckram cover for it, and another of black and red Bruges satin, with images of gold, and a black buckram cover. All Hallows the Great had one of black velvet with dead men's heads, but also one of black camlet with a cross of red *bawdkyn*.[106] Where there was more than one cloth, the differences in appearance or quality could be a means of denoting different categories, such as the cloths of blue velvet with pelicans for adults, and of tawny velvet for children, owned by St Stephen Coleman in 1542.[107] Parish fraternities lent cloths, and some Londoners also were able to borrow the hearse-cloths of the city companies, such as that given to the Drapers in 1518 by Alderman John Milborn and his wife, worth 100 marks, or the surviving one of the Saddlers' Company, of crimson and gold velvet, embroidered with the company's arms and religious symbols.[108]

London parishes seem to have retained their hearse-cloths at the Reformation, though the religious symbols and words, originally intended to attract devotion (and perhaps subliminally seen as offering talismanic

---

[104] Walters, *London churches at the Reformation*, p. 256; GL, MS 2968/1, ff. 48v, 164, 167, 172.

[105] Walters, *London churches at the Reformation*, passim. Damasked and/or embroidered cloths of gold and other colours are illustrated in a number of continental books of hours: Wieck, *Painted prayers*, pp. 120–7.

[106] Walters, *London churches at the Reformation*, pp. 94, 498. *Bawdkyn*, baudekin: a rich embroidered stuff, rich brocade (OED).

[107] GL, MS 4456, p. 19.

[108] W. Herbert, *The history of the twelve great Livery Companies of London*, 2 vols. (London, 1834, 1837; reprint, Newton Abbott, 1968), vol. I, pp. 71–2, 444. The Saddlers' pall is illustrated in K. Oliver, *Treasures and plate: the collection of the Saddlers' Company* (Chichester, 1995), pp. 18–19 and endpapers; the Vintners', in Llewellyn, *Art of death*, pl. 49; the Parish Clerks', in R. H. Adams, *The parish clerks of London. A history of the Worshipful Company of Parish Clerks of London* (London, 1971), pl. II.

protection), were probably amended or deleted to conform to new sensibilities, as in the case of the Saddlers' hearse-cloth.[109] Over the early modern period, the cloth seems to have changed in appearance and somewhat in function, though there is no consistent change of nomenclature. Early examples and illustrations indicate shaped, richly decorated cloths, cut with flaps to hang neatly over a coffin or hearse; later ones show more voluminous examples that draped the coffin more fully and sometimes enveloped the bearers.[110] Probably parishes replaced their embroidered cloths at different dates, according to need or local sentiment. The Parish Clerks' surviving hearse-cloth of crimson and black velvet was either newly made or re-embroidered after 1582, with the new arms of the company granted that year.[111] St Anne Aldersgate in the 1580s had their best hearse-cloth newly embroidered with candlesticks ('xvj new branches'), and edged with cord or fringe, for a cost of at least 33s. 10d.[112] However, though gorgeous cloths remained in use for some time, black or sober colours became more common. In 1615 the parish of St Mary Colechurch paid 9s. 4d. for 'dressing, drawing and dieing' a black hearse-cloth, while in the same year two old hearse-cloths, possibly coloured ones, were made into a carpet for the communion table and a pulpit cloth.[113] In 1624 the parish of St Dunstan in the West paid 58s. 6d. for three and a quarter yards of 'brown blue cloth' for a burial cloth, presumably of good-quality woollen.[114] Black cloths were accepted as an indispensable part of the funeral ritual by the 1640s, required for decency and comeliness and apparently free from Puritan suspicion. The parish of St Anne Aldersgate bought a new black burial cloth in 1653–4, and hired it out for at least 1s.; the parish of St Christopher le Stocks bought a black cloth in 1658; the parish of St Giles Cripplegate bought 'a very good hearsecloth' in 1659.[115]

Parishes had begun to charge for the use of the hearse-cloth from the 1540s onwards, perhaps to replace the income they had formerly gained from wax and lights, perhaps also to maintain one of the possible differentials in the quality of funerals.[116] By the seventeenth century many

---

[109] Oliver, *Treasures and plate*, pp. 18–19.

[110] Litten, *English way of death*, pp. 9, 12–15; Llewellyn, *Art of death*, pp. 73–4.

[111] Adams, *Parish clerks of London*, pp. 18, 32, and pl. II. The new arms eliminated the six 'haly water sprencles' of the older arms, relics of a now-disused ritual. The new cloth was repaired again in 1686.

[112] McMurray, *Records of two city parishes*, p. 63.   [113] GL, MS 66, ff. 15–16.

[114] GL, MS 2968, f. 247v.

[115] McMurray, *Records of two city parishes*, pp. 344, 346; Freshfield, *Vestry minutes of St Christopher le Stocks*, p. 43; GL, MS 6048/1, f. 2v.

[116] The earliest reference to hiring a parish hearse-cloth in London sources that I have found is at St Mary Woolnoth, 1539–40: GL, MS 1002/1A, f. 2. Payments may have been made for fraternity cloths before then: cf. C. Welch (ed.), *Churchwardens' accounts*

parishes had a better and a less good cloth, and charged accordingly for their use. At St Andrew Undershaft in 1638, the black hearse-cloth was lent out at twice the rate of an embroidered one.[117] At St Giles Cripplegate in 1644, 'any of the clothes that cover the corps of the dead ... are freely lent without any pay whatsoever, only what you please to give the sexton for his labour to bring it', but this was unusual, and by 1664 the same parish was charging 2s., 1s. 6d., and 1s. for use of its best, second, and third cloths.[118] Presumably 'best' and 'worst' cloths must have been visibly distinguishable, even if both were black, perhaps because of the quality of the material or the edgings or trimmings.

Parisian parishes supplied both the pall (*poêle* or occasionally *drap*) to cover the body, and the *argenterie*, the silver cross and branches for the candles, for the vigil: it was the gravedigger who delivered them to the house of the deceased, after negotiation with the family and the parish clergy. He also retrieved, cleaned, and folded them afterwards.[119] Many palls, as in London, were the gift of wealthy parishioners or benefactors. In 1542 the *abbé* of Gaillac gave the churchwardens of Saint-Gervais a velvet pall he had had made for the funeral in their church of his brother, François de Voisins, late seneschal of Rouergue, and for his obit. In 1576 the parish had at least three more palls. One was 'ung poisle de velours doublé de toille noire garny de broderie sur le meillieu ou sont les images de Saint-Gervais et Saint-Protais et une orme au meillieu semé et fleurie de lys dor de bassin ayant les ymages des quatre evangelistes aux quatres coings'. Another was of velvet lined with black cloth, with a cross of Bruges satin 'semé de larmes', while a third, given by M. de Charmeaulx, was of black damask.[120] Saint-André-des-Arts in the early seventeenth century had three palls or cloths given by MM. de Thou, Seguier, and de Montholon, local notables, another with the arms of M. Devousay, and another with candlesticks on it. The first of these may be the pall of black velvet with a white satin cross made for the funeral of Christophe de Thou in the church in 1582. The first three palls could be hired for 3 *livres* each, the other two for 16 or 20 *sous*; there were two more 'pour le commun' for which nothing was charged.[121] The same parish in 1687 inventoried three palls of black velvet ('le beau poel', 'le second poel', and 'le commun

of the parish of All Hallows London Wall, 1455–1536 (London, 1912), p. 48, 1509–11: 'Item rec for Sente Sythis clothe for the beryng of moder Adams hosbonde 1d.'.

[117] GL, MS 5026/1, entry for 13 April 1619; LPL, CM VII/94.

[118] GL (printed books), Broadsides 12.79, 4.2. The parish increased its burial fees in 1656–7, but paid some of the surplus to the poor; it also paid some of the hearse-cloth fees to the poor from 1666–7: GL, MS 6047/1, ff. 86, 89, 180v, 183.

[119] For example, at Saint-Jean-en-Grève: AN, LL 805, pp. 253–5; BN, MS Fr. 21609, f. 37.

[120] AN, LL 746, ff. 160, 169.

[121] AN, LL 686, f. 20v, no. 91; *Journal de l'Estoile*, pp. 309–11.

poel') lent for 8, 4 and 3 *livres* respectively; one 'grand poel neuf de damas blanq' lent for 8 *livres*, a second and a third 'poel blanq' lent for 4 and 3 *livres*; a 'petit poel de damas blanq servant aux enfans', for 3 *livres*; and a charity pall, supplied free.[122] Saint-Jean-en-Grève also had a pall for convoys with the lesser choir, and one for transportation by coach.[123]

As noted above, some testators, or their executors, provided cloths for their own funerals, subsequently to be used for their chantry or obit, or given to the church. This was also the case with church vestments and some implements. John Claveryng of London, draper, by his will of 1421, left £20 to buy an entire suit of vestments of black camlet, with deacon, subdeacon, and three choir copes of the same, to be used in his parish church of St Christopher le Stocks; all the vestments were to be embroidered with the words 'Orate pro animabus Johannis Claueryng filii Johannis Claueryng filii Rogeri Claueryng et antecessorum suorum et omnium eorum benefactorum'.[124] It does not appear, from London accounts and inventories, that other individuals chose to have particular vestments, or that the churches charged for their use, though there are a few references that imply that crosses, candlesticks, or other plate were hired.[125] By the time of the Reformation, the London churches had accumulated an immense quantity of vestments and hangings, of fine fabrics and workmanship. Most of these (with the exception of hearse-cloths, as above) were sold during the reign of Edward VI, though some parishes may have been able to recover or restore their use under Mary.[126] After that, vestments and ecclesiastical hangings were no longer an option for funeral display, and many of the parish clergy of Elizabethan London were indeed strongly opposed to liturgical vestments of any kind.[127]

In Paris in the later sixteenth and seventeenth centuries, vestments, hangings, and silverware still formed an important part of the funeral ensemble, and palls and bells could be hired for varying sums. Sometimes the deceased person had selected the trappings he or she wanted before death, in other cases the executors probably made the choice. Pierre de Villiers in 1545 left 25 *livres tournois* to his church of Saint-Etienne-du-Mont, 'tant pour la sonnerie et parements que pour la droict

---

[122] AN, LL 687, ff. 183v–184.   [123] AN, LL 805, pp. 253–5.

[124] Sharpe, *Calendar of wills proved and enrolled in the Court of Husting*, vol. II, pp. 429–30. This could be the 'thre copes one vestement ij deacons of black Tamaske olde' noted in 1552: Walters, *London churches at the Reformation*, p. 228.

[125] GL, MS 1432/1, p. 11 (St Alphege, 1529–30); GL, MS 1002/1A, ff. 15v ff, 31v (St Mary Woolnoth, 1542–3, 1544–5).

[126] Walters, *London parishes at the Reformation*, passim; Merritt, 'Religion, government and society in early modern Westminster'.

[127] Thirty-three London clergy were deprived in the 'vestments controversy' of 1565: Collinson, *The Elizabethan Puritan movement*, pp. 75–8, 84–91; *VCH London* vol. I, pp. 309–11.

de sepulture quant a l'eglise'.[128] Raphael Bonnard in 1616 chose 'les beaux paremens des trepassez' and 'la belle argenterie de ladite eglise'; the choir altar was to be hung with black velvet.[129] Bonnard was a parishioner of les Saints-Innocents, the vestry of which was concerned in the mid-seventeenth century about the cost and quality of their funeral accessories. They concluded in 1644 that their charges for bells, vestments and hangings, and silverware were too low, and raised them to 12 *livres* for their use for a *grand service*, 7 *livres* for a *moyen service* (4 *livres* for a *moyen service* without silverware) and 40 *sous* for little services. Two years later they decided that the present set of black vestments and hangings for the daily mass for the dead was too old, and ordered a new set of black with white orphreys (edges or bands). These were to be available for hire, presumably for funerals and individual commemorative masses, for 8 *livres* 10 *sous*.[130] Saint-André-des-Arts in 1687 offered parishioners a choice between 'les beaux paremens de velours noir de M Dautour' at 8 *livres*, 'les secondes paremens de velours noir' at 4 *livres*, 'les paremens blanqs de M d'Hodier' at 8 *livres*, and 'les seconds paremens blanqs' at 4 *livres*. Anyone who did not hire the *parements* but still wanted chasuble, tunic, and cope paid half the cost of hiring the full set. Similarly, individuals could choose to have the whole set of silver for the convoy and service, comprising twenty candlesticks, two crosses and one *bénitier* (holy-water stock) for 15 *livres*, or only half that number, for half the price.[131] Other parishes charged 10 *sous* per candlestick, used in the house for the vigil or in the church for the service.[132] Though ordinary Parisians hardly participated in the late seventeenth-century phenomenon of exaggeratedly grandiose *pompes funèbres* for the very great, that new tradition drew in part on the old, and on existing conventions: pall, drapes, 'une profusion de lumières et de luxe autour d'un cercueil'. It also encapsulated, in a way that more modest funerals may have echoed, the special character of late seventeenth-century French Catholicism, strongly influenced by Jesuit and Counter-Reformation theology. Certainly the new style could hardly have succeeded without widespread understanding of the funeral performance as an expression of identity, confession, and status.[133]

One more aspect of the funeral performance, also largely under the control of the church, that offered opportunities for the expression of personal

---

[128] Cited in G. de Rot, *mémoire de maitrise*, p. 215.

[129] Chaunu, *La mort à Paris*, pp. 357–8, citing Bruno de Cessole's research.

[130] AN, LL 758, ff. 97, 101.   [131] AN, LL 687, ff. 183r–184.

[132] AN, LL 805, pp. 253–5; AN, L 651/2.

[133] V.-L. Tapié, *Baroque et classicisme* (Paris, 1957), pp. 238–50.

choice and the assertion of status was the ringing of bells. The overt purpose of bellringing was spiritual benefit: the bell was tolled 'when men do
lye in perill of death, wherby the said parishioners having thereof knowledge may pray for him', as the vestry of St Dunstan in the West put
it in 1553/4.[134] A single bell was tolled immediately after the death was
notified, and longer knells or peals were also rung before or during the funeral service, again to attract attention and prayers. But in addition to this
function, bellringing carried a message that could be easily understood.
The tone, the number of bells, and the duration of the ringing advertised
the status of the person for whose benefit the bells were rung. Hard to
ignore but easy to decode, it must have made an extremely important
contribution to the social impact of the funeral event.

Most London churches had between three and six bells at the Reformation, usually up to four named or numbered bells and the sanctus bell.
Each bell sounded a different note, with the great bell being the deep-
est and most impressive. In the early to mid-sixteenth century several
parishes set out charges for ringing different bells.[135] At St Dunstan in
the West in 1553–4, the parish charged 6d. for tolling the great bell at
the time of death, 4d. for the second bell, and 2d. for the third.[136] The
'normal' funeral knell, a single bell tolling, was for six hours, often called
a forenoon's or afternoon's knell, but the bells chosen determined the
price. At All Hallows Staining, a six-hour knell of the great bell cost 6s.
8d., a knell of the fourth bell, 5s., and of the third, 3s. The two smallest
bells seem to have been rung at no extra charge.[137] Peals, of two or more
bells, were briefer but perhaps more impressive. They seem to have lasted
either for the time of the procession ('a peal of two bells to bring the corse
to church'; 'all the peals of all the bells to the dirige and mass') or of the
service.[138] At St Peter Westcheap, it cost 16d. to have peals rung during
a 'solemn burial both dirige and mass', but only 8d. during a low dirge
and mass.[139] A similar distinction was made at St Michael le Querne,
where the knell and peals cost more if rung for a high dirge 'sung by
note' than for a low one. The peals were to be rung for an hour and not
more than two hours in both cases.[140] The principle on which Parisian
parishes rated bellringing – by size, number, or time – is less clear, but

---

[134] GL, MS 2968/1, f. 157v.
[135] St Dunstan in the East was charging 3s. for a knell of the third bell, 5s. for the fourth
bell and 6s. 8d. for the great bell in 1504–5: GL, MS 4887, f. 49 ff. For lists of charges,
see GL, MS 4570/1, f. 118v, GL, MS 645/1, f. 182; GL, MS 2895/1, f. 37v; GL,
MS 4956/2, f. 7; GL, MS 6842, f. 5 bis; GL, MS 1279/2, f. 49; Overall, *Accounts of
churchwardens of St Michael Cornhill*, p. 223.
[136] GL, MS 2968/1, f. 157v.   [137] GL, MS 4956/2, f. 7.
[138] Overall, *Accounts of churchwardens of St Michael Cornhill*, p. 223.
[139] GL, MS 645/1, f. 182.   [140] GL, MS 2895/1, f. 37v.

several prescribed rates for 'la grande sonnerie', and for the second, third, and fourth *sonneries*. These were probably peals, since at both Saint-Jean-en-Grève and Saint-Gervais anyone choosing to have the great bell alone paid the same as for the third *sonnerie*.[141] At Saint-André-des-Arts, anyone who employed more than the minimum choir was also obliged to have 'la grosse sonnerie' and to hire the good hangings and silverware.[142]

Bells were treated with suspicion by Protestant reformers, perhaps partly because of their pagan associations. More explicitly, they were rejected because of their implication with intercession for a dying or dead person, though unlike most other accompaniments to liturgical practice only some specific uses, and not their existence, were proscribed.[143] The Injunctions of 1547 and 1559 forbade bellringing and 'knolling' during services.[144] The bishops' interpretations of 1560–1 allowed that a passing bell could be tolled, but that after death only one short peal could be rung before the burial, and another after, and their interrogatories asked whether parish clerks 'use to ring oft and long peals at the burial of the dead'. Bishop Sandys' 1571 articles for the diocese of London enquired again whether parish clerks exceeded the injunctions.[145] Despite this, bellringing remained an important feature of Anglican practice. Churchwardens' accounts continue to record payments for knells, including 'afternoon's knells', as before the Reformation, and parishes certainly maintained their bells at considerable expense and trouble.[146] In the late sixteenth century, London parishes were charging for passing bells, knells, and peals, including six-hour knells of the great and other bells and peals at burials.[147] Despite the opposition to bellringing voiced by a number of Puritans over the years, it seems to have continued even during the Puritan revolution in many places, including 'parliamentarian Cambridge'.[148] Again, local practice in London probably varied from parish to parish. It appears that the parishes of St Christopher le Stocks and St Bartholomew Exchange – both of which have been characterised as 'truly Presbyterian' at this period – ceased to ring knells for a few years

[141] AN, LL 805, p. 254; AN, LL 752 ff. 60–62v.

[142] AN, LL 687, f. 185. Cf. AN, LL 686, ff. 21v, 25.

[143] Walters, *London churches at the Reformation*, pp. 45–7. Walters says that bells had few 'superstitious' associations, but cf. K. Thomas, *Religion and the decline of magic* (London, 1978), pp. 59, 60, 65, 67, 85.

[144] Hughes and Larkin, *Tudor royal proclamations*, vol. I, p. 399; vol. II, p. 122.

[145] Frere, *Visitation articles and injunctions*, vol. III, pp. 62, 91, 309.

[146] For knells, see e.g. GL, MS 6836, passim; McMurray, *Records of two city parishes*, pp. 376–7. For repairing bells, see ibid., pp. 335–50, 375–93. Bellringing remained a recognisable expression of status in other Protestant communities too, one of the ways in which 'class differences were visible practically throughout Germany': Karant-Nunn, *The Reformation of ritual*, p. 180.

[147] LPL, CM IX/45.   [148] Cressy, *Birth, marriage and death*, p. 425.

after the publication of the Directory of Public Worship in 1645, but had begun to do so again by 1650 or 1651.[149] After the Restoration, bellringing was encouraged again, 'to rehabilitate the ceremonies and customs of the restored Church of England'; the bishop of London, Humphrey Henchman, affirmed the value of tolling the passing bell, as a reminder to the living to consider their own death.[150]

In all this the message of status sounded clearly. At St Dunstan in the West in 1623–4, most of those buried in church had peals as well as knell; only a few of those buried in the churchyard in a coffin had peals, and none of those buried in the churchyard without a coffin had any extra bells.[151] A few parishes charged more for bellringing of any kind if the deceased was buried in the choir or chancel, or in the church as opposed to the churchyard. The vestry of St Bride Fleet Street agreed that the great bell should only be used as a passing bell for officeholders or 'such strangers or parishioners as are of good ability', and not for children.[152] The choice of bells in the later sixteenth and seventeenth centuries must usually have been left to the discretion of executors, and references to bells in wills seem to be extremely rare. Knells and peals nevertheless remained a constant feature of city life, especially as the urban population increased. Despite the increasing noise of city life, and the familiarity of this sound, it could still draw attention. It seems to have been one of the features especially noted during epidemics. In July 1551, Bartholomew Warner wrote to John Johnson that the sudden and sharp epidemic of the sweat in London was believed to be declining; only thirty had died yesterday, compared with 120 the day before, 'nor today I her no bells wher for I trust yt nigh seased'. Dekker's pamphlet on the 1603 plague mentions 'Bells heavily tolling in one place, and ringing out in another', while Wallington, in 1625, stayed in 'this dolfull citie, hearing of belles tolling and ringing out continually'.[153] Pepys noted in 1665 'a sad noise to hear our Bell to toll and ring so often today, either for deaths or burials; I think five or six times.'[154]

Variation and choice in liturgy and paraliturgical accompaniments were evidently central to the meaning of the urban funeral. For the individual, making choices between the many alternatives was a way both of

[149] Freshfield, *Accounts of St Christopher le Stocks*, pp. 103–113; Freshfield, *Account books of St Bartholomew Exchange*, pp. 121–71; Tai Liu, *Puritan London*, p. 79.
[150] Cressy, *Birth, marriage and death*, p. 425.   [151] GL, MS 2968/2, ff. 218–26.
[152] GL, MS 9531/13, pt. 2, ff. 372v–373v, 379–80, 385v–386v.
[153] PRO, SP 46/7, f. 8 (I thank Danae Tankard for this reference); Dekker, 'The wonderful year', in Wilson, *The Plague Pamphlets of Thomas Dekker*, p. 28; GL, MS 204, p. 407.
[154] Pepys, *Diary*, vol. VI, p. 175 (30 July 1665).

asserting a personal identity in the face of death, and of affirming support for an orderly, differentiated, and hierarchical society. Despite the divergence of eschatology between London and Paris, funeral ceremony remained important in both communities, and indeed the flexibility and adaptability of this composite ritual proved to be its great strength. Individual elements in the funeral performance changed or disappeared over time, but new forms and practices replaced them. The confessional change in London meant that specific trappings of the burial ritual – vestments, hangings, lights, intercessory prayer – were abandoned, along with liturgical variation and repetition. The Protestant funeral became less sacramental and sacerdotal; attention was focused instead on secular processions, bellringing, sermons, and feasting, which could still reflect individuality and status but certainly gave the funeral performance a different, and perhaps more sober and secular, feeling. In Catholic Paris, there was a continued emphasis on post-mortem commemoration, and indeed a continuing flow of benefactions towards this end. The presence of the clergy, regular and secular, was enhanced, and the sacramental nature of the rite emphasized.

However, while some of the distinctions in the funeral ritual – such as masses to particular dedications – might be said to be based on disinterested religious devotion, for the most part they were associated with securing advantage, whether spiritual or social. Although charity was often invoked, and the wider sharing of spiritual benefits implied, for instance by the donation of lights, cloths, and vestments, the desire for individual advantage drove the process. Multiple masses, singing, a numerous clerical attendance, and a profusion of lights all won greater spiritual privilege for the deceased, but also set a standard of performance that had attractions for other reasons. By allowing spiritual good to be bought and advertised, the church endorsed the display of status as defined by other criteria. It participated directly in the extension of discrimination in ritual to express differences in secular status when it offered gradations of hangings and hearse-cloths, or of bellringing, which had no direct implication of spiritual benefit. Indeed, by enforcing dues even when the individual was buried elsewhere, or the particular item was not used, parishes appear to have been exploiting a captive market: 'all parishioners dying in the parish and buried else where are notwithstanding to pay the duties to the parson, church clark and sexton as if they had been buried in the same sort at home'.[155] Although it could be argued that it was the church's lay representatives, the vestry, and churchwardens, who invested in this elaboration of distinctions, the clergy were themselves

---

[155] LPL, CM VII/94. For payments for hire of the black cloth, though not used, cf. GL, MS 9235/1 pt. 1, f. 250.

deeply involved. In London, the minister's fee for a burial service was on a sliding scale, tied to the place of burial.[156] Indeed, as one London minister said in 1638, apropos of his income from burials, 'I may say, if people do not die, I cannot live.'[157] They were certainly seen as having a financial interest. Clerical demand for mortuary payment had provoked the notorious case of Richard Hunne in the early sixteenth century; a seventeenth-century Londoner, with a similar point of view, complained of being 'constrained to have a twelve-penny priest, to say something over the grave, and he will grudge it if he have not more than a shilling'.[158] In Paris, the numbers of priests involved in a funeral had a significant impact on its cost, through their fees and the expense of equipping them properly.[159] And the variations in fees and prices charged by parishes received official endorsement, despite their inconsistencies.[160]

But if the church as provider and the laity as consumers were, effectively, collaborating in the commodification of funeral ceremony, as chapters 8 and 9 will show there were many agencies outside the parish church and community that participated in its development. The maintenance of distinction and difference in the funeral was clearly an important part of its continued appeal, and an increasing number of secular customs also became attached to the ceremony. But it must be asked whether continued elaboration and differentiation of funeral display did not begin to overload the medium, leading either to a dilution of the moral import of the event, or to an alienating appearance of conspicuous privilege. Although funeral ceremony and the satisfactions gained by observing tradition remained, and remain, of great importance to many people, it is also clear that some had growing reservations on the subject.

[156] LPL, CM IX/45.
[157] T. C. Dale (ed.), *The inhabitants of London in 1638* (London, 1931), p. 224.
[158] Brigden, *London and the Reformation*, pp. 98–103; Cressy, *Birth, marriage, and death*, pp. 456–7.
[159] Cf. McManners, *Death and the Enlightenment*, pp. 281–6.
[160] GL, MS 9531/13, pt. 2, ff. 372, 378–9, 383, 385, 400.

8 'The whole profit of the funeralls': commercialisation and consumption

'The ceremonies used in the burialls of gentlemen both in this realme and in all Christian kingdomes aymed onlye at two special purposes; those wear the profit of the church, and the honor of the deceased . . . So the whole profit of the funeralls was distributed among two kinde of people, the one priestes, who were supposed to have the care of his soule, the other, officers of armes, that were intended to preserve his honor here on yearthe.'[1] Discussion of the choices made between different liturgical options and paraliturgical accoutrements, and the messages of status that such choices were able to convey, clearly indicates that funeral ritual in early modern London and Paris was carrying a wide range of meaning beyond the devotional. In addition to the choices offered by the church and its representatives, however, there were other more purely material or commercial interests involved, as well as social pressures and expectations. Funerals were becoming a secular, social ritual of consumption. Agencies outside the church and parish community promoted the funeral as a vehicle of honour and social distinction, and competed to control it: 'we finde that between these people [clergy and heralds], there used to be a kinde of strife and contention, which of them sholde challenge most to themselves in these solemnities'.[2] Citizens of London and Paris were not free from outside influences, either in the matter of choice or in that of provision. But although they seem to have resisted the monopolistic claims of heralds and *jurés-crieurs*, there were strong, possibly increasing, social pressures to spend appropriately on funerals, which they could not easily escape. Many of the objects of expenditure, such as feasting, satisfied a number of impulses. The offering of food expressed both general and particular sociabilities, and combined charitable giving with the

---

[1] [Anon.], 'Of the Antiquitye of Ceremonies used at Funerals in England' [9 February 1599/1600], in *A Collection of Curious Discourses written by eminent Antiquaries upon several heads in our English Antiquities, together with Mr Thomas Hearne's preface and appendix to the former edition*, 2 vols. (London, 1775), vol. I, p. 205. I thank Scott Newstrom for this reference.
[2] Ibid.

advertisement of generosity, in proportions that no doubt varied from case to case. The commercialisation of funeral services allowed as well as encouraged a wider spectrum of urban society to engage in the ritual, but it did also provoke critical and cynical responses.

Direction and provision

The College of Heralds in England, and the privileged corporation of *jurés-crieurs de corps et de vin* in Paris, exercised rights of supervision, direction, and in some aspects monopoly supply over funerals of the élite and those who aspired to join the élite. The major part of the heralds' effort was devoted to the funerals of royalty and the aristocracy, but many of these ceremonies took place in the capital city and certainly familiarised the citizen with the heraldic or stately funeral. But, in addition, leading citizens came under the heralds' or *crieurs'* jurisdiction, though they were not bound by the rigid prescriptions that seem to have characterised some German communities, for example.[3] On a personal level, many of London's mercantile élite were claiming gentility and establishing coats of arms in the sixteenth century, though only a small proportion of citizens actually came from country families above yeoman status.[4] A higher proportion of the Court of Aldermen could claim gentle origin, and almost all Lord Mayors, and some other distinguished citizens such as Sir Thomas Gresham, were knighted.[5] Serving Lord Mayors had the status of minor nobility: Sir Cuthbert Buckle (d. 1594) 'was buried as a barron because he dyed in the tyme of his mayoralte'.[6] In Paris, the qualities of *noble* and *honorable* were widespread, and Parisian city councillors and officers of the Hôtel de Ville, not to mention lawyers, *avocats*, and members of the sovereign courts were almost certain to hold one or other rank.[7]

Some role in the conduct of funerals was played in London, perhaps only for a brief period, by the fraternity of Parish Clerks, first chartered in 1442 but substantially revised in function in the sixteenth century.

---

[3] Koslofsky, *The Reformation of the dead*; Karant-Nunn, *The Reformation of ritual*; J. Whaley, 'Symbolism for the survivors: the disposal of the dead in Hamburg in the late seventeenth and eighteenth centuries', in Whaley (ed.), *Mirrors of mortality*, pp. 80–105.

[4] H. Stanford London and S. W. Rawlins (eds.), *Visitation of London, 1568* (London, 1963); J. J. Howard and J. L. Chester (eds.), *The visitation of London anno domini 1633, 1634, and 1635*, 2 vols. (London, 1883); J. B. Whitmore and A. W. Hughes Clarke (eds.), *London Visitation pedigrees, 1664* (London, 1940). Only 6 per cent of 771 new freemen of immigrant origin in 1551–3 were sons of gentlemen or esquires: Rappaport, *Worlds within worlds*, pp. 82–3.

[5] Cf. R. G. Lang, 'Social origins and social aspirations of Jacobean London merchants', *Economic History Review* 27 (1974), 28–47.

[6] Bodl. MS Ashmole 818, f. 45v.

[7] Cf. Diefendorf, *Paris city councillors*, pp. 52–9.

The fraternity comprised both the men serving as clerks in the individual parishes, and others, male and female, who wished to join with them in the spiritual benefits of fraternity. The former group also acted, on request and for payment, at services and funerals in other parishes. Their regulations of 1529 refer to 'the kepyng and maynteyning of all laudabull custume, diriges and masses, processions, obits, buryings and all other causes resonable', not only, it is implied, at the burials of fraternity members. A new set of regulations in 1553 shows that they were a co-operative under the direction of their elected masters and wardens, taking turns at serving at funerals as the opportunity arose, and yielding a proportion of their fee to the common box. Twenty or thirty at a time attended funerals in the 1550s and early 1560s, and their special function was to provide singing. However, although they attempted to exclude non-fraternity members from this office, and could provide an embroidered pall or hearse-cloth on request, they did not succeed in monopolising London funeral provision in the way that the College of Heralds was able to do for the élite.[8]

The characteristics of the heraldic funeral, and the oppressive grip of the College of Heralds on such ceremonies, which ultimately led to their eclipse, have been well described by Gittings and Llewellyn.[9] The role of the College was to ensure that the rank of the deceased was appropriately reflected in the funeral ceremony, using a carefully graded display of attendance, dress, and heraldry itself, and to see that the proper sequence of actions was fulfilled. One or more heralds participated in the funeral (for which they received a fee), effectively acting as master of ceremonies. They aimed both to prevent improper claims to arms and honours, and to ensure that the right standard was maintained; only when this was satisfactorily done would they issue a certificate to that effect. They certainly appear to have been successful in creating a ritualised performance that varied little in its essentials for more than a century, and that may have provided a bridge from pre- to post-Reformation ceremonials.[10] Where their control became oppressive was in the expenditure that 'appropriateness' entailed: the very large quantity of mourners,

---

[8] Adams, *Parish clerks of London*, pp. 20–1, 25–6, 101; J. Christie, *Some account of the Parish Clerks, more especially of the ancient fraternity (brethrene and sisterne) of S. Nicholas now known as the Worshipful Company of Parish Clerks* (London, 1893), pp. 71–2, 148–55.

[9] Gittings, *Death, burial and the individual*, pp. 166–204; C. Gittings, 'Urban funerals in late medieval and Reformation England', in Bassett (ed.), *Death in towns*, pp. 170–83; Llewellyn, *Art of death*, pp. 60–72.

[10] Compare the account of Sir William Roche's funeral in 1523 (Machyn, *Diary*, pp. xxi–xxii) with that of Sir John Leman in 1632 (BL, Add. MS 71131 F, also discussed in chapter 9, below). For examples of heralds' certificates see e.g. *Collectanea topographica et genealogica*, vol. III (London, 1836), pp. 286–94.

black gowns, escutcheons with arms, and hangings for church, street, and house deemed necessary for those of high rank. At the funeral of Sir James Deane, a merchant and former alderman, in the city in 1608, the heralds put in a bill for £54 16s. 4d., which included the fee for the assistance of two heralds, each with an attendant, and for dressing all four in black; the hire of hearse and pall; and the painter's bill of £18 6s., for supplying standard, pennon, coat of arms, helm, crest, mantle, wreath, target, eight dozen scutcheons of arms painted on metal paper or buckram, and four more pennons.[11] The heralds marshalled the funeral procession and especially oversaw the offering of the arms at the altar or communion table.[12] Even ordinary citizens' funerals were subject, at least in theory, to the heralds, and were included in lists setting out the required honours and proceedings.[13]

It is not clear how many city funerals were in practice subjected to the heralds' intervention; after Machyn, who reports a large number of funerals under heraldic direction between 1550 and 1563,[14] most of the evidence comes from the heralds' own notes and archives, which are perhaps more likely to preserve a record of the greater and more elaborate funerals in which they participated, as well as of disputed cases. It is also difficult, therefore, to assess just how uncompromising they were in their requirements, and whether there was evasion or effective resistance. When the earl marshal heard in 1635 that Sir Richard Deane, alderman and late Lord Mayor, was to be buried 'in a private manner no way sutable with his degree and eminent quality of chief magistrate of the citty', he wrote to remind the present Lord Mayor that the king had recently forbidden night funerals, and earnestly desired the City to ensure the due observance of 'the auncient and reverend ceremonies' 'for the solempne and ceremonious enterment' of former Lord Mayors.[15] Gittings, following Lawrence Stone, suggests that it was the huge cost of a full heraldic funeral, and perhaps also the rigid impersonality of the performance, running counter to a more individualistic current in attitudes to death and mourning, that brought about the downfall of the heralds,[16] though as noted below, some citizens were still willing to spend

---

[11] BL, Add. MS 26705, f. 134.

[12] Cf. e.g. Bodl. MS Ashmole 836, pp. 289–90, recording the procession and offering at the funeral of Sir William Webbe, alderman, 26 July 1599.

[13] Nichols, *Illustrations*, pp. 65–74, esp. p. 74, 'The proceedings of a citizen's funeral'. I thank Caroline Barron for this reference.

[14] Machyn, *Diary*, passim.

[15] R. E. C. Waters, *Parish registers in England, their history and contents* (London, 1887), pp. 50–1 (this useful reference is from Woodward, *The theatre of death*, p. 146); Beaven, *The aldermen of the city of London*, vol. II, p. 54.

[16] Gittings, *Death, burial, and the individual*, pp. 188, 195–200.

hundreds of pounds on funerals in the later seventeenth century. If it was not a question of cost alone, other considerations may have contributed to the heralds' decline – the city élite's dislike of being ordered about by a body independent of the municipality, resistance to the court's taste for pageantry, a puritanical hostility to the elaboration of ritual around a religious ceremony.

The *jurés-crieurs de corps et de vin* in Paris were, like the English heralds, a quasi-monopoly body, exercising considerable control, by virtue of their chartered privileges, over the funeral ceremonies and furnishings of the better sort. They were one of the city's medieval corporations, with ordinances dating from 1415. They were limited to twenty-four in number, and were originally criers or announcers of deaths (as well as of the authorised prices of wine) but in time became the organisers and furnishers of funerals.[17] In principle they operated as a collective, with fixed prices and a common stock of goods and profits, again like the heralds, though there were disputes about individuals undertaking private commissions. They came under the jurisdiction of the *prévôt des marchands* and the Bureau de Ville, though the issues of public order as well as corporate privilege involved meant that both the Parlement of Paris and, later, the lieutenant of police at the Châtelet, took an interest in their activities.[18]

By the sixteenth century their role was more to make a formal announcement than to be the first bringers of the news of a decease. The Bureau de Ville heard privately of the death of Jean l'Escalopier, one of the *échevins*, on 15 November 1563, and began at once to make their preparations for his funeral. Sixteen *crieurs* came on the day of the funeral, 16 November, to the Hôtel de Ville, with escutcheons of the arms of the deceased, and proclaimed his death, ringing their handbells and reciting the names and titles of the deceased and asking for prayers. They repeated this *cri* outside in the place de Grève, and shortly afterwards the municipal procession with the *corps de Ville* left the Hôtel de Ville for l'Escalopier's house to escort his body to church.[19] Although there were court-appointed masters of ceremonies for the enormously elaborate funerals of royalty and great public persons, the *jurés-crieurs* also played a part in announcing these events. They came *en corps* to invite the Bureau de Ville to obsequies and services at Notre-Dame for the souls of persons such as the queen of Spain (1611) or the cardinal de Gondi (1616).[20]

---

[17] See Thibaut-Payen, *Les morts, l'église, et l'état*, pp. 74–7; Chaunu, *La mort à Paris*, pp. 351–3, 356.

[18] *RDBVP*, vol. XI, pp. 437–40, ibid., vol. XVII, pp. 32–3; BN, MS Fr. 21609, vol. IV, ff. 106–114.

[19] *RDBVP*, vol. V, pp. 326–7; BN, MS Fr. 21609, vol. IV, f. 106.

[20] *RDBVP*, vol. XV, pp. 117–21; vol. XVI, pp. 383–4. Cf. Giesey, *Royal funeral ceremony*.

Regulations for the *crieurs'* activities make it clear that they were not meant to go to the houses of the deceased and ask to be employed for the funeral unless the widow or widower sent for them; neither were they to seek commissions, or perhaps introductions, from priests, *fossoyeurs*, or others. Although they acted together on great occasions, for most funerals they probably operated singly, reporting their activities and profits to the group. In 1634 the *crieur's* personal fee for attending a convoy from house to church was 3 *livres* 4 *sous*, but their main profit came from the supply of furnishings for the funeral. These were to come from the common stock, and tariffs for the various elements were established in 1595 and again in 1634. These included hangings for house and church, priced mostly by the piece and by the day, a dais for the body to repose on during the vigil at home, frames for candles for the vigil, and cloth to form an altar. Like the parish churches and confraternities, they could also supply palls and silver or silver-gilt candlesticks. All these were for hire; so too, probably, were the formal *manteaux de deuil*, mourning outfits, as distinct from the black gowns that individuals might wish to bequeath to family and dependants.[21] Behind the scenes they purveyed the coffin and bier, coaches, seating, and services and ceremonies as required. Like the heralds, the *crieurs'* share of the total cost of a funeral was considerable: they received 110 *livres*, out of a total of 339 *livres* 8 *sous*, spent on the funeral of Nicolas de Furetière in 1697.[22] Obviously their greatest day was a royal funeral. In order to meet their enormous responsibilities at the funeral of Henri IV, the Bureau de Ville contracted with Gaspard Mellon, *juré-crieur*, to supply serge and velvet to hang the front of the Hôtel de Ville and the church of Saint-Jean-en-Grève, and to decorate them with the arms of the king and of the Ville. This was just for a preliminary service; for the funeral itself, the Bureau bargained with him to hang the porticos of the pont Notre-Dame and several other places on the route to the porte Saint-Denis with black cloth and velvet, for two days, at a cost of 180 *livres*.[23]

The *crieurs'* command of this valuable trade, and their other privileges, earned them considerable criticism. The manufacturers and suppliers of the textiles and other furnishings resented their activity, as did the printers, when the practice of issuing printed invitations developed, but usually their monopoly was upheld.[24] There was an ingenious but unsuccessful attempt in 1617 to create an intermediate monopoly or central depot for the supply of hangings, which it was claimed the *crieurs* were hiring

[21] *RDBVP*, vol. XI, pp. 437–40.   [22] Hillairet, *Les 200 cimetières*, p. 11.

[23] *RDBVP*, vol. XIV, pp. 508–10, 515–16.

[24] Thibaut-Payen, *Les morts, l'église, et l'état*, pp. 74–7.

from the cloth-finishers, who did not own them, rather than the drapers, who did.[25] They were clearly not the only suppliers of such goods, since a judgement of 1641 referred to the other furnishers of 'draps, serges, satins et velours pour les obsèques et funerailles des defunts', though in the event it confirmed the *crieurs'* rights (though not a monopoly right) to supply their clients, even if they did so at greater cost to the customer than their competitors.[26] A list of charges was registered in 1634, to prevent the *crieurs* from claiming or asking more than was fixed, on pain of suspension from their office for three months.[27] There were also disputes with parish vestries over their respective rights to the funeral furnishings, as in 1671, when the *marguilliers* of Saint-Jean-en-Grève resisted the *jurés-crieurs'* claim to a velvet pall that had served at a funeral in their church, and sought confirmation of usage in other churches.[28] Something of the *crieurs'* reputation is indicated by the fact that, at the funeral of Claude de Choilly, *échevin*, in 1603, the torchbearers refused to come into the church lest the *crieurs* should claim that the torches, normally a perquisite of the bearers, belonged to them.[29]

The social and political value of the grand funeral was obviously the aspect that legitimated the heralds' and the *jurés-crieurs'* activities in the eyes of the state. Such funerals served to illustrate order and hierarchy and to evoke respect and deference from onlookers. Elizabeth was a strong supporter of funeral ceremony, and James I, though less so, still acknowledged its value by licensing the use of gold and silver leaf in the arms and ensigns of honour used at funerals, when it was banned in most other contexts.[30] But the heralds and the *jurés-crieurs* were certainly complicit in the commercialisation and elaboration of funeral proceedings, since their own status, and their business success, depended on encouraging a high level of expenditure. It appears, though, that their excessive demands could in the long run be self-defeating. Their control of the process was increasingly resented and the perception of them may have shifted. Viewed as a professional collective or *métier*, in an ordered society of callings and classes, their privileges might be acceptable; viewed as a profit-making, monopolistic corporation in a free marketplace, their activities could seem like exploitation. There was room in this marketplace for the independent entrepreneur as well as for the discriminating client.

[25] *RDBVP*, vol. XVII, pp. 32–3.   [26] BN, MS Fr. 21609, vol. IV, ff. 107–108v.
[27] Ibid., f. 106.   [28] AN, LL 797, f. 4.
[29] Thibaut-Payen, *Les morts, l'église, et l'état*, pp. 69, 76–7; *RDBVP*, vol. XIII, pp. 95–7.
[30] J. F. Larkin and P. L. Hughes (eds.), *Stuart royal proclamations*, vol. I: *Royal proclamations of King James I, 1603–1635* (Oxford, 1973), p. 424.

The heralds undoubtedly served a purpose in purveying the goods and services that their prescriptions required, and it is difficult to see how any substantial funeral could have been mounted without someone prepared to act as co-ordinator and go-between. Given the huge size of the market – at least ten to fifteen thousand deaths a year in mid-seventeenth-century London, even if only a small proportion of these were of middling and wealthy individuals – it is surprising that there is little evidence of any significant development of the undertaking trade before the late seventeenth century, though London in due course led the way in this. It seems to have developed not so much from the drapers and suppliers of mourning, but from coffinmakers who expanded into providing the rest of the funerary furnishings. A single surviving trade card, attributed to *c.* 1675–80, advertised William Boyce, coffinmaker, at the White Hart and Coffin in the Old Bailey. At about the same time, William Russell, painter and coffinmaker, apparently negotiated a preferential deal with the College of Arms that its members would attend funerals he arranged.[31] Once the trade was established, it grew rapidly, both in number and in the scale of business. Richard Phipps, a coffinmaker of the early eighteenth century, had a stock of 157 coffins in his shop, as well as mourning accessories, shrouds, and links or torches.[32]

Similarly, however vigorously the *jurés-crieurs* defended their privileges, they did not have the capacity to supply all upper-status funerals everywhere in Paris, let alone to police infringements. Inevitably there were interlopers: in 1615 the corporation pursued a case against one Marin Poing of the faubourg Saint-Jacques, who was calling himself and usurping the function of *crieur de corps et de vin*. His trade of *menuisier* or joiner suggests that he too was in practice a coffinmaker who was expanding into funeral provision.[33] Probably a number of such entrepreneurs actually got away with it, especially in the suburbs. Certainly a very large proportion of all funerals must have been too modest to attract the *crieurs'* attention, though a mid-eighteenth-century printer estimated that some 4,000 funerals a year (out of 18–20,000) were advertised by printed invitations. However, the *jurés-crieurs* were still organising better-class Parisian funerals, and taking 'the lion's share of the profits', in the eighteenth century.[34]

---

[31] Gittings, *Death, burial, and the individual*, pp. 95–7; Litten, *English way of death*, pp. 16–25.

[32] P. Earle, *The making of the English middle class: business, society and family life in London, 1660–1730* (London, 1989), p. 79.

[33] *RDBVP*, vol. XVI, p. 162.

[34] McManners, *Death and the Enlightenment*, pp. 270–302, esp. pp. 272, 283.

'After all done . . . to ys plase to dener':[35] funeral feasts and food

Different pressures and aspirations influenced the concluding event of the funeral ritual, normally some kind of shared eating or drinking. Feasting or feeding is one of the less clearly defined rituals of funerals – except insofar as it was an expected element – in that there was much variety of practice, and different interpretations of the benefits conferred are possible.[36] Ideally, it expressed ideas of charity and community through the traditional medium of commensality, and perhaps offered an opportunity for participants to reconcile anxieties and griefs; but it was also, literally, an act of conspicuous consumption, and could serve narrower ends of status solidarity and personal advertisement, as well as adding to the cost borne by the heirs or survivors.

Funeral feasting was certainly prominent in London; though evidence is much scarcer for Paris, dinners were served to participants in the great funerals of monarchs, probably to sustain or refresh them during the lengthy proceedings, and there are a few references to dinners after civic funerals too. Private dinners, or just some shared refreshment at a tavern, were probably as common in Paris as in London.[37] Dinners are a frequent feature of Machyn's funeral descriptions, and the majority of the London aldermen and leading citizens whose burials he records left money for such purposes. Almost all of them saw their company hall as the best location for this, aiming to involve the company in the funeral and remembrances. In 1521 Master Allen included in his endowment of a chantry in Mercers' Chapel 5 marks (£3 6s. 8d.) for a dinner for the livery to be kept in Mercers' Hall after his obit. He also left 6s. 8d. for 'two mess of meate' to be given amongst the poor beadmen of Whittington College, to pray for his soul.[38] Sir Richard Dobbes (d. 1556) expressed this equally clearly when he left £10 13s. 4d. to the Skinners for a breakfast or dinner, and for them to have his soul in remembrance in their devotions after dinner.[39] Several others specified £10 as their bequest for the dinner. According to Machyn, Sir William Laxton's bequest of this amount to the Grocers in 1556 produced 'a grett dener as I have sene

[35] Machyn, *Diary*, pp. 271–2.

[36] Cf. Cressy, *Birth, marriage, and death*, pp. 443–9; Gittings, *Death, burial and the individual*, pp. 154–64.

[37] *RDBVP*, vol. V, pp. 54–5, 326–7; McManners, *Death and the Enlightenment*, pp. 276–7. This is an area that would merit further investigation.

[38] L. Lyell and F. D. Watney (eds.), *Acts of Court of the Mercers' Company, 1453–1527* (Cambridge, 1936), p. 529.

[39] PRO, PROB 11/38, f. 47.

at any berehyng, for ther dynyd mony worshepfull men and women'.[40] Ten pounds would certainly have financed a very substantial feast. For only a little more expense, £12, the Carpenters' Company provided an election dinner in 1559 for up to 180 members that included a sirloin of beef, ten legs, two loins, and four breasts and necks of mutton, twenty geese, seventeen capons, and twenty-one coneys. Five kilderkins of ale, seventeen gallons of claret, three gallons of sack, and a pottle of muscadell were drunk, and there were evidently puddings and desserts.[41] Such events – effectively free to members, unlike many other company celebrations – must have played an important part in the social life of the great companies, and in the consolidation of membership. At the same time the companies benefited from the prestige the event gave them, and perhaps also from the residue of more generous bequests. The Grocers' Company converted the 1614 bequest of Philip Rogers for a dinner for the liverymen attending his funeral to the purchase of plate 'to remain forever . . . in remembrance of the testator's love' for the company, but in 1619 Richard Pyott, alderman, left the Grocers £40 for a dinner on the day of his burial as well as £20 for a piece of plate with his arms and name.[42]

Other individuals had more modest aims, spending £6, £5, or less. The £3 6s. 8d. that Henry Herdson left to the Waxchandlers' livery in 1555 must have been for a relatively small affair; Robert Dawbeny's £4 to the Merchant Taylors was for a 'drynkyng' only, and Thomas Grenell left the Waxchandlers 20s. for a repast or drinking.[43] These smaller 'recreations' were sometimes limited to those who had attended the burial in their livery.[44] Similar sums were left by company members through the later sixteenth and seventeenth centuries, but there may have been a growing distinction between the company feast and a neighbourly funeral dinner. Lord Mayor Cuthbert Buckle left £10 to the Vintners for a dinner in 1594, and £6 13s. 4d. for a dinner for the parishioners of his parish, St Mary at Hill.[45] Richard Minge, cordwainer (d. 1622), left £5 to his company for a dinner and supper on the day of his funeral, and £4 for the same for his friends, neighbours, and fellow parishioners.[46]

---

[40] PRO, PROB 11/36, ff. 11, 18; PROB 11/38, ff. 47, 79, 86; PROB 11/45, f. 242; Machyn, *Diary*, pp. 111–12.

[41] B. Marsh (ed.), *Records of the Carpenters' Company*, vol. IV: *Wardens' account book, 1546–71* (Oxford, 1916), pp. vi, 99, 105–6.

[42] Ward, 'Religious diversity and guild unity in early modern London', p. 94; PRO, PROB 11/135, f. 41.

[43] PRO, PROB 11/38, f. 127; PROB 11/41, ff. 139–40; PROB 11/42a, f. 213.

[44] PRO, PROB 11/42a, ff. 235, 285; PROB 11/95, ff. 87, 109v.

[45] PRO, PROB 11/84, f. 87v.   [46] McMurray, *Records of two city parishes*, p. 211.

Only those with significant wealth could endow lavish feasting. Most of the preceding examples are from Prerogative Court of Canterbury wills; wills proved in the Consistory, Commissary, and Archdeaconry Courts of London rarely include such bequests or references. Even when they do, the sums are modest: 10s. for a 'recreation' for those that came to a burial in 1543, or 5s. to poor neighbours to refresh them in 1568.[47] But people of this status did have post-funeral dinners or drinkings, even if they did not always mention them in their wills.[48] In areas of provincial England for which significant numbers of probate accounts survive, expenditure on drink and bread, cakes, or biscuits is normal. It must have been equally common in London, though whether the event usually took place in the deceased's house, in an inn or tavern, or in the churchyard, as Gittings suggests, is not clear.[49] Even paupers' burials warranted some expenditure on 'breade and beere' or occasionally wine.[50] Margaret Harlakenden referred to the distribution of spice bread to neighbours as 'the custom of the city of London' in 1566, and it is attested in other wills and accounts; it may have been similar to the spiced 'cakebread' common at Kentish funerals.[51] This custom appears to have become a convention, and it seems likely that the 'spice bread' was the precursor of the biscuits or wafers noted in later seventeenth-century accounts. Samuel Pepys gave his friends burnt claret and biscuits at his brother's funeral in 1664, and Richard Smyth noted the burial of his friend Cornelius Bee, bookseller, in 1672 'without wine or wafers', as if that were unusual, though his own brother Walter (d. 1676) requested burial without wine or sweetmeats.[52] Wine and sweetmeats were also consumed at Elizabeth White's funeral in 1668.[53]

Attitudes to food as part of the funeral ritual varied. Several London Consistory Court willmakers in the early sixteenth century left money to buy bread for distribution at the funeral, as part of the reward for the attendance and intercession of the poor.[54] Over time, however, the wholesale distribution of food at funerals, like the giving of doles, was increasingly felt to risk disorder, and testators preferred to give money to chosen poor attendants to have a dinner elsewhere, sometimes as well

[47] *Consistory Court Wills*, 155; GL, MS 9171/15, f. 308v.
[48] *Consistory Court Wills*, 178.   [49] Gittings, *Death, burial and the individual*, pp. 155–6.
[50] Freshfield, *Account books of the parish of St Bartholomew Exchange*, pp. 16, 173, 176, 184; cf. McMurray, *Records of two city churches*, pp. 101, 349.
[51] PRO, PROB 11/62, f. 383v; McMurray, *Records of two city parishes*, pp. 231–2; Machyn, *Diary*, pp. 113, 171 ('marchpanes'), 235, 295; Gittings, *Death, burial and the individual*, p. 156.
[52] Pepys, *Diary*, vol. V, pp. 90–1; Smyth, *Obituary of Richard Smyth*, p. 93; PRO, PROB 11/353, f. 65.
[53] CLRO, Orphans' Court Inventory 414; see below, p. 223.
[54] *Consistory Court Wills*, 32, 50; cf. 122, 164.

as endowing a charitable distribution on some other occasion.[55] Giving a dinner was clearly felt as a social obligation, but it is undeniable that regarded as a form of charity it did consume resources that might otherwise have been spent directly on the poor, especially as the bequest for a dinner often equalled or exceeded that for immediate distribution to the poor. Sir George Barne (d. 1558) left £20 to be distributed to and among the poor people of the wards of Broad Street and Coleman Street on the day of his burial, but he also left £20 to the Haberdashers for a dinner on the day of his burial, and 10s. to the poor of the company on the same day.[56] Richard Whethill, citizen and merchant (d. 1565), on the other hand, left £5 to the Merchant Taylors towards a meeting or repast, but desired his executors that 'eschewing all vain and superfluous charges on my said burial or dinner they will chiefly relieve the poor'.[57] Margaret Harlakenden in her will of 1566 shared this concern, leaving £20 or more to be spent on a dinner on the day of her burial, 'as well for the refreshing of the poor of the parish of St Andrew Undershaft as for feasting of the rich'.[58] Though conviviality and the restoration of social bonds was an implicit aim of the practice, some more austere Protestants felt that the material pleasures of the feast could undermine the serious, spiritual aspect of the proceedings. 'Who would not mourn thus every day in the year?', Henry Barrow asked ironically.[59] The *Admonition of the Parliament* (1572) criticised the tradition 'bothe in countrye and citie . . . that breade muste be given to the poore, and offrings in buryall time used, and cakes sent abrode to frendes'.[60] Disapproval, however, failed to stop or even, it seems, to moderate a tradition which literally dispensed comfort and refreshment.

Counting the cost of burial

While the elaboration of ritual and accompaniments to the funeral clearly met some social and spiritual aspirations, their mounting cost was regarded with some ambivalence. On the one hand, it was important to have a funeral fitting one's degree; to spend generously was seen as a mark of substance and status, and parsimony incurred criticism. There are cases where the deceased individual's modest wishes were overruled by his or her heirs in the interests of maintaining family honour and social distinction. On the other hand, overspending was also criticised, as revealing vanity, even hubris, and excess, while some particular objects

---

[55] McMurray, *Records of two city parishes*, p. 235.   [56] PRO, PROB 11/40, f. 100v.
[57] PRO, PROB 11/43, f. 351v.   [58] PRO, PROB 11/62, f. 383v.
[59] Quoted in Gittings, *Death, burial and the individual*, p. 158.
[60] Quoted in Woodward, *The theatre of death*, pp. 59–60.

of expenditure were in themselves undesirable because superstitious or threatening to order. There was concern that too much of an individual's substance was spent on funeral ceremony, to the impoverishment of the heirs.[61] These conflicting views need to be taken into account when considering the actual sums spent on funerals, and whether the individual – or, rather, his or her survivors – was getting satisfaction from what was spent.

Early modern funerals ranged from the minimalist to the magnificent, and their cost did likewise. As Gittings and Houlbrooke have noted, this could range from a few shillings to hundreds or even thousands of pounds.[62] London funerals can be found across the whole spectrum, especially if we include the funerals of figures of national importance, some of which took place at Westminster, others beginning in London before moving elsewhere. Few probate accounts survive for London before the later seventeenth century, however, so the general cost of burials of the middling sort can usually only be known from what testators directed their executors to spend. There are other problems in assessing the cost of funerals, since, while the gift of a black gown suggests that the beneficiary was expected to attend the funeral, it is not clear whether remembrances such as rings and gloves should also be counted as 'funeral expenses', or just seen as part of the wider acknowledgement of ties and affections that willmaking often expressed.

Two modest London funerals from the middle of the sixteenth century, probably fairly representative of the average, cost between £1 and £2. Annys Borde's funeral in 1544 cost 22s. 5d., for burial, pit and knell and bell tolling, for priests and clerks for *dirige* and mass, for tapers and bearers, and for the use of the cushion and cloth; another 6s. was given to poor people on the day of her burial. Katherine Bracy's executor paid a total of £1 12s. 1d. in 1543, the main difference being that she appears to have had more priests and clerks and much more wax, suggesting that there was a longer service, perhaps a high rather than low mass. Bracy's executor also paid 5s. 4d. for the funeral dinner. Margery Thompson accounted for £6 for her husband Thomas Walden's funeral and month's mind in 1543, but gave no breakdown of the costs. Both Annys Borde's and Thomas Walden's funerals cost about 12 per cent of their respective estates.[63]

After the Reformation, though lights and extra services were no longer available, fees for the grave, for hire of the hearse-cloth, and for ringing

[61] See e.g. Houlbrooke, *Death, religion and the family*, pp. 270–2.

[62] Gittings, *Death, burial and the individual*, pp. 180–1, 238–9; Houlbrooke, *Death, religion and the family*, pp. 261, 267–70, 275, 279–81.

[63] *Consistory Court Wills*, 178, 199, 200.

bells, as well as for church officers' attendance, continued to be payable. Churchwardens' accounts sometimes total the funeral charges paid to the parish, but this does not represent the full cost to the estate of the deceased, which would also include the costs of a coffin or a winding-sheet, and any distributions or entertainment. Charges paid to the parish for a modest burial in the churchyard of St Botolph Aldgate in 1586 were only 8s. 9d., suggesting a total cost to the executors of less than £1. Two slightly more elaborate burials in church in the same parish in 1587 incurred fees of around 25s., and their total cost was probably between £2 and £3.[64] On a similar scale, William Oliver, yeoman, of Turnmill Street, Middlesex, asked in 1585 for burial in the church of St Anne Aldersgate, and for 40s. to be spent on his funeral, but this sum did not include his bequests to the poor and of gold rings.[65] Elizabeth Rowley wanted 40s. 'and no more' to be spent on her funeral 'in Christian manner of burial' at Clerkenwell in 1619, but she was probably buried in the churchyard.[66] By way of comparison, the median funeral cost for 101 Kentish yeomen between c. 1580 and 1645 was £2 4s. 8d., though actual cost ranged from under 10s. to over £24.[67] Though prices rose over time, it was still possible for a decent middling-class funeral in London to cost less than £20, the sum William Tyler, goldsmith, specified in his will of 1650.[68] The cost of grave, coffin, service, and very modest refreshments need not have come to more than £10–12. Anna Raymond left £5 to be 'decently interred' at St Bride's in 1660, and another £2 for a sermon; Samuel Pepys' brother Tom was buried for £11 6s. in 1664, including wine and biscuits for up to 150 people.[69] William Ambler, threadman, limited attendance at his funeral to twelve persons, and the total cost to £10.[70]

The civic élite, on the other hand, were prepared to spend lavishly. In the later sixteenth century, Elizabeth Woodroff, widow of David Woodroff, late alderman, wanted £200 to be spent on her burial and funerals.[71] Others, judging by the number of their bequests of mourning, must have been aiming to spend in the order of £50 to £100 or more.[72] Only a handful of Kentish knights, esquires, and gentlemen spent up to £150 on funerals in the later sixteenth and early seventeenth century; most must have spent well under £25.[73] The major expenditure of heraldic funerals in this period was on cloth, given as gowns or cloaks to family,

---

[64] GL, MS 9234/1, ff. 12, 25, 119.

[65] McMurray, *Records of two city parishes*, pp. 231, 208.

[66] GL, MS 9051/6, f. 27.   [67] Gittings, *Death, burial, and the individual*, p. 239.

[68] McMurray, *Records of two city parishes*, p. 237.

[69] GL, MS. 9171/13, f. 15v; Houlbrooke, *Death, religion and the family*, pp. 285–6.

[70] Earle, *Making of the English middle class*, p. 311.   [71] PRO, PROB 11/54, f. 216v.

[72] E.g. PRO, PROB 11/37, f. 67v; PROB 11/38, f. 192; PROB 11/95, f. 81v.

[73] Gittings, *Death, burial, and the individual*, p. 239.

friends, and poor mourners. As one of the heralds wrote to a nobleman about his wife's funeral, 'the greatest charge will be in blacks to such as yr Lordship shall think fit to give mourning to kindred and friends and their servants for the honor and state of the proceeding'.[74] Gowns for the hundred poor men and women attending Sir John Gresham's funeral in 1556 cost £120; Lady Laxton (d. 1576) left gowns to forty poor men and sixty poor women, and smocks, at 20s. each, to the latter as well, suggesting a total expenditure of at least £150.[75] The cost of Lord Mayor Sir Cuthbert Buckle's funeral in 1594 probably came to at least twice that. The herald painter's bill was £28 12s. 10d., the bill for bells and hearse, probably inclusive of grave and service, was £10. Gowns for a hundred poor men must have come to over £100, and forty-six gowns for family and friends at least £100 more. Buckle also left £10 to his company, the Vintners, for a dinner. Several more bequests in his will, such as to the Vintners' almspeople and to Christ's and St Thomas's Hospitals, may also in effect have been payments to promote attendance at the funeral.[76]

In the seventeenth century, the cost of both moderate and substantial funerals continued to escalate. The heralds' and painter's bills for the funeral of Sir James Deane, buried at St Olave Hart Street in 1608, came to £54 16s. 4d., and his executors would also have been obliged to hire hangings for the church and supply mourning to at least some of the cortège of 150.[77] The painter's bill alone for the funeral of Sir William Curteen in 1636 came to £27 15s. 4d.[78] Although John Weever lamented in 1631 that ceremonial rites were 'altogether laid aside', and that noblemen and gentlemen were being buried cheaply and without appropriate dignity, he also complained of the extravagant tombs erected by wealthy merchants and financiers ('the rich quondam tradesman or griping usurer'), and despite the existence of a more Puritan tradition there is no sign that London's civic élite, or the wider merchant class, were keen to abandon funeral ceremonies and processions.[79] Heralds' procession lists or accounts survive for the funerals of at least twelve former Lord Mayors and a handful of other aldermen and citizens between 1606 and 1673, as do certificates that appropriate heraldic honours had been observed at the funerals of other citizens.[80] Though the cost of these funerals is not usually known, Rebecca, widow of Sir John Wollaston, alderman, ordered in

---

[74] Bodl. MS Ashmole 836, p. 119.   [75] PRO, PROB 11/38, f. 192; PROB 11/58, f. 163.
[76] Bodl. MS Ashmole 818, ff. 45–6; PRO, PROB 11/84, f. 87v. Buckle left gowns to 60 poor men in his will, but 100 appear to have attended the funeral.
[77] BL, Add. MSS 71131 B, 26705, f. 134.   [78] Bodl. MS Ashmole 818, f. 36.
[79] Weever, *Antient funeral monuments*, pp. xi–xii. For a fuller discussion of processions, see below, chapter 9.
[80] BL, Add. MSS 71131 A–X, 26705; cf. *Collectanea topographica et genealogica*, vol. III, pp. 286–93, 370–84.

1659 that the charges of her funeral at St John Zachary should not exceed
£800, though this sum was to include all the mourning for her friends
and relatives, and gowns for sixty poor men at 20s. each. Even a more
modest merchant taylor of the same parish allowed £150 for his funeral
expenses in 1661.[81]

The Orphans' Court inventories of the late seventeenth and early eighteenth centuries offer a more statistical sample. Of 207 London citizens
dying between 1665 and 1720, twenty-eight (13 per cent) had funerals
costing over £200, including five costing between £400 and £730. The
majority of these highest spenders were merchants, with total fortunes in
excess of £10,000; the average cost of their funerals was just under £300.
Forty-six citizens, or 22 per cent of the sample, spent between £100 and
£200 on their funeral, and nearly two-thirds of the sample spent less
than £100. The average cost of a funeral for men with fortunes between
£1,000 and £2,000 was £84, for men with fortunes under £1,000, £43.[82]
A breakdown of the expenses of a funeral of generous but not extraordinary scale indicates where the money was going, and that it was the
elaboration of the funeral into a social event, with appropriate dress and
refreshments, rather than the more traditional items of grave, coffin, services, and charitable distributions that was inflating the cost. Elizabeth
White, widow of Thomas White, late citizen, of the Blackamore's Head,
a coffee-house in Cock Lane, was buried in 1668 for a total cost of £148
3s. 8d. Mourning goods and mementoes were the largest single items of
expenditure. Suits of mourning for two couples (one of them the executor) cost £13 6s. 8d. per couple; another woman had mourning at £5; five
more, including the deceased's servants, were dressed in mourning for a
cost of £28 14s. Twelve rings costing £4 14s. were given to 'speciall freinds
at the Funerall'. A milliner supplied ribbons and gloves, presumably to
be worn by more of the congregation, for £24 (ribbons and gloves were
also given to those who appraised the estate), and a hosier supplied black
stockings for 29s. Wine at the burial and the appraisers' dinner cost £11
11s., and a confectioner supplied 'Boxes & Sweet Meats, ribbons etc.'
for £30 10s. Compared with this expenditure on consumables, the costs
of the coffin (£3), grave and church duties (£5 8s.), sickbed visits and
funeral sermon from the minister (30s.), and gifts to the poor at the funeral (24s.) were modest. The whole estate, including debts, was valued
at £598 4s. 3d., so the funeral charges came to nearly 25 per cent of the
whole.[83]

[81] McMurray, *Records of two city parishes*, pp. 237–8.
[82] Earle, *The making of the English middle class*, p. 311, table 11.1, p. 312. I have used Earle's
figures, but recalculated some of them in order to express his findings in a different way.
[83] CLRO, Orphans' Court Inventory 414. I thank David Mitchell for this reference.

The cost of funerals in Paris is harder either to assess or to illustrate. The main source is wills, but only a small percentage of testators in Paris, as in London, specified limits to the expenditure or set out their requirements in such a way that they can be costed. Willmaking ranged across the social spectrum from the artisan to the noble: among the former, in a seventeenth-century sample, a journeyman cobbler limited expenditure on his funeral to 26 *livres*, the widows of a tailor and of a labourer to 30 *livres*, though the widow of a *racousteur de bois* allowed up to 120 *livres*. Paule Attali and Bruno de Cessole estimated that 10 to 15 *livres* (the kind of savings a labourer might be able to accumulate over ten years) would pay for a funeral with priests, hangings, some mourning, and a dozen poor people carrying torches; for 30 to 45 *livres*, of which a significant sum would go the *jurés-crieurs de corps et de vin*, one could have more pomp and more people.[84] However, this may be overly optimistic, as other evidence suggests that church costs alone could reach this amount. At Saint-Gervais in 1675, the cost of the cheapest hangings, pall, minimal silverware, and a coffined grave in the churchyard would come to 28 *livres* 10 *sous*; the cost of a priest, mass, and a *service complet* would add another 10–12 *livres*, while a procession with lights would add still more.[85] This total is closer to a *sentence* of 1691, indicating that 55 *livres* 14 *sous* would pay for a coffin, grave in church, hire of hangings and pall, and the fee for the *curé* of the parish and for the assistance of twenty-four priests at the convoy, service, and burial, and six extra masses.[86]

If any of the separate elements of the total funeral was elaborated or multiplied, the cost rose steeply. Choosing the best hangings, pall, bells, a lead coffin, and grave in church at Saint-Gervais in 1675 would bring the minimum cost payable to the parish up to 118 *livres* 4 *sous*.[87] The total cost of such a funeral, with priests, lights, and the services of the *jurés-crieurs*, would probably be 400 to 500 *livres*. The funeral in 1697 of Nicolas de Furetière, *avocat au Parlement*, in the church of Saint-Louis-en-l'Ile cost 339 *livres* 8 *sous*, of which only 70 *livres* went to the parish and gravedigger, for grave, pall, hangings, silver, etc. The fees to the *curé*, thirty-three assistant priests and the choir came to 63 *livres*, and twenty-four torches (*flambeaux*) and eighteen tapers (*cierges*) cost 96 *livres*. The *jurés-crieurs*' bill came to 110 *livres* 8 *sous* for supplying invitations, hangings for the house and church, children to accompany the cortège, and for bearing

---

[84] Chaunu, *La mort à Paris*, pp. 360–1, citing the *mémoires de maîtrise* of Attali and de Cessole.

[85] AN, L 651/2; Cessole, *mémoire de maîtrise*, p. 228.

[86] Cessole, *mémoire de maîtrise*, pp. 224–5; cf. Thibaut-Payen, *Les morts, l'église et l'état*, pp. 58–68.

[87] AN, L 651/2.

the body.[88] This total did not apparently include money for simultaneous or successive masses. Jeanne Bourgeois' funeral in 1691 cost 224 *livres* 19 *sous*; since this sum included the cost of 200 masses, the provision at the funeral itself may have been quite frugal.[89] None of this includes the cost of mourning, supplied by the *jurés-crieurs* and distributed at least to the household of the deceased. Some attenders may have provided for themselves, but the king gave 300 *livres* for mourning for each of the chief officers of the Bureau de Ville for the funeral of Henri IV; for the obsequies of Marguerite de Valois he gave each 200 *livres*.[90] This probably covered the cost of outfitting servants and attendants on each officer, but still indicates the potentially very high cost of such provision.[91]

Pomp, parsimony, and poverty

It is impossible to say whether Londoners or Parisians were spending more on their funerals, or a higher proportion of their wealth, since the range of costs was so great, as was the wealth and status of the individuals concerned. In both cities, however, it seems clear that the separate elements in the funeral performance were increasingly seen as commodities with a price, as well as a value. However, not all the pressure was in the direction of greater elaboration and expense, and some individuals chose to make a statement of belief or affiliation by rejecting rather than acquiescing in tradition.

The rejection of funeral pomp and of excessive attention to funeral ceremonies and ritual was not confined to Protestant and Puritan approaches to death and burial. In both pre-Reformation London and in Paris throughout the period there were some who deplored the excess of expenditure on funerals and chose for themselves a modest, or on occasion even an ostentatiously humble, one. William Creke, citizen and draper of London, asked in 1440/1 for a speedy funeral 'absque pompa seu mundi vana gloria', and without any month's mind; William Duffelde, citizen and carpenter, asked for his funeral in 1528 to be honestly done without 'any pompe or pride of the world', though he did request two trentals and an obit.[92] A Parisian surgeon, Michel Yvard, chose burial in the Innocents in 1555, '[sans] aulcune pompe ni criée par la ville', though not on account of any reformed sympathies, since he also chose

---

[88] Hillairet, *Les 200 cimetières*, p. 11.   [89] Cessole, *mémoire de maîtrise*, pp. 224–5.

[90] *RDBVP*, vol. XIV, p. 511; vol. XVI, pp. 181–3.

[91] For details of an eighteenth-century funeral costing over 1,200 *livres*, see McManners, *Death and the Enlightenment*, pp. 285–6.

[92] GL, MS 9171/4, f. 57v; McMurray, *Records of two city parishes*, p. 227. Cf. Cressy, 'Death and the social order', p. 105: '"without pomp" was an ambiguous formulation'.

to have the assistance of the city's orphans, 'ces intercesseurs privilégiés qui ont naturel accès au Royaume de Dieu'. Such overt rejection of ceremony was only ever the choice of a small minority: around 2 per cent of a sixteenth-century Paris sample.[93] This current of pious Catholic practice appears to have strengthened during the seventeenth century, alongside, but not necessarily due to, the evolution of Jansenist theology. In eighteenth-century Paris, a growing number of wills 'repudiated the baroque splendours of the traditional funeral', and there are some notable examples of dramatically simple funerals.[94]

There was, however, a Protestant discourse of simplicity which could overlap with the rejection of pomp for personal, economic, or aesthetic reasons. 'Sumptuous and costly burials are not to be commended... [They] only set forth a vain, foolish and boasting pomp', wrote Thomas Becon in 1534.[95] A number of London wills, especially of the mid-sixteenth century, express these sentiments. In most cases they are associated with will preambles invoking the idea of redemption rather than intercession, characteristic – though not diagnostic – of more Protestant sympathies. There is an indication of ideological rejection in the instructions of Henry Forrest, citizen and barber-surgeon, in his will of 1551, that no more than 20s. was to be spent on his funeral, 'without any pompous manner or muche ringing of bells, nor having any number of lights at the same burial'.[96] The majority of those who advocated some degree of austerity, however, including the more advanced Protestants among the civic élite, combined this with a respect for the forms and customs of decent burial. Sir Henry Huberthorn (d. 1556) wished his burial to be honestly done without pomp or vainglory, but he specified that he should be buried in a vault in St Peter Cornhill, where his wife had been buried, and that twenty poor men and women should bring his body to the church.[97] Sir William Locke (d. 1550) was buried in Mercers' Chapel and had forty poor men in attendance, but although he left them gowns he added that his executors should not give out black gowns 'which is waste money spent'.[98] Whether even such limited reservations were observed is another matter. According to Machyn, Locke was buried with sixty poor men, mourners, heralds, and arms, and the street hung with black, with his arms on the cloth; Huberthorn was buried with twenty staff torches

---

[93] Chaunu, *La mort à Paris*, p. 346.
[94] McManners, *Death and the Enlightenment*, pp. 300–2.
[95] *Dives and pauper* (1534), quoted in Cressy, *Birth, marriage and death*, p. 412. Cf. Thomas, *Religion and the decline of magic*, pp. 75, 722.
[96] McMurray, *Records of two city parishes*, p. 231.
[97] PRO, PROB 11/38, f. 127. See also D. J. Hickman, 'The religious allegiance of London's ruling élite, 1520–1603' (unpublished Ph. D. thesis, University of London, 1995).
[98] PRO, PROB 11/33, f. 163.

and four great tapers in gilt candlesticks, arms, 'mony mornars', and black hangings.[99]

A few individuals rejected the use of black, so prominent a part of later sixteenth- and seventeenth-century élite funerals. Stephen Kirton, alderman and merchant of the Staple, in his will of 1552 wished for 'all vain and superfluous charges to be omitted' at his funeral, and left gowns to forty poor men and women of his parish, St Andrew Undershaft, to wear on the day of his funeral, 'of russet or any colour except black or puke'.[100] Alderman Henry Herdson left a number of 'pewke' gowns, but apparently no blacks, in 1555.[101] Richard Whethill, citizen and merchant of the Staple, willed in 1565 to be buried at the discretion of his friends and executors, urging them to eschew 'all vain and superfluous charges', and left sixteen poor men gowns of 'such cloth and colour as may be most commodious for their wearing'.[102] But John Kirton (d. 1566), son of Stephen, while invoking the merits of Christ's death and passion, and renouncing 'all vain and superfluous charges', also left mourning to his close family, and a death's-head ring to his mother.[103]

Night burial, noted in chapter 7 above as a new seventeenth-century development in England, is an interesting example of the invention of a custom in response to changing needs and sensibilities, but the fashion had a limited following in the city. Although some parishes set a fee (double the normal rate) for night burial from the 1590s,[104] relatively few night burials are recorded. Most of these were of élite citizen status, and took place in the church or a private vault.[105] When any motive is given, it seems to have been privacy and the avoidance of 'pompe or prodigalitie', but as with the aristocracy, it was seen as an excuse for a meaner burial than the person's estate warranted.[106] The parish clerk of St Pancras Soper Lane noted that Lady Rowe was buried in their vault on 25 September 1601 between 10 and 11 at night, 'summa cum parsimonia'.[107] Perhaps to avoid such criticism, Dame Anne, widow of Sir James Pemberton, alderman, in 1625, asking for burial by night, without pomp or glory of the world, in the church of St John Zachary, made arrangements for distributions at a later date, so that the poor might

---

[99] Machyn, *Diary*, pp. 1–2, 115–16.
[100] PRO, PROB 11/36, f. 124v. 'Puke' or 'pewke': a bluish-black or inky colour: OED.
[101] PRO, PROB 11/37, f. 276.   [102] PRO, PROB 11/43, f. 351v.
[103] PRO, PROB 11/48, f. 379.
[104] LPL, CM IX/45; GL, MS 9531/13, pt 2, ff. 383–384v, 400; GL, MS 9583/1, f. 53. It is difficult to know whether this was intended to discourage, or merely to profit from, this minority practice.
[105] E.g. *Registers of St Michael Cornhill*, pp. 219, 231, 232; *Registers of St Helen Bishopsgate*, p. 269; *Registers of St Pancras Soper Lane*, pp. 293, 295, 296.
[106] E.g. PRO, PROB 11/135, f. 18; PRO, PROB 11/144, f. 76.
[107] *Registers of St Pancras Soper Lane*, p. 293.

not lose 'by the priuatenes of my funeralls'.[108] The English heralds' own lamenting of the trend towards private and/or nocturnal burial suggests that there was a strong current of feeling in favour of an alternative to the formal and heraldic tradition, though whether this should be seen as a move towards 'individualism' is less clear.[109]

Cynicism, secularism, and perhaps a distaste for the commercialised elaboration and cost of the funeral may have been equal motives for rejecting the pompous funeral. John Chamberlain observed and reported to his correspondents a great variety of public events, including funerals, and perhaps in reaction against the grandiose and sometimes ill-managed public ceremony asked in 1627 for his own funeral to be 'performed with as little trouble and charge as maie bee answearable to the still and quiett course I have allwaies sought to follow in my life tyme'.[110] Walter Smyth, gentleman, citizen, and scrivener (brother of the Richard Smyth who carefully recorded numerous funeral performances), seems to have chosen night burial in 1676 as part of a deliberately low-key and inexpensive ceremony: he wished to be buried in the churchyard of the parish in which he should die, 'deeper than ordinary', in the night-time, and without any sermon, wine, sweetmeats, gloves, rings, or any of the usual funeral gifts except 'only a branch of rosemary'.[111] Sir Richard Browne (d. 1683), John Evelyn's father-in-law, directed his own burial in a churchyard, because he deplored 'this excess of making churches Charnel-houses'.[112] However, the absence of specific instructions from the wills of many Londoners need not imply any distancing from common practice, since the executors, on whom the task devolved, could have been given instructions before the death. Similarly, Parisians' requests for a small-scale (*modique*) funeral may be conventional, like requests for burial with honesty or discretion, or according to degree. Chaunu suggests that Parisian Huguenots used the phrase 'according to my estate' or sought an unaggressive simplicity, as much to avoid hostile attention in their funerals as in a declaration of faith.[113]

Choices such as these ran counter to the trend for elaboration of detail and enhancement of cost, and perhaps asserted an alternative moral universe, but there was another aspect of funeral provision which may have helped to sustain the sense that burial and its ceremonies indeed constituted a

---

[108] McMurray, *Records of two city parishes*, p. 235. Other night burials are recorded in parish registers.

[109] Gittings, *Death, burial and the individual*, pp. 195–9; Woodward, *The theatre of death*, pp. 141, 146.

[110] McClure, *Letters of John Chamberlain*, vol. II, pp. 632–5.

[111] PRO, PROB 11/353, f. 65; cf. Smyth, *The Obituary of Richard Smyth*.

[112] Evelyn, *Diary*, p. 301.   [113] Chaunu, *La mort à Paris*, pp. 319, 346.

meaningful social and religious ritual, not simply an occasion for conspicuous personal display. Obviously, there must have been many in late
medieval and early modern London and Paris who could not pay all or
perhaps any of the costs of their own burial: vagrants, dependent paupers,
abandoned children, and probably many of the independent but precar-
iously surviving poor.[114] The charitable burial of the poor, to which the
rich contributed, if indirectly, may have somewhat redeemed the impact
of the aggressive self-importance of the grand funeral, while throwing
its splendours into relief. London parishes noted that the surplus from
their burial fees went to the support of the poor ('paid to the poor out
of burials in the church this year'), and sometimes that payments for
tombs and monuments did likewise, while the Parisian *jurés-crieurs* paid
into a fund to help the Enfants-Trouvés kept by the ladies of Charity of
the Hôtel-Dieu.[115]

Burial of the poor was a work of Christian mercy, a charge to which
pre-Reformation Londoners responded, individually or collectively. The
parish fraternities and other guilds had as one of their objects the burial of
poor members, but those who could not even join a fraternity were also
assisted. The parish of St Michael Cornhill had a grave in the church
called 'goddys grave', in which they appear to have buried strangers.[116]
The parish of St Mary at Hill in 1512–13 gathered alms in church
towards the burials of poor people and other works of charity.[117] The
parish of St Dunstan in the West paid 3d. 'for beringe of a pore bodye'
in 1541–2, and 21d. in 1543–4 'for buriyng of a pore body that died in
Chauncery Lane'.[118] Other parishes no doubt did the same as occasion
arose. The parish of St Mary at Hill had also agreed earlier that Sir John
Plomer's bell should serve for all poor people (for a knell), on payment
of 1d., while the parish of St Andrew Hubbard decided in 1547 that
the small bell should be 'of charyte rowng for all pouere' without any
cost.[119]

Charitable burial necessarily continued after the Reformation. Many
later sixteenth- and seventeenth-century registers report the burials of
vagrants, foundlings, and dependent poor, for which the churchwardens
or overseers of the poor must have paid. The parish of All Hallows Bread

---

[114] A large proportion of London's population lived at or below the poverty line: Archer,
Pursuit of stability, pp. 152–4.
[115] GL, MS 6047/1, ff. 89, 98, 107, 116, 125, 134v, 148, 157v, 166v, 176, 183; GL,
MS 4887, f. 145v; Freshfield, *Vestry minute book of the parish of St Margaret Lothbury*,
pp. 41, 49; BN, MS Fr. 21609, vol. IV, pp. 107–108v.
[116] Overall, *Accounts of the churchwardens of St Michael Cornhill*, p. 37.
[117] Littlehales, *Medieval records of a London city church*, p. 284.
[118] GL, MS 2968/1, ff. 106v, 112v.
[119] Littlehales, *Medieval records of a London city church*, p. 246; GL, MS 1279/2, f. 47.

Street buried 'a poore wooman that died in the streete who came out of the contrey' and 'a poore man that died in the streete within the compass of our parish' in 1574 and 1593 respectively, and similar references can be found elsewhere.[120] The churchwardens of All Hallows the Great paid 3s. 10d. for the burial of widow Clarke 'that died poor' in 1622, a sum made up of the minister's fee of 1s. 6d., the clerk's of 1s., 1s. for a knell, and 4d. for digging a grave in the churchyard; they waived the duty they themselves would normally have taken.[121] In 1638–9 the churchwardens of St Anne Aldersgate paid 2s. for a winding-sheet for 'old Smith', who had been bedridden and dependent on charity before his death, and also paid the parson's and clerk's fees of 6s. in all. On many other occasions churchwardens record payments of a few shillings for burials of this kind.[122] Parishes had to shoulder a much larger burden in plague years, paying for the burials of numerous individuals whose families could not afford to do so, or who had perhaps no surviving family.[123]

Those who were poor but not destitute benefited from the parish's charity to the extent of having their fees (for grave, services, cloth, and perhaps knell) waived, though no actual money was laid out for them; their own costs, therefore, could have been limited to supplying a winding-sheet and any refreshments.[124] At St Bride's in 1624, a complex statement of charges concluded 'Item, for such as are so poor they be not able to pay duties, allowance be made . . . according to the churchwardens' discretion',[125] and it is clear that all parishes must have made some concession of this kind. Those who paid no burial fees made up a significant proportion of the dead, depending on the size and wealth of the parish population: more than half the forty-one burials at St Bride's in January 1665 paid no fees to the parish.[126]

It is likely that a high proportion of Parisian funerals were burials of charity too; Chaunu suggests that half the population could not afford the 10 to 15 *livres* of a modest funeral, though this is probably no more than a guess.[127] The Parisian parish records make several explicit references to poor and charity funerals, exempting them from fees for the grave

[120] *Registers of All Hallows Bread Street*, pp. 163, 167.
[121] GL, MS 818/1, f. 27v; GL MS 9531/13, pt. 2, f. 378.
[122] McMurray, *Records of two city parishes*, pp. 337, 348, 389, 390. Cf. Hill and Frere, *Memorials of Stepney parish*, p. 158.
[123] E.g. Freshfield, *Account books of St Bartholomew Exchange*, pp. 187–8 (1665); Kitto, *St Martin in the Fields: accounts of the churchwardens*, p. 578 (1603).
[124] Cf. e.g. *Registers of All Hallows Bread Street*, p. 192; GL MS 4438, not foliated: entries for 2 and 9 Sept. 1625, 7 Nov. 1625; GL MS 66, f. 13v; GL, MS 9531/13 pt. 2, f. 400.
[125] GL, MS 9531/13, pt. 2, ff. 372v–373v (consecration); GL, MS 6570/1 (St Bride, parish papers), item 62.
[126] GL, MS 6540/1.   [127] Chaunu, *La mort à Paris*, pp. 360–1.

site, services, or both. The parish of the Innocents charged charity convoys in coffins only 1 *livre* 10 *sous* for the ground, and convoys without coffins were free; Saint-Jean-en-Grève likewise noted 'pour l'ouverture de terre dans le cimetière ne sera payé aucune chose à l'égard des pauvres...Pour les convoys et enterrements de Charité ne sera payé aucune chose'.[128] Saint-André-des-Arts supplied both charity bier and pall free.[129] An eighteenth-century submission, apparently by the *fossoyeur* of Saint-Jean-en-Grève, said that the parish had always had five priests to perform charity burials, two paid by the *curé* and three by the *marguilliers*. The ceremonies, which included in effect a procession, led by the *fossoyeur* with his baton, two torches, utensils (cross and candlesticks), and the body carried on a bier and covered with a pall, were 'à la satisfaction des pauvres', even if not all the priests were present. At such interments, the ladies of Charity were accustomed to supply a shroud for the body and 20 *sous* for the four bearers. Another memorandum of 1752 gave the ordinary cost of a charity burial as 7 *livres* 10 *sous*, with the major cost being the bier, presumably to be understood as a coffin in which the body was buried.[130] It is not clear whether this reflects the pattern and cost of charity burials in the seventeenth century or earlier, but it suggests that such burials were not necessarily minimalist or ignominious. As noted in chapter 2, however, nearly a quarter of all Parisians were dying in hospitals in the later seventeenth century. This alone relieved parishes of the expense of burying quite a large proportion of their poor members, and may have allowed them to treat more generously those they did undertake. Those who were buried from the hospitals, however, were treated pragmatically and sometimes it seems callously, with inadequate protection either for themselves or for the public. Bodies were transported to the cemetery, roughly shrouded, in a loaded cart, overnight or in the early morning, with the minimal ceremony of lanterns or torches and an attendant priest.[131] These individuals were being buried out of charity, it is true, but it is a new understanding of the term, far from the mutuality implicit in medieval notions of charitable exchange.

In the early modern city, funerals had an important part to play in the ongoing negotiation between religious or communitarian values and more secular or self-interested motivations. All the elements discussed in this chapter – professional intervention, the offering of food in various

[128] AN, L 570/33; AN, LL 805, pp. 253–5; AN, L 651/2.
[129] AN, LL 687, ff. 183r–184.
[130] AN, L 663 (un-numbered papers, including eighteenth-century leaves concerning charity burials).
[131] See above, chapters 1, 3; cf. Harding, 'Whose body?', p. 183.

contexts, the mounting expenditure – provoked some resistance or criticism, but it is clear that on the whole the elaborated secular funeral ritual was assimilated into the cultural repertoire of early modern London and Paris. The heralds and *jurés-crieurs* attempted to enforce standards of display and expenditure on a prominent minority of civic society, and helped to normalise the observance of secular rituals and practices across a wider population. Wills, probate accounts, and other commentaries show how ordinary citizens had internalised these priorities and assumptions. The conventions of the funeral were sufficiently well established for them to be used, with a range of interpretation, in contemporary theatrical drama: hangings, mourning, processions, interments played a significant role in the staging and symbolism of plays by both court and oppositional dramatists, which may in turn have enhanced the experience of the real event for playgoing citizens.[132] Funeral protocol was available for ironic inversion and humorous play at a more popular level as well. Nehemiah Wallington noted in 1654 that the Gracechurch Street conduit, which had run dry in the summer drought, had been dressed by the waterbearers with mourning cloth. Two waterbearers, a man and a woman, were dressed in black, and they and others stood around the conduit with their tankards pointing downwards, and declaring 'it is not for bread nor for beer we mourn, but we mourn for water'.[133]

While it would be an exaggeration to say that funerals were, over this period, transformed from sacred rituals to secular celebrations, it is perhaps the case that a rite that was once a complex ensemble of different values was being reduced in the direction of a more one-dimensional occasion, all the elements of which could in practice be measured against a single scale of valuation, that of price. This was true, for example, of the place of burial, especially in church, once reserved for benefactors in a general sense but now often sold to powerful and wealthy parties. It was also true of funeral accessories and performance. Increasingly, though perhaps more in seventeenth-century London than in Paris, the ordering of society was by wealth and respectability; consumption of funeral goods and options helped to tie this new world into the traditions of the old. But whereas once monetary expenditure on the funeral was a means of acquiring benefit created by some other ideology (honour, charity, piety), it was becoming an end in itself; consumption was tending to become its own justification. An appreciation of the funeral as, essentially, an occasion of

---

[132] M. Neill, '"Exeunt with a dead march": funeral pageantry on the Shakespearean stage', in D. M. Bergeron (ed.), *Pageantry in the Shakespearean theater* (Athens Ga, 1985), pp. 153–93.

[133] P. Seaver, *Wallington's world: a Puritan artisan in 17th-century London* (London, 1985), p. 53.

economic significance – detached from any ideological or religious context – is expressed both by the royal order, in 1622, that 'blackes and mourning stuffes' given at burials should be of English wool and manufacture only, and still more strikingly by the 'Burials in Woollen' Acts of 1660 and 1678, which mandated woollen shrouds on penalty of a £5 fine.[134]

The process of commodification, which gradually erodes other measures of status or worth, has never been completed, even long after the end of the period considered here, and it certainly tends to conceal itself. Older value systems are constantly invoked, even in defence of obviously sectional interests. The prescriptions of the English heralds, and their response to resistance to them, employed the rhetoric of honour and dignity, but they did in fact focus on expenditure. This enabled the heralds, however, to engage the crown in their support, by presenting their interests as closely aligned.[135] The *jurés-crieurs* of Paris, on the other hand, retained their privileged position by appealing to history, tradition, and their identity as a quasi-religious commonalty.[136] The funeral feasts of the city companies drew on notions of commensality and fellowship, but in reality gave high-status dining precedence over genuine charitable distribution. And individuals planning their own funerals invoked decency and reverence, and asked for treatment 'as befits' or 'according to my estate', an injunction that recurs in wills in both London and Paris, but one that could be flexibly interpreted. Funerals evidently were valued, in London and Paris, but whether under these changing circumstances they still had the social value, could do the work of containment and restoration, that funeral ritual is traditionally expected to do, is perhaps less certain.

---

[134] Larkin and Hughes, *Stuart royal proclamations*, vol. I, p. 547; Houlbrooke, *Death, religion and the family*, p. 341.

[135] Gittings, *Death, burial and the individual*, pp. 199–200.

[136] *RDBVP*, vol. XVII, pp. 32–3; BN, MS Fr. 21609, vol. IV, ff. 106–14.

9 'The last love and ceremony': funerals, community, and civic identity

If one notable feature of the urban funeral was the way in which the individual, acting through the medium of the will or through his or her executors, could script and shape the performance, selecting from a range of equipment and appurtenances, an equally important aspect is the role the funeral played as a focus of collective and communal observance. As frequent, repeated, familiar, and yet individualised performances in the public spaces of the city, funerals had a large part to play in the creation of a collective urban consciousness. The issue, on any single occasion, was not simply the fate of the particular soul, or the need to show affection or respect for a unique individual; the ceremony had a meaning for the larger community, as a moment of self-definition and as an opportunity to witness a shared belief in a social and confessional order. As with other public rituals, the co-option of the city's inhabitants and fabric into the performance was crucial: the troubled and dirty city put on a new face, peaceable, respectable, orderly, to honour the dead, and friends and neighbours (ideally) forgot their day-to-day disputes and sat down together to share a meal.

The heralds and the *jurés-crieurs*, as discussed above, imposed a programme on the funeral practices of the socially important, at least ostensibly in the interests of a larger vision of society. While their prescriptions may have been resisted by some, and their exactions resented, there seems to have been a high level of compliance. At all levels, and for all sorts of reasons, funeral ceremony needed to involve others, if possible representatives of several different groups. In pre-Reformation London, and in Paris, the attendance or attention of others was essential to the spiritual effectiveness of the funeral: to lack prayers at the moment of death, at the interment, and within the short to medium term, was to jeopardise salvation itself. In consequence, both individuals facing death, and their survivors and successors, were concerned to ensure a good attendance at the funeral and participation in any later ceremonies or commemorations. This is clearly seen in the arrangements many testators made to have extra clerics, religious, and poor people attend. However, the practice had accumulated such social significance that it continued, somewhat modified in detail but on an equal or greater scale, in post-Reformation London. Funerals in Catholic Paris could still draw on the traditional resources of lights, bells, singing, and priestly attendance to make an impression; Londoners did much with numbers, sermons, and civic heraldry.

The early modern funeral, Catholic and Protestant, was a performance with concentric circles of participation. Those who attended a funeral had a role both as actor and as audience; some of the careful variations of service and accoutrements could only be appreciated by those close enough to observe them, while the ensemble of procession and attendance diffused a message to a wider circle of onlookers. Lights and bells, music and singing, served an important function in calling the attention of those who were not actually participants to what was going on; so too did the liveries of fraternity and guild members and the robes of those holding civic or other office. As with other kinds of procession, even the outer ring of spectators had a part to play: the *bourgeois* of Paris were expected to hang their houses with black and to stand outside them with a burning torch when a royal funeral procession passed by. They were also instructed, before Henri IV's funeral in 1610, to clean the street in front of their houses so that the convoy did not encounter the usual mud and filth.[1]

The issue of the reciprocity of prayers and charitable donation was always complicated, and many of its inherent contradictions were never resolved. Essentially, those who left money for the attendance of priests, religious, or others at their funeral, and who endowed commemorative services, were buying prayers for themselves; but the church's services could not be sold, and the goodwill of the intercessor made a vital contribution. Contradictions were partly eased by deeming it appropriate to pay clergy for the time spent on particular services, and by emphasising the gratitude of beneficiaries as a motive for offering prayers. However, even when the question of spiritual benefit was formally eliminated, as in post-Reformation London, there remained a tension between the desire for a good attendance and the wish that it should be, or appear, voluntary and grateful rather than compelled or bought. Some testators explicitly linked their bequests to funeral attendance; others no doubt expected it. The responses of the living were equally complicated, and attendance at a funeral could be regarded either as a moral or social obligation, as a natural expression of respect, or as a voluntary statement of emotional or political solidarity.

---

[1] *RDBVP*, vol. VIII, p. 389; vol. XIV, p. 516.

Intercession and attendance

No proper funeral – except among the most radical Protestant groups – took place without the presence of a priest or minister, to conduct the service and lead the prayers. The parish priest or *curé* was a central figure in the lives of his parishioners, and was expected to participate in the deathbed, witnessing or writing wills, and offering spiritual succour to the dying person. He also led the funeral procession or convoy to the church, where he performed the office of the dead and oversaw the interment. For many testators, however, it seems that the minimum clerical attendance at the funeral was not enough to allay their spiritual anxieties. Given a Catholic theology of salvation that encouraged the multiplication of observances and offerings, the number of individuals attending was of crucial significance, as was their status as intercessors: both the professed religious, and the virtuous laity (poor, humble, or youthfully innocent) were specially valued.[2] To this extent, the testator was still in control, choosing the number and kind of intercessors and rewarding them for their attendance. Pre-Reformation Londoners asked for extra priests or clerks, and sometimes for members of religious orders; Parisians drew on the large numbers of supplementary parish clergy and also chose representatives from a variety of religious orders and houses. Both also asked for children to be present, often as torchbearers, sometimes perhaps as choir. In most cases these people were left small sums for their attendance, but these apparently voluntary contributions became, like bequests for burial in church, the basis for a formal tariff, at least for the parish clergy.[3]

In early sixteenth-century London, the presence of extra clergy was often invoked. Agnes Smyth of St Bartholomew the Little asked 'all the prestes of the church to feche my bode therto', and also for twelve children bearing twelve tapers; Sir William Lankton, priest, asked for 'my corse to be borne to the churche and humate with 4 preestis of the same church... the parson and the preestes with the clerke and childern shall syng dirige and bury my corse with note'. John Cokker, priest, left 4s. to the priests 'that shall bere my body to my sepulture'.[4] In most cases these would have been the chantry and stipendiary priests of the parish, serving offices endowed by lay benefactors, and contributing to the overall provision of services for all parishioners. Most London parishes had at least one permanent chantry, and some had several, producing a local clerical establishment of perhaps four to eight priests, employed in teaching and

---

[2] Cf. C. Burgess, '"A fond thing vainly invented": an essay on purgatory and pious motive in later medieval England', in S. Wright (ed.), *Parish, church and people: local studies in lay religion, 1350–1750* (London, 1988), pp. 56–84.

[3] LPL, CM VII; AN, L 664, no. 6.

[4] *Consistory Court Wills*, 164, 59, 10.

musical performance as well as divine service.[5] One of the main roles of parish clerks was to participate in services in their own church, especially singing. The fraternity of Parish Clerks, as well as maintaining a bederoll and a fraternity life of their own from the mid-fifteenth century, were also employed to augment other funerals.[6] The members of the Pappey, a college or fraternity of priests, were invited to attend or say prayers on several funeral occasions.[7] When chantries, obits, and intercession for the dead were abolished in 1548, the chantry clergy were largely dispersed. Though a few may have found a role as assistants to overworked rectors and vicars, or as freelance preachers, parishes no longer supported a large clerical staff for liturgical purposes. The presence of numerous priests at a funeral was no longer possible or desirable. The Parish Clerks, however, survived, and at least for a few years continued to offer funeral assistance.[8] A new set of regulations for the fraternity in 1553, during the restoration of the Catholic liturgy under Mary, set out their obligations and fees: 8d. each for a funeral in the morning, 12d. for a funeral comprising both afternoon and morrow services, an additional 2d. for carrying the corpse.[9] Some burials in London in 1559 with 'nodur prest nor clarke' suggest a strict interpretation of the new order, but others did still employ the Parish Clerks, sometimes singing in English.[10] They continued to appear in the early years of Elizabeth, but their role as more or less professional funeral attenders outside their own parishes appears to have been taken over by the children of Christ's Hospital.[11] William Braynewoode left 20s. 'to the Company of Clarkes if they accompany me to the grave' in 1586, but he was himself a clerk, and he also left 20s. to the children of Christ's Hospital 'whom I will to be at my burial'.[12]

Parisian parish churches maintained much larger staffs of priests in the later sixteenth and seventeenth centuries, to fulfil both their liturgical and additional intercessory obligations. Jeanne Passavent, *bourgeoise*, wished for the *curé* and all the *prêtres habitués* to be present at her funeral in 1583, and left 4 *écus* to the *curé* and 1 *écu* to each priest. Jeanne Regnault, widow of *noble homme* Jehan Henard, notary and *secretaire du roi*, expected

[5] Kitching, *London and Middlesex chantry certificate*; cf. Burgess, 'Shaping the parish: St Mary at Hill, London, in the fifteenth century'.

[6] Adams, *Parish clerks of London*, pp. 20–1, 25–6; Christie, *Some account of the Parish Clerks*, pp. 71–2, 148–55; *Consistory Court Wills*, 77; Machyn, *Diary*, pp. 17, 21. See above, pp. 209–10.

[7] *Consistory Court Wills*, 10, 23, 36, 38, 39, 171, 215.

[8] PRO, PROB 11/36, f. 11. Thirty Clerks came to the funeral, and a sermon was preached by 'Master Samsum' (Thomas Sampson): Machyn, *Diary*, p. 27.

[9] Christie, *Some account of the Parish Clerks*, pp. 148–55.

[10] Machyn, *Diary*, pp. 191, 193, 199, 211, 212.

[11] Christie, *Some account of the Parish Clerks*, pp. 154–5; see below, pp. 239–40.

[12] GL, MS 9171/17, f. 16.

'les gens d'église de sa paroisse' to be there.[13] Local clerical establishments could include as many as forty priests, and even testators requesting 'un cérémonial allégé' would expect the attendance of the *curé*, his two vicars, some *prêtres habitués* and the choir.[14] By the later seventeenth century, there was some resistance to the cost of employing large numbers of clergy or choir. Saint-André-des-Arts limited the size of its 'choeur ordinaire' to fifteen, but allowed the deceased's family to have as many additional *prêtres habitués* as they wished – provided that, if they did so, they also paid for the best bells, vestments, and silverware.[15]

In addition to the secular parish clergy, city residents could call on members of a wide range of religious orders and houses, both to attend the funeral and to say services simultaneously or subsequently. The friars had located themselves in urban centres in order to fulfil their mission to the laity; their role as confessors placed them in some respects in competition with the parish clergy, and they were always in demand, at least among those of middling and upper status. The four London houses (Greyfriars, Blackfriars, Austin Friars, and Whitefriars) were often represented at pre-Reformation funerals, and asked to perform post-obit services in their own church; the friary churches were also popular places of burial for the merchant class of London as well as the nobility.[16] The London houses were closed in 1538, but the Parisian friaries (Cordeliers, Jacobins, Augustins, and Carmes) remained popular. Both Jeanne Passavent and Jeanne Regnault had the four orders at their burials, as did Raphael Bonnard, *marchand fripier*, in 1616, and the friars appear to have been one of the three categories (the others being children and the poor) most commonly requested in addition to the parish clergy.[17] They also often appeared at civic and public funerals, of the status attended by the Bureau de Ville. In most cases there were probably only a few from each house present, though up to 300 Cordeliers joined the procession for Dr François le Picart in 1556. They came in very large numbers, perhaps the whole of the community, to royal funerals: at Henri IV's funeral there were 224 Cordeliers, 190 Jacobins, 100 Augustins, and 50 Carmes.[18]

The older friars' popularity may have been challenged by the new or revived orders and new mendicant houses established in Catholic-reform Paris. The Minimes, the Billettes, the Blancs-Manteaux, the Capuchins, the Mathurins, and the religious of Sainte-Catherine du Val des Ecoliers

---

[13] AN, L 664, no. 6; AN, L 631/2.   [14] Chaunu, *La mort à Paris*, pp. 357, 513.
[15] AN, LL 797, f. 23; AN, LL 687, f. 185.
[16] McMurray, *Records of two city parishes*, p. 203; cf. Sharpe, *Calendar of wills proved and enrolled in the Court of Husting*, vol. II, p. 649; cf. pp. 125–6 above.
[17] AN, L 664, no. 6; AN, L 631/2; Chaunu, *La mort à Paris*, p. 358.
[18] *RDBVP*, vol. IV, pp. 450–1; vol. V, pp. 326–7; vol. XIV, p. 525.

appeared alongside the older orders of friars at a number of civic and noble funerals in sixteenth- and early seventeenth-century Paris. Four Cordeliers carried the body of *échevin* Claude de Choilly in 1603, but Minimes carried the bodies of *échevin* Jean l'Escalopier in 1563 and the chancellor of France M. de Bellièvre in 1607; the Billettes carried François Courtin, *greffier* of Paris, in 1609.[19] Similar choices occur in the wills of lesser Parisians. Jeanne Regnault wanted the Bonshommes to attend her funeral; Jeanne Passavent wanted the Minimes, the Billettes, and the Blancs-Manteaux.[20] Raphael Bonnard wanted his body to be carried by the so-called Caputs or 'Capulets' de Montaigu, members of the austere Collège de Montaigu, who also attended Jeanne Passavent's funeral and several civic ones.[21] The choices made seem to reflect an appreciation of the fine distinctions between orders and allegiances in the Catholic Reformation.

Both Londoners and Parisians desired the attendance of children. They attended sometimes as choir members, but were most often present as inmates of the city orphanages. There were four main institutions in early modern Paris: the hospitals of the Enfants Rouges, the Enfants de la Charité, de la Trinité, and du Saint-Esprit.[22] Children from all four hospitals attended the largest funerals, such as that of the Cardinal de Birague in 1583; on lesser occasions there might only be children from one or two.[23] London had a very similar institution (closest to the Enfants de la Trinité in its educational function) in Christ's Hospital, founded in 1550 in the premises of the former Greyfriars. The 'children of the hospital' led the procession in a herald's memorandum (probably of the sixteenth century) for the standard proceedings at a citizen's funeral.[24] At the burial of master John Hethe in early 1553, there were 'a C. chylderyn of Gray-freres boys and gyrlles, ij and ij to-gether', all dressed by his bequest, and 'the children of the hospital' or 'the Blue-coat boys' appeared at several civic funerals in the later sixteenth and seventeenth centuries, evidently sometimes by special request and payment.[25] They seem to have stimulated

[19] *RDBVP*, vol. V, pp. 326–7; vol. VI, pp. 111–14; vol. VIII, pp. 352–4; vol. XIII, pp. 95–7; vol. XIV, pp. 211–14, 359–60. For a discussion of the religious orders see Pillorget, *Paris au temps des premiers Bourbons*, pp. 483–509.

[20] AN, L 631/2; AN, L 664, no. 6.

[21] Chaunu, *La mort à Paris*, p. 358; AN, L 664, no. 6; *RDBVP*, vol. VIII, pp. 352–4; vol. XIV, pp. 359–60. The nickname derived from the haircut ('une sorte de capulet') of the scholars: *RDBVP*, vol. IX, pp. 104–6.

[22] Babelon, *Paris au XVIe siècle*, pp. 186–8.

[23] *RDBVP*, vol. VIII, pp. 352–4; vol. XIV, pp. 359–60.

[24] Nichols, *Illustrations*, p. 74. I thank Caroline Barron for this reference.

[25] Machyn, *Diary*, p. 32; Bodl. MS Ashmole 836, p. 295; BL, Add. MSS 71131 D, F; Pepys, *Diary*, vol. VI, p. 114; PRO, PROB 11/95, ff. 87, 121; PRO, PROB 11/135, f. 15v.

some competition from a group of young men, calling themselves 'the youths of the parish of St John of Jerusalem', who offered their services, presumably as a choir, at marriages and funerals, in 1635.[26]

Gittings identifies the presence of children at funerals with a message of social continuity, those starting on life accompanying those leaving it, and some such symbolism may well have contributed to the phenomenon.[27] But they were believed to possess a special spiritual value, as 'intercesseurs privilégiées qui ont naturel accès au Royaume de Dieu', as Michel Yvard, *chirurgien juré à Paris*, called them in 1555.[28] Obviously in Protestant England they were not seen as intercessors, but their presence clearly derived from a Catholic/purgatorial understanding of the funeral ceremony. More explicitly, though, in London, and to an important degree in Paris, they were identified with the city as an institution, and represented it as a charitable commonwealth. In Paris, additionally, processions of children could be an intensely charged occasion, perhaps harking back to children's crusades and even the biblical massacre of the Innocents, and carrying a message of Christian solidarity, anti-heresy, and even martyrdom. The barefoot Enfants de la Trinité, carrying candles, in le Picart's funeral procession in 1556 must have summoned up images of such penitential processions, and perhaps they were already being associated with a defensive confessionalism: le Picart was reverenced as an exemplar of life and doctrine.[29] In January 1589, soon after the assassinations of the duke and cardinal of Guise, little children began to hold liturgical processions in Paris, carrying candles and singing.[30]

Confraternities, charity, and community

If the role of children at funerals shades from that of privileged intercessors to the representation of an idea of the civic community, similar ideas of larger community are expressed in the attendance of the poor, and of smaller, more exclusive communities in the invocation of confraternity and the solidarity of occupation, profession, or office. As with children, the idea of intercession was primary, but in Catholic Paris, as well as in Protestant London, it is easy to see that other considerations came into play. The expression of charity, in all its meanings, was an important element in funeral ritual, and in the city there was no lack of suitable relationships and interactions in which it could be exemplified.

---

[26] Gittings, *Death, burial and the individual*, p. 153.
[27] Ibid., pp. 153–4, 160–1.   [28] Chaunu, *La mort à Paris*, p. 346.
[29] *RDBVP*, vol. IV, pp. 450–1; Taylor, *Heresy and orthodoxy in sixteenth-century Paris*, pp. 213–14.
[30] Lestoile, *Journal de l'Estoile pour le règne de Henri III*, pp. 612, 614.

Fraternities and confraternities were a long-standing feature of late medieval society, not exclusively urban, by any means, but sustained in large numbers in London and Paris both by the resources of the urban population and by their spiritual anxieties. Largely voluntary and limited to groups identifying shared economic, social, or devotional interests, they institutionalised mutual charity as a mode of social relation. Though collective worship or observance was important to all of them, many took funerals and commemoration as a particular responsibility. London had over 150 parish fraternities in the later middle ages, many but not all of which survived up to the Reformation. They have been characterised by Caroline Barron as 'essentially communal chantries', and one of the duties of fraternity members was to attend the burials of their fellows, contributing to the cost if necessary, and certainly making offerings and prayers.[31] As noted above, membership of a fraternity also brought advantages of extra lights and special hearse-cloths. The ordinances of several fraternities specified that they should meet the body of any member who died within ten miles of London outside the city and attend it home.[32] Londoners who belonged to fraternities built them into their planning for the funeral: 'To each brother and sister of the fraternity present at my burial, 4d.'; 'I entreat my brothers of the fraternity of the Trinity that they of their charity should come to pay their respects warmly clad'.[33] Craft guilds, which usually centred on a religious fraternity, similarly expected brethren to attend: 'I bequethe unto the ffelyschep off the Skynners to be present at my obseque, masse and dirrige 6s. 8d.'; 'I bequethe to the Company of Bakers if they come to my buryall, 10s.'; 'to the wardens of my company for their paynes commynge to my buryinge 10s.'[34] The Brewers paid Robert their clerk 4d. for warning the members of the craft to come to the funeral of two almsmen; the Carpenters fined members for failing to attend the collective 'obytt derege and masse' in 1546/7, though this was the last year they did so.[35]

Although religious fraternities were suppressed in 1548, craft-based guilds and companies survived, and their attendance at funerals continued through the Reformation years and afterwards. The post-funeral feast for company members was, as we have seen, a prominent element in remembrance and charity. For Londoners of higher status, the presence of members of the craft guild, dressed in their livery, certainly contributed to the spectacle. The body of Sir William Roche, knight

---

[31] Barron, 'The parish fraternities of medieval London', pp. 23–5.
[32] Basing, *Parish fraternity register*, 139, 140. Cf. Ariès, *The hour of our death*, pp. 185–8.
[33] *Consistory Court Wills*, 12, 53.   [34] Ibid., 79, 127, 229.
[35] GL, MS 5440, f. 269v; Marsh, *Records of the Carpenters' Company*, vol. IV: *Wardens' account book, 1546–71*, p. 7.

and alderman (d. 1523), was accompanied by four leading members of the Drapers' Company in livery; the mourners were followed by the aldermen, the sheriffs, and the liverymen of the Drapers. Many of the funerals noted by Machyn were attended by liveried companymen.[36] Sir Rowland Hill (d. 1561) left 5s. each to the wardens of the Mercery to be at his burial, and 12d. to each of the livery, as well as a large sum for a dinner at Mercers' Hall.[37] Sir Philip Sidney's association with the Grocers' Company brought 120 of them in livery to his funeral procession in 1587.[38] On a more modest scale, John Wase (d. 1561) left 3s. 4d. to the Brewers for taking pains to come to his funeral in livery.[39] The practice certainly continued into the later sixteenth and seventeenth centuries, but as the wording of most bequests suggests, attendance was seen as voluntary, not mandatory; those officers and liverymen who came expected some reward for doing so.[40] As noted in chapter 7, the companies had resplendent hearse-cloths which they lent to members; their arms were also displayed on banners carried around the corpse, and company halls were used both as the starting-point for some processions and for the dinner afterwards.[41] By this date, the involvement of the company and its members in funeral processions and services was more a matter of lending prestige and celebrating a social rather than a religious solidarity, an aspect underlined by the attention paid to funeral feasts. Nevertheless, a significant function of the post-Reformation companies was their accumulation and dispensation of endowments to benefit the poor. They were increasingly identified as trustees or administrators of major charitable foundations, almost the only one of their early functions to survive to the present day. Many of those involving their company in their funerals also made some bequest to the company's charitable funds.[42]

This aspect of charity – benevolence to the poor – remained a central element of funeral ceremony. Pre-Reformation belief stressed the importance of deeds of charity and mercy, and the particular value of the prayers of the poor, and pre-Reformation testators of all social classes took care

---

[36] Machyn *Diary*, pp. xxi–xxiv, 173, 232, 269, 293.

[37] PRO, PROB 11/44, ff. 259. See above, pp. 216–17.

[38] J. Nichols, *The Progresses and public processions of Queen Elizabeth, among which are interspersed other solemnities, public expenditures, and remarkable events during the reign of that illustrious princess*, 3 vols. (London, 1823), vol. II, pp. 483–94.

[39] PRO, PROB 11/44, ff. 225.

[40] E.g. PRO, PROB 11/95, ff. 38, 87, 109v. Cf. PRO, PROB 11/44, f. 259; Machyn, *Diary*, pp. 271–2.

[41] E.g. BL, Add. MSS 71131 D, F, G, for funeral processions starting from company halls; see above, chapter 8, for dinners.

[42] E.g. PRO, PROB 11/84, f. 87v; Bodl. MS Ashmole 818, f. 45. Cf. Ward, *Metropolitan communities*, esp. pp. 113–15.

to include charitable bequests of this kind. Londoners left money to poor men and women to attend their funerals, or arranged for distributions of money on the day of burial that would guarantee their presence. For testators of modest status, numerous small bequests dominated: John Hudson, ironmonger, left 4d. apiece to four poor children for holding four tapers, and 13d. to thirteen poor folk of the parish on the day of his departing; Joan Brytten left 4s. in halfpenny loaves at the time of her burial; Agnes Smyth left 2s. in bread. Margaret Bowman left £3 to be given in 4d. doles at her burial to poor householders of her parish.[43] More affluent Londoners could be more lavish in their benefactions, and the most common bequest was of a gown, sometimes with a kerchief or shift as well, to a number of poor men or women. Sir Henry Amcotts, asking for a Catholic funeral in 1554, left gowns to twenty poor men who would carry torches at his funeral, and the same to twenty poor women; Sir Henry Huberthorn left a frieze gown each to twenty poor men and women to bring his body to the church.[44] These bequests betray a perception of the poor as numerous and ubiquitous, a constant and significant presence who could easily be recruited into a funeral performance. Their presence also added to the scale and solemnity of the proceedings, especially when they were uniformly dressed, or carried lights, and was a very visible testimony to the piety and charity (and substance) of the deceased or his executors.

The poor did not disappear from English funeral processions when the value of their prayers was denied, and if anything the scale of processions may have increased. The practice of inviting numbers of poor men and women to attend the funeral, offering them some return in cash or kind, had become so deeply entrenched, such an essential part of funeral practice, that it survived the abolition of purgatory and the new emphasis on faith not works. Bequests of gowns and the attendance at the funeral of dozens of grateful poor were still standard practice in Elizabethan and Stuart London. Clothing them in black or grey gowns may suggest an evocation of the monastic habit, or at least an imitation of the uniformity and sobriety of religious dress. As a herald noted, perhaps rather self-servingly, it was customary to have as many poor persons as the deceased had years at death,[45] though several testators preferred a round number. A hundred poor men attended the funeral of Sir Cuthbert Buckle in 1594, though his will only specified gowns for sixty;[46] seventy-two were at Sir William Webbe's funeral in 1599, and several seventeenth-century aldermen and civic leaders had eighty to a hundred poor men, constituting a third or

---

[43] *Consistory Court Wills*, 85, 122, 164, 179.
[44] PRO, PROB 11/37, f. 67; ibid., 38, f. 127.   [45] Bodl. MS Ashmole 836, pp. 121–2.
[46] PRO, PROB 11/84, f. 87v; Bodl. MS Ashmole 818, f. 45.

more of the procession.[47] The increased role awarded to the poor in London funerals could have been a way of compensating for the loss of other spiritual and social meanings in the funeral ritual. It is notable that their place near the front of the funeral procession was that still occupied, in contemporary Paris, by the regular clergy. Involving the poor in this way can also be interpreted, of course, both as a more useful and self-less form of charity than endowing prayers, and as the exercise of social control. It was an obvious, even ostentatious, form of giving, and it also offered the possibility of discrimination or local patronage. John Wase (d. 1561) asked his executors (who included Richard Grafton, whose Protestant sympathies are known) 'most earnestly to be good unto the poor of London that be godly'.[48] Lady Isabel Gresham (d. 1565), widow of Sir Richard, wanted gowns, with caps or linen veils, to be given to an equal number of poor men and women, who were to be chosen first from her tenants in Lad Lane in London and Bethnal Green in Middlesex, and secondly from the poor of the parishes of St Lawrence Jewry, St Stephen Coleman Street, and St Mary Aldermanbury, 'so allway that the poore of the parish of St Lawrence be throughlie first sarved'.[49] The establishment of the Poor Law and parochial systems of relief did not af-fect the tradition of inviting the poor to funerals, even though they might now be deemed to be eligible for adequate support from other sources. Several early seventeenth-century willmakers envisaged that the poor of the parish and beyond would 'resorte' or 'assemble' at their funeral for the distribution of bread and alms, and explicitly provided for this.[50] There was nevertheless some anxiety about the wholesale distribution of alms at funerals, both because it failed to distinguish worthy from unworthy recipients, and because it could occasion disorder. Seventeen beggars were 'thronged and trampled to death' at the distribution of the 6d. dole at Leadenhall following the funeral of Lady Ramsey, widow of a former Lord Mayor, in 1601.[51] Sir William Craven, who lived near Leadenhall, and could have witnessed or heard of this event ordered that nothing be given to people in the street on the day of his funeral 'for the avoid-ing of tumults, which be usually occasioned at burials', but left black gowns and 12d. apiece for dinner to a hundred poor men to come to his burial.[52]

---

[47] Bodl. MS Ashmole 836, p. 289; BL, Add. MS 71131 A–X.
[48] PRO, PROB 11/44, f. 225.
[49] Will printed in Gower, *Genealogy of the family of Gresham*, pp. 76–9.
[50] E.g. PRO, PROB 11/95, ff. 87; 121; 135, ff. 15v, 38, 39v.
[51] McClure (ed.), *Letters of John Chamberlain*, vol. I, pp. 134–6.
[52] Strype, *Survey of London*, bk. 2, pp. 67–9.

In Paris, where confraternities, religious orders, and the theology of intercession survived through the early modern period, the poor still had a role to play. Twenty-four *pauvres* walked in the procession for Dr François le Picart in 1556, carrying torches with escutcheons of his arms; a hundred, dressed in mourning, with torches with arms, attended the funerals of the Cardinal de Bourbon in 1557 and the Cardinal de Birague in 1583. Two hundred poor attended the funeral of the duke of Anjou in 1584, and 246 that of the duc de Joyeuse in 1588; 500 were in the funeral procession of Henri IV.[53] These very large displays, however, seem to have been confined to the grandest funerals. For people of lower rank, a much smaller number attended. François Courtin, *greffier* of Paris, equivalent of one of the London aldermen, had twelve poor men at his funeral in 1609, considerably fewer than attended similar events in London. The number twelve occurs elsewhere and may have been standard.[54] Parisians' attitude to the poor was ambivalent, varying from virtual idolisation of their sanctity, as the special protégés of Jesus, to a determination to enclose and reform them on a large scale. A Grand Bureau des Pauvres was established in 1554, but its efforts to round up and enclose the poor were not very successful.[55] It did, however, offer a way of providing and controlling a contingent of poor people at major funerals: the usher or bailiff of the Bureau led the one hundred poor at the funeral of the comte de Brissac in 1569, and the 200 at the funeral of the duke of Anjou in 1584.[56] Early seventeenth-century reforms of poor management and relief were only partially effective, until the establishment of the Hôpital Général in 1656, which created a series of hospitals in which men, women, and children were interned. Even this, however, met considerable opposition from those who saw personal charity to the poor as an essential lifeline to salvation for the rich.[57] Parisians certainly continued to give to the poor, sometimes discriminating carefully between particular objects or recipients, but it is not clear how far they involved them in funeral ritual. Jacques Chaillou and Madeleine Grosjean, husband and wife, together made a will in 1666 leaving 60 *livres* to the most humble (*honteux*) poor to be found on the day of their burial – whom they may have expected to come to the funeral – but this was only a tiny proportion of their

[53] *RDBVP*, vol. IV, pp. 450–1, 472–3; vol. VIII, pp. 352–4, 388–95; vol. IX, pp. 104–6; vol. XIV, pp. 525–6.

[54] *RDBVP*, vol. XIV, pp. 359–60; Chaunu, *La mort à Paris*, pp. 357, 361.

[55] Pillorget, *Paris sous les premiers Bourbons*, pp. 524–6. See also Bernard, *The emerging city*, pp. 132–55.

[56] *RDBVP*, vol. VIII, pp. 388–95; vol. VI, pp. 111–14.

[57] Pillorget, *Paris sous les premiers Bourbons*, pp. 524–6; cf. R. P. Chalumeau, 'L'assistance aux malades pauvres au XVIIe siècle', *XVIIe siècle* 90–1 (1971), 75–86.

total benefaction of 5,810 *livres* to the poor. Their beneficiaries included orphans, prisoners, and converts, but the Hôpital Général received the largest share at 2,000 *livres*.[58]

Confraternities played a major role in medieval and early modern Parisian society. Unlike the London religious fraternities, which disappeared almost without trace, except for those whose identity was subsumed in that of the craft and livery companies, the Parisian confraternities flourished. In the sixteenth and seventeenth centuries there were craft- or occupation-based fraternities, whose activities were severely constrained by the hostility of government to the possibility of combination or collective action, and a wider range focusing on the encouragement of parochial piety, often through devotion to a religious cult or object. Both kinds were based either in parish churches, where they might build or maintain chapels, or in religious houses. The church of Saint-Gervais had five confraternities by the later sixteenth century: two craft ones, of tanners and wine merchants; one dedicated to St Eutropius; and two new ones, dedicated to the Holy Name of Jesus and to St Michael. Many of the new confraternities of the later sixteenth and seventeenth centuries were established to defend or propagate Catholic devotion in the face of the threat of heresy and toleration. The Saint-Gervais confraternity of the Holy Name of Jesus, devoted to the sacrament, was very active in the years of the Ligue and members swore an oath not to recognise Henri IV.[59] In the seventeenth century, many of the trade fraternities declined, but the devotional ones continued to do well, patronised by the élite and even by royalty. One of their objects, as with traditional medieval fraternities, was to offer spiritual support to sick and dying members, and to guarantee their burial and intercession. Masters were charged with maintaining the chapel, ensuring the viaticum was delivered to the sick, and attending members' funerals. The regulations of the seventeenth-century confraternity of the Virgin, St Roch, and St Sebastian at Saint-Gervais included the promise: 'après le décès: service aux dépens de la confrerie'.[60] Members of the confraternity of *parcheminiers* in Saint-André-des-Arts were expected to pray for a dying member, and to attend a service at the expense of the confraternity for the soul of a deceased confrère, or to commune privately to the same intention.[61] Like the London parish fraternities, the Parisian religious confraternities appear to have welcomed sisters as well as brothers. Jeanne Passavent either belonged to or shared a devotion with the confraternity of Notre-Dame in the chapel of the Saint-Esprit in her parish church of Saint-Jean-en-Grève, for she left them 6 *écus sol* to lend

---

[58] Chaunu, *La mort à Paris*, pp. 422–3.   [59] Babelon, *Paris au XVIe siècle*, pp. 384–93.
[60] Pillorget, *Paris sous les premiers Bourbons*, pp. 561–4.   [61] AN, L 630, no. 13A.

her their funeral pall and say a *service complet* for her soul. She also left 6 *écus* to the confraternity of Saint-Claude in the church of Saint-Antoine, probably for a similar service.[62]

For some sections of society, formal membership of a confraternity could perhaps blur into identification with a professional group. Etienne Tonnellier, doctor of theology and *curé* of Saint-Eustache, in his will of 1644 asked 'tous mes confraires pretres habitués en ladite église' to be present at his burial, but it is not clear whether he was referring to a constituted confraternity or just expressing a sense of fellowship between the priests of the church. He also besought the attendance of 'les pretres de la grande confrairie', probably the citywide confraternity of priests and *bourgeois de Paris* of Notre-Dame.[63] The parish *curés* of seventeenth-century Paris claimed the right to function as a corporate body, and demonstrated their solidarity by marching in processions and appearing at the funerals of colleagues.[64] Other professional associations included the university and the law. A great number of doctors of theology, religious and secular, with the dean of the faculty and other beadles and officers, attended the funeral of the popular teacher and doctor of theology François le Picart in 1556.[65] Tonnellier, above, asked that all the doctors and bachelors of the faculty of theology be invited to his funeral, and that those who came should be given 20 or 10 *sous* each.[66] Elite Parisians often combined office and status in several worlds, such as the church and the university, as above, or the law and the military. At the funeral of a *juge-consul* who was also one of the sixteen colonels of the city in 1592, the *juge-consuls*' claim to bear the pall and be present *en corps* exclusively was overruled in favour of the colonels.[67] Nicole le Maistre, canon of Notre-Dame and *conseiller en Parlement*, was buried in 1568 with a ceremony that harmoniously integrated his two identities. His body was covered in the pall of the court of Parlement, one corner of which was taken by another canon and *conseiller*. Two presidents of Parlement and several Masters of Requests were present, but the convoy was led by the vicar of the dean of Paris and was made up of the parish clergy of Saint-Cosme and the *prêtres habitués* of Notre-Dame.[68] The funeral procession of Christophe de Thou, *premier président* of Parlement, in 1582 was attended by all the *présidents* and *conseillers* then in Paris in black, and

[62] AN, L 664, no. 6.

[63] Chaunu, *La mort à Paris*, pp. 508–9; Babelon, *Paris au XVIe siècle*, p. 389.

[64] Golden, *The godly rebellion*, pp. 80–1.   [65] *RDBVP*, vol. IV, pp. 450–1.

[66] Chaunu, *La mort à Paris*, pp. 508–9. Members of the university also participated in state funerals, such as those of the duke of Anjou in 1584 and Henri IV in 1610: *RDBVP*, vol. VIII, pp. 388–95; vol. XIV, p. 526.

[67] *RDBVP*, vol. X, p. 267.   [68] AN, microfilm L 510/27, f. 2v.

several Masters of Requests. The corners of the pall, which was specially provided for this funeral, were held by two *présidents* and the two senior *conseillers* of the Grand Chambre. A large number of princes, dukes, and other nobles followed the body; five bishops were mourners. The personnel of the Sainte-Chapelle – located in the same palace complex as the Parlement – did the office and processed as a body.[69] In London, the legal profession was represented at a number of civic funerals as well as state ones, and came out in force for funerals of their own members, mostly in the western suburbs of the city. Ranulph Cholmely, Recorder of London, straddled the worlds of the law and the city; his funeral at St Dunstan in the West in 1563 was attended by senior aldermen and the Lord Mayor, and by 200 men from the Inns of Court.[70]

Precedence and processions: representing the city

Funeral services were preceded by the transport of the body to the church, and this act became the occasion for a carefully programmed procession or *convoi* through the public space of the streets. The size and grandeur of this procession was a mark of the status and individuality of the deceased, and of the respect paid to the idea of the dead. Both cities had an important tradition of civic and religious procession, which helped to shape the funeral procession and was itself enriched by it. Royal entries, the Midsummer Watch, and the evolving Lord Mayor's Show in London took over the streets of the capital in a largely orderly fashion to express and reinforce a model of structured and harmonious community.[71] Large-scale funerals were also used to underpin the structure of authority and deference, though their ritual language could be usurped by resistant groups to assert an alternative allegiance. Paris had a very long history of royal entries and royal funeral convoys, and its procession tradition gained in political and ideological significance during the later sixteenth century. Processions of relics, or of penitents, had an immense emotional impact and considerable political effect in the tensions of the period. Used to assert Catholic religious unity against the perceived threat of heresy or even toleration, through enthusiastic mass participation in the ritual,

---

[69] Lestoile, *Journal de l'Estoile pour le règne de Henri III*, pp. 309–11. De Thou was buried 'en notable pompe funebre' in his family chapel in Saint-André-des-Arts: ibid., p. 309.

[70] Machyn, *Diary*, pp. 306–7; PRO, PROB 11/46, f. 184. For lawyers' presence at city funerals, cf. BL, Add. MSS 71131 D, E, F, H.

[71] D. M. Bergeron, *English civic pageantry, 1558–1642* (London, 1971); S. Williams, 'The Lord Mayor's Show in Tudor and Stuart times', *Guildhall Miscellany* 1.10 (1959), 3–18; S. Lindenbaum, 'Ceremony and oligarchy: the London Midsummer Watch', in B. Hanawalt and K. Reyerson (eds.), *City and spectacle in medieval Europe* (Minneapolis, 1994), pp. 171–88.

they could threaten public order, and certainly challenged the authority of the royal government. Grand funeral ceremonies, such as that of Charles IX in 1574, could therefore be a counter-assertion of the unity of the state.[72]

Different perspectives on the procession are offered by different observers or participants. Henry Machyn in London focused on equipment and attendance, perhaps betraying a professional interest from his position as parish clerk and member of the Merchant Taylors' Company, the suppliers of cloth and clothing.[73] John Chamberlain refers at times to public funerals in his general account of news and gossip to Dudley Carleton and his other correspondents, sometimes adding a personal opinion on the event.[74] Pierre l'Estoile in Paris was a more professional chronicler, noting funerals as events of public importance, but often offering additionally an alternative and cynical view of them through the printed satires and slanders he transcribed.[75] The vicar of the dean of Paris kept a register of convoys he attended because he was entitled to keep the torches and lights from the procession; the English heralds kept extensive memoranda, both for precedent and for accounting purposes.[76] The members of the Bureau de l'Hôtel de Ville were concerned to record their own involvement, and the status accorded them.[77]

Funeral processions were carefully marshalled, by heralds, masters of ceremonies, or the *jurés-crieurs* in Paris, and the order of proceeding was vital. The corpse and its accompaniment formed the focus of the procession, perhaps two-thirds of the way back; honour graded downwards in either direction. Placement in the funeral procession was crucial. The heralds' memoranda of some London funerals are full of corrections, apparently to ensure that a proper record was kept; the dignitaries in Parisian funerals on occasion came to blows. At the funeral of the Cardinal de Bourbon in 1557, the canons of Saint-Germain-l'Auxerrois were constrained 'à force de coups de poing' to walk ahead of the canons of Notre-Dame; they similarly contested their place at the funeral of the chancellor Olivier in 1560, and there were 'quelques differends et propos d'altercation' over precedence at the funeral of Charles IX.[78] The Bureau de Ville accepted that they should be placed lower than the Parlement

[72] Diefendorf, *Beneath the cross*, pp. 44–8. Cf. Giesey, *Royal funeral ceremony*.

[73] Machyn, *Diary*, pp. viii–ix, xi; I also thank Gary Gibbs and Ian Mortimer for useful discussion on these points.

[74] McClure, *Letters of John Chamberlain* vol. I, p. 193, vol. II, pp. 236–8, 554, 616–17.

[75] Lestoile, *Journal de L'Estoile pour le règne de Henri III*, passim.

[76] E.g. BL. Add. MSS 71131 A–X; Bodl. MSS Ashmole 818, 836.

[77] AN, L 510, microfilm no. 27; *RDBVP*, passim.

[78] *RDBVP*, vol. IV, pp. 472–3; vol. V, pp. 54–5; Lestoile, *Journal de L'Estoile pour le règne de Henri III*, p. 42.

of Paris at major funerals, but were always very conscious of where they were in relation to the representatives of the Cour des Aides and the Chambre des Comptes. They resisted the claims of the Cour des Monnaies to precede them at the funeral of the duke of Anjou in 1584, and after the burial of Chancellor de Bellièvre in 1607 recorded with satisfaction that 'les Generaulx des Monnoyes ne se trouvent point audict convoy'.[79]

The municipalities of both London and Paris rendered full honours to one of their members who died. Aldermen and officers of London government were called on to participate in the ceremonies as 'the last love, duty, and ceremony one to another'. The officers of Paris's Bureau de Ville were invited to the funeral of François Courtin, *greffier*, in 1609, 'afin de rendre par leur presence l'assemblee plus honorable', and on another occasion were thanked by the family of Claude de Choilly, *échevin*, for the honour they had done them in attending his funeral.[80] However, there were significant differences in the way in which the municipalities of the two cities participated, perhaps implicit in the different appeals to 'love' and 'honour'. Parisian funerals seem to have been more formal, representing official status and connections rather than family or friends, and certainly including a major statement of municipal identity in the use of city officers and men-at-arms in liveries, and of torches with the city's arms.[81] Londoners at times had to be coerced into compliance with the forms: the earl marshal wrote to the Lord Mayor in office in 1635, referring to the private funeral of a former Lord Mayor, to desire him in future to ensure the due observance of 'the auncient and reverend ceremonies' appropriate for the funerals of such persons.[82]

The mourning aspect of the funeral procession was very evident in London, with lists of those wearing black cloaks or gowns, and higher place being given to aldermen in mourning than to those in their ordinary gowns.[83] The Parisian municipality appeared in black gowns for some funerals, but on at least some occasions, for funerals of members of the municipality, wore their colourful ordinary liveries. At that of Jean l'Escalopier, *échevin*, in 1563, the *prévot des marchands*, the *échevins*, and the *greffier* wore their *robbes my parties*, the *procureur du roi et de la Ville* his

---

[79] *RDBVP*, vol. V, pp. 54–5; vol. VIII, pp. 45, 389–95; vol. XIV, p. 214; vol. XVI, pp. 383–4.

[80] Munday et al., *Survey of London . . . 1633*, p. 660 (quoted in Nichols' introduction to Machyn's *Diary*, p. xxiv); *RDBVP*, vol. XIV, pp. 359–60; vol. XIII, pp. 95–7.

[81] E.g. *RDBVP*, vol. XIII, pp. 95–7; vol. XIV, pp. 359–60.

[82] Waters, *Parish registers in England, their history and contents*, pp. 50–1; Beaven, *Aldermen of London*, vol. II, p. 54.

[83] Nichols, *Illustrations*, p. 74, 'Proceedings of a citezen's funeral': 'Aldermen in blacks' came before the coffin, 'Aldermen not in blackes' among the mourners following it.

scarlet robe, and the *receveur de la Ville*, his 'bons habits noirs'.[84] As at the funerals of royalty, appearing in robes of office may have been an expression of the continuity of office and government despite the death of a leading establishment figure.[85] Although London funerals were managed by the heralds, and had to bear quite a burden of heraldic symbolism, they still allowed the family an important place. In Paris the chief mourners ('le grand deuil') were separated from the corpse by the civic party, whereas in London family members supported and immediately followed the body, and included both close family and more distant connections, and on occasion small children.[86] Even if this apparent difference of style is a function of the different records kept by the heralds (for London) and the Bureau de Ville in Paris, this in itself suggests that the latter saw funerals as occasions where honour and precedence counted most.

Certainly some of the London records indicate a full attendance of neighbours and family, as well as due respect to position and rank. The funeral procession of Sir John Leman, knight and alderman, in 1632, began with the children of Christ's Hospital; they were followed by 266 poor men, and by several minor officers such as parish clerks, masters of Christ's Hospital, and the beadle of Leman's company, the Fishmongers. Then came the servants of more distinguished men: sending one's servants to join such a procession was an accepted way of paying respect to the dead. Leman's 'freinds in clokes', and his 'kinsmen in cloaks' came next, then 'gentlemen in gownes', divines in gowns, esquires, doctors of physic, and doctors of divinity. These appear to have been men attending as individuals, placed by the heralds in order of their rank, rather than representatives of estates. Next came the aldermen (in reverse order of seniority), and the Lord Mayor with the Swordbearer, the Common Crier, and a trainbearer. The body was preceded by the preacher and the parson of Leman's parish, by his pennon of arms, and by his helm, crest, sword, targe, and coat of arms. Six of the Lord Mayor's officers carried the coffin, and six men bore pennons around it, representing the Goldsmiths' and Fishmongers' Companies, the East India Company, the city, and 'Christ Church' (? Christ's Hospital). The corpse was immediately followed by the family mourners, and then by the Lord Keeper and two Chief Justices with attendants. Finally came Leman's female relatives and

[84] *RDBVP*, vol. V, pp. 326–7; similarly for the funerals of three other *échevins* in 1579, 1585, and 1603: ibid., vol. VIII, pp. 198–9, 502–3; vol. XIII, pp. 95–7. The reference to 'bons habits noirs' may be an explicit distinction from the *deuil* or mourning worn on other occasions.

[85] Cf. Giesey, *Royal funeral ceremony*, pp. 53–61, 66–9; E. Kantorowicz, *The king's two bodies. A study in medieval political theology* (Princeton, 1970), p. 418.

[86] 'Little Simon and Tho. Bennet carried by there 2 maids' were in the procession of Sir Thomas Bennett in 1627: BL, Add. MS 71131 E.

household servants, down to the housemaid and nurse. At the end came members of the city companies, the hospitals, and 'freinds of the parish and others'.[87]

A similar order was followed at other civic funerals ordered by the heralds, with the key participants being, in order, poor men or women; servants, friends, and kinsmen; aldermen and Lord Mayor; parson or preacher; the body; the chief mourners; and the family and household of the deceased.[88] Some extra elements might be added: the Lord Mayor was chief mourner at the funeral of Sir Cuthbert Buckle in 1594, because Buckle died during his mayoral year; the city's Artillery Company attended Sir William Cockayne's funeral in 1626.[89] Funeral honours of this kind were accorded not only to the aldermen and common councilmen, but to their wives and even widows, indicating that there was a sense of an élite class, not just a group of officeholders. A widow clearly kept the identity she had acquired with her husband, even if she outlived him by decades. Sir William Laxton, late Lord Mayor, was buried with a full heraldic funeral and civic attendance in 1556. His widow, Lady (Joan) Laxton, did not die until 1576, but her funeral was attended by all the aldermen (eight of them in black and the rest in violet) and their wives; by the Lord Mayor, Swordbearer, Town Clerk, and Chamberlain; by members of the Grocers' Company and the masters of the city hospitals. The pennons of the city, the Grocers' Company, and the Merchant Adventurers were borne around her corpse.[90] Sir Rowland Hill, alderman and past mayor (d. 1561), requested that all the mayoresses (wives and widows of past mayors) be invited to his funeral dinner.[91] The family connections between members of the élite also reinforced this sense of solidarity, so that some individuals took part in funeral ceremonies both *ex officio* and in a personal capacity. Benedict Barnham attended Sir Cuthbert Buckle's funeral in the multiple identities of assistant mourner, fellow alderman, cousin of the deceased, overseer of his will, and a beneficiary of the will.[92]

The heralds' records for London civic funerals do not describe the formalities before the full funeral procession formed up at the deceased's house or at a company hall. In Paris, the *greffier* recorded the ceremonies at the Hôtel de Ville (the formal *cri* or announcement and invitation) and the procession, with unlit torches, of the officers to the deceased's house.

[87] BL, Add. MS 71131 F.
[88] BL, Add. MSS 71131 A–X. Cf. 'The proceedings of a citizen's funeral' in Nichols, *Illustrations*, p. 74.
[89] Bodl. MS Ashmole 818; BL, Add. MS 71131 D.
[90] Machyn, *Diary*, pp. 111–12; Bodl. MS Ashmole 836, pp. 295, 361.
[91] Machyn, *Diary*, pp. 270–1; PRO, PROB 11/44, f. 259.
[92] Bodl. MS Ashmole 818; PRO, PROB 11/84, f. 87v.

It could be a very large party, comprising the *prévôt des marchands*, the *échevins*, the city's chief officers, and some or all of the twenty-four city councillors; in addition there were usually the *sergents de ville*, a number of members of the three civic corps of archers, *arbalestiers* (crossbowmen) and *hacquebutiers* (harquebus-men), and sometimes the sixteen *hanouars* or salt-porters.[93] These last had the honour of bearing the king's body, or later his effigy, though Paris, but also appeared at other funerals.[94] For the funeral of Jean l'Escalopier, *échevin*, in 1560, the Bureau de Ville ordered sixteen torches with the arms of the Ville, to be carried by the *hanouars*, and sent them ahead of the civic party to the house of the deceased. The *sergents de ville* in their *robbes my parties*, with the silver ship of Paris on the shoulder, preceded the *prévôt des marchands*, the *échevins*, and the *greffiers*, *procureur*, and *receveur* on horseback to l'Escalopier's house in the rue Saint-Denis. There, after vigils were said over the body, they formed a procession led by the four orders of friars and the priests of the church of Saint-Jacques-de-la-Boucherie. The sixteen *hanouars* carried torches round the corpse, which was immediately followed by the civic party, and then by the mourners, and after them a great number of relations and *bourgeois* and merchants of the city.[95] For the funeral of François Courtin, *greffier*, a grander affair, in 1609, the Bureau de Ville commissioned two dozen torches of 2 lbs weight, with the arms of the Ville, and ordered the captain of archers to send thirty of his men. On this occasion, many more religious preceded the corpse (friars, 'Cappettes', Billettes, Blancs-Manteaux, Mathurins) and the *crieurs* were present with their handbells; the city's archers carried the twenty-four torches in the procession. As before, the civic party followed the corpse and preceded the family mourners. The new *greffier* in a black gown led the Bureau de Ville (normally he followed the *échevins*). The tail of the procession was made up of the family of the deceased, the city councillors, and other notables.[96] The role of the Bureau de Ville in the strife of the later sixteenth century, and its identification with the passionate Catholicism of the Ligue, may have encouraged its support for funeral display as an expression of ideological solidarity. Robert Danès, *quartenier*, former *échevin*, and *greffier* of the Chambre des Comptes, was buried at Saint-Jean-en-Grève in 1592, with a civic and governmental following, and a very large number of *bourgeois*, invited and not. The archbishop of Aix, a Parisian *ligueur*, performed the service, and the whole was described in the municipality's records as 'ung des plus beaulx convoys quy ayt esté y a longtemps en ceste ville'.[97]

---

[93] E.g. *RDBVP*, vol. V, pp. 326–7.   [94] See Giesey, *Royal funeral ceremony*, pp. 61–6.
[95] *RDBVP*, vol. V, pp. 326–7.   [96] Ibid., vol. XIV, pp. 359–60.   [97] Ibid., vol. X, p. 280.

The city and the state: the play of power

London and Paris put on ceremonies for their own notables, but they were also co-opted into participation in funerals of national importance; both English and French monarchies were fully aware of the importance of their own representation, and of the contribution the city could make to this.[98] Even if the final resting-place of royalty was outside the city itself, at Westminster or Windsor or Saint-Denis, the capital was crucially involved in the funeral. The human and financial resources of the urban community made an important contribution to processions that could take over its streets and cathedral. Much more was involved in these events than simply the transport and burial of a body, and the political and symbolic meanings of royal funeral ritual have been extensively analysed. Though these studies pay due attention to the linear ordering of the procession itself, there is not always much discussion of the geographical space through which the procession passed.[99] It is clear that, for funerals as well as other civic processions, the streets, houses, and points of entry such as gates and bridges made an important contribution to the overall conception. The presence of an appropriately behaved crowd was also necessary.

These were undoubtedly great occasions in the city's internal life, as well as in its connection to national politics. The way the city honoured a dead monarch complemented the way in which it received a new one. Henry Machyn was equally impressed by Queen Mary's entrance into the city of London on 3 August 1553 and by the funeral of Edward VI five days later at Westminster Abbey; likewise, he reports in detail the procession of Mary's body from St James's to Westminster in 1558.[100] On the whole, royal funeral processions bypassed the city of London, being focused on the west end, but the Lord Mayor and aldermen were still involved as representatives of a significant estate in the realm. They were placed with quite high honour (below knights and barons) in the funeral procession of Elizabeth I. They also shared in the first procession of James I, which did pass through the outskirts of the city, when the body was brought from Theobalds to Denmark House. It reached Smithfield at about nine at night and continued from there through Holborn, Chancery Lane,

---

[98] S. Anglo, *Images of Tudor kingship* (London, 1992), pp. 99–106; D. Howarth, *Images of rule. Art and politics in the English Renaissance, 1485–1649* (London, 1997), pp. 2–3, 174–7.

[99] Fritz, 'From "public" to "private": the royal funeral in England, 1500–1830', pp. 61–79; Gittings, *Death, burial and the individual*, pp. 216–34; Woodward, *The theatre of death*; Giesey, *Royal funeral ceremony*. Interestingly, this approach to the subject mirrors contemporary representations of such processions, which wind across the page or picture-space, divorced from any physical setting.

[100] Machyn, *Diary*, pp. 39–41, 182–4.

8 The Lord Mayor of London in the funeral procession of Elizabeth
I, 1603. Anonymous contemporary coloured drawing (London, British
Library, Add. MS 35324. By permission of the British Library).

and the Strand.[101] The city – as a location and as an institution – played a major part in the highly political and politically opportune funeral of Sir Philip Sidney in 1587. Killed in the Low Countries in November 1586, his body was brought back to England and remained at the Minories in east London for some three months, before being taken in a major procession for interment at St Paul's on 16 February 1587, a few days after the execution of Mary Queen of Scots. Though not a 'state' funeral, it overruled heraldic precedent to heighten the sense of the occasion by giving him honours of a higher rank than he possessed. The involvement of his father-in-law, Sir Francis Walsingham, in financing the event is also regarded as significant. The procession route led through the city from Aldgate to St Paul's, and was enhanced by the attendance of the Lord Mayor and Swordbearer and eighteen aldermen in their violet robes, all on horseback, emphasising the military aspect of the occasion. They were followed by 120 of the Grocers' Company in livery, and by some 300 men of the city's trained bands, marching three and three and trailing their arms and ensign.[102] It was certainly reported to be an effective spectacle: the streets were so crowded that the procession could hardly pass, the houses along the route were similarly full of people, 'of which great multitude ther wear few or none that shed not some tears as the corps passed by them'.[103]

The city's involvement in such events was not always free from contention. Shortly before Elizabeth's funeral, the Lord Mayor wrote to the Exchequer to remind them that it was customary for black to be supplied for 104 city officers, including the Lord Mayor and aldermen; although this had been omitted on some occasion in the past, this should not be made a precedent. In effect, he asked that the custom be observed so that they could properly support the forthcoming funerals of the late queen.[104] In 1619 the Mayor and aldermen appear to have been 'forgotten or neglected' altogether from the funeral ceremonies for Anne of Denmark, so that the king in a gesture of conciliation ordered a similar ceremony at St Paul's the following Sunday, which was attended by all the aldermen and officers in black.[105]

---

[101] Woodward, *The theatre of death*, pp. 92, 115, 196, 210–13.

[102] Ibid., pp. 75–7; Nichols, *The Progresses and public processions of Queen Elizabeth*, vol. II, pp. 483–94; S. Bos, M. Lange-Meijers, and J. Six, 'Sidney's funeral portrayed', in J. van Dorsten, D. Baker-Smith, and A. F. Kinney, *Sir Philip Sidney: 1586 and the creation of a legend* (Leiden, 1986), pp. 38–61.

[103] Bos, Lange-Meijers, and Six, 'Sidney's funeral portrayed', pp. 57–8, quoting Thomas Lant (1587).

[104] W. H. and H. C. Overall, *Analytical index to the Remembrancia*, p. 437.

[105] McClure, *The letters of John Chamberlain*, vol. II, p. 241.

Control of the rituals of honour, including funerals, was equally important for those seeking legitimacy for usurped authority. As Ian Gentles has
shown, Parliamentarians used all the traditional trappings at the funerals
of John Pym in 1643 and the earl of Essex in 1646. Pym had a heraldic
funeral in Westminster Abbey, with many members of Parliament and of
the Assembly of Divines, though as a mere gentleman he did not merit
noble honours. The earl of Essex, however, had a full-scale funeral procession from Essex House (hung with mourning) to the Abbey, with an
effigy, a hearse in Westminster Abbey, and a very large number of soldiers and military musicians. As many nobles as could be collected were
present as mourners or assistants, and the coffin was followed by members of the Houses of Lords and Commons, the Recorder and aldermen
of London, and the London Militia Committee.[106] As is well known,
proceedings at the 'superb funeral' of Oliver Cromwell replicated royal
precedent, down to the use of effigy and regalia. The procession from
Somerset House to Westminster Abbey was attended by heralds, guards
of honour, and 'innumerable mourners'.[107] Soon after the Restoration,
in a calculated reversing of this regal interment, Cromwell's body and
those of other regicides were exhumed from the Abbey and hanged and
reburied at Tyburn.[108]

The city of Paris was prominently involved in the funeral ritual of the
kings of France and other members of the royal family in the fifteenth to
early seventeenth centuries.[109] Wherever the king died, there would be
a procession through the city and a service at Notre-Dame ('l'église de
Paris'), before the body was taken to Saint-Denis. The Bureau de Ville
had a privileged role in this procession through the city. At the funeral of
Charles IX in 1574, the city's officers in black, with some 200 men from
the city's companies, wearing mourning caps and hoods and carrying
torches with the arms of the Ville, went to the porte Saint-Antoine to meet
the body. An enormous cortège was then formed, in which representatives
of the Ville occupied a notable position. The *hanouars* or salt-porters of
Paris carried the effigy, and the city's leading officers held a canopy of
mourning over or behind it, as far as Notre-Dame. The body stayed in the
cathedral overnight, and the next morning the Bureau de Ville returned,
still in mourning, along with the representatives of the Parlement and
the sovereign courts, to attend the service. In the afternoon the body
and effigy were carried in the same state to the porte Saint-Denis, where

---

[106] Gentles, 'Political funerals during the English Revolution', pp. 205–24. Essex's hearse
copied that of Henry prince of Wales (d. 1612): Howarth, *Images of rule*, p. 172.

[107] Gittings, *Death, burial and the individual*, pp. 229–31, quoting John Evelyn.

[108] Pepys, *Diary*, vol. I, p. 309, vol. II, pp. 26–7.   [109] Giesey, *Royal funeral ceremony*.

they were surrendered to the men of the king's household.[110] The event was not without incident – altercations broke out between members of the Parlement and other nobles and ecclesiastics, over their place at the ceremony – and the presence of the city's men-at-arms in such numbers was at least partly in the interests of crowd control, 'pour renger le peuple et vuider les rues'.[111] The religious and political tensions of the period increased the importance attached to this very public display of royal authority: this funeral reasserted the royal presence in Paris, not long after the city had been completely out of control on St Bartholomew's Eve in 1572. It clearly did not quell all dissent, however. After describing the funeral, Pierre l'Estoile transcribed a 'tombeau satirique' that circulated at the time, attributed by some to a Huguenot who could not forget St Bartholomew, by others to a strongly Catholic *avocat* of the Parlement. It accused Charles IX of being crueller than Nero, more deceitful than Tiberius, hated by his subjects, and one who had presided over a reign of horrible carnage.[112]

The funeral of Henri III's brother, the duke of Anjou, in 1584, was conducted with equal ceremony, for 'la seconde personne du Royaume' but also the last Valois heir. It reflected the king's taste for procession and ceremony, and perhaps also an attempt to repair his relations with Paris.[113] As before, the effigy was carried by the *hanouars* while it was in the city, and the canopy by *échevins* and councillors. The city supplied 200 torches for the procession, and distributed escutcheons of the city's arms for the torches that the *bourgeois* were to place in front of their houses while the procession passed. They ordered the *quarteniers* to send four *bourgeois* and archers from each *quartier* to join the procession; the guilds were each to send between four and twelve individuals (seventy-eight in all) in mourning.[114] No ritual or ceremonial could, however, do anything to defuse the escalating political and confessional tensions in Paris over the next few years; funerals and obsequies became occasions for the expression of extreme feelings. On the death of Catherine de Medici in January 1589, the Sixteen, in effective control of Paris, threatened that if her body were brought to the city for burial at Saint-Denis, they would drag it in the mud or throw it in the river.[115] News of the assassination of Henri III was greeted with rejoicing in Paris; the Bureau de Ville referred to it as 'advenu comme par ung fouldre celeste'. Obviously, there could be no possibility of his having the traditional royal funeral treatment while

[110] *RDBVP*, vol. VII, pp. 193–4.
[111] Roelker, *The Paris of Henry of Navarre*, p. 33; *RDBVP*, vol. VII, p. 194.
[112] Lestoile, *Journal de l'Estoile pour le règne de Henri III*, pp. 37–8.
[113] Babelon, *Paris au XVIe siècle*, pp. 464–8.   [114] *RDBVP*, vol. VIII, pp. 388–95.
[115] Ibid., p. 605.

the capital remained in the hands of the Ligue and there was no agreement on his successor. It was only at the burial of Henri IV, in 1610, that Henri III's corpse was transferred from Compiègne to Saint-Denis for burial in the vault of his parents and brothers.[116]

The funeral of Henri IV was particularly magnificent, perhaps as a way of celebrating the unity and peace his reign had brought and outfacing the crisis into which his assassination had plunged the country. The Bureau de Ville searched their own registers for information on what they were accustomed to do on such an occasion, and determined to do all as well as before, and better if possible. They may also have wished to acknowledge the restoration of good relations between the city and the monarchy; Henri IV, after beginning his reign with a devastating siege of Paris, had subsequently concentrated his attention and resources on the city, to rebuild its economy and morale, as well as to reshape its architecture.[117] Underlining the mutual benefit and honour the ceremony bestowed, the new king gave the Bureau 2,400 *livres* to buy mourning for each of the eight principal officers, and also sent money for mourning for the twenty-four councillors. The city itself had the considerable expense of supplying mourning for its own troops and servants, paying their wages, and hanging the front of the Hôtel de Ville, and several arches and gates of the city, with mourning. They also had the church of Saint-Jean-en-Grève hung with black for the two services they held there for the king's soul. The city provided 400 torches for the funeral procession, and escutcheons for the torches that citizens living along the processional route were themselves to provide. The latter were also expected to hang the fronts of their houses with black. Hanging the arches and gates for two days cost 180 *livres*, and the making of 2,000 escutcheons for torches some 350 *livres*, at 42 *sous* per dozen, but the total cost to the city must have been several thousand *livres*.[118] The funeral procession itself was enormous. Starting from the Louvre at 2 p.m., it took seven hours to reach Notre-Dame, going by way of the Pont Neuf, the quai des Augustins, and the Pont Saint-Michel. There were over 900 friars and regular clergy in the procession; clergy from all the parishes of Paris, and seventeen bishops and archbishops; 500 poor; representatives of the sovereign courts and of the Châtelet and the municipality of Paris; the king's household, guards, and esquires; military bands; ambassadors and nuncios; princes, nobles and gentlemen. As was customary, the salt-porters of Paris carried the effigy and the Bureau de Ville carried the canopy while the procession was in the city. The first

---

[116] Roelker, *The Paris of Henry of Navarre*, pp. 182–3; *RDBVP*, vol. IX, p. 420; vol. XIV, p. 524.

[117] *RDBVP*, vol. XIV, pp. 510, 517–18. Cf. Ballon, *The Paris of Henri IV*, esp. pp. 250–5.

[118] *RDBVP*, vol. XIV, pp. 508–11, 515–17.

9 Funeral procession of Henri IV, 1610. The royal effigy, carried by officers of the Parlement in crimson robes, followed by the canopy carried by four nobles. Documentary sources attribute these roles to the salt-porters of Paris and the Bureau de Ville respectively, while the procession was inside the city. Seventeenth-century print by Francesco Vallegion and Catarin Doini, D.D.D, entitled 'Pompe funerali fatte in Parigi nella morte dell' invitissimo Henrico IIII re di Francia e Navarra' (Paris, Bibliothèque Nationale, Cabinet des Estampes, Hennin XVIII, ff. 31–5. Cliché Bibliothèque Nationale de France, Paris).

10 Funeral procession of Henri IV, 1610. The captains, lieutenants and ensigns of the city of Paris, cloaked and hooded in black, followed by the archers and harquebus-men in cloaks and hats, trailing their weapons. Seventeenth-century print by Francesco Vallegion and Catarin Doini, D.D.D, entitled 'Pompe funerali fatte in Parigi nella morte dell' invitissimo Henrico IIII re di Francia e Navarra' (Paris, Bibliothèque Nationale, Cabinet des Estampes, Hennin XVIII, ff. 31–5. Cliché Bibliothèque Nationale de France, Paris).

day concluded with vespers and vigils for the dead in Notre-Dame; on the second day, after a service and funeral oration lasting four hours, the procession re-formed, and took the body by way of the Pont Notre-Dame and the rue Saint-Denis to the porte Saint-Denis, where the city surrendered it to the household esquires. On the third day, the Bureau de Ville and others returned to the basilica of Saint-Denis for another mass, offertory, and funeral oration, ending in the interment and a dinner. Five days later, the Bureau held another service at Saint-Jean-en-Grève.[119]

Parisian funeral ceremonies also maintained two traditions eliminated from the Protestant liturgy: casting holy water on the corpse, and holding funeral services for persons dying and buried elsewhere. Casting holy water became a ritual of honour in itself, separate from any other liturgical ceremony, and might even be offered to an effigy rather than a corpse.[120] Catholic monarchs honoured their counterparts in other countries (to whom they were in any case often related) by celebrating funeral services for them in their own capitals. Henry VIII commanded such a service for the wife of the emperor Charles V, at St Paul's in 1539. The cathedral was hung with black, a hearse with the arms of the Empire was set up, and numerous peers and bishops attended; it was 'as rich a thing and as honourably done as ever was seen'. The bells were rung in all the parish churches of London from Saturday noon to Sunday at night.[121] Elizabeth, in the first year of her reign, ordered obsequies for Charles V, at Westminster, using the same hearse as for Mary's funeral, with dirge and morrow mass.[122] Respects and commemorations of a restrained kind continued in Protestant England, but the full religious ceremony flourished in Paris. In the later sixteenth and early seventeenth centuries the Bureau de Ville attended obsequies for, among others, Mary of Guise, Don Carlos of Spain, Elizabeth de Valois, queen of Spain, the emperor Maximilian, the king of Portugal, and the queen of Spain. On these occasions, when there was obviously no funeral convoy, the Bureau processed from the Hôtel de Ville to Notre-Dame, where representatives of many other offices and institutions gathered. The civic party, in black, was accompanied by a party of the archers or *arbalestiers* of the city, and by the *sergents de ville* in livery. Issues of precedence focused on their seating inside the cathedral, whether they were placed on high or low chairs, and where they were in relation to other estates and offices.[123] Services on these occasions were

[119] Ibid., pp. 525–33.
[120] Ibid., vol. VIII, p. 391; vol. XIV, p. 524; vol. XVI, pp. 181–3; Lestoile, *Journal de l'Estoile pour le règne de Henri III*, pp. 355–8. For the use of the funeral effigy, see Giesey, *Royal funeral ceremony*, esp. chs. 6 and 7, pp. 79–124.
[121] M. St.-C. Byrne (ed.), *The Lisle letters*, 6 vols. (Chicago, 1981), vol. V, p. 528.
[122] Machyn, *Diary*, p. 184.
[123] *RDBVP*, vol. V, pp. 59–61; vol. VI, pp. 56–7, 64; vol. VIII, pp. 45, 224–5; vol. XVI, pp. 117–21.

hardly less imposing than those for French royalty. At the service for the queen of Spain in 1611, the cathedral was hung with black cloths and velvet, a *chapelle ardente* of 800 or 900 candles was provided, and the hearse was covered in a pall of cloth of gold. Two hundred poor were dressed in mourning, and princes, nobles, bishops, and ambassadors attended.[124]

An important development in Paris at the end of the period under consideration was the introduction of a grandiose Italianate or baroque genre of *pompe funèbre* for the very great. A strong tradition of formal and elaborate funerary performance was obviously already present, but this new development elevated it to an art. It focused on the construction of huge pageant-like edifices within the church of interment or commemoration, framing and displaying the coffin. Essentially static and temporary, these were nevertheless displays of impressive grandeur and huge expense. The style originated in Italy in the sixteenth century, but was actively promoted in France from the mid-seventeenth, by those who stood to gain most from it: clerics and architects. The Jesuit Père Menestrier was a leading figure in this. He came to Paris in 1670, and participated in several such *pompes* in the 1670s and 1680s. He advocated a complexity and richness of classical allegory and Christian allusion, combining 'tentures noires... lumières et... chant lugubre de l'Eglise' with inscriptions, paintings, and representations. The emphasis here was not so much on participation in a ceremony but on witness of spectacle. Such *pompes* focused on individuals whose honour reflected on the state (even if the state did not necessarily pay for them) – Chancellor Séguier, Turenne, the prince de Condé; they also affirmed an almost militant Catholicism, allying 'l'idéologie religieuse de la Contre-Reforme et... la sensibilité d'une société aristocratique'. The number of such events must have been limited, but they gained a wider currency from the publication of Menestrier's treatise *Des décors funèbres* in 1684, and the circulation of pictorial representations. Like the developing genre of funeral orations, they were intended to attract attention and comment, and to evoke awe and respect, in a larger circle than those who attended them in person.[125]

There can be no doubt that funerals on the grand scale had a major impact on the city in which they took place, though whether all responded with the emotions they were expected to produce seems doubtful. Even the most powerful rituals could hardly be expected to succeed in uniting all disparate interests and varied perspectives in the motley urban

---

[124] Ibid., vol. XVI, pp. 117–21.

[125] W. D. Howarth, *Life and letters in France*, vol. I: *The seventeenth century* (London, 1965), pp. 155–67 and plate VI; Tapié, *Baroque et classicisme*, pp. 238–50 and illustrations facing pp. 176, 177, 192, 193; J. Wilhelm, *La vie quotidienne des Parisiens au temps du Roi-Soleil, 1660–1715* (Paris, 1989), pp. 133–6.

population. Impressive as the spectacle of the funeral of the duke of Anjou was, some emotions may have been assumed: the duke of Guise looked 'fort triste et melancolique', but the observer Pierre L'Estoile believed he was thoughtful rather than sad, and that the Guise were pleased at the event which allowed them to advance their political designs.[126] L'Estoile was ambivalent, if not cynical, about several of the individuals whose funerals he reported, giving as much or more space to the printed libels and satires that circulated, even for such a respected figure as Christophe de Thou, 'regretté par tous'.[127] Chamberlain described the funeral of Anne of Denmark as 'a drawling tedious sight'; the numerous gentlemen and ladies 'made but a poore shew...laggering along even tired with the length of the way and the weight of their clothes'.[128] Pepys was frankly unimpressed by the funeral of Sir Thomas Vyner in 1665, preferring 'for ease and coolness' to go shopping for a new suit. Although he later stopped to watch the procession, 'the show being over' he went on his way to Westminster.[129]

Nor did the event always pass off as planned. Although most convoys must have passed in an orderly fashion, without incident, disorders did occur. In Paris, struggles for precedence marred a number of state funerals, as noted above, and the competition between parishes and other religious institutions for the bodies and burial of individuals led to some unseemly incidents. When someone had willed burial elsewhere, the parish priest was supposed to convoy the body to the chosen church and to hand it over, certifying that the individual had died in communion with the church, for which he would share the lights of the convoy with the house of burial. However, there were several cases in seventeenth-century Paris when either the legality of the will provision was contested, or the body was delivered with an ill grace, dumped at the convent gate, and stripped of the parish's hearse-cloth and lights. There was an actual affray in the street between the priest of Saint-Paul and the Jesuits in 1655, before Parlement settled that bodies must be conveyed into the nave of the burial church before being handed over.[130] The dean of Paris's vicar kept his register of convoys because he was entitled to keep the torches and lights from the procession as a reward; usually he agreed amicably with other claimants, waiving strict protocol in the interests of a seemly funeral, but more than once he resorted to litigation after the event to enforce his rights.[131]

---

[126] Lestoile, *Journal de L'Estoile*, pp. 355–8.   [127] Ibid., pp. 309–11, 318.
[128] McClure, *Letters of John Chamberlain*, vol. II, pp. 236–7.
[129] Pepys, *Diary*, vol. VI, p. 114.
[130] Thibaut-Payen, *Les morts, l'église, et l'état*, pp. 20–2, 40–66; Golden, *The godly rebellion*, pp. 106–7.
[131] AN, L 510, microfilm no. 27.

Certainly the importance accorded to funeral processions as representations of power and legitimacy opened the practice to oppositional appropriation. As noted above, Parliamentarians gave Pym and Essex traditional funerals in the 1640s, but more remarkable was the exploitation of these rituals of power by popular followings. Two Leveller figures, Colonel Thomas Rainborowe and Robert Lockyer, were given heroes' funerals in the city. The former, killed by royalist agents in 1648, was brought back to London and taken in a procession of nearly 3,000 people through the main streets of the city and out to Wapping in the east end for burial. The critical satires on this event, intending to disparage it, emphasise the level of popular participation – 'Will the weaver, Tom the tapster, Kit the cobler... trudg'd very devoutly both before and behind' – though also allowing that some hundreds followed in coaches and on horseback. Lockyer was executed (in St Paul's churchyard) in 1649 for his part in a mutiny over pay, and his funeral clearly focused tensions and hostilities among Londoners towards the government at Westminster. His funeral procession made an indirect but significant circuit through the centre of the city and out to the New Churchyard beyond Bishopsgate, and attracted 4,000 people, according to contemporary estimates. It was joined by hundreds of soldiers and also numbers of women, and seems to have borrowed several symbols, such as trumpeters, a draped charger, and the wearing of ribbons or colours, from official heraldic or military funeral ritual.[132] Similar exploitation of the genre occurred in rebellious Paris. The Sixteen, emerging as a controlling force in Paris, gave an impressive cortège to their leader Charles Hotman in 1587.[133] In the same month, January 1589, that the Sixteen threatened to degrade the body of Catherine de Medici, there were services in Notre-Dame for the assassinated duke and Cardinal of Guise, with 'great lamentations' and 'a tremendous crowd of people as if it were the funeral of a king of France'. The Bureau de Ville called on the councillors, *quarteniers*, and city troops to attend with them, in mourning, or black, or livery, as appropriate, and paid part of the cost of the whole event.[134]

As these oppositional stagings suggest, there was despite the formality a good deal of emotional force in grand funeral ritual. There would always be some for whom the death was a personal loss, and others for whom it meant political jeopardy or disaster. But many were simply affected by the event and the spectacle. Londoners wept at the funeral of Sir Philip Sidney, and at that of Elizabeth 'there was such general sighing and

---

[132] Gentles, 'Political funerals during the English Revolution', pp. 205–24.
[133] M. Greengrass, *France in the age of Henri IV. The struggle for stability* (Harlow, 1984), pp. 40–1.
[134] Roelker, *The Paris of Henry of Navarre*, pp. 168, 172; *RDBVP*, vol. IX, pp. 271, 276–7, 277n, 553–4.

groning, and weeping and the like hath not been seene or knowne in the memorie of man'.[135] Numerous people came to pay their respects to the popular preacher le Picart, 'l'ung des plus beaulx myrouers d'exemplarité de vie et de doctrine', in 1556; the poor and simple brought their books and paternosters and touched them to his hands. During the procession, the streets were crowded with people anxious to see the corpse (or, by now, the coffin) for the last time.[136] At the Bureau de Ville's requiem mass for the assassinated Henri IV, the crowd of people, 'chacun fort affligé et pleurant la mort de son Roy', was too great to fit into the church of Saint-Jean-en-Grève.[137] We need not dismiss these descriptions as purely conventional, nor the exhibition of emotion as factitious.

An essential aspect of the funeral in the early modern city was that it con- nected the individual to a larger community or communal identity. This community might be as limited as the parish, but often other groups were represented too: the religious, the poor, some devotional or occupational association. On a personal scale, realising or visualising the other orders of society in this way helped to place one in an ordered and integrated society, as effectively as the material trappings of the funeral served as tokens of status. Apart from the very clear spiritual benefits that wide participation in obsequies brought to Catholic believers, incorporating representatives of other orders into one's own ceremony seemed to bring merit by association. And there was a strong sense that funerals were an important, communal, collective ritual of solidarity and sympathy, and that to share in them benefited everybody. There was considerable popular resistance to the ban on funeral assemblies in time of plague in London, when their sociable and restorative function seemed even more necessary: Pepys deplored 'the madness of people of the town, who will (because they are forbid) come in Crowds along with the dead Corps to see them buried'.[138] Observation of these seemingly timeless rituals helped to overcome the sense of interruption and discontinuity.

In the larger civic frame, funerals were explicit re-presentations of or- der, both demonstrating the hierarchical order of society and invoking the orderly behaviour of a coherent and compliant populace. The fu- nerals of substantial citizens and officeholders could be very elaborate affairs, especially when the heralds in London or the *jurés-crieurs* in Paris

---

[135] Bos, Lange-Meijers, and Six, 'Sidney's funeral portrayed', pp. 57–8; Woodward, *The theatre of death*, p. 88, quoting Stow's *Annales*.
[136] *RDBVP*, vol. IV, pp. 450–1. Le Picart's funeral procession is also recorded in the regis- ters of the Collège de Navarre, and quoted at length in Taylor, *Heresy and orthodoxy in sixteenth-century Paris. François le Picart*, pp. 213–14.
[137] *RDBVP*, vol. XIV, pp. 508–10.
[138] Pepys, *Diary*, vol. VI, p. 211 (3 September 1665); Slack, Impact of plague, pp. 296–8.

took a hand, prescribing a wealth of hangings and attendants and carefully choreographing the procession and church service. Obviously this fits in with the evolution of civic ceremonial in a more general sense, and with the ruling group's evolving sense of itself, but it also offers points of value for the present discussion. When members of the civic élite died, their survivors put on a tremendous performance. A funeral procession such as Lord Mayor Sir Cuthbert Buckle's in the middle of the difficult 1590s offered a model of the order of society, expressing very clearly a view of the hierarchy of wealth, rank, and office. It presented the poor as submissive and grateful beneficiaries of the deceased's charity, and demonstrated the continuity of the structure and business of government notwithstanding the loss of the city's figurehead, already succeeded in office. Funerals like this also expressed a kind of class solidarity, with the participation of London aldermen and officers of city government. The Parisian Bureau de Ville took very seriously its contribution to funeral ceremonies, both of its own members and of figures of national importance. Protocol and *placement* were of great significance. Arguably, the attachment to civic ritual became stronger as the real power of the municipality waned: London's aldermen ruled a diminishing proportion of the population and territory of the metropolis in the sixteenth and seventeenth centuries, while Paris's municipality had a very restricted range of competence, of which the management of ceremonial formed an important part.

Obviously, funerals like these affirmed the position of the individual in his or her social circle, and demonstrated that he or she could exert influence and secure co-operation well beyond that, but did not necessarily succeed in all their objectives.[139] Presenting a model of society is not the same as ensuring that everyone else accepts it, and many were probably indifferent, cynical, or even hostile to the message. But funeral performances had sufficient attractive features – spectacle, solemnity, religious piety, largesse – to encourage wide acquiescence. Certainly quite large numbers of people received benefits, in the form of gowns and doles, even if the majority of the expenditure went on hangings, heraldry, and gowns, gloves, and rings for friends and family. The ideals of conviviality and commensality were invoked, even if not always fulfilled: larger funerals were followed by substantial dinners, and even more modest persons made provision for distributions to neighbours and poor folk. The caveats expressed earlier – about the overloading of funeral performance with detail and difference, and the increasing secularisation and commodification of all its aspects – must be taken in conjunction with

---

[139] Cf. Karant-Nunn, *The Reformation of ritual*, p. 192.

the evidence for its continuing value in urban society. Though there were certainly challenges, and the character of the funeral may have changed, there is little evidence of substantial dissent from the notion that funerals were important and meaningful social rituals, as is shown by their appropriation by opposition groups for their own purposes.

10   Conclusion

This book began with the premiss that the study of death, or rather of the actions and procedures surrounding the dead body, would prove a useful approach to understanding early modern London and Paris, and some of the differences between them. Death was a recurrent feature of life in the early modern city; the death of the other was all around, the death of the self never far off. To a much greater extent than is now the case, the living and the dead co-existed, and sometimes competed; they shared the same physical space, they had an ongoing relationship of reciprocal benefit. Exploring that relationship, tracing the interactions of living and dead, illuminates a significant aspect of urban society.

The approach taken has been to focus on two main themes, the location of burial, and the composite nature of urban funerary ritual. In the large and complex metropolitan environment individuals had multiple identities and loyalties; where and how they were buried represented a compromise between the desirable and the possible, both of which were conditioned by the crowded and competitive urban milieu. The struggle to resolve these issues was in some ways constructive, helping to build social relations within the city and within its constituent communities. The practical problems large-scale urban mortality created forced local community leaders to address the issue of burial directly, to find ways of imposing order on the disorderly bodies of the dead. Insofar as they were able to solve the problem of how and where to dispose of the dead at a practical level, while still respecting popular traditions and sensibilities, the process could contribute to the affirmation of social relations and the maintenance of order. A too pragmatic response, however, that precluded such respect, might be effective in material terms but could not repair the social damage caused by high mortality. Burial traditions and practices played an important role in the constitution of early modern metropolitan society, but the relationship between living and dead appears to have worked better in practice in London than in Paris.

If death is destabilising, and societies have to work to restore the disturbed equilibrium, in early modern London and Paris that task was daunting. The dimensions of mortality and the burial problem were enormous. In normal times mortality rates were probably three to four times those prevalent in modern societies, at 30 to 40 per thousand per annum. The annual death toll in London in the late sixteenth century was 3–4,000 a year; Paris's was probably higher. Both cities were recording nearly 20,000 deaths per annum in the 1670s. In time of epidemic or crisis, mortality escalated to unbelievable heights. London probably lost between 10 and 20 per cent of its population in each of the the five major plagues of the period; Paris is said to have lost a third of its population in the siege.[1] But the incidence of mortality was unevenly spread, both geographically and socially. Deaths from all causes were higher in peripheral and suburban parishes than in the centre, and infant and child mortality was significantly worse.[2] Most deaths in the early modern city were of juveniles or dependent adults: 40 to 50 per cent of all deaths in non-plague years were of children under fourteen; probably at least another 10 per cent were in their mid-teens to early twenties. Of the remainder, most of the women and some of the men would have been in some sense dependants: wives, adult servants, lodgers, pensioners, and paupers. However, most decisions about individual burials were made by a small and largely male group, the householders, the group from whom all the governors of local and civic society were drawn. Almost all burials were performed according to rules and priorities set by an even smaller group, the parish officeholders and clergy. These men formulated priorities for access to burial space, agreeing or refusing to allocate space to individuals, and using prices and incentives to influence choices. With an appreciation of the value placed on display, they created elaborate structures of charges for the trappings of funerary performance, as well as for attendance and services. Their monopoly of the burial options of the local community was another source for the exercise of that compound of patronage, deference, charity, authority, and compromise, with which early modern cities were largely ruled.

Vestries certainly had a number of practical considerations in mind when formulating their burial policies. It is not surprising that they charged more for adult graves than for children's; more for burial in a coffin than in a shroud alone; much more for burial in a lead coffin than in a wooden one. In their approach to pricing grave sites, they were influenced partly by the amount of space available, but also by a strong sense of what was

---

[1] See above, chapter 2; Babelon, *Paris au XVIe siècle*, p. 176.
[2] Finlay, *Population and metropolis*, pp. 50, 101, 108.

socially appropriate. They imposed a kind of rationing by price which translated into concrete terms a broad metaphor of social centrality and marginality. Vestries in London and Paris both before and after the Reformation operated on similar assumptions about the desirability of certain spaces for burial, attaching a higher monetary value to sites of greater honour or sanctity, which also happened to be prominent places in the parish church, the centre of communal worship; more distant sites were given a much lower value. Such policies effectively matched social status to spatial location, especially in the literal marginalisation of the socially marginal, the poor. In this they paralleled the organisation of seating in the church, which assigned pews or *bancs* according to status, and also the linear ordering of classes in the funeral procession. The costs involved were not in themselves very great, so it may be more that the notion of differential pricing supported the social value placed on specific locations, rather than that individuals of middling rank or above were excluded from certain spaces because of price. These policies were effective, in that to a very great extent *noblesse*, gentlemen, and merchants were buried in churches, and more modest tradesmen and servants in churchyards. Parishes making *ad hoc* decisions about the burial of foundlings, paupers, and pensioners for which they had to pay also usually opted for cheaper, marginal spaces.

The spatial paradigm was reinforced in early modern London by the creation of new churchyards (parochial and other) on the periphery of the metropolis. In Paris, the picture was complicated by the dual identity of the Innocents as both a pauper and a traditional citizen burial ground, but the grounds at la Trinité and outside the city were clearly for social outcasts. In both cities, much plague burial took place in peripheral and even temporary graveyards. Burial location was thus a means both of defining status within the community, and of marking exclusion from that community. Suicides, excommunicates, and heretics were all in theory excluded from burial in consecrated ground; nonconformists, and especially Quakers, often chose burial elsewhere. The conflict over Huguenot burial in Paris is symbolic of the importance attached to burial in traditional and time-sanctioned locations.

The principle of charging different prices for different burial options was extended across the whole range of funeral services and accessories, according to a rationale of desirability that resulted in distinctions either audible or visible. Urban funeral ritual was complex but flexible, allowing it to be moulded to fit individual circumstances and to satisfy a range of needs. It was able to express individual and shared identities in language and ceremony that a wide audience could read. Its richness and variety drew on the wealth of the urban population and the resources of service, commodities, and craftsmanship available to them; it may also reflect anxieties about transience and mortality that were ever present to city-dwellers. Whether Catholic or reformed, the church had a vested interest in order and hierarchy, and in the effective representation of these to the laity.[3] The clear evocation of inequality in burial location and trappings may have been mitigated by the fact that many funerals were acts of charity, though, at the same time, to dispense charity is to exert a form of control, and having this power underwrote the authority of local officers. Parishes made another distinction that helped to identify the local community, in charging higher fees to non-parishioners, but, as has been argued, this in the long run worked to undermine notions of natural community, in that it allowed outsiders to buy their way in, thereby perhaps reinforcing the translation of more subtle differences into monetary value. By the late seventeenth century, parishes in both London and Paris had gone a long way towards the complete commodification of burial.

In time of crisis society drew strength from observing what it saw as its own traditions, which explains the efforts of the London parishes to maintain normal burial practice for as long as possible in time of plague. Curtailing normal funeral procedures, and resorting to burial in mass graves or in extra-urban locations, was seen as a shocking breach of custom, an offence to dignity: 'the poor man is hurried to his Grave, by nasty and slovenly Bearers, in the night, without followers, without friends, without rites of burial commonly used in our Church, due to our Religion, to our Nation, to the Majesty of our Kingdom; nay, to the decency of a Christian'.[4] The 'misplacement' of élite plague victims in Paris was sometimes corrected by their later re-interment in a place appropriate to their status.[5] Similarly, occasions of national crisis, such as the assassination of Henri IV, evoked a public response that made use of funeral ceremonial on a grand scale, clearly demonstrating a belief in the political value of such a performance.

Over a period of 150 years of dramatic social and cultural change, 'timeless' burial practices naturally underwent some modification. While arguing that they continued to function in a broadly similar way, it is important not to overlook the shifts that did take place. The attachment to traditional sites, though strong, was in practice forced to allow for the pragmatic relocation of burial to new and more distant spaces. The unitary Christian community of the medieval city, accommodated entirely

---

[3] Karant-Nunn, *The Reformation of ritual*, p. 192.
[4] Thomas Dekker, 'A rod for run-awaies', in Wilson (ed.), *Plague Pamphlets*, pp. 144–5; Harding, 'Burial of the plague dead', pp. 58–9.
[5] BN, MS Fr. 32589, entry for 15 Sept. 1591.

within a single parochial and civic framework, was replaced by a wider variety of religious congregations, not all of them territorially defined, and some of them consciously gathered or separated. In Protestant London, a number of specific accoutrements to the funeral disappeared, to be replaced by a greater emphasis on the remainder, and on new secular traditions, though the increasing professionalisation and commercialisation of the whole process was common to both cities. Even more significantly, in Protestant eschatology the attentions paid to the dead had to concentrate on the funeral and interment rather than any repeated liturgical commemorations. The longer-term relationship of the dead and the living became a physical rather than a spiritual one, that of co-existence in a material world rather than interaction and reciprocity with a view to a future spiritual existence.

Continuities, Catholic and Protestant

Further light is cast on the importance of burial traditions and access to traditional places of burial when the part these played in the contests of the Reformation in sixteenth-century London and Paris is considered. For much of this study, the emphasis has been on continuities and similarities, though with due regard for particularity of place and practice. But the sixteenth and seventeenth centuries are characterised, for most historians, by rupture and discontinuity, and there was a marked divergence between the experiences of London and Paris. During this period, religion, formerly a unifying force in social and cultural spheres, became a divisive one. Both cities experienced religious upheaval, though it was far more violent in Paris. In both, religion became a political issue, but whereas in London the victory of Protestantism virtually silenced the expression of surviving Catholic dissent within a generation, in Paris the passionate Catholicism of the majority failed to suppress the equally fervent Protestantism of a minority even after years of bitter fighting and bloodshed.

Even the revisionists allow that London was a partial exception to their view of a slow and reluctant acceptance of reformed practice. A wealthy and literate society, in contact with continental ideas, under the eye of the crown and, during Edward's reign, of an energetically reforming bishop, Londoners were confronted by change and had to come to terms with it. However, different interpretations of the result are possible. Susan Brigden's account of the Reformation in London concludes that by 1560 the social fabric of city and parish had been severely damaged: 'the world of shared faith was broken . . . and the Christian community divided'.[6]

---

[6] Brigden, *London and the Reformation*, p. 639.

This sense of irreparable loss and the destruction of a source of communal solidarity and solace obviously connects with other modern perspectives on the Reformation in its wider context, notably the accounts of Scarisbrick, Haigh, and Duffy.[7] As well as religious upheaval, sixteenth-century London faced a host of economic and social problems, the result of its rapid expansion, trade fluctuations, national population growth and price rises. Nevertheless it remained relatively peaceful and harmonious, and other writers focusing on London have been less pessimistic, insisting on the continuing integrity of parishes, wards, and city companies. London's governors weathered the Reformation by virtue of caution and policy, though these might be expressed by individuals in compliance with the varying injunctions issued by the crown, or in strategic retirement from the public scene; the maintenance of unity among the élite was a significant factor in the maintenance of order.[8]

Rituals of death and burial seem to have retained an important place in this changing society, and it may be that this was due to those characteristics – flexibility, adaptability, an absence of doctrinal absolutism – that allowed them to survive fundamental challenges to their theological rationale at the Reformation. Their adaptability to changing circumstance resulted from their richness and variety, and from the fact that the programme of any individual funeral had long been a matter of choice within a wide range of options. This ability to choose also meant that the ceremony reflected social concerns and meanings as well as spiritual ones: wealth, status, family, occupational, and local affiliations were all expressed in the funeral and commemoration. These elements of social value were not undermined by theological challenges, and may have provided the necessary framework for the relatively smooth transition from Catholic to reformed ritual. A parallel case – of survival despite a fundamental challenge to the rationale – would be the city companies. Their religious basis was uprooted but their importance as institutions of sociability and social control, economic regulation and protection, civic government, and charitable activity, ensured their survival.[9] In both cases, though, the survival of rituals or institutions contributed something important to London's stability in the sixteenth and seventeenth centuries: a sense of tradition and continuity (even if this glossed over quite substantial changes), and a means of affirming the importance of status and structure in social relations.

---

[7] J. J. Scarisbrick, *The Reformation and the English people* (Oxford, 1984); C. Haigh (ed.), *The English Reformation revised* (Cambridge, 1987); Duffy, *The stripping of the altars*; C. Haigh, *English Reformations: religion, politics, and society under the Tudors* (Oxford, 1993); P. Marshall (ed.), *The impact of the English Reformation, 1500–1640* (London, 1997).

[8] E.g. Archer, *The pursuit of stability*; Hickman, 'The religious allegiance of London's ruling élite, 1520–1603'.

[9] Cf. e.g. Ward, *Metropolitan communities*.

In Paris, the great majority of the populace remained Catholic; for them, the economy of salvation was unchanged and the spiritual merits attributed to liturgy and 'pararitual' were not questioned. Masses and commemorative services remained central to the treatment of the dead. The religious houses, with their promise of special spiritual care, continued and indeed multiplied; devotional fraternities, suppressed in London, flourished in Paris, stimulated by the heightened interests and passions of the confessional conflict. In these ways, therefore, early modern Parisian funeral traditions obviously differed from practice in London, which had abandoned these particular elements. In some other ways, however, developments in Paris paralleled or even converged on those in London. Obviously these too are not independent variables, in that they must be influenced by the experience of religious conflict and by the evolution of Catholic reformed thought, itself a response to the challenge of Protestantism.

Pre-Reformation burial ritual in London had many secular elements which served a social rather than a spiritual purpose, and it would certainly be a mistake to suppose that burial ritual in sixteenth- and seventeenth-century Catholic Paris carried any less social import. Status distinctions continued to be significant, with perhaps a larger range of elements to play with, since the multiplication of masses and the host of attendant priests in the parish churches had not been abolished, and lights and vestments were still highly valued. Commercialisation and commodification were equally characteristic. As in London, parishes charged a range of prices for the location of burial and for the ornaments hired. Funeral ritual and the place of burial were at least as much a representation of social distinctions in Paris as they were in London. If anything, they were more so, given the pervasive respect for rank which allowed ancient and noble families to privatise parts of parish churches for burial vaults and family chapels. Burial in church could be bought, in most cases; burial in a private vault was a fairly exclusive privilege, proclaiming family and descent. It gave the newly deceased a place 'avec ses ancestres' and allowed him or her to share in the commemorative traditions established by the family.

Another parallel between developments in Protestant London and Catholic Paris concerns the attachment to the past and respect for the provisions of one's ancestors. This was by no means sacrosanct in Paris, nor freely ignored in London. In both cities there was a flourishing tradition of monumental commemoration, that may indeed have reached new heights of elaboration and expense. However, this co-existed with more casual and sometimes directly hostile attitudes. It is certainly true that popular iconoclasm and the destruction of superstitious images and allusions was a facet of Protestant activism. In London, Cheapside cross, a maypole, and the statue of St Thomas Becket at the church of St Thomas of Acre were prominent victims of such destruction, while in Paris early Protestants attacked statues of the Virgin in particular but also relics, liturgical objects, and most of the material trappings of Catholic worship.[10] The sale of tombstones and brasses, recorded in some London parish registers in the 1540s, suggests a deliberate break with past commemorations, while John Stow, writing at the end of the century, criticised his contemporaries for their failure to maintain the tombs and monuments of their ancestors and predecessors.[11] But in fact, while there may have been more stones and brasses (with their now suspect inscriptions) sold in the 1540s, this had been part of the parishes' practice of burial management for at least a century.[12] And this was also the case in Paris: theft (rather than overt sale) of memorials from the Innocents, failure to maintain the fabric and monuments in private chapels, ejection of the longer dead to make way for the more recent, all occur in parish records. The churches were quite pragmatic about reducing endowed services on money grounds. Jeanne Passavent had endowed an obit and three masses a week in 1582, but a revision of such services in 1685 reduced this to one weekly mass. At the same time the services of another forty-three endowments were similarly reduced, and thirty-three discharged completely.[13] While the assertion of tradition and respect for the past was an important aspect of the Catholic claim to authority, it was not in practice a binding obligation.

Conflict

Despite the many continuities and similarities in practice between traditional Catholic funeral rituals and reformed Protestant ones, serving at least some of the same functions in both societies, burial did become controversial in the conflict of Catholic and Protestant in early modern Paris. This is perhaps understandable. Traditional burial practices were founded upon hierarchy and discrimination, in a way that normally helped to underwrite and reconfirm social stability. But such discrimination – already expressed in marked inequalities and exclusions – could also offer an opportunity, a foothold, for parties to sectional conflicts of other kinds to co-opt burial practices into the terms of their dispute,

---

[10] Brigden, *London and the Reformation*, pp. 429–31, 433, 592–3; Babelon, *Paris au XVIe siècle*, pp. 404–5.

[11] Stow, *Survey*, vol. I, p. xxxi.

[12] E.g. GL, MS 2968/1, f. 98v; Littlehales, *Records of a London city church*, p. 389; Overall, *Accounts of churchwardens of the parish of St Michael Cornhill*, pp. 10, 15.

[13] AN, LL 805, esp. p. 50.

especially when, in fact, there were many common themes. An issue that divided the community, as the response to reformed thought did in Paris, encouraged its protagonists to look for ways of focusing and expressing their hostilities, and burial location proved to be very vulnerable to co-option for such a purpose. Burial could be presented as an issue in itself, and used as an occasion for identifying and excluding the other. Protestantism was always a minority religion in Paris; the hostility of the majority of the Parisian populace to Huguenots and their religion in general was extreme, and there was no tradition of religious pluralism on which to draw.[14]

Massacre and the desecration of the dead are features of internecine strife, as we know all too well from modern conflicts; we are also familiar with the degradations historically imposed on the corpses of suicides, excommunicates, heretics, and traitors. These aspects of the disposal of the dead, hostile anti-types of Christian burial, came to the fore in sixteenth-century Paris. Disputes centred on the Huguenots' claims to continue burial in the city's ancient churchyards, using their own rites. To many Catholics, this constituted pollution of especially sacred sites within the enceinte of the city. Canon law excluded the heretic and excommunicate from burial in consecrated ground, but it was the strength of popular Catholic feeling that really pushed this issue into the forefront. In 1562 a riot ensued after Catholics disinterred and threw into the gutter a corpse buried according to reformed rites in the Innocents; another such incident occurred in 1564. The massacre of St Bartholomew's Eve included the degradation of victims' corpses, starting with Coligny's, and many of them were thrown into the river. The pacification of May 1576 offered Parisian Huguenots use of the cemetery of la Trinité, on the margin of the city though still within the walls, which they shared with the poor and plague victims, and indeed the victims of fifteenth-century massacres. In the years of the Ligue these privileges were reduced, and there were complaints of burial refused, graves attacked, bodies exhumed.[15]

Burial remained a troublesome issue through the seventeenth century. Even after official toleration, Huguenots suffered all kinds of humiliations and penalties. Funeral processions had to take place in the early morning or evening (though interment could be during the day), and be protected by an archer of the watch. The Edict of Nantes was intended to guarantee secure burial for Huguenots by granting them three churchyards

---

[14] P. Benedict, 'Un roi, une loi, deux fois: parameters for the history of a Catholic – Reformed coexistence in France, 1555–1685', in O. P. Grell and R. Scribner (eds.), Tolerance and intolerance in the European Reformation (Cambridge, 1996), pp. 65–93, esp. p. 81.

[15] Diefendorf, Beneath the cross, pp. 69, 73, 93–106; Benedict, 'Un roi, une loi, deux fois', pp. 65–93.

in Paris, part of La Trinité, and two cemeteries in the faubourg Saint-Germain and the faubourg Saint-Denis. Catholics were forbidden to exhume Protestant corpses. However, the Huguenots were dispossessed of their cemetery in the faubourg Saint-Germain by an *arrêt* of Parlement in 1604, so that it could be used for Catholic plague burials, and had to obtain an alternative; they had great difficulty in securing the third cemetery promised. The partitioning of churchyards between Catholics and Protestants was prohibited in 1634, and the foundation of new churchyards very restricted. Vexatious prosecutions and an increasingly rigorous application of the law combined to make life more and more difficult, until the revocation of the Edict of Nantes in 1685. The bodies of those who died outside the church were therafter liable to exemplary punishment, including being dragged through the mud.[16]

The association of heresy with a ritualised destruction of the body is obviously an important element here, apparently legitimising the brutality with which Huguenot corpses and burials were treated. Natalie Davis argues that 'official acts of desecration of the corpses of certain criminals anticipate some of the acts performed by riotous crowds', which included exhumation, disembowelling, castration, and burning.[17] It is significant that in 1681 the masters of the Hôtel-Dieu stated that they gave the bodies of heretics (that is, Protestants) for anatomizing, but not those of Catholics, though they did say that the flesh and bones must be returned for burial according to their religion.[18] A contributory factor to the vehemence of Catholic crowds may have been the association of Protestantism with iconoclasm, and specifically with the destruction and despoliation of tombs in the first religious war.[19] Apart from the *geste* of violence, however, the aim seems to have been to exorcise heresy and eliminate pollution, by excluding heretic corpses from the sacred space of the churchyard. The marginalisation of Huguenot cemeteries to the suburbs emphasized their unacceptability in Paris, the most Catholic city; it also metaphorically and literally placed them with plague and pauper burials. In the eighteenth century the proposal to remove burial from the city centre to the suburbs was strongly opposed, on the grounds that it equated the faithful with the Huguenots.[20]

It was in fact the continuities in burial practice and expectations that made it both a factor for stability in London and a potential source of

[16] Hillairet, *Les 200 cimetières*, pp. 265–72; Thibaut-Payen, *Les morts, l'église et l'état*, pp. 157–85.
[17] N. Z. Davis, 'The rites of violence', in N. Z. Davis, *Society and culture in early modern France* (Stanford, 1975), p. 162.
[18] Brièle, *Collection de documents*, vol. I, p. 218.
[19] Salmon, *Society in crisis. France in the sixteenth century*, p. 137.
[20] BN, MS Joly de Fleury 1207, ff. 15–21. See above, pp. 116–18.

conflict in Paris. Protestants in both London and Paris retained many traditional ritual practices and attitudes to the body: they did not dismiss the corpse as insignificant or its fate as unimportant, though a strict interpretation of Protestant eschatology might have suggested this. The corpse deserved respect (degrading rituals would have no impact if this were not so) and the place where it was buried was a marker of the deceased's place in an integrated society. In particular, burial in traditional locations and styles was a way of laying claim to the past and thereby legitimating the present. In London, the gradual transformation of religious practice permitted a range of beliefs and allowed them to evolve at their own pace, within the framework of broad uniformity. Though many traditions of the past were rejected, much was retained, and the process of Reformation was such that Protestant Londoners were able to possess their own history. Those accepting the Anglican settlement did not need to dispute possession of burial sites and funerary rituals with any subgroup in society. They were able effectively to ignore or exclude such Catholic recusancy as survived in the capital, and it was not until the growth of separatism and nonconformity that there was any real dissociation from the past, in the rejection of the parochial basis for congregations and worship, and of the parish church and churchyard as the prime location of burial. This was not the case in Paris. Protestants as well as Catholics claimed the past and expressed the same need for identification with it, including use of churches and churchyards, but this could only be realized by a process of exclusion rather than accommodation. They were competing for possession of the same tradition. They were not prepared to share the past, and in practice they could not share the spaces of the present. There are many other aspects to the conflict, of course, but burial and the disposal of the dead was a key area of dispute and an important indicator of the strength of feeling. The antagonism of Catholics to Protestant burial may actually have strengthened solidarity within the Catholic community, but at a considerable price for the city as a whole.

London and Paris

To the question, did the way in which London and Paris dealt with death actually help to constitute and strengthen the 'networks of order', the answer must be a qualified yes. Disposing of the dead required local authorities, individuals, and wider but more marginal social groups to interact, and engaged them in a process that had to include negotiation, accommodation, and acknowledgement of a range of divergent interests. Because of the eschatological significance of the issue, ideas of piety and charity figured largely, moderating utilitarian or pragmatic responses to the problem. Burial spaces and the way they were used consolidated a whole set of assumptions about communal rights and social priorities; burial practices helped to realise a vision of local society as hierarchical, respectful of rank, exclusive of outsiders, protective of its own, tempered by charity. Burying the dead among the living fundamentally shaped the physical form of the city, and also its moral environment: it implied the integration of the past with the present, the acknowledgement of a wider community than the immediate and mundane, and constituted a reminder – even if imperfectly received – that present existence is not the only reality.

But in general the process worked better in London than in Paris. London parishes were smaller and more numerous (130 to Paris's 48 by the 1670s), so the size of the problem many of them faced was less, though it was certainly an increasing one. Local government traditions of participation and elective office were stronger, despite the growth of select vestries. London was much less class- and caste-ridden than Paris; if London churchwardens and vestrymen were an élite, they were at least rooted in the locality and not far distant socially from the majority of their fellow parishioners. And their burial practices, though reflecting hierarchies of wealth and status, and increasingly strained by shortage of accommodation, were not crudely polarised, and maintained a modicum of respect for sensibilities. London dealt with the increase in burials by opening more burial grounds and doubling up burials in existing ones. The increasing use of coffins may have limited the brutal impact of reopening graves to add further burials, though there are still plenty of references to inadvertent uncovering of remains. London burial remained under-planned and under-resourced, and indeed became increasingly chaotic, until the agitations of reformers in the nineteenth century brought about wholesale change.[21] Ironically, the failure to find a comprehensive solution to the burial problem in the early modern period, while it allowed environmental unpleasantness to multiply, was perhaps less damaging to social equilibrium than a more dirigiste approach. In this it may resemble London's attitude to plague, in which the parishes were largely left to handle the problem as best they could, while the attempts of central government to impose a more rigorous programme of control were resisted or ignored.[22]

This was less clearly the case in Paris. While burial practices resembled those in London to a considerable extent, and could function affirmatively

[21] Walker, *Gatherings from graveyards*, passim.

[22] Slack, *Impact of plague*, pp. 144–69; Slack, 'Metropolitan government in crisis', pp. 60–81; Champion, *London's dreaded visitation*; Harding, 'Burial of the plague dead', pp. 53–64.

within the community in the ways outlined above, there is a sense that the system was under greater strain and that on occasion it failed. Paris's more pragmatic treatment of the majority of the dead, resulting in part from the city's greater size over a long period, could not make the most of the restorative potential of burial tradition and ritual. All early modern burial practices, being to some extent discriminatory, helped to define the community and its hierarchies, but when burial policies too blatantly offered privileges to the few at the expense of the many, they may have contributed to a sense of alienation or disaffection. The contrast between what was available to the rich and what was left for the poor was very marked in Paris. Many Parisian parishes appear to have been very willing to assign special spaces to noble and honourable families, effectively privatising parts of the church and churchyard, to a much greater degree than was the case in London. When the parish's representatives invited bids to build private chapels, guaranteeing a private burial vault and an altar dedicated to the benefactors' intention, they were in effect selling off parts of a common resource for a largely private benefit and use. The church was enlarged and beautified at minimal common expense, and the quantity and perhaps quality of services, notably masses, being performed there was increased, but it is debatable whether a succession of masses to special intentions, celebrated in private chapels, really benefited the parish's collective worship. By contrast to the secluded spaces of the rich, the poor, and some even of the middling sort, were buried in the open graveyard, often it seems in mass graves or *fosses communes*, which in the course of time would be opened, emptied, and reused. Even more brutal was the treatment of the bodies of the destitute who ended their lives in one of the city's hospitals – which, by 1670, may have been as much as a quarter of the city's population. Bodies were carted to the graveyard at la Trinité, or, from the 1670s, the new burial ground at Clamart, roughly shrouded, and there buried in mass graves with minimal ceremony. There is little sense that these were seen as embodied individuals, let alone souls; the prevailing image is of waste disposal. Though the dead-carts became part of the urban mythology of Paris, it is hard to see that treating a significant proportion of the city's dead in this summary fashion did anything to mitigate the trauma of high urban mortality, let alone strengthen social relations or encourage integration and stability.

The polarisation of the burial experience of rich and poor, the crude 'depersonalisation' of many Parisian bodies,[23] as an important weakness of the city's burial practice, had parallels in other areas. In a number of instances, bodies were treated either as commodities or as negligible

---

[23] See Harding, 'Whose body?', pp. 171–6.

matter – in either case, as having no right to a place or even to respect. There were recurrent disputes over the possession of bodies for burial, usually between parish clergy and a religious house, in the sixteenth and seventeenth centuries. Similarly, even though the practice of charnelling exhumed bones effectively transmuted skeletal remains into sanctified relics, there was a potential danger, in that the expedient of exhumation and relocation was available for adoption by others with different motivations. So long as reverent preservation was the aim and end of mass burial and subsequent exhumation, anxieties about the process were appeased and it remained acceptable; but if that was disregarded then the moral sanction for it evaporated. Even though in theory the remains were carefully relocated, the demolition of the southern *charnier* at the Innocents, and the appropriation of a broad strip of ground to widen the rue de la Ferronerie in 1669 was a significant assault by the state on the integrity of the Innocents – a place of high significance in the myth of Parisian identity and a major symbol of religious and civic piety.[24] This deed also provided a kind of precedent for more wide-ranging proposals to close and clear the city churchyards in the eighteenth century, finally achieved after the Revolution.[25] The words of the parish clergy on that occasion, though clearly self-interested, can be applied to the situation in the sixteenth and seventeenth centuries, as a way of illustrating the damage that inconsiderate treatment of the dead could do. They argued that 'all the people of the world, but especially the French, have always respected the mortal remains of those who were dear to them; for them it is a real consolation, however sad, that they are not separated from them . . . They are outraged and distressed by any act that undermines the tribute they owe to affection, blood, and memory.'[26] This attribution of transcendent meaning to the dead body can also help to explain why burial became such a passionately contested issue in the conflict between Catholic and Protestant. Responses to the body could be either sentimental or brutal, and sometimes perhaps both, depending on how it was identified; the nuanced discriminations of the traditional burial order legitimised, but were ultimately overwhelmed by, a more violent opposition of sanctification and degradation.

It would be a mistake to argue that burial practices had in themselves a decisive impact on the workings of urban society; they were deeply embedded in social relations, which they undoubtedly helped to shape, but

[24] AN L 570, item 26; Brièle and Husson, *Inventaire-sommaire*, vol. II, p. 123; Brièle, *Collection de documents*, vol. I, pp. 187–8; Bernard, *The emerging city*, pp. 190–1.
[25] BN, MS Joly de Fleury 1207; Foisil, 'Les attitudes', pp. 303–32.
[26] BN, MS Joly de Fleury 1207, esp. ff. 15–21.

they were not an independent variable. On the whole they were positive and consolidating, supporting order and assisting society to survive a testing situation. They figured or revealed existing dysfunction, rather than creating it; the brutal treatment of the bodies of the poor in Paris was the result, not the cause, of a sharply polarised understanding of society. Nor can burial practice can be neatly mapped onto the social and political structure of a particular community. There are too many variables of historic practice, contingency, and spatial and social particularity. In London and Paris, the choices that were made between different options and approaches in the early modern period were constrained by decisions previously taken, and coloured by prejudices and preferences already formed, as well as by the events of the moment. Nevertheless, we would do well to incorporate an appreciation of the impact of death, and the response it evoked, into our assessment of early modern urban life. If we believe that ritualised patterns of behaviour express underlying assumptions and anxieties, in the individual or in the collectivity, we can learn much from exploring, describing, and analysing the burial customs and practices of these two metropolitan societies.

Death was frequent and devastating in the early modern city; death rituals had a lot of work to do if they were to limit or repair the damage. To a significant extent, in both London and Paris, they did this work effectively: their complexity and variety enabled them to represent hierarchy and social difference, while at the same time affirming continuity in the face of change. Practices retained their force through significant religious change and during the devastating mortality of epidemics. There were limits, however, to what they could do, and the sheer weight of numbers, the size of the metropolitan population, was overwhelming subtle discriminations and sensitivities by the later seventeenth century. The meaning and moral value of burial ritual was weakened by the increasing secularisation and commercialisation of urban society. And in Paris, over the whole period, such rituals could only partially work to reintegrate a society that was tending to institutionalise polarisation and stratification, and in which confessional and factional strife were given such free rein.

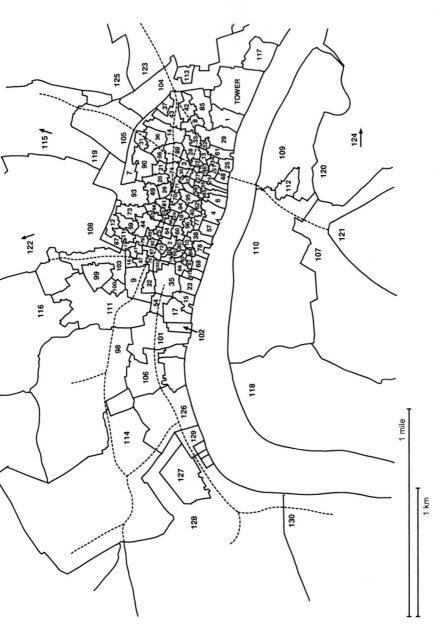

Map 1   Sketch map of parishes in London, *c.* 1664, based on maps in C. Spence, *London in the 1690s. A social atlas* (London: Centre for Metropolitan History, 2000); D. Keene and V. Harding, *A survey of documentary sources for London before the Great Fire* (London: London Record Society 22, 1986); P. Laxton, *The A to Z of Regency London* (London: London Topographical Society 31, 1985). The numbers refer to the list of parishes in appendix 1, from the Yearly Bill of Mortality for 1664. Not all parishes and non-parochial spaces within the Bills could be shown.

Appendix 1: Mortality in the London parishes, 1664

From Guildhall Library, printed books section, *Bills of Mortality 1649–85* (G. 1.33)

	Parish	Buried	Whereof of the plague
	BURIED IN THE NINETY-SEVEN PARISHES WITHIN THE WALLS		
1	All Hallows Barking	86	
2	All Hallows Bread St	20	
3	All Hallows Gracechurch/Lombard Street	18	
4	All Hallows the Great	90	
5	All Hallows Honey Lane	9	
6	All Hallows the Less	43	
7	All Hallows on the Wall	93	
8	All Hallows Staining	38	
9	Christ Church Newgate Street	140	
10	Holy Trinity the Less	31	
11	St Alban Wood Street	46	
12	St Alphage	51	
13	St Andrew Hubbard	27	
14	St Andrew Undershaft	56	
15	St Andrew Wardrobe	81	
16	St Anne Aldersgate (St Anne and St Agnes)	42	
17	St Anne Blackfriars	97	
18	St Antholin	13	
19	St Augustine Watling Street	13	
20	St Bartholomew Exchange	22	
21	St Benet Fink	29	
22	St Benet Gracechurch	13	

23	St Benet Paul's Wharf	70
24	St Benet Sherehog	13
25	St Botolph Billingsgate	23
26	St Christopher le Stocks	16
27	St Clement Eastcheap	15
28	St Dionis Backchurch	31
29	St Dunstan in the East	102
30	St Edmund Lombard Street	20
31	St Ethelburga	23
32	St Faith	30
33	St Gabriel Fenchurch	18
34	St George Botolph Lane	13
35	St Gregory by St Paul's	118
36	St Helen	25
37	St James Duke's Place	41
38	St James Garlickhithe	40
39	St John the Evangelist	5
40	St John Walbrook	31
41	St John Zachary	23
42	St Katherine Coleman	44
43	St Katherine Cree	87
44	St Lawrence Jewry	45
45	St Lawrence Pountney	38
46	St Leonard Eastcheap	14
47	St Leonard Foster Lane	37
48	St Magnus	36
49	St Margaret Lothbury	33
50	St Margaret Moses	14
51	St Margaret New Fish Street/Bridge Street	26
52	St Margaret Pattens	17
53	St Martin Ironmonger Lane	11
54	St Martin Ludgate	51
55	St Martin Orgar	25
56	St Martin Outwich	17
57	St Martin Vintry	76
58	St Mary Abchurch	30
59	St Mary Aldermanbury	46
60	St Mary Aldermary	20

61	St Mary at Hill	23	
62	St Mary Bothaw	22	
63	St Mary Colechurch	5	
64	St Mary Le Bow	21	
65	St Mary Magdalen Milk Street	19	
66	St Mary Magdalen Old Fish Street	42	
67	St Mary Mounthaw	12	
68	St Mary Somerset	73	
69	St Mary Staining	7	
70	St Mary Woolchurch	22	
71	St Mary Woolnoth	21	
72	St Matthew Friday Street	9	
73	St Michael Bassishaw	38	
74	St Michael Cornhill	36	
75	St Michael Crooked Lane	46	
76	St Michael Le Querne	17	
77	St Michael Paternoster Royal	22	
78	St Michael Queenhithe	47	
79	St Michael Wood Street	24	
80	St Mildred Bread Street	12	
81	St Mildred Poultry	24	
82	St Nicholas Acon	14	
83	St Nicholas Coleabbey	31	
84	St Nicholas Olave	18	
85	St Olave Hart Street	37	
86	St Olave Jewry	29	
87	St Olave Silver Street	42	
88	St Pancras Soper Lane	12	
89	St Peter Cornhill	36	
90	St Peter le Poor	22	
91	St Peter Paul's Wharf	23	
92	St Peter Wood St	13	
93	St Stephen Coleman Street	133	
94	St Stephen Walbrook	19	
95	St Swithin	41	
96	St Thomas Apostle	29	
97	St Vedast Foster Lane	25	
	Total	3,448	0

BURIED IN THE SIXTEEN PARISHES WITHOUT THE WALLS

98	St Andrew Holborn	843	
99	St Bartholomew the Great	90	
100	St Bartholomew the Less	44	
101	St Bride	412	
102	Bridewell precinct	34	
103	St Botolph Aldersgate	187	
104	St Botolph Aldgate	785	1
105	St Botolph Bishopsgate	545	
106	St Dunstan in the West	265	
107	St George Southwark	259	
108	St Giles Cripplegate	1,353	1
109	St Olave Southwark	829	
110	St Saviour Southwark	605	
111	St Sepulchre	851	
112	St Thomas Southwark	54	
113	Holy Trinity Minories	12	
	At the Pest House	0	
	Total	7,168	2

BURIED IN THE TWELVE OUT-PARISHES IN MIDDLESEX AND SURREY

114	St Giles in the Fields	931	1
115	Hackney parish	80	
116	St James Clerkenwell	313	
117	St Katherine by the Tower	200	
118	Lambeth parish	236	
119	St Leonard Shoreditch	424	
120	St Mary Magdalen Bermondsey	305	
121	St Mary Newington [Surrey]	235	
122	St Mary Islington	58	
123	St Mary Whitechapel	671	3
124	Rotherhithe parish	40	
125	Stepney parish	1,392	
	Total	4,885	4

BURIED IN THE FIVE PARISHES
IN THE CITY AND LIBERTIES OF
WESTMINSTER

126	St Clement Danes	534	
127	St Paul Covent Garden	133	
128	St Martin in the Fields	1,242	
129	St Mary Savoy	80	
130	St Margaret Westminster	807	
	At the Pest House	0	
	Total	2,796	0

CHRISTENED	Males	6,041	
	Females	5,681	
	In all	11,722	
BURIED	Males	9,367	
	Females	8,928	
	In all	18,297	
	Of the plague		6

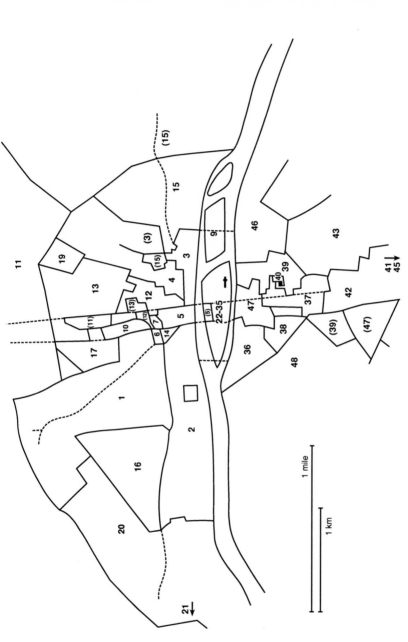

Map 2 Sketch map of parishes in Paris, c. 1670, based on Le Fer's map of 1697, with information from A. Friedmann, *Paris, ses rues, ses paroisses du Moyen Age à la Révolution. Origine et évolution des circonscriptions paroissales* (Paris: Plon 1959) and D. Chadych and D. Leborgne, *Atlas de Paris. Evolution d'un paysage urbain* (Paris: parigramme, 1999). The numbers refer to the list of parishes in appendix 2, from the Etat des Baptêmes, 1670. Not all parishes and non-parochial spaces could be shown, and some boundaries are uncertain.

Appendix 2: Mortality in the Paris parishes, 1670

Summed from the monthly bills in BN (Réserve), LK[7] 6745

	Parishes	Total
	VILLE	
1	Saint-Eustache	1,621
2	Saint-Germain-l'Auxerrois	930
3	Saint-Gervais	528
4	Saint-Jean-en-Grève	326
5	Saint-Jaques-de-la-Boucherie	368
6	Les Saints-Innocents	23
7	Saint-Josse	6
8	Saint-Jaques-de-l'Hospital	1
9	Saint-Louis, Ile Notre-Dame	183
10	Saint-Leu–Saint-Gilles	169
11	Saint-Laurent et la Villeneuve son annexe	1,202
12	Saint-Mederic	330
13	Saint-Nicolas-des-Champs	1,423
14	Saint-Opportune	28
15	Saint-Paul et Sainte-Marguerite annexe	1,517
16	Saint-Roch	579
17	Saint-Sauveur	372
18	Saint-Thomas-du-Louvre	6
19	Le Temple	34
20	La Ville l'Eveque	107
21	Chaillot, au faubourg de la Conference	28
	Total	9,781
	CITE	
22	Saint-Barthelemy	192
23	La basse Sainte-Chapelle du Palais	7
24	Sainte-Croix	15

25	Saint-Christophe	7
26	Saint-Germain-le-Vieux	122
27	Saint-Genevieve-les-Ardents	27
28	Saint-Jean-le-Rond	13
29	Saint-Landry	40
30	Sainte-Madeleine	37
31	Sainte-Marine	6
32	Sainte-Martial	22
33	Saint-Pierre-des-Arcis	19
34	Saint-Pierre-aux-Boeufs	18
35	Saint-Symphorien	29
	Total	554

UNIVERSITE

36	Saint-Andre-des-Arts	184
37	Saint-Benoît	221
38	Saint-Cosme	99
39	Saint-Etienne-du-Mont	715
40	Saint-Hilaire	77
41	Saint-Hyppolite	153
42	Saint-Jaques-du-Haut-Pas	330
43	Saint-Jean-de-Latran	29
44	Saint-Medard	540
45	Saint-Martin	103
46	Saint-Nicolas-du-Chardonnet	308
47	Saint-Séverin	465
48	Saint-Sulpice, faubourg Saint-Germain	1,676
	Total	4,900
	De la religion pretendue reformee	357
	Hôtel-Dieu	4,812
	Other hospitals (see below)	1,073

The 'hospitals' section of the bill (added from February 1670) lists figures under the following headings:

> Hôtel-Dieu: Malades, premier du mois; entrez pendant le mois; enfans baptisez; morts; convalescens sortis; malades restez au dernier du mois
>
> Hospital des Quinze-vingts aveugles: enfans baptisez; mariés; morts
>
> Hospital de la Charité des Hommes, faubourg Saint-Germain: malades; morts

Hospital de la Charité des Femmes de la Place Royale et Raquette:
  malades; morts
Hospital des Incurables: malades; morts
Hospital de Saint-Louis: malades; morts
Hospital des petites maisons et ses annexes: pauvres et infirmes
Hospital de la Trinité: pauvres enfans; morts
Hospital du Saint-Esprit: pauvres enfans; morts
Hospital de Saint-Gervais: pauvres enfans; morts
Hospital des Enfants Trouvés: en nourrice ou dans la maison
Hospital Général (listed separately for Maison de la Pitié; Bicêtre;
  la Salpetrière; Scipion; la Savonnerie): pauvres valides enfer-
  mez; morts

Appendix 3: Funeral provision of Joan Brytten, 1540

LMA, Consistory Court Wills, Original wills, bundle I. 27. Printed in *Consistory Court Wills*, 122.

I Joan Brytten of the parish of St Michel Wood Street, sick in body, bequeath my soul to Almighty God and our blessed Lady and all the holy company of heaven, and my body to be buried in the parish church of St Gregory by St Paul's, under a stone there prepared all ready for me.

To the high altar of St Michael's for tithes forgotten, 8d.

I will have at the time of my burial, half a trental of masses, 5s. 4d.

I will have six priests beside the parson, the clerk and the sexton, and bequeath them for their labour 4s. 10d.

I will have a forenoon's knell, 20d., [and] the peals, 6d.

I will have 5 1-lb tapers, at 15d., and to the children to bear them before the cross, 10d.

I will that 4s. be distributed in halfpenny loaves at the time of my burial.

I will that a dinner be made on the day of my burial for those entrusted with my will, to cost 3s. 4d.

My goods to be inventoried, appraised and sold, and the residue, after debts and burial expenses, to pay a priest to sing for my soul and the souls of my master Milard, his wife, and all Christian souls, in the church of St Gregory for half a year, and in the church of St Michael for a quarter of a year, or as far as the goods will extend. The priest's wages to be at the rate of £6 13s. 4d. a year.

[etc.]

Appendix 4: Funeral provision
of Jeanne Passavent, 1582

AN, L 664 Saint-Jean-en-Grève, papers

Box with papers and parchments (originals and copies) in eighteenth-century folders, concerning foundations in the church.

no 6. (memorandum) Foundation by Jeanne Passavent, wife of Bertrand Lefebvre, 1583, of one obit, 30 August, and 3 low masses a week for ever. Reduced to an obit and 51 low masses a year by order, 1685.

Copy testament of Jeanne Passavent, 28 Aug 1582.

Honorable femme Jeanne de Passavent, wife of *honorable homme* Bertrand Lefebvre, merchant and *bourgeois de Paris*, lying sick in her house in the place de Grève, being nevertheless sound of mind etc., considering that nothing is more certain than death or less certain than the hour of the same, and not wishing to die intestate, etc., made her will as follows.

In the name of the Father, the Son and the Holy Spirit, as a good Catholic she recommends her soul when it shall leave her body, begging him to pardon her faults and receive her in paradise by the intercession of the glorious Virgin Mary, St Michael the Angel, Saints Peter, Paul, and all the saints of the heavenly court of Paradise.

5 *sous* to be distributed as usual; her debts to be paid.

To be buried in the morning in the church of Saint-Jean-en-Grève, facing and below the crucifix of the said church, nearby where her late mother was buried.

The curé and all the *prestres habitues* to be present at her convoy, and to be paid, the curé 4 *écus* for attending the convoy and for the service, and one *écu* to each priest.

Also at her convoy, the four mendicant orders, the Minimes, the children of the hospitals of the Saint-Esprit and la Trinité and the Enfants Rouges, the Capettes de Montagu, the religious of the Billettes and the Blancs-Manteaux are to be present; and to each of the convents, hospitals and Capettes be distributed 3 *écus sols* on the charge that each say a *service complet*.

For lights, 4 dozen torches, each of 2 lb.

3 *services complets*, with vigils, lauds and *recomandances* to be sung in the church of Saint-Jean, after each of which be sung a *salve regina*.

To each of the convents of the Avemaria, the Filles de Pénitence and the *Cordellières* of Saint-Marcel, 3 *écus* for a *service complet* in each of their churches.

To the confraternity of Our Lady of Siesse [?Liesse?] founded in the chapel of the Saint-Esprit [in Saint-Jean] en Grève, Paris, 6 *écus sols*, both for lending the confraternity's pall and so that the masters of the confraternity shall have said in the said chapel a *service complet* for her benefit.

To the confraternity of Saint-Claude in the church of Saint-Antoine, 6 *écus*.

To 200 poor on day of her interment, 1 *sou* and a loaf of the same value, on the charge that they assist at the service and offertory.

[etc.]

Appendix 5: A note on sources

Since a major aim of this study was to compare experiences in London and Paris, comparability of source material was a vital consideration. In broad terms this could be achieved: the two cities had many similar institutions, such as parishes and municipal guilds, which generated similar forms of record. They also both had tiers of local institutions and municipal and national authorities with responsibility, or at least concern, for some areas relevant to this study, though there were much greater differences between the structures and records of these institutions. In both London and Paris there was a numerous, educated, property-owning, and spiritually aware urban middle class (citizens and gentry in London, *bourgeois*, *noblesse de robe*, and other lesser nobility in Paris) who used wills and testaments to express their concerns about death and salvation and to establish palliative practices, often using similar discursive conventions.

What distinguishes the cities as far as source material goes is their subsequent history: archives for the study of early modern London have suffered only minor depredations, while those of Paris have been decimated by revolutions and disaster. London is very well recorded for the early modern period, with the only serious gap, for the purposes of this study, being a virtual absence of probate inventories and accounts. The Parisian sources are very limited for the early sixteenth century, and indeed are uneven throughout the period, though they become more plentiful from the mid-sixteenth century and, with some exceptions, through to the later seventeenth.[1] Paris's losses have been particularly serious for three of the source groups used in this study, the records of the Etat Civil (the recording of baptisms, marriages and burials), those of the municipality of Paris, and of the Hôtel-Dieu, Paris's great sick hospital. All of these were wholly or partly destroyed in 1871; fortunately, in each case,

---

[1] V. Harding, 'Medieval documentary sources for London and Paris: a comparison', in J. Boffey and P. King (eds.), *London and Europe in the later Middle Ages* (London, 1995), pp. 35–54; Harding, 'From compact city to complex metropolis: records for the history of London, 1500–1720'; F. Gasnault, 'Les archives de Paris: mutilation, démembrement, recomposition', in M. V. Roberts (ed.), *Archives and the metropolis* (London, 1998), pp. 43–9.

some surveys, extracts, or even calendars had already been compiled and published. One important bonus of the comparative approach is that it involves asking questions that the source material for one city alone might not encourage one to formulate. It also tempts extrapolation, to bridge gaps and fill lacunae, sometimes no doubt a risky strategy.

Both England and France instituted the recording of births, marriages, and deaths in the first half of the sixteenth century. The city of London, with over a hundred parishes, has a good level of record survival, not always from the earliest possible date of 1538, but in many cases from 1558. There are gaps in the seventeenth century, as some parishes lost their current registers in the Fire of 1666. A useful number of these registers are available in print.[2] In France, universal registration of baptisms began in 1539, and of marriages and burials in 1579, though several parishes appear to have had records predating the official orders.[3] Paris had at least some records dating from 1527, and others from the 1540s and 1550s, probably very similar in form to those kept elsewhere in France or in London. All of these, however, were destroyed in the burning of the Hôtel de Ville in 1871; copies kept in the Palais de Justice were burnt at the same time. Nevertheless there is some valuable material deriving from these registers. Eighteenth-century antiquarians and genealogists made copious extracts from the registers of a small number of parishes, and these now survive largely in the Bibliothèque Nationale's MSS Français and Joly de Fleury collections. These concentrated on the descents of particular families, and are therefore extremely selective. Even for the most fully recorded parish, Saint-André-des-Arts, it is unlikely that the extracts cover more than 10 per cent of all burials.[4] For other parishes the data is even more sketchily recorded; Saint-Gervais and Saint-Jean-en-Grève are the next best.[5] Nevertheless, this does provide some information on burial location, and especially the choices made over a period of time by members of one family or lineage; on services and commemorations; and on the speed of interment.[6]

The records of London's government survive well (apart from accounts, lost in the Chamber fire of 1786). However, apart from plague

---

[2] See Guildhall Library, *Handlist of parish registers*, part 1, *City of London* (5th edn, 1984). This also notes the registers in print, mostly published by the Harleian Society, as does J. M. Sims, *London and Middlesex published records, a handlist* (London Record Society, Occasional Publications 1, 1970).

[3] Babelon, *Paris au XVe siècle*, p. 160.

[4] BN, MS Fr. 32589, Saint-André-des-Arts, incl. burials from 1550.

[5] BN, MS Fr. 32838, Saint-Gervais, burials 1639–1712; BN, MS Fr. 32588, Saint-Jean-en-Grève, burials 1623–32; BN, MS Fr. 32585, Saint-Landry, burials 1527–1711; BN, MS Fr. 32585, Saint-Medard, testaments and burials 1544–80; BN, MS Fr. 32594, Saint-Sulpice, *régistres mortuaires* 1604–1714. See M. Barroux, *Les sources de l'ancien Etat civil Parisien. Répertoire critique* (Paris, 1898).

[6] Cf. below; and Harding, 'Whose body?', pp. 170–87.

orders, London's rulers were normally content to leave the administration of burial to the parishes, and their records yield comparatively little. On a few occasions they were sufficiently concerned about the burial problem to investigate the possibility of opening new grounds, but took little direct action in this between 1569 and 1665.[7] They were necessarily more active in plague years. The records of the Parisian municipality were largely destroyed in 1871, but before that date a significant number of the early modern Registres des Délibérations du Bureau de la Ville de Paris had been transcribed and published, covering the years 1499–1632. Since one of the municipality's limited number of functions was the management of ceremonial in the city, these include descriptions of major funerals in Paris, of both local and national figures, and were especially valuable for chapter 9.[8] However, the complete loss of the later seventeenth-century material truncates the story of funeral ceremony in Paris at a critical point. A similar disaster, though not resulting in such comprehensive destruction, befell the records of the Hôtel-Dieu: some were burnt in 1871, but most survived, and earlier calendaring and publication saved much information from total loss. Much of the most interesting material from both minute books and accounts is available in print, in Brièle's *Inventaire-sommaire* and *Collection des documents*, though not all record series were so comprehensively excerpted.[9] In other areas too, nineteenth-century enthusiasm has done much to compensate for archival losses. The 'Histoire Générale de Paris' was responsible for publishing both Raunié's *Epitaphier du vieux Paris* (1890–) and Adolphe Berty's *Topographie historique du vieux Paris* (1866–97), two ambitious projects that recovered and reconstructed significant amounts of data of great value for this study. Numerous records of the Parlement of Paris, which took a major part in the administration of the capital, also survive, and provide the basis for Jacqueline Thibaut-Payen's detailed and valuable study of the clash of church and state over burial in the area of the Parlement's jurisdiction.[10]

Parishes in London and Paris shared many objectives, including the maintenance of collective worship with the appropriate apparatus, and

[7] E.g. CLRO, Repertory 26 (pt. 2), f. 388v; Repertory 44, f. 95; W. H. and H. C. Overall, *Analytical Index to the Series of Records known as the Remembrancia*, no. I. 331.

[8] *Régisters des délibérations du Bureau de la Ville de Paris*, ed. F. Bonnardot, A. Tuetey, P. Guérin, et al. (Histoire Générale de Paris), 20 vols. (Paris, 1883–1984).

[9] Fosseyeux, *L'Hôtel-Dieu de Paris aux XVIIe et XVIII siècles*; Jehanno, 'Les comptes de l'Hôtel-Dieu de Paris au Moyen Age'; Brièle and Husson, *Inventaire-sommaire*, vol. II; Brièle, *Collection des documents*. The surviving archives of the Hôtel-Dieu are now at the Archives de l'Assistance Publique, 7 rue des Minimes.

[10] E. Taillemite, *Les Archives Nationales. Etat général des fonds*, vol. I: *L' Ancien Régime* (Paris, 1978), pp. 649–63; Thibaut-Payen, *Les Morts, l'église et l'état*. Cf. J. H. Shennan, *The Parlement of Paris* (Stroud, 1998); Hamscher, *The Parlement of Paris after the Fronde*, pp. 247–57.

the defence of religious orthodoxy and discipline. As institutions they developed similar structures and procedures, with committees of leading parishioners, known as the vestry or *fabrique*, making policy and authorising action, normally carried out by two or three elected officers with executive powers, serving for a limited period of time, known as churchwardens or *marguilliers*. They also employed small staffs of waged servants such as sextons, clerks, and gravediggers or *fossoyeurs*. It seems likely that in both cities the parishes created similar sets of administrative records (financial accounts of the officers, minutes of the deliberative or administrative committee) as well as muniments such as cartularies and formal record books. However, the parish records of Paris have been severely damaged or dispersed over time, probably mostly at the Revolution. While some accounts and minutes (*comptes*, *déliberations*), do survive, they are patchy and incomplete, compared with the excellent survival and quantity of those for London.[11] Rather more of the formal record books such as obituary lists, lists of foundations, etc., have survived, and in some cases eighteenth-century papers or extracts illuminate earlier practice.[12] Surveys for this project could not be comprehensive, of either the London or the Paris material. In both cases, I chose to focus on the records of a small number of parishes, selected principally for their archival quality and for their coincidence with other records such as burial registers or extracts; other parish archives were sampled or explored if they appeared promising. The fact that accounts and/or minutes from several London parishes are available in print has been extremely useful. When offering examples to illustrate a point, I have often cited a printed source, provided it is supported by other material elsewhere, to allow the reader to verify the matter more easily if wished.

Wills constitute the remaining major source for the book. Londoners' wills were proved in one of several courts (the Consistory, Commissary, and Archdeaconry Courts of London, the Prerogative Court of Canterbury, and the city's Court of Husting) and the registers or rolls of these courts are for the most part extant, voluminous, and accessible.[13] It was relatively easy to skim and sample registers, or to check the wills of individuals. The only major absence is of probate (executors') accounts, of the kind that provided such useful data on funeral expenses in Berkshire,

---

[11] See Guildhall Library, *Vestry minutes of parishes within the city of London. A handlist* (London, 1964); *Churchwarden's accounts of parishes within the City of London. A handlist* (London, 1969); Keene and Harding, *Survey of sources for property holding in London before the Great Fire* (London, 1984).

[12] Taillemite, *Les Archives Nationales. Etat géneral des fonds*, vol. I. Parish records are largely in series H^5, L, LL, and S.

[13] See A. J. Camp, *Wills and their whereabouts* (London, 1963).

Kent, Lincolnshire, and Somerset for Clare Gittings' study.[14] At the very end of the period studied, however, some of the inventories compiled for the City's Court of Orphans do yield valuable information.[15] In Paris, willmaking may have been even more widespread: many married women made wills, which was uncommon in England, and the spiritual duty of willmaking, even more than its practical value, was impressed on individuals. But there are no probate registers. Wills were drawn up by notaries and copies preserved in the archives of the numerous notarial practices or Etudes. Among these voluminous archives, wills, though numerous, constitute only a tiny fraction of the whole: according to Chaunu, they form less than 2 per cent, and in the sixteenth century often less than 1 per cent, of the material in those archives.[16] Though the notarial archives have been declared public records, and most of the surviving ones deposited in the Minutier Central section of the Archives Nationales,[17] the sheer bulk of the collections is such that it would be impossible for a single researcher to get far with sampling these, even as the main focus of study. An appreciation of the value of the source, but also of the magnitude of the task of exploiting it, inspired the major enterprise led by Professor Pierre Chaunu in the 1970s. I acknowledge with admiration and gratitude the work of his students, who between them read and noted over 8,000 wills from the notarial archives, and whose research and resulting *mémoires de maîtrise* form the acknowledged foundation of Chaunu's *La mort à Paris*. I have drawn extensively on the information presented in that book, and also consulted those *mémoires* deposited at the Archives Nationales.

Several other sources, some of them unique to one city, have also been important. I found much of value in the English Heralds' memoranda in the British and Bodleian Libraries, in the eighteenth-century descriptions of Parisian burial practice (part of the proceedings concerning the proposed closure of the Innocents and the parish churchyards) in the Bibliothèque Nationale, in a range of contemporary and near contemporary writings on death and burial, and in the records of the urban commentators and chroniclers. For areas outside my scheme of approach, such as sermon literature or collections of personal papers and diaries, both of which offer important insights, I have depended on those historians who have worked through these sources and put so much of them into the public domain.

---

[14] Gittings, *Death, burial and the individual*, esp. pp. 235–42.
[15] The Orphans' Court inventories are in CLRO. See Earle, *The making of the English middle class*.
[16] Chaunu, *La mort à Paris*, p. 225.
[17] R. Marquand, *Les Archives Nationales. Etat général des fonds*, vol. IV, *Fonds divers* (Paris, 1980).

Bibliography

MANUSCRIPTS AND EARLY PRINTED PAPERS

ARCHIVES NATIONALES, PARIS

Taillemite, E., *Les Archives Nationales. Etat général des fonds*, vol. I: *L'Ancien Régime* (Paris: Archives Nationales, 1978)

Marquand, R., *Les Archives Nationales. Etat général des fonds*, vol IV: *Fonds divers* (Paris: Archives Nationales, 1980)

Saint-André-des-Arts
H^5 3749: 18C papers: rents, foundations
L 630: title deeds and miscellaneous papers
L 631: foundations and bequests
L 632: papers concerning chapels, in bundles
L 633: papers concerning chapels, in bundles
LL 686: Délibérations (minutes), 1589–1627
LL 687: Délibérations, 1657–93
LL 691: Register of masses, obits, services, etc., 1621
LL 692: Obituary list, 1546
S 3308–11, S* 3311, S* 3312: papers

Saint-Germain-l'Auxerrois (cemetery of the Innocents)
H^5 3816 (1, 2): burial registers, 1667–1731
L 570: papers concerning the cemetery, incl. L 570/28–33, 18C depositions and counter-claims
L 571: papers concerning the cemetery, incl. L 571/1, 'Estat des charniers du cimetiere des Saints Innocens', *c.* 1599; L 571/3, mid-18C *mémoire* concerning the cemetery and its use; L 571/5, 7, bundles of permissions to erect tombs granted by St Germain l'Auxerrois, 1411–1651.
LL 434/B: Epitaphier

Saint-Gervais
L 651: Papers, incl. L 651/2, printed pamphlet, fees and duties 1675
LL 746: 16C book of foundations
LL 747: Book of foundations
LL 748: Délibérations, 1684–1704
LL 752: 18C book of foundations

LL 753: book of depositions, 1691
LL 754: book of foundations, 1730
LL 756: cartulary
S 3359: papers and titles, incl. dossier 3, concerning cemetery, 1385–1763

Saint-Jean-en-Grève
L 663: papers concerning chapels and foundations, and charity burials; incl.
   L 663/10, late 18C handwritten book on history of parish
L 664: papers concerning foundations in church
LL 797: Déliberations, 1671–9
LL 798: Déliberations, 1674–1719
LL 804: 16C foundation book
LL 805: 17C foundation book
S 3401: papers
S 3402, S 3405: papers concerning cemetery, etc.

Saints-Innocents (parish)
LL 758: Déliberations, 17C

Other
L 510 (microfilm) no. 27: Register of burials and convoys by dean of Paris,
   1567–97

ARCHIVES DE L'ASSISTANCE PUBLIQUE, HÔPITAUX DE PARIS,
7 RUE DES MINIMES, PARIS

Comptes de l'Hôtel-Dieu
Déliberations de l'Hôtel-Dieu
Register of testaments at the Hôtel-Dieu: cat. 6358 (layette 330, liasse 1413(1)).
Registres de l'Hôtel-Dieu

BIBLIOTHÈQUE NATIONALE, PARIS

Réserve (printed works)
LK^7 6745: collected Etat des Baptêmes

Manuscripts section
MS Clairambault 448, collection of papers, incl. printed Etat des Baptêmes for
   May 1680
MS Fr. 21609: N. Delamare, *Traité de la police, où l'on trouvera l'histoire de son
   établissement, les fonctions et les prérogatives de ses magistrats, toutes les lois et les
   règlements qui la concernent*, 4 vols. (2nd printed edn, Paris 1722–38)
MS Fr. 32585 (Saint-Landry, burials 1527–1711; Saint-Médard, testaments and
   burials 1544–80)
MS Fr. 32588 (18C extracts from the registers of Saint-Jean-en-Grève, 1623–32)
MS Fr. 32589 (18C extracts from the registers of Saint-André-des-Arts, 1550–
   1670)

MS Fr. 32594 (Saint-Sulpice, *registres mortuaires* 1604–1714)

MS Fr. 32838 (18C extracts from the registers of Saint-Gervais, 1639–1712)

MSS Joly de Fleury 1207, 1208 ('Cimetières de Paris, 1763–5': *mémoires* and depositions concerning burial in Paris)

MS Joly de Fleury 1317: Bound volume of papers, 'Assemblées de police, cimetières'; includes printed Etat des Baptêmes for September 1684

MS Joly de Fleury 2530: volume of collected papers and printed notices, incl. printed Etat des Baptêmes for June 1684

BODLEIAN LIBRARY, OXFORD

Bodl. MS Ashmole 818: heralds' memoranda

Bodl. MS Ashmole 836: heralds' memoranda

BRITISH LIBRARY, LONDON

Add. MS 12222: St Giles Cripplegate, CA 1570–1607

Add. MS 26705: Volume of memoranda of Robert Wever, including notes on funerals and expenses

Add. MSS 71131 A–X: Heralds' notes of funeral processions of Lord Mayors, etc. of London, 1605–73

Harl. Roll H 28: lightwardens' account, St Andrew Holborn, 1477–8

MS Harl. 877: St Mary Woolnoth, BR: 16–17C

MS Harl. 2252: Collections of John Colyns, incl. notes on tithes, burial fees, etc.

MS Sloane 2177: includes notes on funeral of John Fox, 1596

CORPORATION OF LONDON RECORDS OFFICE, LONDON (CLRO)

Journals (minutes of the Court of Common Council)

Letterbooks

Orphans' Court Inventories

Plans: Comptroller's City Lands Plans, 142, 270

Plans: Railways: North London Railway, City Branch, 1860 (678F, plan 122)

Repertories (minutes of the Court of Aldermen)

GUILDHALL LIBRARY, LONDON: MANUSCRIPTS SECTION

Parish Records

See *Handlist of parish registers*, part 1, *City of London* (Corporation of London, 5th edn, 1984); *Churchwardens' accounts of parishes within the City of London. A handlist* (Corporation of London, 2nd edn, 1969); *Vestry minutes of parishes within the city of London. A handlist* (Corporation of London, 2nd edn, 1964)

All Hallows Honey Lane

MS 5022: BR 1538–1667

MS 5026/1: CA 1618–1743

All Hallows London Wall
MS 5090/1–2: CA 1455–1536, 1566–1681

All Hallows Staining
MS 4956/1–3: CA 1491–1706

All Hallows the Great
MS 818/1: CA 1616–1708

Christ Church Newgate Street
MS 9163: incl. CA 1593–5

St Alphege
MS 1432/1–4: CA 1527–1677

St Andrew Hubbard
MS 1278/1: register book
MS 1279/1–3: CA 1454–1712

St Botolph Aldersgate
MS 1454/1–103: CA 1466–1636
MS 1455/1: CA 1637–79

St Botolph Aldgate
MS 9220–3: BR 1558–1625
MS 9229: BR 1653–4
MS 9234/1–7: parish clerks' memorandum books, 1583–1597
MS 9235/1–2: CA 1547–1691
MS 9237: Portsoken Ward, poor and CA 1622–78

St Botolph Bishopsgate
MS 4515/1–4: BR 1558–1677
MS 4524/1–2: CA 1567–1662
MS 4526/1: VM 1616–90

St Bride Fleet Street
MS 6540/1: BR 1653–72
MS 6552/1: CA 1639–78
MS 6554/1: VM 1644–65
MS 6570/1: parish papers

St Christopher le Stocks
MS 4424: Record book, 1483 to 18C

St Dionis Backchurch
MS 4215/1: CA 1625–1729

St Dunstan in the East
MS 4887: Record book 1433–1556, and CA 1494–1509

St Dunstan in the West
MS 2968/1–5: CA 1516–1681
MS 3016/1–2: VM 1588–1701
MS 10342–8: BR 1558–1669

St George Botolph Lane
MS 4791: BR 1390–1597

St Giles Cripplegate
MS 6047/1: CA 1648–69
MS 6048/1: VM 1659–1808

St Helen Bishopsgate
MS 6830/1–2: BR 1575–1670
MS 6831/1–2: BR 1598–1630, 1651–86
MS 6836: CA 1565–1654; VM 1558–78
MS 1101: Drawings of tombs, etc.

St Lawrence Pountney
MS 7882/1–2: CA 1635–84

St Margaret Pattens
MS 4570/1–3: CA 1506–1760

St Martin Orgar
MS 959/1: CA 1469–71 and 1550–1707

St Martin Outwich
MS 6842: CA 1508–46
MS 11394/1: CA 1632–1743

St Mary at Hill
MS 1239/1: CA 1420–31, 1477–1559

St Mary Colechurch
MS 64: VM 1612–1701
MS 66: CA 1612–1700
MS 4438: BR 1558–1666

St Mary Magdalen Milk Street
MS 2596/1–2: CA 1518–1667

St Mary Woolnoth
MS 1002/1: CA 1539–1641

St Michael Cornhill
MS 4070/1–2: CA 1455–76, 1547–1702
MS 4072/1: VM 1563–1697

St Michael le Querne
MS 2895/1–2: CA 1514–1717

St Olave Silver Street
MS 6534: BR 1561–1770

St Pancras Soper Lane
MS 5019/1: VM 1626–99

St Peter Westcheap
MS 645/1–2: CA 1435–1702

St Sepulchre
MS 3146/1–2: CA 1648–83
MS 3149/1–2: VM 1653–83

St Stephen Coleman Street
MS 4456: record book, 1466–1832
MS 4457/1–3: CA 1486–1509, 1586–1685

St Stephen Walbrook
MS 593/1–4: CA 1474–1748

St Paul's Cathedral
MS 12190: petition, 1700
MS 19934: lease 1552
MS 25175: copies of presentments
MS 25189: plan of Pardon churchyard, *c.* 1666
MS 25190/8: surveys incl. land near cathedral, 1665
MS 25498: accounts, 1570–84
MS 25499: accounts, 1622–6, 1628–36
MS 25532: verger's notebook, late 16C
MS 25632: Parliamentary surveys
MS 25634: accounts, 1525–6
MS 25635: rough chamberlain's accounts, 1535–6
MS 25636: accounts, 1548–9
MS 25637/1: accounts, 1553–5
MS 25638: accounts, 1592–4
MS 25639: accounts, 1608–10
MS 25641: Receiver-general's accounts, 1663–4
MS 25642: Receiver-general's accounts, 1663–4?
MS 25643/1: chamberlain and receiver-general's accounts, 1666–79
MS 25741: register of burials, 1760–1812

Episcopal administration
MS 9060A: Visitation book, 1662
MS 9531/13, 14: Bishop's registers, 1559–1624, 1604–21
MS 9537/17: Visitations
MS 9538/1: Visitations, 1693
MS 9583/1: Visitations, 1633–40

Livery Company records
MS 5440: Brewers' Company, accounts, 1418–39

Wills
MS 9051: Archdeaconry Court of London, will registers
MS 9171: Commissary Court will registers

Other
MS 204: Nehemiah Wallington, 'A record of god's mercies', 1630
MS 2480/2: MS volume of 'Monumental inscriptions and armorial bearings in
    the churches within the city of London', by A. J. Jewers, 1910–19

GUILDHALL LIBRARY, LONDON: PRINTED BOOKS

Broadsides 12.79, 4.2
Bills of Mortality G. 1.33

LAMBETH PALACE LIBRARY, LONDON

CM (Cartae Miscellanee) VII: Returns to an inquiry *c.* 1635–6 about parish
    government and fees in the city parishes
CM IX/14: St Martin Orgar, CA 1517–1637
CM IX/45: A table of the highest and lowest rates of duties, n.d., ?1592
MS 1485: Monumental inscriptions from London churches, *c.* 1638
MS 3390: Holy Trinity Minories, CA and VM, 1567–1686

LONDON METROPOLITAN ARCHIVE, LONDON

Consistory Court of London, wills and will registers

PUBLIC RECORD OFFICE, LONDON

PROB 11: Wills
SP 46/7: Johnson family correspondence

PRINTED PRIMARY SOURCES

[Anon.], 'Of the Antiquitye of Ceremonies used at Funerals in England'
    [9 February 1599/1600], in *A Collection of Curious Discourses written by*

eminent Antiquaries upon several heads in our English Antiquities, together with Mr Thomas Hearne's preface and appendix to the former edition 2 vols. (London: Benjamin White, 1775), vol. I

Arnold, Richard, *The customs of London, otherwise called Arnold's Chronicle, containing among divers other matters the original of the celebrated poem of the Nut-Brown maid* (London: privately printed, 1811)

Aubrey's Brief Lives, ed. O. L. Dick (London: Secker and Warburg, 1958)

Balmford, J., *A Short Dialogue concerning the Plagues Infection* (London, 1603)

Basing, P. (ed.), *Parish fraternity register: Fraternity of the Holy Trinity and SS. Fabian and Sebastian in the parish of St Botolph without Aldersgate* (London Record Society 18, 1982)

Beaune, C. (ed.), *Journal d'un bourgeois de Paris* (Paris: Livres de Poche, 1990)

Bertillon, J., *Des recensements de la population: de la nuptualité, de la natalité, et de la mortalité à Paris pendant le XIX siècle et les époques antérieures* (Paris, Imprimerie Municipale, 1907; Annexe à l'Annuaire statistique de la ville de Paris pour 1905), pp. 11–15

Brièle, L., *Collection de documents pour servir à l'histoire des hôpitaux de Paris*, 4 vols. (Paris: Imprimerie Nationale, 1881–7)

Brièle, L. and M. A. Husson, *Inventaire-sommaire des archives hospitalières antérieures à 1790. Hôtel-Dieu*, 2 vols. (Paris: Imprimerie Nationale, 1866, 1884)

Brigg, W. (ed.), *The register book of the parish of St Nicholas Acons, London, 1539–1812* (Leeds: Walker and Laycock, 1890)

Brooke, J. M. S. and A. W. C. Hallen, *The transcript of the Registers of the united parishes of St Mary Woolnoth and St Mary Woolchurch haw in the city of London, 1538–1760* (London: Bowles and Sons, 1886)

Browne, Sir Thomas, 'Hydriotaphia. Urne-buriall, or a brief discourse of the Sepulchrall Urnes lately found in Norfolk', in L. C. Martin (ed.), *Sir Thomas Browne. Religio Medici and other works* (Oxford: Clarendon Press, 1964), pp. 90–125

Burgess, C. (ed.), *The church records of St Andrew Hubbard Eastcheap, c. 1450–1570* (London Record Society 34, 1999)

Byrne, M. St.-C. (ed.), *The Lisle letters*, 6 vols. (Chicago: University of Chicago Press, 1981)

Calendar of State Papers Domestic, 1654 (HMSO)

Collectanea topographica et genealogica, 8 vols. (London: John Bowyer Nichols and Son, 1834–43)

A collection of the yearly Bills of Mortality from 1657 to 1758 inclusive (London, printed for A. Millar in the Strand, 1759)

Commission municipale du vieux Paris, année 1904. Procès-verbaux (Paris: Imprimerie Municipale, 1905), pp. 55–118

Corrozet, G. and N. B[onfons], *Les antiquitiez, histoires, croniques et singularitez de la grande et excellente cité de Paris...Avec les fondations et bastiments des lieux: les sepulchres et epitaphes des princes, princesses et autres personnes illustres* (Paris: Nicolas Bonfons, 1597)

Dale, T. C. (ed.), *The inhabitants of London in 1638* (London: Society of Genealogists, 1931)

Darlington, I (ed.), *London Consistory Court wills, 1492–1547* (London Record Society 3, 1967)

Defoe, D., *Journal of the plague year, being observations or memorials of the most remarkable occurrences, as well public as private, which happened in London during the last great visitation in 1665* (Harmondsworth: Penguin Classics edn, 1966; reprinted 1987)

Dekker, Thomas, *The wonderful year* (1603), in Wilson (ed.), *The Plague Pamphlets of Thomas Dekker*, pp. 28–9

   A rod for run-awaies (1625), in Wilson (ed.), *The Plague Pamphlets of Thomas Dekker*, pp. 158–9

Delamare, N., *Traité de la police, où l'on trouvera l'histoire de son établissement, les fonctions et les prérogatives de ses magistrats, toutes les lois et les règlements qui la concernent* (2nd printed edn., Paris: 1722–38)

Dérens, J., *Plan de Paris par Truschet et Hoyau 1550, dit Plan de Bâle 1552–9* (Zurich: Seefeld, 1980)

Dufour, Abbé V., *La danse macabre des Saints-Innocents à Paris* (Paris: L. Willem, 1874)

Dugdale, Sir William, *The history of St Paul's Cathedral in London* (1st edn, 1658) *with a continuation and additions by Henry Ellis* (London: Longman, Hurst, Rees, Orme and Brown, 1818)

The endowed charities of the city of London, reprinted . . . from 17 reports of the Commissioners for inquiring concerning charities (London: M. Sherwood, 1829)

Evelyn, John, *The diary of John Evelyn*, ed. J. Bowle (Oxford: Oxford University Press, The World's Classics, 1985)

Fisher, Payne, *The tombes, monuments and sepulchral inscriptions lately visible in St Paul's Cathedral (and St Faith's beneath it) previous to its destruction* (London: printed for the author, 1684; reprinted edition by G. Blacker Morgan, London: privately reprinted, 1885)

Frere, W. H. (ed.), *Visitation articles and injunctions of the period of the Reformation*, 3 vols. (London: Alcuin Club Collections, Longmans, Green and Co., 1910)

Freshfield, E. (ed.), *Accomptes of the churchwardens of the paryshe of St Christofer's in London*, 2 vols. (London: Rixon and Arnold, 1885–95)

   Minutes of the vestry meetings and other records of the parish of St Christopher le Stocks in the city of London (London: Rixon and Arnold, 1886)

   The vestry minute book of the parish of St Margaret Lothbury in the city of London, 1571–1677 (London: Rixon and Arnold, 1887)

   The account books of the parish of St Bartholomew Exchange in the city of London, 1596–1698 (London: Rixon and Arnold, 1895)

Giese, L. L., *London Consistory Court depositions, 1586–1611: list and indexes* (London Record Society 32, 1995)

Glass, D. V. (ed.), *London inhabitants within the walls, 1695* (London Record Society 2, 1966)

Graunt, John, 'Natural and political observations upon the Bills of Mortality' (1676), in Hull (ed.), *The economic writings of Sir William Petty, together with observations on the Bills of Mortality*, vol. II, pp. 314–435

Hill, G. W. and W. H. Frere, *Memorials of Stepney parish. That is to say the vestry Minutes from 1579 to 1662, now first printed with an introduction and notes* (Guildford: Billing and Sons, 1890–1)

Howard, J. J. and J. L. Chester (eds.), *The visitation of London anno domini 1633, 1634, and 1635*, 2 vols. (London: Harl. Soc., 15, 17, 1880, 1883)

Howarth, W. D., *Life and letters in France*, vol. I: *The seventeenth century* (London: Nelson, 1965)

Howgego, J., *Printed maps of London, c. 1553–1850* (Folkestone: Dawson, 1978)

Hughes, P. L. and J. F. Larkin (eds.), *Tudor royal proclamations*, 3 vols. (New Haven: Yale University Press, 1969)

Hull, C. H. (ed.), *The economic writings of Sir William Petty, together with observations on the Bills of Mortality*, 2 vols. (New York: Kelly Reprint, 1963–4)

Jupp, E. B. and R. Hovenden (eds.), *The registers of christenings, marriages and burials of the parish of Allhallows London Wall within the city of London, from the year of Our Lord 1559 to 1675* (London: Chiswick Press, 1878)

Kitching, C. J. (ed.), *The London and Middlesex chantry certificate of 1548* (London Record Society 16, 1980)

Kitto, J. V. (ed.), *St Martin in the Fields: the accounts of the churchwardens, 1525–1603* (London: Simpkin Marshall Kent Hamilton and Co., 1901)

Larkin, J. F. and P. L. Hughes (eds.), *Stuart royal proclamations*, vol. I: *Royal proclamations of King James I, 1603–1635* (Oxford: Clarendon Press, 1973)

Lebeuf, J., *Histoire de la ville et de tout le diocèse de Paris*, new edn. by H. Cocheris, 3 vols. (Paris, 1863–7)

Lestoile, Pierre de, *Journal de L'Estoile pour le règne de Henri III, 1574–89*, ed. L. R. Lefèvre (Paris: Gallimard, 1943)

Journal de L'Estoile pour le règne de Henri IV, ed. L. R. Lefèvre and A. Martin, 2 vols. (Paris: Gallimard, 1948, 1958)

Lewis, Thomas, *Seasonable considerations on the indecent and dangerous custom of burying in churches and church-yards, with remarkable observations, historical and philosophical, proving that the custom is not only contrary to the practice of the Ancients but fatal in case of infection* (London, 1721)

Lindley, K. and D. Scott (eds.), *The journal of Thomas Juxon, 1644–1647* (London: Camden Society 5th series 13, 1999)

Littlehales, H. (ed.), *Medieval records of a London city church, A.D. 1420–1559* [St Mary at Hill] (London: Early English Text Society original series, 125, 128, 1904–5)

Lyell, L. and F. D. Watney (eds.), *Acts of Court of the Mercers Company, 1453–1527* (Cambridge: Cambridge University Press, 1936)

Machyn, Henry, *The diary of Henry Machyn, citizen and merchant-taylor of London, from A.D. 1550 to A.D. 1563*, ed. J. G. Nichols (London: Camden Society 42, 1848)

MacLure, M., *Register of sermons preached at Paul's Cross, 1534–1642* (Ottawa: University of Toronto Centre for Reformation and Renaissance Studies, Occasional Publications vol. VI, 1989)

Maitland, W., *The history and survey of London from its foundation to the present time*, 2 vols. (London: T. Osborne, J. Shipton, and J. Hodges, 1756)

Marsh, B. (ed.), *Records of the Carpenters' Company*, vol. IV: *Wardens' account book, 1546–71* (Oxford: Oxford University Press, 1916)

Masters, B. R., *The public markets of the city of London surveyed by William Leybourn in 1677* (London: London Topographical Society, 1974)

Masters, B. R. (ed.), *Chamber accounts of the sixteenth century* (London Record Society 20, 1984)

McClure, N. E. (ed.), *The letters of John Chamberlain*, 2 vols. (Philadelphia: American Philosophical Society, 1939)

McMurray, W., *The records of two city parishes: a collection of documents illustrative of the history of SS Anne and Agnes, Aldersgate, and St John Zachary, London* (London: Hunter and Longhurst Ltd, 1925)

Munday, Anthony, et al., *The Survey of London . . . begun first by the Paines and Industry of Iohn Stow, in the yeere 1598 . . . And now completely finished by the study and labour of A.M., H.D. and others, this present yeere 1633* (London: Elizabeth Purslow, 1633)

Newcourt, R., *Repertorium ecclesiasticum Parochiale Londinense*, 2 vols. (London: printed by Benj. Motte, 1708–10)

Nichols, J., *Illustrations of the manners and expences of antient times in England, in the fifteenth, sixteenth, and seventeenth centuries, deduced from the accompts of churchwardens and other authentic documents collected from various parts of the kingdom, with explanatory notes* (London: printed by and for J. Nichols, 1797)

The Progresses and public processions of Queen Elizabeth, among which are interspersed other solemnities, public expenditures, and remarkable events during the reign of that illustrious princess, 3 vols. (London: printed by and for J. Nichols, 1823)

Overall, W. H. (ed.), *The accounts of the churchwardens of the parish of St Michael Cornhill, 1456–1608* (London: Alfred James Waterlow, 1871)

Overall, W. H. and H. C. Overall, *Analytical index to the series of records known as the Remembrancia preserved among the archives of the City of London, A.D. 1579–1664* (London: E. J. Francis and Co., 1878)

Pepys, Samuel, *The Diary of Samuel Pepys, 1660–69*, ed. R. Latham and W. Matthews, 11 vols. (London: Bell and Hyman, 1970–83)

Petty, W., 'Five essays in political arithmetick' (1686/7), reprinted in Hull (ed.), *The economic writings of Sir William Petty, together with observations on the Bills of Mortality*, vol. II, pp. 519–44

'Two essays in political arithmetick concerning the people, housing, hospitals, etc. of London and Paris' (1687), reprinted in Hull (ed.), *The economic writings of Sir William Petty, together with observations on the Bills of Mortality*, vol. II, pp. 501–13

Port, M. H. (ed.), *The commissions for building fifty new churches* (London Record Society 23, 1986)

Powicke, F. M. and C. R. Cheney (eds.), *Councils and synods with other documents relating to the English church*, vol. II: A.D. 1205–1313 (Oxford: Clarendon Press, 1964)

Prockter, A. and R. Taylor (eds.), *The A to Z of Elizabethan London* (London: London Topographical Society, 1979)

Registers of All Hallows Bread Street (1538–1892) and of St John the Evangelist, Friday Street (1653–1822) (London: Harl. Soc. Register Section 43, 1913)

Registers of Christ Church Newgate Street, 1538–1754 (London: Harl. Soc. Register Section 21, 1895)

Registers of St Antholin, Budge Row (1538–1754) and of St John the Baptist upon Walbrook (1682–1754) (London: Harl. Soc. Register Section 8, 1883)

Registers of St Benet and St Peter Paul's Wharf, 4 vols. (London: Harl. Soc. Register Section 38–41, 1909–12)

Registers of St Clement Eastcheap and St Martin Orgar, 1539–1853, 2 vols. (London: Harl. Soc. Register Section 67–8, 1937–8)

Registers of St Dionis Backchurch, 1538–74 (London: Harl. Soc. Register Section 3, 1878)

Registers of St Helen Bishopsgate, 1575–1837 (London: Harl. Soc. Register Section 31, 1904)

Registers of St Lawrence [Jewry], 1538–1812, and St Mary Magdalen Milk Street, 1677–1812, 2 vols. (London: Harl. Soc. Register Section 70–1, 1940–1)

Registers of St Mary Aldermary, 1558–1754 (London: Harl. Soc. Register Section 5, 1880)

Registers of St Mary le Bow, All Hallows Honey Lane, and St Pancras Soper Lane 1538–1852, 2 vols. (London: Harl. Soc. Register Section 44–5, 1914–15)

Registers of St Mary Magdalen, 1558–1666, and St Michael Bassishaw, 1538–1892, 3 vols. (London: Harl. Soc. Register Section 72–4, 1942–4)

Registers of St Mary Mounthaw, 1568–1849 (London: Harl. Soc. Register Section 58, 1928)

Registers of St Mary Somerset, 1557–1853, 2 vols. (London: Harl. Soc. Register Section 59–60, 1929–30)

Registers of St Mary the Virgin Aldermanbury, 1538–1859, 3 vols. (London: Harl. Soc. Register Section 61–2, 65, 1931–5)

Registers of St Mildred Bread Street [1658–1853] and St Margaret Moses, Friday Street [1558–1650] (London: Harl. Soc. Register Section 42, 1912)

Registers of St Michael Cornhill, 1546–1754 (London: Harl. Soc. Register Section 7, 1882)

Registers of St Olave [Hart Street], 1563–1700 (London: Harl. Soc. Register Section 46, 1916)

Registers of St Peter Cornhill, 1538–1774, 2 vols. (London: Harl. Soc. Register Section 1, 4, 1877–9)

Registers of St Stephen Walbrook and St Benet Sherehog [1547–1860], 2 vols. (London: Harl. Soc. Register Section 49–50, 1919–20)

Registers of St Thomas the Apostle, 1558–1754 (London: Harl. Soc. Register Section 6, 1881)

Registers of St Vedast (1558–1836) and St Michael le Quern (1685–1836), 2 vols. (London: Harl. Soc. Register Section 29–30, 1902–3)

Registres des délibérations du Bureau de la Ville de Paris, ed. F. Bonnardot, A. Tuetey, P. Guérin, et al., 20 vols. (Paris: Histoire Général de Paris, Imprimerie Nationale, 1883–1990)

Report from the Select Committee on the improvement of the health of towns (Parl. Papers 1842 (X), no. 327)

Schofield, J., *The London surveys of Ralph Treswell* (London Topographical Society, 1987)

Sharpe, R. R. (ed.), *Calendar of wills proved and enrolled in the Court of Husting, 1258–1688,* 2 vols. (London: Corporation of London, 1889–90)

Simpson, W. S. (ed.), *Registrum Statutorum et consuetudinum Ecclesiae Cathedralis Sancti Pauli Londiniensis* (London: Nichols and Sons, 1873)

Sims, J. M., *London and Middlesex published records, a handlist* (London Record Society, Occasional Publications 1, 1970)

Smyth, Richard, *The Obituary of Richard Smyth, Secondary of the Poultry Compter, London, being a catalogue of all such persons as he knew in their life, extending from AD 1627 to AD 1674*, ed. H. Ellis (London: Camden Society 44, 1849)

Spelman, Sir Henry, *De sepultura*, in *The English works of Sir Henry Spelman, kt., published in his lifetime, together with his posthumous works relating to the laws and antiquities of England . . . together with the life of the author now revised* (London: D. Browne, W. Mears, F. Clay, etc., 1723)

Stanford London, H. and S. W. Rawlins (eds.), *Visitation of London, 1568*, 2 vols. (London: Harl. Soc. 109–10, 1963)

Stow, John, *A Survey of London* (1603), ed. C. L. Kingsford, 2 vols. (Oxford: Oxford University Press, 1908; reprinted 1968)

Strype, John, *A survey of the cities of London and Westminster . . . written at first in the year MDXCVIII by John Stow . . . now lately corrected, improved and very much Enlarged . . . by John Strype*, 2 vols. (London: A. Churchill, J. Knapton, R. Knaplock, J. Walthoe, E. Horne, B. Tooke, D. Midwinter, B. Cowse, R. Robinson, and T. Ward, 1720)

Tate, Mr, 'Of the Antiquity, Variety and Ceremonies of Funerals in England' [30 April 1600], in *A Collection of Curious Discourses written by eminent Antiquaries upon several heads in our English Antiquities, together with Mr Thomas Hearne's preface and appendix to the former edition*, 2 vols. (London: Benjamin White, 1775), vol. I

Thomassin, L., *Ancienne et nouvelle discipline de l'église, touchant les Bénéfices et les Bénéficiers*, 3 vols. (Paris, 1725)

Walker, G. A., *Gatherings from graveyards, particularly those of London, with a concise history of the modes of interment among different Nations from the earliest periods and a detail of the dangerous and fatal results produced by the unwise and revolting custom of inhuming the dead in the midst of the living* (London: 1839)

Walters, H. B., *London churches at the Reformation* (London: SPCK/Church History Society, 1939)

Waters, R. E. C., *Parish registers in England, their history and contents, with suggestions for securing their better custody and preservation* (London: Longmans, Green and Co., 1887)

Weever, J., *Antient funeral monuments of Great Britiain, Ireland and the islands adjacent . . . whereunto is prefixed a discourse on funeral monuments* [1631] (London: W. Tooke, 1767)

Welch, C. (ed.), *Churchwardens' accounts of the parish of All Hallows London Wall, 1455–1536* (London: Blades, 1912)

Whitmore, J. B. and A. W. Hughes Clarke (eds.), *London visitation pedigrees, 1664* (London: Harl. Soc. 92, 1940)

Wilson, F. P. (ed.), *The Plague Pamphlets of Thomas Dekker* (Oxford: Clarendon Press, 1925)

SECONDARY WORKS

Adams, R. H., *The parish clerks of London. A history of the Worshipful Company of Parish Clerks of London* (London: Phillimore, 1971)

Alsop, J. D., 'Religious preambles in early modern English wills as formulae', *Journal of Ecclesiastical History* 40 (1989), 19–27

Anglo, S., *Images of Tudor kingship* (London: Seaby, 1992)

Appleby, A. B., 'Nutrition and disease, the case of London, 1550–1750', *Journal of Interdisciplinary History* 6 (1975), 1–22

  Famine in Tudor and Stuart England (Liverpool: Liverpool University Press, 1978)

  'The disappearance of plague – a continuing puzzle', *Economic History Review*, 2nd ser. 33 (1980), pp. 161–73

Archer, I. W., *The pursuit of stability. Social relations in Elizabethan London* (Cambridge: Cambridge University Press, 1991)

  'The government of London, 1500–1650', *London Journal* 26 (2001), pp. 19–28

Ariès, P., *The hour of our death*, translated by Helen Weaver (London: Peregrine Books, 1983); originally published in France as *L'homme devant la mort* (Paris: Editions du Seuil, 1977)

Arnold, A. P., 'A list of Jews and their households in London, extracted from the census lists of 1695', *Jewish Historical Society of England, Transactions* 24 (1970–3), 134–50

Atkinson, A. G. B., *St Botolph Aldgate, the story of a city parish* (London: Richards, 1898)

Babelon, J.-P., *Nouvelle histoire de Paris. Paris au XVIe siècle* (Paris: Hachette, 1986)

Ballon, H., *The Paris of Henri IV. Architecture and urbanism* (New York and Cambridge, Mass.: Architectural History Foundation and MIT Press, 1991)

Banker, J. R., *Death in the community. Memorialization and confraternities in an Italian commune in the late Middle Ages* (Athens, Ga.: University of Georgia Press, 1988)

Barker, F. and P. Jackson, *London, 2000 years of a city and its people* (London: Papermac, 1983)

Barroll, L., *Politics, plague and Shakespeare's theater, the Stuart years* (Ithaca and London: Cornell University Press, 1991)

Barron, C. M., 'The parish fraternities of medieval London', in C. M. Barron and C. Harper-Bill (eds.), *The church in pre-Reformation society. Essays in honour of F. R. H. du Boulay* (Woodbridge: Boydell Press, 1985), pp. 13–37

  'Centres of conspicuous consumption: the aristocratic town house in London, 1200–1550', *London Journal* 20 (1995), 1–16

Barron, C. M. and J. Roscoe, 'The medieval parish church of St Andrew Holborn', *London Topographical Record* 24 (1980), 55–9

Barroux, M., *Les sources de l'ancien Etat civil Parisien. Répertoire critique* (Paris: 1898)

Bassett, S. R. (ed.), *Death in towns. Urban responses to the dying and the dead, 100–1600* (Leicester: Leicester University Press, 1992)

Beaven, A. B., *The aldermen of the city of London, temp. Henry III–1908*, 2 vols. (London: Corporation of London, 1908, 1913)

Beier, A. L. and Finlay, R. (eds.), *London 1500–1700, the making of the metropolis* (London: Longman, 1986)

Beier, L. M., 'The good death in seventeenth-century England', in Houlbrooke (ed.), *Death, ritual and bereavement*, pp. 43–61

Bell, W. G., *The great plague in London in 1665* (London: John Lane, The Bodley Head, 1924)

Benedict, P., *'Un roi, une loi, deux fois:* parameters for the history of a Catholic–Reformed coexistence in France, 1555–1685', in O. P. Grell and B. Scribner (eds.), *Tolerance and intolerance in the European Reformation* (Cambridge: Cambridge University Press 1996), pp. 65–93

Benedict, P. (ed.), *Cities and social change in early modern France* (London: Routledge, 1992)

Bergeron, D. M., *English civic pageantry, 1558–1642* (London: Edward Arnold, 1971)

Bernard, L., *The emerging city. Paris in the age of Louis XIV* (Durham, N.C.: Duke University Press, 1970)

Berty, A., H. Legrand, and L. M. Tisserand, *Topographie historique du vieux Paris*, 6 vols. (Paris: Histoire Général de Paris, 1866–97)

Binski, P., *Medieval death: ritual and representation* (London: British Museum Press, 1996)

Biraben, J. N., *Les hommes et la peste en France et dans les pays européens et méditerranéens*, 2 vols. (Paris: Ecole des Hautes Etudes en Sciences Sociales, Centre de Recherches Historiques, 1975–6)

Bird, R., *The turbulent London of Richard II* (London: Longmans, Green, 1949)

Blayney, P. W. M., *The bookshops in Paul's Cross churchyard* (London: The Bibliographical Society, 1990)

Blench, J. W., *Preaching in England in the late fifteenth and sixteenth centuries: a study of English sermons, 1450–c. 1600* (Oxford: Blackwell, 1964)

Bloch, M. and J. Parry, 'Introduction', to M. Bloch and J. Parry (eds.), *Death and the regeneration of life* (Cambridge: Cambridge University Press, 1982), pp. 1–44

Boase, T. S. R., *Death in the Middle Ages: mortality, judgment, and remembrance* (London: Thames and Hudson, 1972)

Bos, S., M. Lange-Meijers, and J. Six, 'Sidney's funeral portrayed', in J. van Dorsten, D. Baker-Smith, and A. F. Kinney, *Sir Philip Sidney: 1586 and the creation of a legend* (Leiden: Leiden University Press, 1986), pp. 38–61

Bossy, J., *Christianity in the West, 1400–1700* (Oxford: Oxford University Press, 1985)

Boulter, C. B., *History of St Andrew Undershaft, St Mary Axe, in the City of London*; with a description of the monuments and coloured glass therein (London: privately printed, 1935)

Boulton, J., *Neighbourhood and society. A London suburb in the seventeenth century* (Cambridge: Cambridge University Press, 1987)

'London widowhood revisited: the decline of female remarriage in the 17th and early 18th centuries', *Continuity and Change* 5 (1990), 323–55

'Wage labour in seventeenth-century London', *Economic History Review* 49 (1996) 268–90

'Food prices and the standard of living in London in the "century of revolution", 1580–1700', *Economic History Review* 53 (2000), 455–92

'London', in P. Clark (ed.), *Cambridge urban history of Britain*, vol. II: *1540–1840* (Cambridge: Cambridge University Press, 2000), pp. 315–46

Brett-James, N. G., *The growth of Stuart London* (London: G. Allen and Unwin, 1935)

Brigden, S., 'Tithe controversy in Reformation London', *Journal of Ecclesiastical History* 32 (1981), 285–301

London and the Reformation (Oxford: Clarendon Press, 1989)

Briggs, R., *Communities of belief. Cultural and social tensions in early modern France* (Oxford: Clarendon Paperbacks, 1995)

Brochard, L., *Saint-Gervais. Histoire du monument, d'après de nombreux documents inédits* (Paris: Desclée de Brouwer, 1938)

Saint-Gervais. Histoire de la paroisse, d'après de nombreux documents inédits (Paris: Firmin-Dodat, 1950)

Brockliss, L. and C. Jones, *The medical world of early modern France* (Oxford: Clarendon Press, 1997)

Brodsky, V., 'Widows in late Elizabethan London: remarriage, economic opportunity and family orientations', in L. Bonfield, R. Smith, and K. Wrightson (eds.), *The world we have gained* (Oxford: Blackwell, 1986), pp. 122–54

Brooke, C. N. L. and G. Keir, *London 800–1215: the shaping of a city* (London: Martin Secker and Warburg, 1975)

Brown, E. A. R., 'Burying and unburying the kings of France', in E. A. R. Brown, *The monarchy of Capetian France and royal ceremonial* (Aldershot: Variorum, 1991), pp. 241–66

'Death and the human body in the later Middle Ages: the legislation of Boniface VIII on the division of the corpse', in E. A. R. Brown, *The monarchy of Capetian France and royal ceremonial* (Aldershot: Variorum, 1991), pp. 221–70

Burgess, C., ' "A fond thing vainly invented": an essay on purgatory and pious motive in later medieval England', in S. Wright (ed.), *Parish, church and people: local studies in lay religion, 1350–1750* (London: Hutchinson, 1988), pp. 56–84

'Late medieval wills and pious convention: testamentary evidence reconsidered', in M. Hicks (ed.), *Profit, piety and the professions in later medieval England* (Gloucester: Alan Sutton, 1990), pp. 14–33

'Shaping the parish: St Mary at Hill, London, in the fifteenth century', in J. Blair and B. Golding (eds.), *The cloister and the world: essays in medieval history in honour of Barbara Harvey* (Oxford: Clarendon Press, 1996), pp. 246–86

Bynum, C. Walker, *The resurrection of the body in western Christianity, 200–1336* (New York: Columbia University Press, 1995)

Camp, A. J., *Wills and their whereabouts* (London: published by the author, 1963)

Campbell, B. M. S., J. A. Galloway, D. Keene, and M. Murphy, *A medieval city and its grain supply: agrarian production and distribution in the London region c. 1300* (London: Historical Geography Research Paper Series 30, 1993)

Cannadine, D., 'War and death, grief and mourning in modern Britain', in Whaley (ed.), *Mirrors of mortality*, pp. 196–202

Carlin, M., *Medieval Southwark* (London: Hambledon Press, 1996)

Chalumeau, R. P., 'L'assistance aux malades pauvres au XVIIe Siècle', *XVIIe Siècle* 90–1 (1971), 75–86

Champion, J. A. I., *London's dreaded visitation. The social geography of the great plague in 1665* (London: Historical Geography Research Paper Series 31, 1995)

Champion, J. A. I. (ed.), *Epidemic disease in London* (London: Centre for Metropolitan History Working Paper Series 1, 1993)

Chapman, R., I. Kinnes, and K. Randsborg, *The archaeology of death* (Cambridge: Cambridge University Press, 1981)

Chaunu, P., *La mort à Paris: XVIe, XVIIe, XVIIIe siècles* (Paris: Fayard, 1978)

Chaunu, P., M. Foisil, and F. de Noirfontaine, *Le basculement religieux de Paris au XVIIIe siècle* (Paris: Fayard, 1998)

Cherry, B., 'New types of late medieval tombs in the London area', in L. M. Grant (ed.), *Medieval art, architecture, and archaeology in London* (London: British Archaeological Association Conference Transactions, 1990), pp. 140–54

Christie, J., *Some account of the Parish Clerks, more especially of the ancient fraternity (bretherne and sisterne) of S. Nicholas now known as the Worshipful Company of Parish Clerks* (London: privately printed, 1893)

Cobb, R., *Death in Paris: the records of the Basse-Géole de la Seine, October 1795–September 1801* (Oxford: Oxford University Press, 1978)

Cohen, K., *Metamorphosis of a death symbol. The transi tomb in the late middle ages and the Renaissance* (Berkeley and London: University of California Press, 1973)

Collinson, P., *The Elizabethan Puritan movement* (London: Jonathan Cape, 1967; reprinted in paperback, Oxford: Clarendon Press, 1967)

Colvin, H. M., *Architecture and the afterlife* (London: Yale University Press, 1991)

[Corporation of London] *Bunhill Fields Burial Ground: proceedings in reference to its preservation, with the inscriptions on the tombs* (London: Hamilton Adams and Co., 1867)

Couzy, H., 'L'église des Saints-Innocents à Paris', *Bulletin Monumental* 130 (1972), 279–303

Cox, J. E., *The annals of St Helen Bishopsgate* (London: Tinsley, 1876)

Cox, M., *Life and death in Spitalfields, 1700–1850* (York: Council for British Archaeology, 1996)

Cox, M. (ed.), *Grave concerns: death and burial in England, 1700–1850* (York: Council for British Archaeology, Research Report 113, 1998)

Cressy, D., *Bonfires and bells: national memory and the Protestant calendar in Elizabethan and Stuart England* (London: Weidenfeld and Nicolson, 1989)

'Death and the social order: the funerary preferences of Elizabethan gentlemen', *Continuity and Change* 5 (1989), 99–119

Birth, marriage and death. Ritual, religion and the life-cycle in Tudor and Stuart England (Oxford: Oxford University Press, 1997)

Crouzet, D., *Les guerriers de Dieu: la violence au temps des troubles de religion (vers 1525–vers 1610)* (Seyssel, France: Champ Vallon, 1990)

Daniell, C., *Death and burial in medieval England* (London: Routledge, 1997)

Davis, N. Z., 'The rites of violence', in N. Z. Davis, *Society and culture in early modern France* (Stanford: Stanford University Press, 1975)

de Certeau, M., *The practice of everyday life*, translated by S. Rendall (Berkeley: University of California Press, 1984)

de Viguerie, J. and E. Saive-Lever, 'Essai pour une géographie socio-professionelle de Paris dans la première moitié du XVIIe siècle', *Revue d'Histoire Moderne et Contemporaine* 20 (1973), 424–9

Descimon, R., 'Paris on the eve of Saint Bartholomew: taxation, privilege and social geography', in Benedict (ed.), *Cities and social change in early modern France*, pp. 69–104

Descimon, R. and J. Nagle, 'Les quartiers de Paris du Moyen Age au XVIIIe siècle. Evolution d'un espace plurifonctionnel', *Annales ESC* 34 (1979), 956–83

Dethan, G., *Nouvelle histoire de Paris. Paris au temps de Louis XIV* (Paris: Hachette, 1990)

Diamond, A. S., 'The community of the resettlement, 1656–84', *Jewish Historical Society of England, Miscellany* pt. 6 (1962), 73–141

Diefendorf, B., *Paris city councillors in the sixteenth century. The politics of patrimony* (Princeton: Princeton University Press, 1983)

    Beneath the cross. Catholics and Protestant in sixteenth-century Paris (Oxford: Oxford University Press, 1991)

Dinn, R., 'Death and rebirth in medieval Bury St Edmunds', in Bassett (ed.), *Death in towns*, pp. 151–69

Duby, G. (ed.), *Histoire de la France urbaine*, 5 vols. (Paris: Seuil, 1980–5)

Duffy, E., *The stripping of the altars: traditional religion in England, c. 1400–1580* (New Haven: Yale University Press, 1992)

Durston, C. and J. Eales (eds.), *The culture of English Puritanism, 1560–1700* (Basingstoke: Macmillan, 1996)

Dyer, A., 'The English sweating sickness of 1551. An epidemic anatomized', *Medical History* 41 (1997), 361–83

Dymond, D., 'God's disputed acre', *Journal of Ecclesiastical History* 50 (1999), 464–97

Earle, P., *The making of the English middle class: business, society and family life in London, 1660–1730* (London: Methuen, 1989)

Etlin, R. A., *The architecture of death: the transformation of the cemetery in eighteenth-century Paris* (Cambridge, Mass.: MIT Press, 1984)

Favier, J., *Nouvelle histoire de Paris. Paris au XVe siècle, 1380–1500* (Paris: Hachette, 1974)

Fenn, R. K., *The persistence of purgatory* (Cambridge: Cambridge University Press, 1995)

Finlay, R., *Population and metropolis, the demography of London 1580–1650* (Cambridge: Cambridge University Press, 1981)

Finlay, R. and B. Shearer, 'Population growth and suburban expansion', in Beier and Finlay (eds.), *London 1500–1700, the making of the metropolis*, pp. 37–59

Fisher, F. J., 'Influenza and inflation in Tudor England', *Economic History Review* 2nd. ser. 18 (1965), 120–9

Foisil, M., 'Les attitudes devant la mort au XVIIIe siècle: sépultures et suppressions de sépultures dans le cimetière parisien des Saints-Innocents', *Revue Historique* 251 (1974), 303–30

Forbes, T. R., *Chronicle from Aldgate: life and death in Shakespeare's London* (New Haven: Yale University Press, 1971)

'By what disease or casualty: the changing face of death in London', in C. Webster (ed.), *Health, medicine and mortality in the sixteeenth century* (Cambridge: Cambridge University Press, 1979), pp. 117–40

Fosseyeux, M., *L'Hôtel-Dieu de Paris au XVIIe et XVIIIe siècles* (Paris: Berger-Levrault, 1912)

'Les épidémies de peste à Paris', *Bulletin de la Société Française d'Histoire de la Médicine*, 12.2 (1913), 115–41

Foster, F. F., *The politics of stability. A portrait of the rulers in Elizabethan London* (London: Royal Historical Society, 1977)

Friedmann, A., *Paris, ses rues, ses paroisses du Moyen Age à la Revolution. Origine et évolution des circonscriptions paroissiales* (Paris: Plon, 1959)

Fritz, P. S., 'From "public" to "private": the royal funerals in England, 1500–1830', in Whaley (ed.), *Mirrors of mortality*, pp. 61–79

Garrioch, D., *Neighbourhood and community in Paris, 1740–1790* (Cambridge: Cambridge University Press, 1986)

The formation of the Parisian bourgeoisie, 1690–1830 (Cambridge, Mass. and London: Harvard University Press, 1996)

Gasnault, F., 'Les archives de Paris: mutilation, démembrement, recomposition', in M. V. Roberts (ed.), *Archives and the metropolis* (London: Corporation of London, 1998), pp. 43–9

Geary, P. J., *Living with the dead in the Middle Ages* (Ithaca and London: Cornell University Press, 1994)

Gentles, I., 'Political funerals during the English Revolution', in S. Porter (ed.), *London and the Civil War* (London: Macmillan, 1996), pp. 205–24

George, D. M., *London life in the eighteenth century* (London: Kegan Paul, 1925; republished Harmondsworth: Penguin, 1966)

Geremek, B., *The margins of society in late medieval Paris* (Cambridge: Cambridge University Press, 1987)

Giesey, R., *The royal funeral ceremony in Renaissance France* (Geneva: E. Droz, 1960)

'The Presidents of Parlement at the royal funeral', *Sixteenth-Century Journal* 7 (1976), 25–34

Gittings, C., *Death, burial and the individual in early modern England* (London: Croom Helm, 1984)

'Urban funerals in late medieval and Reformation England', in Bassett (ed.), *Death in towns*, pp. 170–83

Glass, D. V., 'Notes on the demography of London at the end of the seventeenth century', in Glass and Revelle (eds.), *Population and Social Change*, pp. 275–86

Glass, D. V. and R. Revelle (eds.), *Population and social change* (London: Edward Arnold, 1972)

Golden, R. M., *The godly rebellion. Parisian curés and the religious Fronde, 1652–1662* (Chapel Hill: University of North Carolina Press, 1981)

Gordon, B. and P. Marshall (eds.), *The place of the dead. Death and remembrance in late medieval and early modern Europe* (Cambridge: Cambridge University Press, 2000)

Gower, G. W. G. L., *Genealogy of the family of Gresham* (London: printed for private circulation, 1883)

Grainger, I. and Duncan Hawkins, with Paul Falcini and Peter Mills, 'Excavations at the Royal Mint Site, 1986–88', *The London Archaeologist* 5.16 (Autumn 1988), 429–36

Greengrass, M., *France in the age of Henri IV. The struggle for stability* (Harlow: Longman, 1984)

The French Reformation (Oxford: Basil Blackwell, 1987)

Gwynn, R. D., *Huguenot heritage. the history and contribution of the Huguenots in Britain* (London: Routledge, 1985)

Hadwin, J. F., 'Deflating philanthropy', *Economic History Review* 2nd ser. 31 (1978), 105–17

Haigh, C., *English Reformations: religion, politics, and society under the Tudors* (Oxford: Clarendon Press, 1993)

Haigh, C. (ed.), *The English Reformation revised* (Cambridge: Cambridge University Press, 1987)

Hallam, E., J. Hockey, and G. Howarth, *Beyond the body. Death and social identity* (London: Routledge, 1999)

Hamscher, A. N., *The Parlement of Paris after the Fronde, 1653–1673* (Pittsburgh: University of Pittsburgh Press, 1976)

Harben, H. A., *A dictionary of London* (London: Herbert Jenkins Ltd, 1908)

Harding, V., '"And one more may be laid there": the location of burials in early modern London', *London Journal* 14.2 (1989), 112–29

'The population of London, 1550–1700: a review of the published evidence', *London Journal* 15 (1990), 111–28

'Burial choice and burial location in later medieval London', in Bassett (ed.), *Death in towns*, 119–35

'Burial of the plague dead in early modern London', in Champion (ed.), *Epidemic disease in London*, pp. 53–64

'Medieval documentary sources for London and Paris: a comparison', in J. Boffey and P. King (eds.), *London and Europe in the later Middle Ages* (London: Centre for Medieval and Renaissance Studies, Queen Mary and Westfield College, 1995), pp. 35–54.

'Burial on the margin: distance and discrimination in the early modern city', in Cox (ed.), *Grave concerns*, pp. 54–64

'From compact city to complex metropolis: records for the history of London, 1500–1720', in M. V. Roberts (ed.), *Archives and the metropolis* (London: Corporation of London, 1998), pp. 83–92

'Mortality and the mental map of London: Richard Smyth's *Obituary*', in *Medicine, mortality and the book trade*, ed. M. Harris and R. Myers (Cheam: St Paul's Bibliographies, 1998), pp. 49–71

'Memento mori: la peur de l'agonie, de la mort et des morts à Londres au XVIIe siècle', *Histoire Urbaine* 2 (Dec. 2000), 39–57

'Whose body? A study of attitudes towards the dead body in early modern Paris', in Gordon and Marshall (eds.), *The place of the dead*, pp. 170–87

'City, capital and metropolis: the changing shape of seventeenth-century London', in J. F. Merritt (ed.), *Imagining early modern London: perceptions and portrayals of the city from Stow to Strype, 1598–1720* (Cambridge: Cambridge University Press, 2001), pp. 117–43

'Controlling a complex metropolis, 1650–1750. Politics, parishes and powers', *London Journal* 26 (2001), pp. 29–37

Henderson, J., 'The parish and the poor in Florence at the time of the Black Death: the case of S. Frediano', *Continuity and Change* 3 (1988), 247–72

Piety and charity in late medieval Florence (Chicago: University of Chicago Press, 1994)

Herbert, W., *The history of the twelve great Livery Companies of London*, 2 vols. (London, 1834, 1837; reprint, Newton Abbott: David and Charles, 1968)

Herlan, R. W., 'Social articulation and the configuration of parochial poverty in London on the eve of the Restoration', *Guildhall Studies in London History* 2(2) (1976), 43–53

Hertz, R., *Death and the right hand*, translated by R. and C. Needham (Glencoe, Ill.: The Free Press, 1960)

Hildesheimer, F., *La terreur et la pitié? L'Ancien Régime à l'épreuve de la peste* (Paris: Publisud, 1990)

Hill, G. W. and W. H. Frere (eds.), *Memorials of Stepney parish. That is to say the vestry minutes from 1579 to 1662, now first printed with an introduction and notes* (Guildford: Billing and Sons, 1890–1)

Hillairet, J., *Les 200 cimetières du vieux Paris* (Paris: Les Editions de Minuit, 1958)

Hoffbauer, T. J. H., *Paris à travers les ages* (new edn, annotated by P. Payen Appenzeller, Paris: Editions Tchou, 1982)

Hohl, C., 'Les épidémies et leurs consequences sur l'organisation des hôpitaux au XVIe siècle à Paris', *Bulletin de la Société de l'Histoire de Paris et Ile de France* 89 (1962), 33–6

Hollaender, A. E. J. and W. Kellaway (eds.), *Studies in London history presented to P. E. Jones* (London: Hodder and Stoughton, 1969)

Hollingsworth, M. F. and T. H. Hollingsworth, 'Plague mortality rates by age and sex in the parish of St Botolph's without Bishopsgate, London, 1603', *Population Studies* 25 (1971), 131–46

Holmes, Mrs Basil, *The London burial grounds. Notes on their history from the earliest times to the present day* (London: T. Fisher Unwin, 1896)

Holmes, M., 'A source-book for Stow?', in Hollaender and Kellaway (eds.), *Studies in London history*, pp. 257–85

Holt, M., 'Putting religion back into the Wars of Religion', *French Historical Studies* 18 (1993), 524–51

The French Wars of Religion, 1562–1629 (Cambridge: Cambridge University Press, 1995)

Houlbrooke, R. A., 'The Puritan death-bed, c.1560–c.1660', in C. Durston and J. Eales (eds.), *The culture of English Puritanism, 1560–1700* (London: Macmillan, 1996), pp. 122–44

'Death, church, and family in England between the late fifteenth and the early eighteenth centuries', in Houlbrooke (ed.), *Death, ritual and bereavement*, pp. 25–42

Death, religion and the family in England, 1450–1750 (Oxford: Oxford University Press, 1998)

Houlbrooke, R. A. (ed.), *Death, ritual and bereavement* (London: Routledge, 1989)

Howarth, D., *Images of rule. Art and politics in the English Renaissance, 1485–1649* (London: Macmillan, 1997)

Hutton, R., 'The local impact of the Tudor Reformations', in Haigh (ed.), *The English Reformation revised*, pp. 114–38

Hyde, R., J. Fisher, and R. Cline, *The A to Z of Restoration London* (London: London Topographical Society, 1992)

Imray, J., *The charity of Richard Whittington. A history of the trust administered by the Mercers' Company* (London: Athlone Press, 1968)

Jacquart, J., 'Le poids démographique de Paris et de l'Ile de France au XVIe siècle', in *Annales de démographie historique, 1980* (Paris: Ecole des Hautes Etudes en Sciences Sociales, 1980), pp. 87–96

Janaway, R., 'An introductory guide to textiles from 18th and 19th century burials', in Cox (ed.), *Grave concerns*, pp. 17–32

Jéhanno, C., 'Les comptes de l'Hôtel-Dieu de Paris au Moyen Age. Documents pour servir à l'histoire économique et sociale', *Etudes et documents (Comité pour l'histoire économique et financière)* 9 (1997), 502–27

Johns, A., *The nature of the book. Print and knowledge in the making* (Chicago and London: University of Chicago Press, 1998)

Jones, E., 'London in the early seventeenth century: an ecological approach', *London Journal* 6 (1980), 123–34

Jordan, W. K., *The charities of London, 1480–1660. The aspirations and achievements of the urban society* (London: Allen and Unwin, 1960)

Jupp, P. C. and C. Gittings (eds.), *Death in England: an illustrated history* (Manchester: Manchester University Press, 1999)

Kantorowicz, E. H., *The king's two bodies. A study in mediaeval political theology* (Princeton: Princeton University Press, 1970)

Karant-Nunn, S. C., *The Reformation of ritual. An interpretation of early modern Germany* (London: Routledge, 1997)

Keene, D. and V. Harding, *Survey of sources for property holding in London before the Great Fire* (London Record Society 22, 1984)

Historical gazetteer of London before the Great Fire, 1, Cheapside (Chadwyck-Healey microfiche, 1987)

King, P. M., 'The English cadaver tomb in the late fifteenth century: some indications of a Lancastrian connection', in J. H. M. Taylor (ed.), *Dies illa. Death in the Middle Ages* (Liverpool: Cairns, 1984)

Kingsford, C. L., *The Greyfriars of London: their history with the register of their convent and an appendix of documents* (Aberdeen: British Society of Franciscan Studies, 1915)

Knight, C. (ed.), *London*, 6 vols. (London: Charles Knight, 1841–4)

Koslofsky, C. M., *The Reformation of the dead. Death and ritual in early modern Germany, 1450–1700* (Basingstoke: Macmillan, 2000)

Kselman, T. A., *Death and the afterlife in modern France* (Princeton: Princeton University Press, 1993)

Landers, J., *Death and the metropolis. Studies in the demographic history of London, 1670–1830* (Cambridge: Cambridge University Press, 1993)

Lang, R. G., 'Social origins and social aspirations of Jacobean London merchants', *Economic History Review* 27 (1974), 28–47.

Laqueur, T., 'Cemeteries, religion and the study of capitalism', in J. Garnett and C. Matthews (eds.), *Revival and religion since 1700: Essays for John Walsh* (London: Hambledon, 1993), pp. 183–200

Laurence, A., 'Godly grief: individual response to death in seventeenth-century Britain', in Houlbrooke (ed.), *Death, ritual and bereavement*, pp. 62–76

Lavedan, P., *Nouvelle histoire de Paris. Histoire de l'urbanisme à Paris* (Paris: Hachette, 1975)

Le Goff, J., *The birth of purgatory* (Chicago: University of Chicago Press, 1984)

Lefebvre, H., *The production of space*, translated by D. Nicholson-Smith (Oxford: Basil Blackwell, 1991)

Lemoine, H., 'L'église Saint-Jean-en-Grève, ses cimetières et sa démolition', *Bulletin de la Société Historique de Paris* (1922), 71–6

Light, A. W., *Bunhill Fields*, 2 vols. (London: Farncombe, 1915, 1933)

Lindenbaum, S., 'Ceremony and oligarchy: the London Midsummer Watch', in B. Hanawalt and K. Reyerson (eds.), *City and spectacle in medieval Europe* (Minneapolis: University of Minnesota Press, 1994), pp. 171–88

Litten, J., *The English way of death. The common funeral since 1450* (Robert Hale, London, 1991)

Llewellyn, N., *The art of death: visual culture in the English death ritual c.1500–c.1800* (London: Reaktion, in association with the Victoria and Albert Museum, 1991)

   Funeral monuments in post-Reformation England (Cambridge: Cambridge University Press, 2000)

Lobel, M. D. (ed.), *The British atlas of historic towns*, vol. III: *The city of London from prehistoric times to c. 1520* (London: Scolar Press, 1990)

Lucenet, M., *Les grandes pestes en France* (Paris: Aubier, 1985)

MacDonald, M. and T. R. Murphy, *Sleepless souls. Suicide in early modern England* (Oxford: Clarendon Press, 1990)

Maltby, J., *Prayer book and people in Elizabethan and early Stuart England* (Cambridge: Cambridge University Press, 1998)

Manley, L., *Literature and culture in early modern London* (Cambridge: Cambridge University Press, 1995)

Marshall, P. (ed.), *The impact of the English Reformation, 1500–1640* (London: Arnold, 1997)

McCullough, D., *Tudor church militant. Edward VI and the Protestant Reformation* (London: Penguin Books, 1999)

McDonnell, K. G., *Medieval London suburbs* (Chichester: Phillimore, 1978)

McKellar, E., *The birth of modern London. The development and design of the city, 1660–1720* (Manchester: Manchester University Press, 1999)

McManners, J., *Death and the Enlightenment. Changing attitudes to death among Christians and unbelievers in eighteenth-century France* (Oxford: Oxford University Press, 1981; paperback edn, 1985)

   'Death and the French historians', in Whaley (ed.), *Mirrors of mortality*, pp. 107–30

Medvei, V. C. and J. L. Thornton (eds.), *The royal hospital of St Bartholomew, 1123–1973* (London: The Royal Hospital of St Bartholomew, 1974)

Merritt, J. F., 'Puritans, Laudians, and the phenomenon of church-building in Jacobean London', *Historical Journal* 41.4 (1998), 935–60

Métayer, C., *Au tombeau des secrets. Les écrivains publics du Paris populaire. Cimetière des Saints-Innocents, XVIe–XVIIIe siècles* (Paris: Albin Michel, 2001)

Metcalf, P., 'Introduction', in P. Metcalf and R. Huntingdon (eds.), *Celebrations of death. The anthropology of mortuary ritual* (Cambridge: Cambridge University Press, 1991), pp. 1–22

Milne, G., *St Bride's church, London. Archaeological research 1952–60 and 1992–5* (London: English Heritage, 1997)

Molleson, T. and M. Cox, with A. H. Waldron and D. Whitaker, *The Spitalfields project*, vol. II: *The anthropology. The middling sort* (York: Council for British Archaeology Research Report 86, 1993)

Moore, N., *The history of St Bartholomew's Hospital*, 2 vols. (London: C. Arthur Pearson Ltd, 1918)

Morrison, J. J., 'Strype's Stow: the 1720 edition of "A Survey of *London*"', *London Journal* 3 (1977), 40–54

Mousnier, R., *Paris au XVIIe siècle* (Paris: typescript lectures, 3 fasc. in 1, 1961)

'Recherches sur les structures sociales parisiennes en 1634, 1635, 1636', *Revue Historique* 507 (1973), 35–58

La stratification sociale à Paris aux XVIIe et XVIIIe siècles. L'échantillon de 1634, 1635, 1636 (Paris: A. Pédone, 1976)

Mouton, L., 'L'affaire de la Croix de Gastine', *Bulletin de la Société de l'Histoire de Paris et Ile de France* 56 (1929), 102–13

Mullett, C. F., *The bubonic plague in England. An essay in the history of preventive medicine* (Lexington: University of Kentucky Press, 1956)

Murray, J., 'Kinship and friendship: the perception of family by clergy and laity in late medieval London', *Albion* 20.3 (1988), 369–85

Naphy, W. G. and P. Roberts (eds.), *Fear in early modern society* (Manchester: Manchester University Press, 1997)

Naz, R., *Dictionnaire du droit canonique*, 7 vols. (Paris: Letouzey et Ané, 1935–65)

Neill, M., '"Exeunt with a dead march": funeral pageantry on the Shakespearean stage', in D. M. Bergeron (ed.), *Pageantry in the Shakespearean theater* (Athens: University of Georgia Press, 1985), pp. 153–93

Norris, M., 'Later medieval monumental brasses: an urban funerary industry and its representation of death', in Bassett (ed.), *Death in towns*, pp. 184–209

Oliver, K., *Treasures and plate: the collection of the Saddlers' Company* (Chichester: Phillimore, 1995)

Panofsky, E., *Tomb sculpture: its changing aspects from Ancient Egypt to Bernini* (London: Thames and Hudson, 1964)

Pardailhé-Galabrun, A., *The birth of intimacy. Privacy and domestic life in early modern Paris* (Cambridge: Polity Press, 1991)

Pearl, V., *London and the outbreak of the Puritan revolution* (Oxford: Oxford University Press, 1961)

'Change and stability in seventeenth-century London', *London Journal* 5 (1979), 3–34

Pendrill, C., *Old parish life in London* (London: Oxford University Press, 1937)

Phillips, H., *Church and culture in seventeenth-century France* (Cambridge: Cambridge University Press, 1997)

Picon, A. and J.-P. Robert, *Un atlas Parisien. Le dessus des cartes* (Paris: Pavillon de L'Arsenal/Picard, 1999)

Pillorget, R., *Nouvelle histoire de Paris. Paris sous les premiers Bourbons, 1594–1661* (Paris: Hachette, 1988)

Pillorget, R. and J. de Viguerie, 'Les quartiers de Paris aux XVIIe et XVIIIe siècles', Revue d'Histoire Moderne et Contemporaine 17 (1970), 253–77

Plongeron, B., *Le diocèse de Paris*, vol I: *Des origines à la Révolution* (Histoire des diocèses de France, vol. XX, Paris: Beauchesne, 1987)

Porter, S., 'Death and burial in a London parish: St Mary Woolnoth, 1653–99', *London Journal* 8 (1982), 76–80

The Great Fire of London (Stroud: Sutton Publishing, 1996; 2nd edn, 1998)

Power, M. J., 'East London housing in the seventeenth century', in P. Clark and P. Slack (eds.), *Crisis and order in English towns, 1500–1700* (London: Routledge and Kegan Paul, 1972), pp. 237–62

'East and West in early modern London', in E. W. Ives, R. J. Knecht, and J. J. Scarisbrick (eds.), *Wealth and power in Tudor England* (London: Athlone Press, 1978), pp. 167–85

'London and the control of the "crisis" of the 1590s', *History* 70 (1985), 371–85

'A "crisis" reconsidered: social and economic dislocation in London in the 1590s', *London Journal* 12 (1986), 134–45

'The social topography of Restoration London', in Beier and Finlay (eds.), *London 1500–1700, the making of the metropolis*, pp. 199–223

Rapley, E., *The dévotes. Women and church in seventeenth-century France* (Quebec: McGill-Queen's University Press, paperback, 1993)

Rappaport, S., *Worlds within worlds: structures of life in sixteenth-century London* (Cambridge: Cambridge University Press, 1989)

Raunié, E., *Epitaphier du vieux Paris. Recueil général des inscriptions funéraires des églises, couvents, collèges, hospices, cimetières et charniers depuis le moyen âge jusqu'à la fin du XVIIIe siècle*, vol. I (Paris: Histoire Général de Paris, 1890)

Reddaway, T. F., *The rebuilding of London after the Great Fire* (London: Jonathan Cape, 1940)

Reeve, J. and M. Adams, *The Spitalfields project*, vol. I: *The archaeology: across the Styx* (York: Council for British Archaeology Research Report 85, 1993)

Richet, D., 'Aspects socio-culturels des conflits religieux à Paris dans la seconde moitié du XVIe siècle', *Annales. ESC* (1977), 764–89

Robertson, J. C., 'Reckoning with London: interpreting the *Bills of Mortality* before John Graunt', *Urban History* 23 (1996), 325–50

Roche, D., *The people of Paris, an essay in popular culture in the 18th century* (Berkeley and Los Angeles: University of California Press, 1987)

Roelker, N. L. (ed.), *The Paris of Henry of Navarre, as seen by Pierre de l'Estoile. Selections from his mémoires-journaux* (Cambridge, Mass.: Harvard University Press, 1958)

Rosenthal, J., *The purchase of paradise. Gift giving and the aristocracy, 1307–1485* (London: Routledge and Kegan Paul, 1972)

Rosser, G., *Medieval Westminster, 1200–1540* (Oxford: Clarendon Press, 1989)

Rowell, G., *The liturgy of Christian burial; an introductory survey of the historical development of Christian burial rites* (London: SPCK for the Alcuin Club, 1977)

Royal Commission on the Historical Monuments of England, *An Inventory of the historical monuments in London*, 5 vols., vol. IV: *The city* (London: HMSO, 1924)

Salmon, J. H. M., *Society in crisis. France in the sixteenth century* (London: Methuen, 1979)

Saunders, J., 'London burials', in C. Knight (ed.), *London*, vol. IV, pp. 161–74

Scarisbrick, J. J., *The Reformation and the English people* (Oxford: Basil Blackwell, 1984)

Schofield, J., *Medieval London houses* (New Haven: Yale University Press, 1994)

Schofield, R., 'Did the mothers really die? Three centuries of maternal mortality in "The world we have lost"', in L. Bonfield, R. Smith, and K. Wrightson (eds.), *The world we have gained: histories of population and social structure* (Oxford: Basil Blackwell, 1986), pp. 231–60

Scribner, R. W., 'Ritual and popular religion in Catholic Germany at the time of the Reformation', *Journal of Ecclesiastical History* 35 (1984), 47–77

Popular culture and popular movements in Reformation Germany (London: Hambledon Press, 1987)

Seaver, P., *The Puritan lectureships. The politics of religious dissent, 1560–1662* (Stanford: Stanford University Press, 1970)

Wallington's world: a puritan artisan in 17th-century London (London: Methuen, 1985)

Shennan, J. H., *The Parlement of Paris* (Stroud: Sutton Publishing, 2nd edn, 1998)

Shrewsbury, J. F. D., *A history of bubonic plague in the British Isles* (Cambridge: Cambridge University Press, 1971)

Simpson, W. S., *Gleanings from old St Paul's* (London: Elliott Stock, 1889)

St Paul's Cathedral and old city life: illustrations of civil and cathedral life from the 13th to the 16th centuries (London: Elliott Stock, 1894)

Sjoberg, G., *The pre-industrial city. Past and present* (New York: The Free Press, 1960)

Slack, P., 'The disappearance of plague – an alternative view', *Economic History Review* 2nd ser. 34 (1981), 469–76

The impact of plague on Tudor and Stuart England (London: Routledge and Kegan Paul, 1985)

'Metropolitan government in crisis: the response to plague', in Beier and Finlay (eds.), *London 1500–1700, the making of the metropolis*, pp. 60–81

Spence, C., *London in the 1690s. A social atlas* (London: Centre for Metropolitan History, 2000)

Spencer, T., *Death and Elizabethan tragedy. A study of convention and opinion in the Elizabethan drama* (Cambridge, Mass.: Harvard University Press, 1936)

Spicer, A., '"Rest of their bones": fear of death and reformed burial practices', in Naphy and Roberts (eds.), *Fear in early modern society*, pp. 167–83

'"Defyle not Christ's kirke with your carrion": burial and the development of burial aisles in post-Reformation Scotland', in Gordon and Marshall (eds.), *The place of the dead*, pp. 149–69

Stannard, D., *The Puritan way of death. A study in religion, culture, and social change* (New York: Oxford University Press, 1977)

Stock, G., 'Quaker burial: doctrine and practice', in Cox (ed.), *Grave concerns*, pp. 129–43

Strocchia, S., *Death and ritual in Renaissance Florence* (Baltimore: Johns Hopkins University Press, 1992)

Sutcliffe, A., *Paris: an architectural history* (New Haven: Yale University Press, 1993)

Sutherland, I., 'When was the great plague? Mortality in London, 1563–1665', in Glass and Revelle (eds.), *Population and social change*, pp. 287–320

Tai Liu, *Puritan London. A study of religion and society in the city parishes* (London: Associated University Presses, 1986)

Tapié, V.-L., *Baroque et classicisme* (Paris: Librairie Plon, 1957)

Taylor, L. J., *Heresy and orthodoxy in sixteenth-century Paris. François le Picart and the beginnings of the Catholic Reformation* (Studies in Medieval and Reformation Thought, vol. LXXVII, Leiden: Brill, 1999)

Thibaut-Payen, J., *Les morts, l'église et l'état: recherches d'histoire administrative sur la sépulture et les cimetières dans le ressort du Parlement de Paris aux XVIIe et XVIIIe siècles* (Paris: Editions Fernand Lanore, 1977)

Thiriet, J.-M., 'Mourir à Vienne aux XVIIe–XVIIIe siècles: le cas des Welsches', *Jahrbuch des Vereins für Geschichte der Stadt Wien* 34 (1978), 204–17

Thomas, K., *Religion and the decline of magic* (London: Peregrine Books, 1978)

Thompson, D., *Renaissance Paris. Architecture and growth, 1475–1600* (Berkeley and Los Angeles: University of California Press, 1984)

Thompson, G. L., *Paris and its people under English rule: the Anglo-Burgundian regime, 1420–36* (Oxford: Clarendon Press, 1991)

Thomson, J. A. F., 'Tithe disputes in later medieval London', *English Historical Review* 78 (1963), 1–17

Todd, B., 'The remarrying widow: a stereotype reconsidered', in M. Prior (ed.), *Women in English society, 1500–1800* (London: Methuen, 1985), pp. 54–92
    'Demographic determinism and female agency: the remarrying widow reconsidered . . . again', *Continuity and Change* 9 (1994), 421–50

Tolmie, M., *The triumph of the Saints. The separate churches of London, 1616–1649* (Cambridge: Cambridge University Press, 1977)

Trout, A., *City on the Seine. Paris in the time of Richelieu and Louis XIV, 1614–1715* (New York: St Martin's Press, 1996)

Twigg, G., *The black death: a biological reappraisal* (London: Batsford, 1984)
    'Plague in London: spatial and temporal aspects of mortality', in Champion (ed.), *Epidemic disease in London*, pp. 1–17

Vance, J. E., 'Land assignment in the pre-capitalist, capitalist, and post-capitalist city', *Economic Geography* 47 (1971), 101–20

Vauchez, A., *The laity in the Middle Ages. Religious beliefs and devotional practices*, translated by M. J. Schneider (Notre Dame and London: University of Notre Dame Press, 1993)

Victoria history of London: including London within the bars, Westminster and Southwark, vol. I, ed. W. Page (London: Constable, 1911)

Victoria history of the county of Middlesex, vol. X: *Hackney parish*, ed. T. F. T. Baker (Oxford: Oxford University Press, 1995)

Victoria history of the county of Middlesex, vol. XI: *Early Stepney with Bethnal Green*, ed. T. F. T. Baker (Oxford: Oxford University Press, 1998)

Villefosse, R. H. de, *Solennités, fêtes et réjouissances parisiennes. Nouvelle histoire de Paris* (Paris: Hachette, 1980)

Wall, C., *The literary and cultural spaces of Restoration London* (Cambridge: Cambridge University Press, 1998)

Ward, J. P., *Metropolitan communities. Trade guilds, identity and change in early modern London* (Stanford: Stanford University Press, 1997)

'Religious diversity and guild unity in early modern London', in E. J. Carlson (ed.), *Religion and the English people, 1500–1640. New voices, new perspectives*, Sixteenth-century Essays and Studies, vol. XLV (Kirksville, Mo.: Thomas Jefferson University Press, 1998), pp. 77–97

Webb, E. A., *The records of St Bartholomew's Priory and of the church and parish of St Bartholomew the Great, West Smithfield*, 2 vols. (London: Oxford University Press, 1921)

Werner, A., *London bodies. The changing shape of Londoners from prehistoric times to the present day* (London: Museum of London, 1998)

Whaley, J., 'Symbolism for the survivors: the disposal of the dead in Hamburg in the late seventeenth and eighteenth centuries', in Whaley (ed.), *Mirrors of mortality*, pp. 80–105

Whaley, J., (ed.), *Mirrors of mortality: studies in the social history of death* (London: Europa Publications Ltd, 1981)

White, W., *Skeletal remains from the cemetery of St Nicholas Shambles, city of London* (London and Middlesex Archaeological Society Special paper no. 9, 1988)

Wieck, R. S., *Painted prayers. The book of hours in medieval and Renaissance art* (New York: George Brazillier Inc. in association with the Pierpont Morgan Library, 1997)

Wilhelm, J., *La vie quotidienne des Parisiens au temps du Roi-Soleil, 1660–1715* (Paris: Hachette, 1989)

Williams, S., 'The Lord Mayor's Show in Tudor and Stuart times', *Guildhall Miscellany* 1(10) (1959), 3–18

Wilson, F. P., *The plague in Shakespeare's London* (Oxford: Clarendon Press, 1927, 2nd edn, 1963)

Woodward, J., *The theatre of death. The ritual managment of royal funerals in Renaissance England* (Woodbridge: The Boydell Press, 1997)

Wrigley, E. A. and R. Schofield, *The population history of England, 1541–1871, a reconstruction* (Cambridge: Cambridge University Press, 1981)

Wunderli, R. M. and G. Broce, 'The final moment before death in early modern England', *Sixteenth-Century Journal* 20 (1989), 258–75

Zell, M., 'The use of religious preambles as a measure of religious belief in the sixteenth century', *Bulletin of the Institute of Historical Research* 50 (1977), 246–9

UNPUBLISHED PAPERS

Hickman, D. J., 'The religious allegiance of London's ruling élite, 1520–1603' (unpublished Ph.D. thesis, University of London, 1995)

Keene, D., 'The poor and their neighbours in seventeenth-century London' (unpublished seminar paper, Centre for Metropolitan History, Institute of Historical Research, London, n. d.)

Kellaway, W., 'Burial in medieval London' (unpublished seminar paper given at Institute of Historical Research, London, 1980)

Merritt, J. F., 'Religion, government and society in early modern Westminster, c. 1525–1625' (unpublished Ph.D. thesis, University of London, 1992)

Miles, A., 'Number One Poultry: post Great Fire burial ground, London' (post-excavation assessment and updated project design, MoLAS, November 1997).

Mémoires de maîtrise, written under the supervision of Professor Pierre Chaunu, and deposited at the Archives Nationales, Paris: Raymond Adeline, Paule Attali, Evelyne Blanc, Patrice Alexandre Carré, Bruno de Cessole, Elisabeth de Chanterac, Geneviève Delaporte, Christine Genin, Patrick Landier, Catherine Martin, Michèle Massucco, Jean de Mathan, Martine Rossignol, Gilbert du Rot, and Emmanuel Tranchant.

Index

Acarie, Pierre, *ligueur*, 152
Adelmare, Sir Julius Caesar, 156; tomb of, 156, 162, 167
Admonition of the Parliament (1572), 219
Aix, archbishop of, 253
Aligret, François, 153
Aligret family, chapel in Saint-André-des-Arts, 153
Allen, Master, 216
Alligret, Olivier, 153; tomb of, 150
Ambler, William, threadman, 221
Amcotts, Sir Henry, 243
Amery, Jean, 183
anatomizing, 278; sale of bodies for, 115, 116
Anjou, François duke of, 245, 250, 258, 264; heart of, 126
Anne of Denmark, *88*; funeral of, 256, 264
anniversaries *see* obits and anniversaries
Ariès, Philippe, 7, 111
arms and heraldry, 12, 210, 211, 226, 242, 245, 250, 251, 257, 258, 259, 267; on tombs, 164
Ars Moriendi, *arts de mourir*, 8, 177, 180, 182
Artillery Company, London, 252
Assembly of Divines, 257
Attali, Paule, 224
Aubrey, John, 65
Aubry, Christophe, *curé* of Saint-André-des-Arts, 152
Austrie, Ralph, fishmonger, 122

Backliffe, Andrew, 136
Bacon, Sir Nicholas, Lord Keeper, 143
Bakers' Company, 241
Balmford, J., 66
Barber, Thomas, preacher, 98
Barne, Sir George, 219
Barnham, Benedict, alderman, 252
Barron, Caroline, 241
Barrow, Henry, divine, 219

Barton, John, mercer, 121–2
bearers, 192, 220, 231
Beaulne, René de, lieutenant of *prévôt de Paris*, tomb of, 170
Becon, Thomas, 226
bederoll, 237
Bee, Cornelius, bookseller, 218
Bellièvre, M. de, chancellor of France, 239, 250
bells, bellringing, *sonnerie*, 13, 129, 136, 139, 177, 179, 180, 189, 201, 202–5, 206, 235, 238, 262; knells, 177, 203, 220, 221, 222, 224, 226, 229, 230, 294; passing bells, 204, 205; peals, 139, 177, 203, 294
Bemon, Jehan, 170; widow of, tomb, 155
Bentham, Thomas, bishop of Coventry and Lichfield, 196
Bethnal Green, 244
biers, 109, 185, 213, 231
Bills of Mortality, 15, 95, 100
Binski, Paul, 143, 148
Birague, Cardinal de, 239, 245
black, hangings and garments, 77, 129, 136, 139, 189, 197, 201–2, 204, 206, 211, 213, 214, 221, 224, 226, 227, 233, 235, 247, 252, 257, 259, 262, 263, 265, 267; rejection of, 227; stockings, 223; *see also* gowns and cloaks, black
Blayney, Peter, 86
Bonde, Sir William, alderman, tomb of, 161
bones and burials, clearance of, 65, 72, 81, 94, 110, 140, 276, 282
bones made into bread, 112
Bonnard, Raphael, *marchand fripier*, 194, 197, 202, 238, 239
booksellers, 87, 89, 93
Borde, Annys, 220
Borow, Baptyst, of Milan, 196
Bouchart, Louis, chevalier, tomb of, 167
Bourbon, Cardinal de, 245, 249

331

Printed in the United Kingdom
by Lightning Source UK Ltd.
122547UK00002B/98/A